The Lost Data on
The Chariots of the Elohim

(and other Secret Teachings and Hidden Mysteries)

by Martha Helene Jones A.A.,A.A.S
April 30, 2008

"Sing to Elohim make melody!…
in YAH name-*shem* (*i.e.,* Yah of Shem) of Him and be joyful…
YHVH He shall tabernacle always,
the thousand thousand chariots (lit. *rkb*-ride) of Elohim.
Adonai (my Lord) is in them,
in Sinai in holy *eshmim* (the heavenly) place...
Kingdoms of Earth sing! to Elohim…
to ride (*lrkb*) in heavens of heavens of old...
give strength to Elohim…
pride and strength of Him in (the) skies."
Ps. 68:4,16-17 & 33-34

This book is intended as a reference point for students of the Judeo/Christian religions, providing research not often presented in orthodox, mainstream and fundamentalist teachings, and so it is dedicated to them.

For a free online search-able PDF with active links go to:
http://butsuri.~~homelinux.net/MHJ~~
allowed.org/MHJ>)

(If any links no longer work try searching for the title or a key phrase from quoted sources.)

To purchase a printed version of this book you can go to:
<http://www.lulu.com/content/5532143>

ISBN 978-1-304-19311-7

To John & Darlene

In appreciation for all
the help in my time of need.

Martha
8608475912

Foreword

Who are the Elohim? Why are there depictions and descriptions of their vehicles (aka "Chariots of the Gods") throughout the histories and ancient religions of the world? If they are still watching us, why don't they communicate with us or give us any evidence of their presence, or have they?

If they are here why don't they contact the authorities? Could it have something to do with the same reason the early Israelites had no kings (the military leaders of their time Gen. 36:31), and a refusal to acknowledge the right of anyone, except the Creator, to rule His children. This especially would mean those using violence to profit and protect their own interests and those of their political alliances, and who do their best to deny any higher authority than their own?

Why have large groups of people spotted strange lights in the sky, appearing and disappearing at will, and performing feats no earthly aircraft could manage? If they are all hoaxed, how could a multitude of strangers at a distance from each other, make simultaneous videotapes of them? (see the Mexico City eclipse, 7/11/91).

Why are humans capable of skills so far beyond all the other animals? What are the hidden mysteries and secrets of the kingdom of heaven (Luke 8:10-11) that came down from the time of the Old Testament to Jesus, and of which he spoke? What secret teachings did he speak of to his disciples (of which, according to Matt. 13:11; Mark 4:11, he only dared speak of in parables to the masses).

How did revelation of these secrets eventually contribute to the motives for his murder, and the murder of his disciples, when they were mentioned publicly? Learn these things and the verses where he is quoted mentioning them. Learn about the word Elohim (SHD 430 - gods, plural of SHD 433 Eloah - god) which Jesus translated as "Gods" - plural when he quotes Ps. 82:6 in John 10:34 "Is it not written in your law? I said ye are Gods(Elohim). " Learn about how 'elohim' eventually came to be translated as "God" singular, along with YHWH's holy name which was never used as a plural word. And learn the originating motives behind all these events and other murders, perpetuating the continuation of a cover-up, lasting from long before his birth until now.

This book also contains information on the following subjects; the Magi who followed the star as it moved across the sky; lost continents and the Great flood; the Shemsu Hor and the winged disk of the Egyptians; the sons of the Elohim who took wives from the daughters of the Adam; mention of the little people in the bible; and the Rh negative bloodline, lacking in the earthling primate rhesus gene.

Table of Contents

This is not one of those books where it is possible to skip around focusing only on parts of interest. The information in each section of this book builds on the definitions, background, understanding, and groundwork established in the previous sections.

The lying pen of the Levite scribes; The Levite usurpers of the priesthood; The Levitican hygiene laws; The Second priesthood; The Second temple; Tithing; The Torah redacted; Deuteronomy; The oldest serial murder mystery in the world; This kind goes not out but by prayer and fasting; Yeschu/Joshu/Jesus' Passover of bread and wine; Paul the apostle who was never a disciple; Historic evidence

Before fire and weapons; The curse of Alzheimer's; B12 from microorganisms; Diseases with a correlated and studied incidence, related to animal food diets; Life not subject to destruction/health; Cancer; Placebos, faith and prayer; Judge not; The hidden mysteries; The secret of the Kingdom of Heaven

Worldwide survivors of the flood; The flood story of the Americas; Japanese flood stories; The countries of Shem, Ham and Jaffeth; India/Vindja; Shem/Shum/Semites/Shumeria; Ham/Khem/Khemit/Egypt; Japheth/Java/Japan/Asia; The sunken continent in the Pacific

Are the Elohim still watching?; Problems with radiometric dating; Epilogue

Chapter One

THE ELOHIM

"In melodies we shall shout to Him, that All Great <u>YHWH, king over all of the Elohim</u>...we shall worship and we shall bow down, we shall kneel before YHWH Maker of us." Ps. 95:2-6

See <<u>http://www.scripture4all.org</u>>

YHVH'S HOLY[1] ELOHIM ([1]as they are called in Dan. 4:8 & 5:11)

To begin to understand how the Hebrew language lost its understanding of the records[2] of YHVH Elohim (the Modern Hebrew spelling which will be discussed further on), we must begin with an open mind. We must fearlessly re-examine everything taught about the word "*Elohim*" אלהים, since the time of the Levite scribes, beginning with Ezra. Only then can the original meaning of the word Elohim, be comprehended with all the connotations the earlier Israelites of Moses' times understood it to have. See Appendix 32 of the Companion Bible, David Ginsburg and others including the following source quoted here. [2](which records are by most, recognized historically to have been redacted by the Levite scribes called Sopherim (approx. 400-600 BCE), in the Old Testament, hereafter OT)

> "Ezra was the first in a long line of *Sopherim* (Scribes) who were given the task of refining the scriptures..." Lane, Jack M. *The Family of God, Part 2.*

> <<u>http://Livingstone/atmospherically</u>> Wheelock, Dean. *The Emendations of the Sopherim.* <<u>http://www.oocities.org/~hebrew_roots/html/hr-2-1-02.html</u>>

Although "Elohim" has now come to include the definition of "God" and be used to mean "God" singular, Strong's Hebrew Dictionary (hereafter SHD) of the Old Testament also defines Elohim as; (SHD 430) elohiym (*el-o-heem*) <u>plural of god</u> (eloah/SHD 433); or that is "gods," plural. Using verses from the OT, with the Hebrew words YHVH and Elohim intact we can clarify some of this lost and/or hidden knowledge of YHVH Elohim (or *YHVH aleim*[3]).

<<u>http://experienced/a/Elohim_-_Etymology/id/1289579</u>>

Note for linguists, one argument (to the theory that the word's plurality reflects early Judaic polytheism), is sometimes given that "Semitic etymologies are actually generally based on postconsonantal roots, which the proposal completely ignores." That argument itself ignores the possibility that "although most roots in Hebrew seem to be tri-radical, many of them were originally bi-radical..." Zuckermann, Ghil'ad. *'Language Contact and Lexical Enrichment in Israeli Hebrew.* <<u>http://en.wikipedia.org/wiki/Triliteral</u>>

[3]Godfrey Higgins in his classic *Anacalypsis* gives the etymology of Elohim, as originally transcribed *aleim*. He states: "Perhaps there is no word in any language about which more has

been written than the word *Aleim*; or, as modern Jews *corruptly* call it, Elohim (SHD 0430). *al* (El), the root of the word *Aleim*, as a verb or in its verbal form, means to mediate, to interpose for protection, to preserve; and a noun, a mediator, an interposer. In its feminine it has two forms … *ale*, and … *alue*. In its plural masculine it makes … *alim*, in its plural feminine … *aleim*. IT IS BY NO MEANS SINGULAR. It is like that made by *ozim*, she-goats, *dbim*, she-bears, etc." Higgins, Godfrey. *Apocalypses. Vol. 1.* p.p. 64-65, 67.

Modern Hebrew asserts that the first letter (*aleph*) in the Hebrew word אלהים makes no sound unless it has vowel points. But discoveries of ancient Hebrew tablets, written without them, attest that this cannot be true for the ancient Hebrew language, since it contained no vowel points, and people were still able to read and pronounce the letter *aleph* as representing some sound. Modern Hebrew is asserted to be a purely consonantal language, however, Aleph is known as one of the "consonantal vowels" or *matres lectiones,* they include *Vav, Yod, Hey,* and sometimes *Aleph.* These 'vowels' were even said to have been inserted by the Sopherim, for example the vowels from Adonai were inserted into YHVH's name, so the vowel sounds in *Adonai* (spelled *aleph, daleth, nun* and *yod* therefore containing the 'vowels' *aleph* and *yod*) were recognized by them and asserted to be the same as the vowels in YHVH. This is evidence that these so-called 'consonantal vowels' served as true vowels for Ancient Hebrew.

<http://www.hebrew4christians.com/Grammar/Unit_Two/Introduction/introduction>

Modern Jews, having lost the ability to speak Hebrew (during the times when it was a dead language, more on this later), also lost their understanding of how to pronounce אלהים; and the vowel points were invented; this was long after the original writings of the *Torah* (meaning "The Law"; the first five books of the Bible attributed to Moses).

> "J. Paterson Smyth, B.D., LL.D., Litt. D., author of several books on the Bible, maintained that "these marks are of comparatively modern date, certainly not older than about 500 or 600 AD." And he added; "We can imagine then what a sensation was produced when Elias Levitt, a very famous Hebrew scholar, about the year 1540, proved to the world that these vowel marks were not in existence for hundreds of years after the time of our Lord!" Of course this caused some controversy at the time, but Dr. Smyth concluded that "no scholar now thinks of doubting the comparatively recent origin of the Hebrew vowel points." Reinhold Press. *Ancient Hebrew.*
>
> <http://www.historyinsidepictures.com/Pages/AncientHebrewisanAncientForgottenLanguagewithNoWrittenVowels.aspx>
>
> "Sometime beginning around 600 A.D., a group of scribes in Tiberias called the Masoretes (mesora means "tradition") began developing a system of vowel marks (called neqqudot) to indicate how the text was traditionally read." from *Introduction to Hebrew vowels.*
> <http://www.hebrew4christians.com/Grammar/Unit_Two/Introduction/introduction.html>

This book will discuss in depth the history of the word now translated as the Hebrew word Elohim, containing the Hebrew letters *aleph* א, *lamed* ל, *heh* ה, *yod* י, & *mem* ם - אלהים (Elohim is capitalized to clarify that it is a proper name; although Hebrew is actually written from right to left with no capitals); and discuss evidence on how the plural word Elohim came to be used as "God," singular. However, it cannot be emphasized too strongly that the vowel points were not used in ancient Hebrew and the present system was developed in the Middle Ages, long after the exile into Babylon (dated 586-536 BCE). During the exile Hebrew ceased to be a commonly spoken language and most Israelites were illiterate (Neh. 8:8). This loss of the understanding of their own language left Israel dependent on the Levite scribes and Ezra, as to the correct interpretation. Modern Judeo/Christian scholarship generally subscribes to the Levite interpretations, but this book will present evidence indicating that their interpretation was flawed in many ways. A great deal will be revealed about the motives these Levite scribes had for committing multiple murders in their rise to power and how those motives may have influenced their decision to alter or 'redact' the texts in their possession.

This book is meant to be read and easily understood by the average person, so rather than trying to discuss the entire Hebrew language, a simple analysis and history of the name that is now translated as Elohim (and a few other Hebrew words) will be presented (mostly in the English transliterations used by <scripture4all.org>). The word אלהים is often transcribed as *aleim* and transliterated as Elohim. The spelling is indeterminate since the first letter, *aleph,* now corresponds to many sounds including "E" or "A." The spelling *aleim* is thus considered by many scholars to be equivalent to Elohim and is used interchangeably with Elohim throughout the online interlinear Bible at <scripture4all.org> quoted frequently in this book. The Modern Hebrew spelling is Elohim and since it is the most familiar form of the word to readers of English, it will often be used throughout this book, referring to YHVH's 'holy gods' (as they are called in Dan. 4:8 & 5:11) in Hebrew and other ancient languages (this does not imply that the vowels added by modern Hebrew scholars are necessarily the correct pronunciation, which is actually unknown to all modern scholars since Hebrew was lost and then revived as a spoken language).

> "...the idea that scholarship has nothing to do with power is an innocent one-or more exactly, it is a naive one. It is not truly an innocent one, for we cannot say that no one is harmed by it. It is not an innocent idea if it serves to sustain power-holders in their power." *Philology and Power,* published in *On the Way to the Postmodern: Old Testament Essays.*
>
> <http://www.shef.ac.uk/bibs/DJACcurrres/Postmodern2/Philology.html>

It is clear that the original Hebrew name contained only five letters and it should also now be clear that the vowel points, and the interpretations of modern Hebrew, as to pronunciation is conjecture from long after the original writings; *and* it will become clear that the meaning of Elohim as precisely synonymous to YHVH, was also conjecture by the Levite scribes and others. With those concepts in mind this book will attempt to present evidence supporting a deeper analysis of what the ancient Israelites meant by the word before it was redacted by the Levite scribes the Sopherim, under Ezra.

As this book proceeds, other OT verses and Hebrew transliterations, taken from the online Interlinear Concordance site given in the next paragraph, will accompany these interpretations. The interlinear concordance on that Internet site has no connection with this author, and is a purely disinterested source, available for the public at large. Even then it can easily be seen in a side by side comparison between the standard Hebrew versions and the oldest Hebrew texts (like the Leningrad Codex @ <http://www.tanach.us/Tanach.xml>) that there are many other differences in spelling, word usage, phrases, etc., from that which standard translations are based upon. How many more subtle changes there have been, it would take a team of scholars to say, but this book will consider only those translations easily available for anyone to see and understand, especially the further liberties taken with translations into English, in the King James Version, hereafter KJV.

Remember that without the original Hebrew words in place, the Bible verses quoted in this book will not be found as they would read with those Hebrew names in place, in many biblical texts after the KJV. However, one *can* find these references if they are read in a Hebrew/English interlinear concordance. A freely available online Hebrew Interlinear Concordance is available @: <http://www.scripture4all.org>. A Strong's Concordance with Hebrew and Greek Lexicon (Strong's Hebrew Dictionary referenced as SHD accompanied by the number.) is available @:

<http://www.tgm.org/bible.htm> & <http://www.eliyah.com/lexicon.html>

Much as I enjoy them, this is not one of those books where it is possible to skip around focusing only on parts of interest. Like learning algebra, the information in each section of this book builds on the definitions, background, understanding, and groundwork established in the previous ones. So all who enter here prepare for a process of discovery with an open mind and be prepared to apply the definitions learned as we go along. Consider the evidence presented, with diligent effort in applying the new definitions presented, and it will hopefully be a duly rewarding and exciting process of discovery and enlightenment.

The argument has been given that the first verse of the Bible uses a singular verb with Elohim, *bara or bra* (SHD 01254), translated as created, past tense, however, *bara* is also used simply as create (for example Ps. 51:10; Isa. 4:5). The argument is that if Elohim were plural it would be accompanied by the plural verb ending in "u" (*waw* or *vav*) as in *baru* בראו, but *bara/bra* need not necessarily be accompanied by the 'u' to form 'Elohim they create' any more than it is necessary to always say (for example) 'men they build' instead of 'men build,' although it might occasionally be phrased this way.). To say 'Elohim they create' is as redundant as saying 'men they toil' or 'people they build'.

> "The subject of the (Hebrew) verb can be identified by a proper name...<u>or</u> a pronoun...It is also common in Biblical Hebrew to include a noun or proper noun for the subject of the verb....The object of the verb can be identified by a noun, proper name or a pronoun."

<http://ancientness-Hebrew/37_lesson02.HTML> &

<http://ancientness-Hebrew/37_lesson04.HTML>

So while it may be common to include a pronoun with the proper name, it is not a universal rule (for example Gen. 33:6 in which the addition of the "u," to the end of a verb describing a plural number of people acting, is *not* present). Thus some people writing ancient Hebrew (before the name אלהים came to mean God singular), clearly understood that it is not *always* necessary to place the pronoun 'they' ("u" added to the verb) in the sentence as long as the subject is already called by a proper name. *Furthermore* the phrase 'they created,' coupled with a proper name, is not found *anywhere* in Biblical Hebrew,[4] so the argument is not only inconclusive, it is misleading because this is a modern verb form not found in Biblical Hebrew. The form *baru* is found in another related Semitic language, Akkadian, and it simply meant 'create' not 'they create' so even if it were found it would not necessarily mean that *all* Israelites of Moses time originally would have understood it to include the pronoun 'they'. [4](ancient Hebrew before the vowel points were invented in the Middle Ages.)

<http://www.christianleadershipcenter.org/Bara.htm>

Much more in this light, on the Genesis creation story will be given in the chapter on Genesis Revisited. But first this book will provide numerous examples in the form of Bible verses (like the verse quoted at the beginning of this chapter), that demonstrate that the word Elohim was originally used to refer to a council of godlike beings, created by YHVH, and ranking beneath Him, and only later came to mean God singular. It will also provide citations that show that variations of the word Elohim, in the Bible and throughout other religious writings of the ancient Middle East, made reference to a council of "gods." There is no question that over time Elohim came to be used to mean the Creator (in Hebrew known as YHVH along with many other names), however, the main point in the first part of this book is to ask the reader to consider that usage of Elohim, to mean the Creator, may have come from the ancient understanding that the "Council of Elohim" (mentioned in Ps. 89:5-7 & Dan. 4:8; 5:11) were one *in* Him.

> "Words, in fact are like fossils; they preserve for us older modes of thought and belief embedded within the skeleton of their outward form. Elohim would never have *come* to denote the singular "God" had it not *first* denoted the plural 'gods.'" Sayce, A. H. *Polytheism in Primitive Israel,* p. 25, *The Jewish Quarterly Review, Vol. 2, No. 1* (Oct., 1889) pp. 25-36. <http://www.jstor.org/pss/1450128>

It is acknowledged by Hebrew scholars that the word Elohim has a plural morphology. That is, it was originally a plural word that eventually came to indicate the singular "God" of Israel. The above quote refers to that acknowledged fact; the history of how it came to mean "God" singular provides the founding premise of this book, i.e., that the ancient Israelites prior to the time of Ezra originally understood that YHVH had created "holy gods," as they are called in Dan. 4:8 & 5:11, and that these were finite "gods" with human-like form, who served the Great Holy Spirit of all the living[5], YHVH the infinite Creator (who has no image Lev. 26:1 & John 1:18). "But who is able to build him an house, seeing the heaven and heaven of heavens cannot contain HIM?" II Chr. 2:6

> [5]"And he is saying Elohim, she, the earth, shall bring forth, <u>living soul to species of her, beast, and moving animal of the land and HE IS BECOMING SO (*uiei*[6])</u>." Gen. 1:24
> [6]*uiei* -He is Becoming is a variation of I Am or I am becoming-*aeie*, another of YHVH's names, see section following on I Am Becoming. To check the Hebrew spellings and meanings in this verse see: <http://scripture4all.org/Online Interlinear/OTpdf/gen1.pdf>

A theory as to the historical process by which the Hebrew word for gods-plural (SHD 430) Elohim, also came to mean god-singular, will be examined in this book. This is a theory, it should be remembered, however, that all the traditional religious teachings as to the meaning of the name Elohim are also only imperfect theories created by imperfect men. No human is all-knowing as only YHVH is omniscient.

Objections to the use of the plural form of this word say that we must accept, without question, the accumulated wisdom of present-day biblical scholars on the subject of the universal use of Elohim as a singular word. Their interpretation often goes unquestioned even when the biblical context shows that there is more than one individual or group under discussion in the same sentence, or when the Hebrew names YHVH *and* Elohim are present in the same text as different beings interacting with each other. They point out verses that have singular verbs and grammatical terms, often ignoring the numerous times when the name Elohim is accompanied by plural verbs, plural predicators and other plural grammatical terms. They then use the predominance of 'singular' instances to support the unilateral use of the word Elohim to mean God, singular, even when the context indicates otherwise.

They apply this premise even when the context shows that YHVH is addressing His holy council of Elohim (mentioned in Ps. 89:5-7 & Dan. 4:8; 5:11) or when YHVH and the Elohim are mentioned as two different entities, often in the same sentence. (Isa. 7:13; 44:6; 48:1; Ps. 97:7&9; 138:1&5; etc). These verses, fully quoted further on, must be read in Hebrew or an interlinear version for an accurate comparison.) The stance (that Elohim means God singular in the OT), is then demanded without providing any ancient records showing evidence, from the time of the original writings of the OT (before Ezra), that this must be so. Rather it is customary to cite traditions from other relatively modern biblical scholars, who also base their assumptions on modern Judeo-Christian religious doctrine and interpretation, formulated since the time of the Levite Sopherim.

> "Judah they come forth swearing in name of YHWH *and* in Elohim of Israel." Isa. 48:1 (note that Jesus' heritage was from Judah. Hebrews 7:14)

There is no ancient Hebrew authority from before the alterations by the scribes, the Sopherim, that asserts that this plural word must always be considered as a singular entity. There is only the relatively recent analysis by traditional biblical scholars, of the use of singular verbs, and other singular grammatical considerations, and we are apparently supposed to ignore the numbers of times that plural verbs are used.

Even then they do not always render it as a singular word; we are often left dependent merely on whim and tradition as to when it is rendered singular and when it is rendered as plural (for example Elohim is used when referring to many false gods). That Hebrew was lost as a spoken language actually leaves us for the most part subject to scholarship from the last two hundred years or so. Additionally, during the exile into slavery in Babylon, many early Israelites were forced to adopt the language of Babylon. They lost the understanding of their own language, Hebrew, and became dependent on the interpretations of the Levite scribes, the Sopherim, whose motives will be shown to have been tainted and whose own records in the Massorah indicate that they altered many texts. Noggin, Nick. *The Massorah,* <http://www.biblestudysite.com/30.htm> & Goggin, Nick. *The Eighteen Emendations of the Sopherim.*

<http://www.biblestudysite.com/33.htm >

> "Trust not in words of falsehood (because) they say; the temple of YHWH, the temple of

YHWH, the temple of YHWH...How can you say; We are wise for we have the law of YHWH, when actually the lying[7] pen of the scribes has handled it falsely?" (Jer. 7:4 & 8:8) This verse was altered to read "vain pen" instead of "pen of falsehood" as it stands in Hebrew.

[7]Sheqer SHD 8267 from 8266 lie or falsehood This word for a lie or a falsehood is previously translated in Jer. 7:4 (and elsewhere) as falsehood; if it was used as falsehood in that verse (by the same author, Jeremiah) it shows that he would have also meant it as falsehood in Jer.8:8, but that it was modified to 'vain' by someone at a later date to prevent the understanding that Jeremiah was accusing the scribes of being dishonest in their renderings of the 'law' of the OT.

See <http://scripture4all.org/OnlineInterlinear/OTpdf/jer7.pdf>

& <http://scripture4all.org/OnlineInterlinear/OTpdf/jer8.pdf>

The above verses clearly demonstrates that according to the Bible itself, and the prophet Jeremiah, protesting the efforts of these same scribes in his own time, the version of the OT we received from the scribes is at least partly falsehood! It has been established that Ezra and the Levite scribes after him (the Sopherim) had the final compilation and editing of the version of the OT commonly available today. Their emendations, although noted in the Masoritic text, were furthermore not included in most versions of the King James Bible.

"You shall not add to the word which I command you, nor take anything from it…" Deu. 4:2

The Sopherim, under Ezra, based the authority of their priesthood in part on Ezra's descent from the line of Aaron (Ezra 7:1). Said authority being then enforced upon the remaining Israelites (by a non-Israelite king) under penalty of death, banishment, fine or imprisonment (Ezra 7:26). Aaron was priest over the Levites servers in the tabernacle of the congregation (who were not allowed to approach the altar of the children of Israel, Num. 18:1-5). The Levites were staunch promoters of animal sacrifice, this was prescribed by the Levites as an atonement for sin.

"For I spoke not unto your fathers, nor commanded them in the day that I brought them out of Egypt, on matters of burnt offerings and sacrifices. But rather this thing I instructed them to say; Listen to my voice, and I will become your Elohim, and you shall become my people...They set their abominations in the house which is called by my name, defiling it." Jer. 7:22-23

<http://scripture4all.org/Online Interlinear/OTpdf/jer7.pdf>

The presence of the above verse from Jeremiah in the OT should serve as evidence for Jews and Christians that not all Israelites from OT times subscribed to the stance of the Levites that animal sacrifice was a requirement, (rather than merely an option, based on laws in Leviticus on how to perform sacrifices hygienically). This verse provides clear evidence that the Levites simply chose to so interpret and interpolate the Levitican guidelines as commandments that *required* everyone to bring animals for sacrifice. And for Christians there is further support to Jeremiah's position in the following verse from Acts in the NT.

"They made a calf in those days and led sacrifice to the idol…Turns yet the God (*Theos*) and besides (instead) gives them to be offering divine service to the host of heaven (Greek-*stratia ho ouranos*[8], Hebrew-*tzba eshmim*); as it is written in the scroll of the prophets, no slayed ones and sacrifices you offered to Me (God) for forty years in the wilderness, house of Israel." Acts 7:42 (see <http://www.scripture4all.org>). This verse clearly disputes the Levite interpolations inserted into the text of the OT (discussed in detail later), advocating animal sacrifice, and just as clearly demonstrates that Jesus had taught his followers the falsehood of the requirement of animal sacrifice. [8]"In Greek mythology the sky god was known as *Ouranos*." Goodgame, Peter. *Domination by Deception.* <http://www.redmoonrising.com/Giza/DomDec6.htm>

The Levite Sopherim from Ezra's time and on even went so far as to change, in one of their alterations a (apparently to them) derogatory passage about Aaron in Num.12:12, so as to make it appear that Aaron was not afflicted with the plague of leprosy for eating flesh[9]. Hebrew Roots. *More Emendations.* [9](This was perhaps because their lineages from Aaron were the basis of their authority to re-institute, practice, and enforce the practice of animal sacrifice. II Chr. 34:21)

<http://www.geocities.com/~hebrew_roots/html/hr-2-3-02.html>

The moral authority of this school of Levite scribes, to make their substitutions is suspect, as by their own record, they used a newly "found" (II Chr. 34:15-24) rendering of the "Law of Moses" to instigate King Josiah to order, at their behest, multiple murders of other priests who thwarted the Levite's authority. According to the OT these Levite "priests of the second order," (II Kings 23:4) in spite of the commandment "Thou shalt not kill," instigated and condoned the murder of many priests of Judah, after they would not attend the then newly instituted Levite animal sacrifice for Passover. (II Chr. 34:21) They were murdered because they chose to attend their own Passover ceremony, where they ate unleavened bread, instead of attending the animal sacrifice of the Levites. II Kings 23:9

The record was then, after they had first been invited to attend (apparently recognized as true followers of YHVH since outsiders were forbidden at Passover Ex 12:43), written so as to make it appear that they were guilty of some heresy (namely burning incense to the host of heaven. *tzba eshmim*[10]). Their murders were instigated by the Levite priests of this 'second' order, under Ezra's great-grandfather Hilikiah (Ezra 7:1). Hilikiah, who "found" the copy of the Law, (this copy at the very least cannot be established as an original version of Moses' Law, since the chain of custody was admittedly broken), was also a Levite, descended from Aaron of the tribe of Levi. (II Kings 22:8 & 23:3-22)

[10]The *tzba eshmim* were YHVH's Elohim, His heavenly hosts who were in oneness with Him. "Praise YHWH, all His heavenly hosts, you his servants who do his will." Ps. 103:21 "Therefore hear the word of YHWH, I saw YHWH sitting on His throne and all the host of the heavens (*tzba eshmim*) standing on His right and His left." I Kings 22:19 "Praise Him, all His angels; praise Him all His heavenly hosts." Ps. 148:2

Moses had already refused the Levite claim to the priesthood once during his own lifetime (Num. 16:8-10). Aaron, Moses brother, was however, Moses' high priest over the Levite servers, whose job was to hygienically sacrifice animals in the tabernacle of the congregation to be served to the mixed multitude. These Levite butchers and servers were therefore forbidden to "<u>come near the vessels of the sanctuary and the altar</u>" (Num. 18:1-5 see also Num. 18:32). Although Exodus, in ch. 40:29 was later changed from ascent and present offering to read that a meat offering was offered there, meat was actually forbidden on this altar, "You shall make an altar...You shall offer no meat offering...thereon." Ex. 30:1&9

Upon the urging of the Levite 'priesthood' of this so-called 'second order', King Josiah during his reign ordered all people who refused to partake of this newly instituted (II Chr. 34:21) animal sacrifice of the Levite's, to be slain (II Kings 23:21-22). That the Levites obtained their power by participating in and condoning the breaking of the commandment, "Thou shalt not kill," in order to promote their own self-interest surely makes their claim to the holy priesthood suspect. According to the NT Jesus himself also questioned the authority of the Levite school of scribes, calling them 'the sons of those who murdered the prophets'. (Matt. 23: 29-31 & Hebrews 7:11-14) The record of some of their changes and an account of their crimes will come under much closer scrutiny in a later chapter.

Many biblical scholars apparently refuse to acknowledge the presence of the plural verbs that provide exceptions to their assumption that the singular interpretation of "God" can be applied universally, to instances where Elohim was used as God, singular. If they can pick and choose when to use Elohim as a singular noun, ignoring examples where it is accompanied by a plural verb, then would this not allow everyone else the same freedom to ignore those verses having singular verbs, and apply a plural meaning universally? A multitude of verses will be presented throughout this book that demonstrate that the former has been, and continues to be the case concerning the word Elohim in the OT.

The word Elohim was used to refer to any Elohim who was a member of YHVH's council of holy gods or a congress of sorts, with one leading Elohim. They all served under, yet were one with YHVH, so of course it often appears to use singular verbs in these references. Just as the words fish and sheep can mean one or many, Elohim could mean one or many. However, YHVH is the only One who is the All. (1 Cor. 15:28)

> "When ever yet may be subjected to <u>HIM THE ALL</u> (*Auto Ho Pas*) then he the son shall be subjected <u>to the One</u> who subjected all to him, that may be *Ho Theos* (the Deity in Greek – i.e., YHVH, KJV God) <u>THE ALL IN ALL</u>." 1 Cor. 15:28

> (see <<u>http://www.scripture4all.org/OnlineInterlinear/Greek_Index.htm</u>>)

The Supreme Deity, the One can have no human image or any other image (John 1:18 "Not yet one has seen God at any time.") since He is infinite (II Chr. 2:6). This is obviously one reason why images were forbidden, so we would not try to make of Him some limited form. "You were shown these things so that you might know that YHWH is *the* Elohim (Note that the "e" in "eAleim" means "the" Elohim) and there is no other aside from Him." Deu. 4:35 also Deu. 4:39 YHVH is the only One who is "the Elohim"[11] since He is the only Pre-existent One who can be "All *in* all" (1 Cor. 15:28) and therefore one with His Elohim, and there is no other who can make that claim.

[11]Cyrus Gordon in *Elohim Its Reputed Meaning of Rulers, Judges* (1935) points out that <u>the</u>

phrase "the Elohim" was eliminated from Deu. 15:17, if these, as some have argued, simply referred to "the Elohim" as human judges why else would it have been so changed? Yet the phrase "the Elohim" (*eAleim*), with the plural predicator "the," was not completely eradicated from the OT. The fact that it still occurs 365 times makes it seem likely that these remnants somehow, perhaps because of their context, survived the editing[12] processes by the Sopherim. The OT text underwent this editing or redacting by the Sopherim, at the same time they concealed the references to YHVH's Elohim by changing the phrase "YHVH Elohim," plural, to "Adonai Elohim" and interpreting it to mean Lord God singular. [12](although the scribes definitely transcribed YHVH as *Adonai*/Lord, there also seems to be evidence of other editing that took place later on by rabbis protesting the trinity. See Professor Alan Segal's book, *Two Powers in Heaven*)

"Thus the heavens and the earth were finished, and all the host of *them* (plural)." Gen. 2:1

This early understanding of "the Elohim" (*eAleim*, remember the "*e*" stands for the word "the," a plural predicator) shows up from as far back as Genesis. Enoch walked with "the Elohim." (Gen. 5:22) Abraham spoke to "the Elohim." (Gen. 17:18); "The Elohim" appeared to Jacob and actually specifies that he make an altar to; "*Al* (or *El*) *the one* appearing to you" (*eAleim* Gen. 35:1&7), this was as opposed, obviously, to other Elohim (*Aleim*); and Moses was afraid to look at "the Elohim." (Ex. 3:6). Since they were so often called "the Elohim," with the plural predicator "the," the early Israelites clearly must have understood that frequently YHVH spoke through his "holy gods" (as they are called in Daniel including Dan. 4:8 & 5:11 translated as gods plural & Jos. 24:19 translated as god singular; yet both contain the plural spelling), and that they were "the Elohim" over whom YHVH was king (Ps. 95:2-6) because they were one with YHVH the Creator of gods (*Al Alim* Dan. 11:36). The Torah clearly recognized the existence of the Elohim, for example comparing YHVH's superiority to them in Exodus 15:11.

It must be understood that while YHVH sometimes speaks as a disembodied voice, He also often speaks through His council of holy Elohim, especially the one single Elohim (often *Eloah/Eloi/Ale*, etc.) at the head of His council, as seen for example in Isa. 40:28. Aside from the possible change in usage from Moses time to Isaiah's time, when Isaiah mentions that "Elohim does not faint...there is no searching of his understanding," it must be remembered that this is a human attempt to discuss the deity not YHVH himself speaking.

With all due respect to Isaiah the prophet, even if his words were not altered by the Levite scribes, Isaiah was, as we all are, apt to use the terminology of his own time, which was long after Moses' *Book of the Law* and *Testimony* (originally carried in the ark, by Levite servers, Ex. 40:20, Deu. 31:26). So Isaiah's usage was perhaps not reflective of the meaning of Elohim as Moses and the early Israelites would have understood it at the time Moses created his original *Book of the Law*. There is also the fact that examples of this sort can equally refer to "Elohim" as the speaker of a group in a state of unified agreement, in oneness with the will of YHVH. The same concept can apply elsewhere in the OT, that is, as YHVH speaking through His Elohim, the holy council and its head ruler and speaker who was also simply referred to as "Elohim."

Just as we would say that; "congress spoke of some legislation," the Elohim often spoke, (singular) through a head speaker, of decisions they, in unity with YHVH, had made concerning mankind, so of course it is often, though not always, accompanied by a singular verb. Traditional modern biblical scholars often insist that the phrase "the Elohim" means "the God" par excellence. Yet they do not cite any ancient authority to prove this, instead they quote each other in a system of circular reasoning, insisting that this must be so, therefore allowing themselves the freedom to avoid explaining the numerous biblical discussions of "the Elohim" with the plural predicator.

Since Elohim is not always accompanied by singular verbs (sometimes the verb is not singular and sometimes there are more than one Elohim described in various passages, appearing together and speaking as one) this shows that the accepted traditional explanation is inconsistent. The explanation given in this book, that the Elohim often speak as one with YHVH, that YHVH speaks through them and that the Levite scribes tried to obliterate references to YHVH's Elohim (perhaps including the accompanying verbs), can account for all the varieties of instances, singular and plural. The traditional interpretations, arbitrarily switching back and forth, ignoring the times when plural grammatical forms are used, does not. The Levites were bold enough to change YHVH's holy name to Adonai, why would anyone think they would hesitate to change the accompanying verbs?

There are many scholars who have addressed the discrepancies and anachronisms in the handling of Deuteronomy, which will be elaborated upon in a later section specifically dealing with Deuteronomy; some of those discrepancies and the relationship those changes may have to the Sopherim, the scribes, will also be discussed later. It will be demonstrated that at the same time they obliterated the compound expression YHVH Elohim (with the plural 'im' ending) first occurring in Gen.2:4, changing it to "Adonai Elohim," they also had a self-serving motive for changing these references to YHVH Lord of the Elohim or YHVH's host of heaven (including especially Deu. 4:19). And thus a motive for changing many of the accompanying verbs, etc., to follow suit with their newly adopted term "Adonai Elohim" and their limited interpretation of monotheism that excluded YHVH's council of holy Gods.

Elohim may have been used by some of the later prophets, as the Levite scribes used it, rather than as it is frequently found in the Torah. These instances must also be considered in light of the study of a multitude of other anachronistic changes (cited later) made by the Sopherim scribes in their handling of Deuteronomy.

The name "Elohim" *is*, however, still sometimes used to denote a plural number of entities, accompanied by plural verbs, and other grammatical terms, as will be seen. These instances make it clear that most biblical scholars apparently think they have a right to pick and choose which passages where Elohim will be interpreted in the plural and which as a singular entity. However, if one adopts that position, the mentions of a holy council of Elohim (Ps. 82:1-7), or "holy gods" must still be addressed. "My God 'Eloah' (singular) in whom is the spirit 'Ruch' of the holy gods 'qdishin Elohim' (plural)" (Dan. 4:8: 5:11). The possibility of their spokesman (*Eloah*) speaking for them, as in oneness with YHVH on any given subject, must also be considered by any who claims to be open to examining and accounting for *all* the recorded evidence.

It might be said that the problem began when the name YHVH (*Yod Heh Vav Heh*) was recorded in the Massorah by the Sopherim, as the word *Adonai* (Lord), and the plural word Elohim (meaning gods) was transcribed as meaning God singular, purportedly to avoid speaking the name YHVH. However the fall away from knowledge of YHVH's oneness with His council of Elohim, had probably been accumulating prior to that (Because of the similarity between eloih and elohim the pronunciation elohim may have been confused, especially among the illiterate, beginning as early as the time of Moses, however, the decision to use elohim almost exclusively to mean the Creator was effectively enforced by the Levite priesthood). If it really were critical for even YHVH's prophets to avoid using or writing YHVH's holy name *altogether*, as the Sopherim interpreted it, then surely it would have been specified in the Ten Commandments. Instead the Israelites were just instructed not to take His name in vain.

This loss of knowledge eventually resulted in the use of "Adonai Elohim" or "Lord God," instead of the compound title YHVH Elohim, (YHVH Lord of the gods or YHVH gods depending on the context. YHVH was often used to mean Lord, depending on the time in history.) which was used prior to that, as we would perhaps say, Lord of the gods or YHVH's Elohim depending on the context. YHWH originally occurred 6,823 times and Adonai originally occurred 449 times. YHVH was changed to ADONAI, all capitals, by the Sopherim, and the instances where "Adonai" already occurred in lower case letters, was left as it was, remaining unchanged, even further confusing the two names. *The Emendations of the Sopherim.*

<http://www.oocities.org/hebrew_roots/html/hr-2-1-02.html>

ATON/ADON/ADONIS/ADONAI

There has always been and continues to be the tendency for historians to take the descriptive titles, for various gods, lords and kings, as the actual name of these beings. It cannot be emphasized too strongly that when this problem is properly addressed it can often show a continuity of understanding among the wiser of the ancients concerning these titled beings (The Creator and His gods, lords and sons of the gods and even various mortal kings). The theme, of a Supreme Creator and His council of gods, pervades religions all down through many ancient cultures. So often it is not that they were talking of a different Creator or different Elohim, or different a council of 'gods' beneath Him, it was often just that they were speaking of Him and them in their own language. Of course in the transmission of any story there is the tendency of getting it confused or putting one's own interpretation on it (just as the Levites did). But there is clearly a core idea that threads through all the stories of the ancient cultures, referring to the Creator and to a council of lessor gods. When we restore our understanding, through learning how different languages spoke of the same beings it can help us come closer to a common understanding in the present.

The many languages have confounded our understanding of the beginnings of history ever since the time of the tower of Babel. In time to come "YHWH He is becoming (*UEIE IEVE*) king over all the earth, in that day, YHWH, He shall become One (*Achad/Echad*) and His name One." Zech. 14:9

"For then I will make the peoples pure of speech, so that they all invoke YHWH by name and serve Him with one accord" (Zeph. 3:9)

One such confusing title, Adon or Adonai, is the actual Hebrew-Chaldean-Egyptian word for "lord." The title "Adon" is inter-changeably used as "master," for example; "Elohim has made me lord (*adon*) of all Egypt" (Gen. 45:9). And as in; "if his master (*adon*) have given him a wife." (Ex.21:4) Adonai derives from the same root as the words *Adon/Aton/Aten* associated with the worship of the Syrian and Egyptian Adonis or *Aton/Aten/Aden/Adon*. Adon, or Adonis of Babylon. Also later on, Adon became the great war-god, Odin or Wodan, as is well known. Moustafa Gadalla, *Tut-Ankh-Amen* & Hislop, Alexander. *The Two Babylons.*

<http://www.biblebelievers.com/babylon/sect41.htm>

Aton is perhaps most well known as the monotheistic One God enforced during the reign of Akhenaten, after he attempted to obliterate all carvings of the previously worshiped Amon Ra as the head of the pantheon of gods (more on this in the section on Om/Aum etc). It is perhaps less well known that Aton was already in existence as a little known sun god who was simply adopted by Akhenaten. And as usual scholars tend to stick to the name itself rather than translating it to "Lord" as the history of the word shows it to mean. The Levites are identified by Osman as the select group of noble relatives of Akhenaten who made up the Egyptian priesthood of Aton and served in the temple of Aton in Egypt. There is a village in Egypt that still retains its name Mal-lawi or Mal-levi, meaning the city of the Levites. *The Gospel According to Egypt.* Citing Ahmed Osman. <http://www.domainofman.com/ankhemmaat/moses.html>

> "Apollodorus. Theocritus, Idyll. Theocritus is speaking of Adonis as delivered by Venus from Acheron, or the infernal regions, after being there for a year; but as the scene is laid in Egypt, it is evident that it is Osiris he refers to, as he was the Adon (lord) or Adonis of the Egyptians." Hislop, Alexander. *The Two Babylons.*
>
> <http://www.biblebelievers.com/babylon/sect41.htm>
>
> & Theocritus. *Idylls 1-4.* <http://www.theoi.com/Text/TheocritusIdylls1.html.>

In Hebrew the last two letters added on to the end of the name Adon, is a Hebrew pronoun meaning "my" or "mine" making it possessive. Thus Adonai means Adon-Mine or My Lord. This word for master or lord, adopted by the Sopherim (the Levite scribes) in place of YHVH, then coupled with the word elohim translated as "God" singular, changed the earlier understanding of the definitions, connotations, and associations with the compound name YHVH Elohim.

Adonai was never used in the Torah as precisely synonymous with YHVH. This understanding had previously been passed down through various priests from Moses time and forward for the next four hundred years or so. This included oral teachings and songs (psalms) among the priests of Judah, who were murdered along with many idolatrous priests, at the behest of the Levite priests of the 'second order,' for burning incense to the Host of Heaven, YHVH's Elohim. (II Kings 23:5) These priests of Judah taught the people the rule of YHVH's council of Elohim and other meanings lost when Moses' *Book of the Law* and *Testimony* was lost along with the Ark of the Covenant. (Ex. 40:20, Deu. 31:26) This was before the priesthood was assumed by the later Levite scribes, when they elevated themselves to become priests; just as Moses foresaw their

13

desires to be moving in that direction already in his own lifetime (Num. 16:10). Their interference is seen especially in the handling of Deuteronomy, which will also be addressed in depth much later.

> "Before the exile, Israelite religion affirmed a council of gods...after the exile, the gods became angels...170 instances of plural Elohim... (occur) in the Qumran (Essene) material alone. Many of these instances are in the context of a heavenly council. If a divine council of gods had ceased to exist in Israelite religion by the end of the exile, how does one account for these references?"[13] Dr. Michael S. Heiser, *Are Yahweh and El Distinct Deities?*

> <http://www.thedivinecouncil.com/HIPHILDeut32%20Psa82%20article.pdf>

[13]The position of this book is that the references are there because the Essenes were closer to the truth than the Levites, and possessed documents outside of the Levite influence, concerning YHVH's "holy gods." The Levite Sopherim edited the version that is now given in the KJV. That we all descended from the Elohim as mentioned in (Gen. 1:27) is a truth that John 10:34-35 shows Jesus to also have embraced when he said "is it not written in your law...I said ye are gods?" Later we will go into evidence showing that Jesus, was known as a Nazarene, and that the Nazarenes as a whole were closely aligned with the Essenes.

Along with the true meaning associated with YHVH, a name understood as describing the infinite Creator thus meaning far more than the name Adonai, which is only a "master" or "lord," the meanings of the associated plural word, "Elohim" also came to be eventually lost and changed to "God" singular. At the time of the exile into slavery in Babylon, the people mostly became illiterate, many even losing the ability to speak Hebrew, adopting the language of Babylon instead. Aramaic was the language of Babylon during the Jewish exile there. (note # 6 from article *The Meaning of the word Nephilim, Fact vs. Fantasy,* by Michael S. Heiser Ph.D., Hebrew Bible and Ancient Semitic Languages, Univ. of Wisconsin-Madison)

> "We're used to thinking of that term (Elohim) as denoting a being who possesses unique, unshared attributes-the *Elohim* of Israel, as it were. That just isn't true. While it's true that the word came to be used as a name for the God of Israel, the term itself has no essence that must be equated with Yahweh. The Old Testament passages...that have demons and spirits of the dead as *Elohim* forbid such an equation. This equation must be dispensed with. The word *Elohim* more broadly does not refer to "deity attributes. (such as "mighty" or "majesty," MHJ) Rather it points to a plane of existence. An *Elohim* is simply a being whose proper habitation is the spirit world." Michael Heiser, *So What Exactly is an Elohim?* (excerpt from his forthcoming book @

> <http://www.thedivinecouncil.com/What%20is%20an%20Elohim.pdf >)

Heiser and a few other biblical scholars like Wade Cox of the Church of Christ (ccg.org) have recognized the existence of YHVH's holy council of Elohim. This recognition was long obscured by the substitutions of the Levite scribes, but most mainstream Christians have yet to reject, as Jesus did, the other literary contributions of the Levite scribes (the Sopherim) to the OT. Jesus had a slight advantage over modern scholars. As a Nazarene he was closely associated with the

Essenes, who having their own versions of the OT, historically disputed the Levite version. And as a rabbi himself (by which title he is many times called in the NT, these verses will be cited further on) he most likely encountered some of these copies of Moses original *Book of the Law* (Ex. 40:20, Deu. 31:26). Not having come under the "editing" and "redacting" of the Levites, these would have been much closer to the true "Law of Moses."

> "Scholars also frequently assert that no explicit denial of the existence of other gods occurs until the time of Deutero-Isaiah and thereafter (6th century BCE) in a presumed campaign by zealous scribes to expunge such references from the sacred texts." Michael Heiser, Ph.D., Introduction, *Monotheism, Polytheism, Monolatry, or Henotheism?*

<http://digitalcommons.liberty.edu/cgi/viewcontent.cgi?article=1276&context=lts_fac_pubs>

The reason for the change to the name "Adonai Elohim," Lord God, must also be considered in light of the popularity of the (Egyptian) name Adon/Aton/Aten/Adonis/Adonai, at the time of the Levites rise to power. And this should be understood, when considering why the Levite scribes made the decision to substitute the word *Adonai,* or Lord in place of YHVH's holy name.

The exposure of Jewish thought to the strict monotheism of the Magi of the Zarathustrian Ormazdian religion, while in exile for two hundred years in Babylon should also be considered. Perhaps there was a perceived jealousy of their philosophy of monotheism, and the desire not to be out done by "The One God Ormazd" or the monotheism of the worship of the Egyptian Aton. The influence of these beliefs should also be considered when analyzing the motives of these scribes, in their zealous efforts to rewrite the "Law of Moses," and other books of the OT obliterating YHVH's holy name and the records of His Elohim. That the Levites have been identified as the select group of noble relatives of Akhenaten who made up the Egyptian priesthood of Aton and served in the temple of Aton in Egypt explains, in part, their motives to substitute the title Adon/Aton in place of YHVH.

Tertullian, Jerome, and other fathers of the church, inform us, that the Gentiles celebrated (well before the time of Jesus) on the 25th of December, the birth of the God Sol, under the name of Adonis (in Persia he was known as Mithra; in Egypt, Phoenicia and Biblis, Adonis). At the same time in Egypt, Phrygia, and Syria, were celebrated the deaths and resurrections of Osiris, Atys, and Adonis. Mead, G. R. S. *Did Jesus Live 100 Years BC.* pp. 104,135-138,177,256,334,335,408 &410

In addition to the 6,823 above-mentioned changes from YHVH Elohim to Adonai Elohim, *Adonai* in lower case letters was actually substituted for the name YHVH another 134 times. The instances of the alterations of YHVH to Adonai/Lord in 134 places, by the Sopherim, are at appendix 32 of the Companion Bible. Many of these alterations were in areas where verses mentioned YHVH and Adonai in the same sentence or context, and thus would have made it obvious that more than one being was under discussion. Additionally these changes occurred at a time when most of the Israelites were illiterate; having just come out of exile in Babylon and so went unquestioned in their time. <http://wordstudy.org/cbaps/ap032.htm>

> "When Joshua was coming into Jericho, he lifted up his eyes and, Behold, he saw a man standing in front of him, his sword drawn in his hand. And Joshua went to him and said,

"Are you for us or for our foes?" And he is saying, "Not that, I am chief of the host of YHWH, now I came." And Joshua fell on his face, to the earth, and bowed down to him and said, Adonai (lord of me) what have you to say to your servant?" Jos. 5:14

Now this verse demonstrates a number of things, it demonstrates that YHVH's Adonai or Lord, having a human shape, was a one time human. It demonstrates that YHVH had a heavenly host, of whom this Adonai was the leader. Most importantly it demonstrates, according to this "Adonai" who served YHVH, that YHVH and Adonai are NOT *one and the same being,* for by his own words he stated that he, Adonai, was the chief of YHVH's hosts.

THE MASTER'S TEACHINGS AGAINST THE "LAW' INTERPRETED BY THE LEVITE SCRIBES

"If therefore perfection were through the Levite priesthood (for under it the people received the law) what further need was there that another priest (Jesus) should rise up of the order of Melchisedek (see Gen. 14:18, Heb. 7:1) and NOT according to the order of Aaron? For the priesthood being changed, <u>there is also the necessity of changing the law</u>...For it is evident that out of Judah[14] the master (Jesus) has risen." Hebrews 7:11-14

[14]Jesus line came out of the priesthood of Judah, rather than the false priesthood presumed by the Levite descendants of Aaron and others. (Through no fault of Aaron's, however, who performed his duties as directed by Moses, as a priest over the Levite servers.) Many of the earlier priests mentioned in the OT were of Judah, *not* descended from the Levites (who had murdered in their rise to power). This position on the necessity of changing the law as handled by the Levites shows that Jesus and his early followers did *not* respect the biblical input of the so-called Levite priesthood. This book will show that the Levite scribes, during their control of these texts of the OT, added much of their own input to the present version we now have. Through the KJV carrying forward their alterations, they thus still influence to this day many preachers and church followers *away* from the necessity of changing the "law" as taught by Jesus to *his* followers, and mislead them back toward the imperfect practices of the Levite priesthood.

So as good students of the master let us scrutinize the so-called "Law," as we have received it from the hands of Ezra and the Levite scribes, for the input, substitutions, alterations and falsehoods of the Levite school (and also look for their false teachings in later books of the OT). This school was descended from the same Levite scribes who, through murder (see II Kings 23:3-22 & Matt. 23: 29-31) had instituted themselves as the "priesthood." So it is still a necessity that we change our understanding of the law, back as close as possible, to the original "Law of Moses." For this is what Jesus prescribed, but was prevented from accomplishing by his murder at the hands of the followers of that corrupt system. We must, by finding all the Levite input, complete the changing of "the law" (the false law promoted by the Levites), as a necessity understood to be required of Jesus' followers as shown above in Hebrews 7:11-14.

Therefore we must also consider whether the copy of the OT we have is perfect or whether it has been altered by human error and by the self-interest of the Levites, who Jesus repeatedly rebuked. This is perhaps not as important for those whose faith is in YHVH, but it may be important for those whose faith is in the, perhaps flawed, human record of the presence of YHVH and His holy Elohim. The Bible is simply a guidebook not meant to be worshiped, we are meant to worship YHVH, the pre-existent All One, not the Bible.

So for the moment this must include suspending judgment on the presence of many singular verbs, until it can be seen whether the Levites can be shown to have made other changes to Moses teachings to suit their own interpretation. If this proves to be the case, then the presence of these singular verbs, in a majority of cases may be seen to be merely the only remaining spindly leg, which the established school of thought, based on the Levite's input, has left to stand on. As such the presence of many singular verbs will then represent the *almost* complete revision of post-exilic thought; and the remaining unchanged plural verbs will be seen to point to cases where they were overlooked by post-exilic scribes or left in because the context demanded it.

Jesus had no fear of rejecting the orthodox teachings of the religious establishment of his time, i.e., the Levite school and their false priesthood, because besides his faith and oneness with YHVH Elohim, he had learned the truth, that we are all descended from the Elohim. (Genesis 6:1-2) And he knew of and is quoted in the NT mentioning that the Levites had murdered in their rise to power (Matt. 23: 29-31) and he knew that the "law" of animal sacrifice, prescribed by the Levite school, was unnecessary and untrue as shown by the following verse.

> "I desire kindness[15,] not sacrifice. And the knowledge of Elohim instead of burnt offerings." Hos. 6:6 [15](mercy in KJV). This verse is twice quoted by Jesus, disputing the stance of the Levite scribes in the promotion of animal sacrifice to receive healing and forgiveness of sin. Matt. 9:13&12:7.

When Jesus tried to publicly reveal that the Levite "law" (Heb. 7:5) of tithing 1/10 of an animal sacrifice, to heal people of their sins, was only there to indulge the rapacity (ravenous appetites) of their false priesthood (Matt. 23:25) he incited the wrath of this so-called priesthood. For this, and mostly because he disputed their rise to power through murder, they eventually instigated his murder also, Luke 23:10). The NT clearly reflects Jesus teachings on the Levite false "priesthood" in Hebrews 7:11-14 where it says that the teachings of the Levite school and their substitutions, alterations, contributions and falsehoods into the "Law" must be changed.

The obliteration of references to YHVH Elohim by the Levite scribes and its significance was well understood by Jesus. He rejected the teachings of those scribes, and he rebukes their school as the descendant's of the murderers of the (true) prophets and yet he still tries to explain to them, that even they were gods. (John10:34-35) He knew and embraced the knowledge that the scribes had rejected, and tried to obliterate, that we are all sons of the Elohim (*ben Elohim*) (and daughters of the Elohim Gen. 1:27). For it was the sons of the Elohim who had inter-bred with the "daughters of the Adam." (Genesis 6:1-2) *Adam* besides becoming the name of an individual is in fact also the Hebrew word for humanity (SHD 119, 120, 122, 127).

> "And he is creating Elohim the Adam in image of him, he creates them male and female he creates them." Gen. 1:27 (These female descendants of the Elohim were present even before the later creation of the specialized woman now known as "Eve" in Gen. 2:21-22.)

17

<http://scripture4all.org/OnlineInterlinear/OTpdf/gen1.pdf>

These were the very same Elohim whom the OT says ride through the heavens of heaven in their chariots (Ps. 68:17&33) and who were present when YHVH ordained the creation of the earth, the sun and the moon. (Job 38:1-7; Ps. 8:3; Jer. 10:11) "He is calling Elohim to atmosphere..." Gen. 1:6-8 "And He is blessing Elohim in the seventh time[16] (*bium*) ...He ceases from all of work *which He creates Elohim to make* these genealogical annals in the time (of) YHVH Elohim making the earth and the heavens" Gen. 2:3-4 ([16]KJV translated as day)

Who was calling the Elohim if not YHVH, and who was blessing them if not YHVH? Who is this "He" who here blesses the Elohim? Why YHVH of course although not specified by the name YHVH at that time (spoken of instead as "He is becoming" a variant of I Am/I am becoming). But He blessed His Elohim, after which they ceased from the work *He* created them for, to make a record of it. (See http://www.scripture4all.org)

> "And He is answering, YHWH...where were you when I laid the foundations of the earth...and the morning stars jubilated together and all the sons of the Elohim shouted for joy?" Job 38:1-7

We will discuss further on, the oneness of the Elohim with YHVH (YHVH Elohim, *YHVH Echad*, Duet 6:4) and consequentially the full meaning of the compound term YHVH Elohim. This will perhaps help explain why the Levite scribes replaced its occurrence in the OT with their substitution, "Adonai Elohim." This (Adonai Elohim or Lord God) is a name by which YHVH was not originally known, in the Hebrew version of Genesis and the rest of the Torah. This was a later interpolation, by Ezra and the Sopherim, some of which was then handed down to us in the also much altered KJV. (including but not limited to Gen. 2:4; 2:7; 2:8; 2:9; 2:15; 2:16; 2:18; 2:19; 2:21; 2:22; 3:9; 3:14; 3:21; 3:22; 3:23; 24:12; Ex.3:19; 9:30; 29:46; Num. 27:16. For other instances it is possible to do a search for "Lord God" on eBible @ <http://www.ebible.com/>

In a later chapter the motive these scribes had for rejecting Jesus' teaching them that, "ye are gods" (John10:34-35) will become clearer, and how that motive connects to the murders Jesus referred to when he called them "the sons of those who murdered the prophets." (Matt. 23: 29-31) Who the prophets were that they murdered, in their rise to power, will also be discussed. Their rage over his revelations of these murders, and the resulting affront to their presumed authority, resulted in his own murder. When he revealed that we are all gods, along with teaching against the Levite practice of animal sacrifice, and revealing the murders committed in establishing the Levite school, it eventually resulted in the murders of Jesus and many of his followers. One of these was Stephen who was also murdered for discussing these murders. (Acts 7:52)

Apparently unlike Jesus, many biblical scholars think it would be heretical and are afraid to question the input into the Bible of these murderous Levite scribes. Probably for the most part because it would mean questioning those parts of the Bible written by known members of the Levite school of thought (like Ezra the scribe turned priest). And it would mean questioning the presence of a multitude of anachronistic changes, additions, and alterations to Moses' original writings that apparently date to the time of this Levite school, and after the exile, rather than to the time of Moses himself. Some of these anachronistic and out of place changes (historically speaking, for they are written as if from the point of view of one looking back to the time of Moses), will be addressed further on in a section on Deuteronomy.

ELOHIM/ALEIM/EL/AL

"I YHWH am the first and the last, there are no Elohim without Me." Isa. 44:6 (also see Isa. 45:18) See <http://www.scripture4all.org>

If YHVH, king over all the Elohim (Ps. 95:2-6), knew Himself by the name "Elohim" and meant for us to acknowledge Him by that name, why would He use for other beings, a name which He recognized as His own? Why, if as traditional scholars insist, Elohim is YHVH's own name, would He use it to refer to other lessor beings, some of whom were false gods, and all of whom He had created?

From this verse alone (Isa. 44:6) it can be seen that YHVH is the Creator of the Elohim. And, unlike the name Elohim, YHVH, as the name for the infinite Pre-existent-One, has never been taken to mean anything except the name of the Omni-present Holy Living Spirit. The Holy Spirit is also known as the *Ruach hakodesh.* (*Ruach*, a feminine noun, a wind or a breath, spirit SHD 7307, coupled with; *hakodesh* pure or sanctified SHD 6942.) The Father, as the Creator of all life, from whom all the living receives spirit, which is seen in the phrase, "spirit of the living ones," *ruch chiim* and by one of YHVH's other names, *Al or El Chiim* the All[17] Life, SHD 2416. (Gen. 6:17 & 7:15) This is the same concept, for the Creator, as is called the Great Spirit among American Indians and by people in other cultures around the world. Coincidentally the root of the Greek word for spirit, *pneuma* also means "wind" or breath along with the Hebrew word *Ruach.* [17]See the section following, THE ALL, on the Hebrew *Al or El* having also the ancient meaning of "all."

> "… YHWH supreme one being feared, great king over all the earth… make melody you Elohim make melody, make melody to king of us..." Ps. 47:2-6

Dr. David Blumenthal, discourses on verse 9-10 of the "*Sefer Yetsirah*" (written 120 CE-600 CE), in his book "Understanding Jewish Mysticism." He tells us that it was at one time understood that the "*ruch Elohim hayyim*" (Gen. 1:2) the Elohim's breath (breath from breath, that is derived from YHVH's breath) was secondary to the *Ruach Hakodesh*. Ruach Hakodesh is more precisely the Holy Spirit, it was not rendered as "Holy Ghost" until the appearance in 1611 of the King James Version of the Bible. Spong, John Shelby. *Liberating the Gospels,* p. 222. & *The Kabbalah.* <http://www.mystae.com/restricted/streams/scripts/kabbalah.html>

Prior to their exile many of the few Israelites who could read would no doubt have questioned the Levite decision to use a plural word for a singular entity. Why would a word, used by the Israelites and other peoples throughout the Middle East, to denote a plural number of gods, now be said by the Levites to be precisely synonymous with YHVH, the infinite All One? (1 Cor. 15:28) The end of their previous understanding, and of Moses' original *Book of the Law* (Ex.

40:20, Deu. 31:26), reached its fulfillment when the compound title, YHVH Elohim, meaning YHVH Lord of the gods or YHVH's gods (plural) depending on the context, was replaced with the title Adonai Elohim, interpreted as Lord God (singular) by the Levite scribes, the Sopherim. The history of the Sopherim records that this had been accomplished around the time of Ezra.

> "YHWH He reigns...bow down to Him all of Elohim...that you YHWH, Supreme over all of the earth, exceedingly you are ascendant over all of Elohim." Ps. 97:7&9

In modern times few people can begin to contemplate translating YHVH Elohim literally as YHVH Lord of the Gods or YHVH's Gods, because the understanding that YHVH has a council of Elohim, through whom He works in part, was lost in the distant past. After released from their exile in Babylon, according to the Bible at the time of Ezra, few of the Israelites could read Hebrew (Neh. 8:8) and many no longer even spoke it, speaking Aramaic instead, so the change went unquestioned and therefore unexplained. In more recent times Hebrew became a dead (unspoken) language in the Middle Ages, un-revived until 1881, (Revived by Elizer Ben-Yehuda) so that even few scholars and modern Jews, who had to relearn to speak the language, rarely thought to question this decision.

http://www.jewishvirtuallibrary.org/jsource/biography/ben_yehuda.html

Our word data derives from an ancient Hebrew word *da'at,* SHD 1847, meaning knowledge, a word included in one of the many names of YHVH given in the Bible, *Al De'ot,* or *Al Douth,* the All[18] Knowledge ("*Al Douth YHVH*" 1 Sam. 2:3). This verse has been translated as El[19] *of* Knowledge, but there is in fact no word "of" in the name, YHVH is *Al De'ot,* period. Therefore He is "All Knowledge" and by another of His names, *Al Amth or Emeth.* (Ps. 31:5, sometimes rendered as "faithful" however SHD 571 gives this word *amth or emeth* as "truth," the understanding is that truth and faith are one, as those who have faith remain truthful) So He is also All[18] Truth. *YHVH is Aur* (Isa. 9:2) the Light of All True Knowledge. [18]See following section on THE ALL as part of the definition of the word *Al or El.* Parsons, John J. *The Hebrew Names of God.* <http://www.hebrew4christians.com/Names_of_G-d/El/el.html>

[19]The word El is literally *Al* in Hebrew, as can be seen throughout the text of the <http://www.scripture4all.org> online interlinear concordance. Al, usually translated El, is actually the Hebrew letters *alef,* corresponding to the letter "A" and *lamed* corresponding to "L." "El" is confusing, because spelled with an "e" the first letter might seem to be closer to the Hebrew letters *hei* or *hey* plus *lamed,* making an "h" sound as in the Hebrew word for "shine" halal #1984 from Brown, Driver, Briggs, SHD 1984 shine, bright, etc. The Hebrew letter *hey,* however, is also used for "H," so it would further confuse the subject. Therefore in this text, except in the name Elohim and when the context requires otherwise, the more correct and literal spelling "*Al*" may be used instead of this commonly accepted and perhaps somewhat inaccurate "El." This is also the transliteration used by the interlinear Bible @

 <http://www.scripture4all.org>

The original Hebrew *data* of the Old Testament itself, defines the work of the Elohim for YHVH, their relationship to YHVH, and their relationship to humanity. Down through history this extensive record of their contacts with us has almost been obliterated by the numerous re-translations and miss-interpretations of the Hebrew terminology by the Levite Sopherim, mainstream Christianity, and Rabbinic Judaism.

Obviously there is a great deal more evidence concerning various biblical dogma, theories, and beliefs, than can be contained in this book. Therefore, this book will focus on developing a particular line of evidence; this line of evidence will become very clear by the end of the book. When it comes to religion, there is and always was the ability to pick and choose to accept whatever set of beliefs were most appealing to the individual. As this book proceeds it will be seen that while Ezra, the Levites and others thereafter have chosen to promote beliefs that suited them, it will become clear that there still *is* evidence to support another line of reasoning. That set of evidence will demonstrate that the Levite interference obscured much of the previous understanding associated with the visitations of YHVH's Elohim.

So we must begin with a recursion through the abundance of etymological data, covered elsewhere in part, and mentioned in passing in different texts, by many other authors. However, to make a comprehensive case it is important to compile as much evidence as possible from some of our foremost secular and non-secular scholars and then examine OT verses with the Hebrew names in place, in conjunction with that understanding.

It is certainly the right of the various authors of the accepted interpretations, from organized religions, to give their version of the Hebrew information on the Elohim. It is certainly also the right of all those who seek the truth, to question that presumed authority and consider the etymological evidence for themselves. While this evidence is strongly disputed amongst many sects, when taken in conjunction with ancient evidence in the form of verses of the OT transliterated directly from their Hebrew renderings (at the above websites and in other interlinear concordances) presented herein, it may allow for an expansion of current understanding.

Quoting a multitude of sources by scholars skilled in areas outside my scope creates a much greater chance of error. However, I ask the experts to still consider the whole argument, not dispensing with it because of any transcribed mistake (based on any presumed authority), which may occur. (If there is evidence that shows any of the facts presented in this book to be false constructive criticism, coupled with *conclusive evidence*, is welcomed, not however, mere opinions based only on religious belief.)

Through fear of damnation, organized religions have controlled and restricted the understanding of the minds of their followers, for too long in this matter. Faith should not be driven by fear, for where there is faith in YHVH, who is *Al Da'at,* All[20] Knowledge, there should be no fear of examining any true evidence. I claim no authority based on scholastic merit, but rather simply ask the reader to consider the logic and the evidence in question. [20]See the following section on The All.

Those previous interpreters, under the auspices of organized religion, have an equal right to assert their meaning and promote it. However, it will become obvious that they have presented no solid proof of their assertions and that the evidence of verb usage that they point to, to justify translating Elohim as God-singular, is itself equally open to the interpretation of any number of YHVH's Elohim speaking as one.

Even when the verbs were suited to a plural noun the verbs were sometimes changed to suit the singular noun, god. In Gen. 35:7, for example, the term Elohim/gods has a plural verb but is translated, "God was revealed," rather than "Gods were revealed" as it actually reads in Hebrew. The Socino (the First Rabbinic Bible - *The Socino Bible* 1488-94 AD) notes that the rabbinical authority Abraham ibn Ezra understood this text to refer to angels. Cox, Wade. *The Elect as Elohim.* <http://www.ccg.org/english/s/p001.html>

Jacob's story tells us; "This is none other but the house of gods" (*beth-Elohim*); and he set up a "pillar" and called it *beth-el* --"the house of God" (Gen. 28:17-19). And Elohim (gods) came to him in a dream and said: "I am the El of Beth-el" (Gen. 31:13); and Jacob built there an altar and called the place Beth-el, "because there *ha-Elohim* or *ealeim* (the-gods) <u>they</u> were revealed unto him" (Gen. 35: 7). Here the Hebrew text expressly uses the plural, noun and verb; "the-gods *were* revealed"; but the Authorized Version falsely translates it as: "God appeared unto him." The Revised Version correctly reads "revealed," but uses wrongly the singular "was."

The verbs used, for the most part, in the Hebrew texts with the plural Elohim are generally singular. The actual verb plural-forms (which in Hebrew is the tiny *vav* or "u" tacked on the end, as we add "s" in English to form the plural of various verbs), although mostly missing, is however, a number of times to be found. It is undeniable that instances exist mentioning the plurality of *ha-Elohim (ealeim),* the Elohim.

Some other examples are; "When Elohim they caused (plural: *hith-u*) me to wander from my father's house" (Gen. 20:13) "Israel, whom gods (Elohim) they went (plural: *balk-u*) to redeem ... from the nations and their gods (Elohim)" (2 Sam. 7:23). In the verse following the OT uses the plural adjective with the plural noun Elohim: "has heard the voice of the living gods (*Elohim chiim*)" (Deu. 5:26).

Even though the defenders of the version we have now, have often chosen to overlook the little "u" plural-sign of the Hebrew verbs and the unobtrusive "im" of the adjective, the fact that they left out the instances named here shows that there were Elohim who served YHVH. Who are these editors to pick and choose, to sometimes translate Elohim as singular and sometimes as plural? All that is asked is please be consistent. The understanding of the use of Elohim to denote YHVH's council meets the necessary requirements in both cases, it can be used with singular and plural verbs, *and* it can account for all the verses where there are multiple entities to which the Bible is referring. The OT provides many instances that witness to the case for multiple Elohim under YHVH.

> "At the mouth of two witnesses, or at the mouth of three witnesses, shall the matter be established" (Deu. 19:15). The many verses already cited and those following will show that the OT itself provides witness to far more than two or three instances, providing evidence that many witnesses, for the defense of the case presented here, clearly exist.

Many modern interpreters try to assert the use of the plural form "the Elohim" merely denotes "mighty." While the word Elohim eventually came to mean mighty, there were also a multitude of pagan god-heads-Elohim that were according to the Bible also mighty, because they are also called Elohim. The frequent use of the singular form, Eloah, also displays the inconsistency of this argument. If Elohim is singular then why switch back and forth between El, Eloah and

Elohim? It was clearly not a question of which Elohim were mighty. It is a question of whether the Elohim spoken of were the same Elohim who existed before the earth was created, who came here in their "fiery chariots" when YHVH called them and ordained them to participate in its creation, and were blessed by YHVH for their work.

> "The *mrkb*/ride of Elohim are tens of thousands of thousands, *shnan* (repeated, i.e., *times* tens of thousands of thousands more) Adonai (my Lord) is in them." Ps. 68:17 (SHD 430) in this significant verse, the use of the phrase 'Chariot of Elohim,' (to describe an obviously plural number of *mrkb*/chariots) has been arbitrarily translated as "chariot of God" (singular).

The significance of Ps. 68:17 is twofold. First it tells us that the "rides" of the Elohim are numbered as "thousands times thousands." Second it tell us that Adonai the "the Lord is among them" this tells us that they are the good guys and not false gods/Elohim, as may be argued concerning many other references to Elohim/Gods. Along with the next verse, Ps. 135:5, we can also come to understand that this "Lord" Adonai was one chosen from among all of the Elohim and was not YHVH Himself.

> "For I know that YHWH is great, and that the Lord of us is *from* all of Elohim." Ps. 135:5

In the next verse the phrase "a little lower than the Elohim" was changed to "a little lower than the angels" concealing the implication that YHVH made the Elohim and ranked humans beneath them. "*YHVH Adninu* (Lord of us) ...What are mortal humans that you are mindful of him and the sons of earthlings that you are visiting him? And you made him (man) a little lower than the Elohim (*m-Aleim*) and have crowned him with glory and honor." Ps. 8:1-5

> "I will praise You with all my heart: before Elohim I will sing praise unto You...For the glory of YHWH is great." Ps. 138:1&5

In Gen. 21:17, the name Elohim has been changed to "the angel of Elohim." Another verse where the term Elohim has been changed to the word angel, causing it to no longer demonstrate that YHVH's Elohim are humanoid in form and that they serve beneath YHVH is Gen. 28:12. "And he (Jacob) dreamed, and behold! A ladder set up on the earth, and the top of it reached to heaven: and behold Elohim messengers/*malaki Elohim* (were) ascending and descending upon it. And behold! YHVH was stationed *above* it and proceeded to say I am YHVH, the Elohim of Abraham and the Elohim of Isaac."

> "And you said, Behold, YHWH He showed us our Elohim, His glory and His greatness, we have heard his voice out of the midst of fire: we have seen this day that Elohim do speak with man, and he lives." Deu. 5:24

There were many other changes added at the time of the "Sopherim," the Levite scribes who, for example, replaced the words "to your gods" (*alelik*[21]) with "to your tents." 1 Kings 12:16, II Chr. 10:16 and II Sam. 20:1. ([21]Any astute observer can see that this word contains the same root as *Aleim*-gods or Elohim, and again attests to their efforts to remove references to the gods, the Elohim.) Besides the numerous changes by the Sopherim concerning the use of YHVH and Elohim, there is a great deal of evidence showing that the Sopherim altered many verses where the names seemed to show that YHVH and the Elohim were distinctly different entities.

A serious study of the ancient usage of the name Elohim, in Hebrew and variations of it in other ancient languages of the Middle East would rather seem to indicate that a different meaning from that understood in ancient times has merely been asserted since the Levite Sopherim. In the Amarna letters the Pharaoh is referred to as an Elohim, of course, because he too was head of his council of advisors, modeled after spiritual knowledge of YHVH's council of Elohim, renowned throughout Egypt and the Middle East. Every upstart god or god-king or religion wanted to create the impression that they too were just as equally suited to lead mortals as head of a council of Elohim, as were YHVH and His council of Elohim.

Just as we might say congress "said" this or that, or a council "said" so and so, it follows that one could also say; "Elohim said…," it is not necessary that it always be phrased that the Elohim "say" something to include a plural meaning. Even then, it is sometimes the case that a plural verb *is* used. So if when the Elohim said something to humans they spoke as a body, in this case the title would be accompanied by a singular verb, like "said." So when it says Elohim said, instead of Elohim say, it can be understood that they spoke as one.

> "The title 'sons or children of God' is familiar from Ugaritic mythology, in which the 'children of El'…the sons/children of God are also found in Phoenician and Ammonite inscriptions." *Oxford Companion to the Bible*

Elohim is *Elhm* in Ugaritic, *Ilum* in Akkadian, *Elahim* in Chaldee, and the Council of the Elder Elohim has linguistic counterparts in Ugaritic texts where *El* presides over a council of gods. Elohim, Elim[22] or Elhm are referred throughout the cosmology of the Middle East from Sumeria to Egypt, showing that the existence of a hierarchy of a council of Elohim was widely known and understood in those cultures. *Gods, Goddesses and Myths of Creation,* Harper and Row, New York, 1974, pp 21-25. & Pelican, *The Greek Myths: 1,* 1986, 28:3, p.144. [22]Elim is considered to be the plural of El and Elohim the plural of Eloah.

Dictionaries

Akkadian search for god-*allallu*

<http://www.premiumwanadoo.com/cuneiform.languages/dictionary/dosearch.php?searchkey=3177&language=id>

Il-god <http://www.oldtestamentstudies.net/hebrew/akkadengdict.asp?item=17&variant=0>

Chaldee search for gods (the Hebrew spelling will be seen to be '*aleph, lamed, yod, mem*' - *alim*)

<http://books.google.com/books?ct=result&id=EB2dl3KQNIkC&dq=online+%22Chaldee+Dictionary%22&pg=PP5&lpg=PP5&q=eloah>

Woodard, Roger D. *The Ancient Languages of Syria-Palestine and Arabia.* Containing some Ugaritic - search for gods (some alternate spellings will be seen to be *ilm & alonim*)

<http://books.google.com/books?id=vTrT-bZyuPcC&pg=PA10&lpg=PA10&dq=online+%22Ugaritic+Dictionary%22&source=web&ots=Hbs8SSqyJP&sig=fGSzspgrro47XLLR00r427_pfAc&hl=en&sa=X&oi=book_result&resnum=4&ct=result>

> "There are several general phrases for a council of gods that provide a conceptual parallel

24

with the Hebrew Bible: *phr 'ilm* - "the assembly of El/the gods..." *phr bn 'ilm* - "the assembly of the sons of El/the gods..." *mphrt bn 'il* - "the assembly of the gods (from the presence of the term *bn* this should probably also be assembly sons of *'il*, mhj)." Michael Heiser Ph.D., Note #7 & 36 *Monotheism, Polytheism, Monolatry, or Henotheism?*

<http://digitalcommons.liberty.edu/cgi/viewcontent.cgi?article=1276&context=lts_fac_pubs>

"Allah," the Aramaic *"Elah,"* is also equivalent to the Hebrew "El" or *"Ilu,"* so what is all the fighting about? "My prophet is bigger or better than yours? We all have the same Creator do we not?" The term Al/El was not only used in the Bible, it was also a common general description of a deity in the ancient Middle East."In Daniel 2:27, both singular and plural forms appear as, *your Elah [is] an Elah of elahin...*Interestingly, *Elah* (not to be confused with the person, Elah) is the Aramaic equivalent of the Arabic *Allah.*" Article on Elah (Elahin, plural). *The Hebrew Bible King James Edition of 1769 Holy Name & Divine Titles Restored.*

<http://www.israelect.com/bible/>

> "In the Ras Shamra texts "El," in the form *'il*, is used both as a general term for any deity and also for the supreme god in the Ugaritic pantheon. The word is also used in the plural, *'ilm*, to denote a number of gods. Occasionally another plural form, *'ilhm*, occurs; and the expression *bn.'il* (sons of god) can also be used to denote more than one god...El is often called Tor-il, the Bull El[23]." Kapelrud, Arvid. *The Ras Shamra Discoveries* p. 57, 59.

[23]The ancient Hebrew pictograph (primitive letters comprising the beginnings of Hebrew) of El or Al, the name used repeatedly in the Bible, is the head of a Bull and a shepherd's crook. From this pictograph we now derive the alef or aleph, like the capital 'A' inverted, the two legs originally being horns above the pointed snout of a bull's head. When accompanied by a shepherd's crook (*lamed* now an "L") denoting a "strong Controller" this clearly implies the One who leads the strongest leader of the herd. This understanding may have degenerated over time into to the worship of the graven image of a bull or bull calf, and this is perhaps one reason the worship of images had to be expressly forbidden. Parsons, John J. *The Hebrew Names of God.* <http://www.hebrew4christians.com/Names_of_G-d/El/el.html>

In most modern translations and re-translations of biblical texts, Elohim and many other divine names, singular and plural have now frequently come to be translated as the singular word, God. This has been misleading and at the very least has greatly confused the original story, as to how many different individuals are being discussed. This is evidenced by verses from the OT itself, with literal usage of the original Hebrew divine names, as they are found in the oldest versions of the OT available to us.

Throughout this book are some of those verses that show the substitution of the original Hebrew words *YHVH, Eloi/Eloah* (God) *Elohim*, or *e-Aleim* (the Gods), *Adonai* (lord), angel of YHVH (*malak YHVH*), and the angel or angels or messengers (*malakhim*), of the *Elohim* (*malakhim Elohim*) replacing these names with the word God. Notice the *-im* ending, which can be seen to pluralize, as in one *malakh*, two *malakhim*, one cherub, two cherubim, one seraph, two seraphim, one *qedos*, two *qedoshim*, one *Adonai*, two *Adonaim*, one Eloah, two Elohim… etc.

Note that there is never any pluralization of YHVH, since it would be impossible for there to be more than one Pre-existent All One. Never is a plural pronoun used in place of YHVH, (unless accompanied by "Elohim" which is in fact a reference to YHVH Elohim – YHVH Lord of the Gods or YHVH Gods depending on the context) and nowhere does it have a plural verb or adjective associated with it."A masculine noun receives a suffix –im that shows it is plural, and a feminine noun in the plural will have a suffix –ot. In some cases, though, a masculine noun will add the suffix –ot in the plural, and sometimes a feminine noun will have the suffix –im for its plural…"

(some common examples) *sus* (horse) – *susim* (horses), *melek* (king) – *melakim* (kings), *dabar* (word) – *dabarim* (words) *har* (mountain) – *harim* (mountains), *is* (man) – *anasim* (men)

From page 111-112 "How Biblical Languages Work" By Peter James Silzer, Thomas (to be found online in Google books)
<http://www.google.com/url?sa=U&start=4&q=http://books.google.com/books%3Fid%3DfojpYW0xbeAC%26pg%3DPA111%26lpg%3DPA111%26dq%3D%2522im%2522%2Bmasculine%2Bplural%2Bending%2BHebrew%26source%3Dweb%26ots%3DLIdJi8lhrg%26sig%3DZrHvR38vvepY5i-2YonGSioVl_8&usg=AFQjCNHp6xhrahPjqyg9g0lFSe8-3gIxwA&oi=book_result&resnum=4&ct=result>

The names discussing a council of Elohim (gods) as well as others, including the sons of the Elohim (in Hebrew *ben* or *b'nai Elohim or ben haElohim*) and sons of the Most High (*ben elyon*) have frequently been translated to the name for a single entity. That entity is now designated by the word God, thus preventing the understanding that these different names were originally used deliberately by the ancient Hebrews, before the time of Ezra and the Sopherim. These different names distinguished amongst these distinctly different entities denoting YHVH's gods, lords, messengers and the descendants of YHVH's Elohim.

YHVH Elohim can thus be seen to be a title differentiating them from the false gods or earthly Elohim, who did not serve YHVH. The others were relatively recent upstarts, who arose to power after YHVH Elohim, YHVH's 'gods' originally participated in the creation of the Earth. Their work was to assist YHVH, and it is for this reason YHVH's council of Elohim were known as YHVH Elohim.

> "(1ˢᵗ) Acclaim to YHWH...(2ⁿᵈ) acclaim to *lalei eAleim* (God of the gods)...(3ʳᵈ) acclaim to *ladni eAdnim* (Lord of the lords)..." Ps 136:1-3 (These verses shows that there are many gods and lords, and that acclaim to YHVH comes before any acclaim accorded to the others.) See <http://www.scripture4all.org>

The use of the different terms, YHVH and Elohim can appear in the same sentence as two distinctly separate beings; i.e. with YHVH speaking *to* the Elohim (Isa. 44:6, Ps. 82:1&6) or Adonai (the Lord) being among the Elohim in their "chariots." (Ps. 68:17) This clearly shows that these terms were not originally interchangeable and have only recently, that is in the last few thousand years, come to be replaced in the modern Bible by the substitution of the singular word "God."

Therefore it is possible that the Levites, in their efforts to eliminate any references that seemed to indicate anything contrary to their limited definition of monotheism, may have changed some of the verbs along with their other changes, without recording such trivial alterations. Given all the other evidence against the Levite efforts, it should be remembered that some of the remaining singular verbs may also be accounted for in this fashion. After considering all the other apparent changes they made, it would certainly seem probable to anyone thinking discriminatingly.

"Remember your creators (*burai-k*) in the days of your youth" (Ecc. 12:1). This verse was changed to read creator singular in the KJV. No doubt this refers to YHVH and His Elohim as pro-"creators" not the Great Holy Spirit of the One, the Creator YHVH who breathes the breath of life into all his creatures. The Hebrew word for Creator is the plural form of the word "*bara.*" The plural of Creator is also seen in Isaiah 54:5, where the prophet states: "For thy Maker is thy husband, YHVH of Hosts is His name." (Young's Literal Translation, 1898) In this verse the word "Maker" is the plural form of the word "*bara,*" which means to form or make.

The name YHVH first appears in Genesis 2:4, accompanied by the word "Elohim." When the understanding of the plural form, Elohim, is seen and used correctly, it becomes clear that "*YHVH Elohim*" literally means; YHVH Lord of the Gods or YHVH's Gods depending on the context. YHVH's council of "godlike" spiritual beings who, in service to all, had become one with YHVH, the Infinite Great Holy Living Spirit, The Pre-existent Universal All-One.

We will learn more about the role of the Elohim in the Creation story anon, and YHVH's presence with the Elohim, as the "I Am" which is literally in fact "I Am Becoming" (Ex. 3:2&14). With the Hebrew words in place, we will discuss YHVH's oneness with His myriad thousands of Elohim. I.e., "*YHVH Elohenu, YHVH Echad*" (Duet 6:4). Echad is Hebrew for one and/or united together (SHD 259) and we will also examine the understanding of oneness in depth, a little further on. (YHVH *Elohenu* literally means; YHVH Elohim of us or, YHVH Lord of the *gods* of us)

> "You shall not revile the gods[24] nor curse the ruler of your people." Ex. 22:28 ([24]Strangely enough, Elohim was here correctly translated as the "gods" in the KJV)

In one quote Jesus is quoted as he actually spoke, in the native tongue of Jewish people of his time, Aramaic, as opposed to the Greek in which the New Testament (hereafter NT) was later written, he uses the <u>singular</u> form *Eli,* or *Eloi.* In Mark 15:34 he says; "*Eloi, Eloi lama sabachthani.*" This is a Greek transliteration of the Aramaic, "*Eli Eli lamah 'azabthani.*"

Clearly, among Christians, Jesus is to be considered the foremost authority of his time as to the correct form to use. He does not say Elohim, Elohim, and note also that he does not say God, God, because the Jews, from which he descended, the tribes of Judah, did not use the word God at that time, when referring to YHVH.

According to the NT account, when he was accused by the Jews seeking to stone him, in John 10:30-35, of making himself God, because he had said; "I and my father are one," he tries to explain; "Is it not written in your law, I say you are gods?" (John 10:34, he is obviously quoting Ps. 82:6 which says 'I say you are Elohim'-gods plural) This reference by Jesus shows that he too recognized the word Elohim to mean "Gods" plural. Once again regaining this hidden mystery of our human heritage, as it was written in the original "Law of Moses" will help enlighten us as to the relationship YHVH's Elohim have to earthlings and why their presence is still seen in the skies, and now often called UFOs. And it will help us to understand how it is that Jesus could number even those who sought to stone him among the descendants of the gods, making them of course also gods.

Jesus tried to teach them that we are "gods" and they rejected his teaching, saying he was claiming to be a god. There will be many who will still refuse to understand concerning YHVH's Elohim, nevertheless, the NT goes on to say; "If he called gods, those *against* whom the word of God came...the scripture cannot be nullified." (John 10:35) Paul goes on to explain further; "For even though there be those that are called gods, whether in heaven or earth, as there be gods many, and lords many, there is to us one god, the Father." Cor. 8:5 With the decision to cease calling the Creator by His name, YHVH, and begin referring to Him as "God" the history of YHVH's Elohim was not incorporated into the NT or the Catholic religion's interpretation of the OT. " In spite of the admission in the NT that there are many gods, the interpretation favored by Constantine and his council of bishops, has influenced most people to now believe that YHVH, the All One, had created no gods who served Him.

ALL MIGHTY

"Al (often rendered El but remember Al is actually the more correct spelling in Hebrew) is stationed in the congregation of the Elohim; Al in among the Elohim He is Elohim ...I say you are gods[25] and all of you are children of the most High (*Oliun*) all of you...but as man you die, and as one of the heads you fall." [25]Ps. 82:1-7 (Many texts have "shall" die, however *Young's Literal Translation* gives the "literal" rendering; "as man you die." So as to say that like men, in their original state they were created to live and die. Thus, rather than some future occurrence, this can be viewed as a quality of these "gods," reminding them of their common mortal beginnings with humans, that unlike YHVH they "die" and that they could still "fall" from their present office. For if they had been, like the infinite Supreme uncreated and pre-existent YHVH, it could not have been said that as man they die, nor could they be brought down.

Organized religion has attempted to say that "Al," "El" or "Elohim" is used as a title denoting "great" or "mighty" saying that the "im" ending indicates the "majestic plural." While through years of usage it came to mean that, there is nothing about calling the infinitely omnipresent YHVH by the name Elohim that logically adds majesty to His already infinitely glorious nature. Not any more than modern people calling God by the term "gods," would to add majesty to that title or thus make God sound more "mighty." There is however a certain infinite quality to the interpretation of this word *Al,* as scholars like Higgins (cited in the next section) who would have it that an alternate meaning, one that still includes "God," is the definition, "All."

"Psalm to David grant you to YHWH sons of Elim[26] grant you to YHWH glory and strength." Ps. 29:1 ([26]this word was translated as 'mighty' preventing awareness that *alim*/Elim is another cognate of Elohim-gods. And obviously these sons of Elim were of a plural number again showing that Elim and Elohim are not precisely the same as YHVH.)

The Hebrew word for "mighty" or "great" is actually *gibbor* or *gabar* (1396) and is used as such in one epithet of the deity, *Al Gibbor*-All Mighty. (Isa. 9:6) If *Al or El*, meant mighty it would make that title redundant nonsense, because *Al Gibbor* would come out to be; the "Mighty Mighty." So clearly the word *Al-El* did not simply imply "mighty" to Isaiah or to any of the other ancient Hebrews who used the term *Al Gibbor*.

It can easily be seen from this and other instances that *Al or El* actually also in this context means "<u>All</u>" and *Gibbor* means Mighty, and has been translated as just that, and that thus *Al or El* was also understood as the word for the divine spirit of "All." The biblical scholars cannot have it both ways either the *Al Gibbor* means "All Mighty" or it does not. If *Al or El* can mean "All" in this instance then it may be applied in others as well. They cannot just decide to arbitrarily translate *Al* as "All" in the phrase "All Mighty" and exclude that meaning elsewhere, especially when it makes more sense to use it.

There is no where in the OT that says that adding the "im" ending means any such thing as mighty or great, and certainly not in any ancient Hebrew literature that was already in existence before the Sopherim's change from YHVH Elohim to Adonai Elohim. This has merely been conjectured, to explain the presence of the plural name Elohim, because the Sopherim scribes had previously changed "YHVH Elohim" to "Adonai Elohim." This was done in their rise to power, after the Israelites came out of exile in Babylon, during which time the Israelites lost their records and the understanding of their history. This change was necessary for the Levite scribes, to defend their new definition of monotheism, that of only one "God," instead of the Supreme Pre-existent All One, the head of a pantheon of Elohim, YHVH's host of heaven, whose prophets Jesus accused them of murdering.

Loflin, Lewis. (*Judaism Meets Hellenism and the Logos.* <u>http://www.sullivan-county.com/id2/jud_logos.htm</u>) makes the statement that; "In Hellenistic Judaism as developed by Philo, this notion (that the universe itself is divine, a living being whose soul is God) of Logos is unacceptable, because for Jewish (sic) God created the universe and transcends it." But this objection is itself in conflict with one of the Jewish names for the Creator, used as far back as Abraham, *Al Oulm or Olam*. (Gen. 21:33, Ps. 90:1-3, 93:2, Isa. 26;4) *Al Olum* means world without end (elsewhere also worlds), SHD 5769, 5865, 5957, forever & 361 *eylam meaning* space). According to John J. Parsons the Hebrew word *Olam* means everlasting time and space, the Infinite Living Universe, YHVH's material manifestation; and whose spirit pervades it all. Parsons, John J. *El and El Constructs Given in the Tanakh.*

<u>http://www.hebrew4christians.com/Names_of_G-d/El/el.html</u>

To reject this understanding is to reject the history of their language, as it appears in the story of Abraham in Genesis. This understanding is also found in another name for YHVH, *Al Hashamayim* (Ps. 136:26) or *lAl Eshmim*, "All[27] the Heavens," translated as "God *of* the Heavens" but there is in fact no word "of," in the phrase, YHVH is "All the Heavens," period. [27]See the next section on the dual meaning of *Al/El* as the All. Parsons, John J. *El and El Constructs Given in the Tanakh.* <u>http://www.hebrew4christians.com/Names_of_G-d/El/el.html</u>

> "Allodial land…land for which a man owes no suit or service…was the land of God – of *Al* (*alef and lamed* aka El, combined with di - *yod dalet*) *Al-di*…From the Pandaean system the name of Al,[28] came to mean ALL…The word *kl* or *kol* has the meaning of ALL, and probably in its origin is *k* (*kaf*) – "as," and *Al* (*alef lamed*) meaning *as all, as God*…*kl* (the Hebrew word *kol*) has also the meaning of the *heavens,* and here we have the Latin coel-um." (Higgins, Godfrey. *Anacalypsis,* Vol. 2, 1992 reprint, pp. 284 & 408. Note; the page numbering of the hard copy of *Anacalypsis* does not correspond with the page numbering of *Anacalypsis* online at Google books, the online version has been much edited thus changing the page numbers.)

> [28]God - *alef lamed* SHD 5920 *Al*, perhaps from SHD 5927 *alah*; SHD 411 gives el also as a demonstrative particle, these or those (but only in the plural sense); an association should possibly be studied in connection with 193 *Uwl* "to twist" so, implying one combined whole or that is, "all" since both of these definitions (these/those and all) can be used to imply united.

At the time I began my researches, I found Higgins enlightening input on this much studied word, *Al* (or El). The above mentioned quote, inspired investigations in to ancient meanings, in an attempt to understand why this understanding was apparently held by a scholar of multiple ancient languages such as Higgins, who died in 1833. This was before the time when Hebrew ceased to be a dead language and again began to be a spoken language (Revived by Elizer Ben-Yehuda in 1881). Higgin's understanding of this much studied word has since faded into obscurity. Higgins position, however, as a scholar of multiple ancient languages, apparently went much deeper than the existing modern understanding of the word, variously spelled *Al, El,* and anciently *Ilu.* Following his lead has led to the following research into ancient meanings some even from before the time of Moses.

The word *Al or El* (aleph lamed) is another word that contains the fossilized remnants of prehistoric meanings, from a time long before Moses would have begun writing the originals of anything that now appears in the OT. As such its meaning, in cultures that existed before *and* at the time when Moses wrote his originals, cannot be ignored by anyone who wants to understand all it must have implied to Moses and to the Israelites.

It is necessary to study the ancient records from before the time when Moses began writing the originals, to ascertain what general meanings it held for Moses and people throughout the ancient Middle East and Egypt, all of whom interacted and communicated with similar words. These meanings would have been much more significant to Moses, at the time he began writing, than the later meanings given to it by religious movements like the Levite Sopherim that came along afterward. A cognate of the word Al or El was already in use in the written languages of Middle Eastern cultures at the time of Moses. That word is Ilu, and the biblical scholars Brown, Driver and Briggs recognize it as such.

Brown, Driver, Briggs 410 gives El or Al as a cognate of the word spelled in Assyrian as *Ilu.* (#410 Brown, Driver, Briggs, *Gesenius Hebrew and English Lexicon*, Pub. Hendrickson, 1979, p. 42. Note that this reference, present in the hard copy, is not included in the online versions of BDB.) Since *Ilu* was a recognized cognate of *Al or El,* meanings associated with it must also be considered when attempting to understand what remains to us of Moses' writings and the ancient Middle Eastern cultural understanding of the word *Al, El, Ilu, Il, etc.*

The online article *THE CHALDEAN LEGEND* tells us; "Of the dead sciences of the past, there is a fair minority of earnest students who are entitled to learn the few truths that may now be given to them." It goes on to quote; "In Chaldea the great First Cause as the ONE, the primordial germ, the unrevealed and grand ALL, existing through himself -- was Ilu." This was the Kabbalistic En-Soph (No-thing). THEOSOPHY, Vol. 52, No. 6, April, 1964 (Pages 175-182; Size: 22K)

<http://www.blavatsky.net/magazine/theosophy/ww/additional/ListOfCollatedArticles/TheChaldeanLegend.html>

The Zohar is an ancient book written in Hebrew, by Jews studying and trying to derive meanings and understand the spiritual relationships in the Jewish religion, it has been described as the; "Hebrew/Aramaic Rabbinical Kabbalistical work that is one of the most important sources for Kabbalah, and was very influential with Chasidim[29]" (The Chassidic Rebbes. *Chassidus Teachings Of Judaism.* Section on "z" <http://www.chassidus.net/glossary.htm>). "In the Zohar, God is described as Ein-Soph, the No-Thing, the endless, the infinite and <u>The All</u>." [29]Much more on the Chasidim/Kasdym etc. in a later chapter. El-Koussa, Karim. *The Kabala: The Authentic Tradition.*

<http://www.szirine.com/2004/05/30/the-kabala-the-authentic-tradition/>

> "THE SUPREME GOD ILU The supreme god the first and sole principle from whom all other deities were derived was Ilu whose name signifies God par excellence. Their idea of him was too comprehensive, too vast to have any determined external form or consequently to receive in general the adoration of the people." Dobbins, Frank Stockton. *Gods and Devils of Mankind,* Samuel Wells Williams Isaac Hollister Hall, p.127-128.
>
> <http://books.google.com/books?hl=en&id=escOAAAAIAAJ&dq=Dobbins,+Frank+Stockton.+Gods+and+Devils+of+Mankind&printsec=frontcover&source=web&ots=M1vRo2ZLdH&sig=s1mpF8MEyZjMmbG9BPWIIdUVkI >

There are many names, given in the OT as synonyms of YHVH, which start with the word *Al (or its variant El).* Some of these include *Al Chaiyim, or Al Chii* (as in Ps. 42:8) which with the meaning "all" would be the All Living or YHVH All Life, the Great Holy Spirit who is All. If the meaning mighty is put in place that makes it the nonsensical title of the "Mighty Living" or "Mighty Life" which makes little or no sense whatsoever, and likewise with the word "great." YHVH *Al Chii*, the Spirit of All Life, is the living organizing First Cause and principle, the All Motion that is in opposition to entropy. Entropy is the tendency, recognized by the science of physics, of inanimate matter, not moved by living spirit, to equilibrate to its lowest energy state.

Another of YHVH's names is *Al Haggadol,* which would, with the inclusion of "All" as part of the definition, be the All Great. If the word mighty or great is read for Al/El, it becomes another nonsensical title; "Mighty Great" or "Great Great." The same problem arises with YHVH's name, *Al Hakadosh,* which with the concept of "All" becomes the aptly fitting All Holy, however, with the meaning "mighty" or "great" it becomes "Mighty Holy" or "Great Holy." With YHVH's name "*The Al Elyon,*" (*lal Oliun,* Gen. 14:19) it obviously makes better sense again as "The All Highest"; which with the meanings mighty and great become the awkward phrases "The Mighty Highest" and "The Great Highest."

This same problem occurs repeatedly with other names of YHVH which with the meaning "All" become; *Al Roi,* the All Seeing; *Al Hakavod,* the All Glory; *Al HaNe'eman,* the All Pleasant; *Al Kedem,* the All Eternal; *Al Olam,* the All Time and Space; *Al Rachum,* the All Merciful; *Al Selichot,* the All Forgiving; and *Al Yeshuati,* the All Salvation. Which become respectively, with the definition "mighty," the illogical and utter nonsense titles of; "Mighty Seeing"; "Mighty Glory"; "Mighty Faithful"; "Mighty Eternal"; "Mighty Time and Space"; "Mighty Forgiving" and "Mighty Salvation." And with the meaning "great" they are equally ridiculous.

It should be clear to all but the most stubbornly entrenched, from these examples that the understanding of the *Al or El,* actually the correct spelling is closer to *Al* (the Hebrew letters aleph & lamed), makes much more sense when the inclusion of the definition "All" is used and understood, whenever it is reasonable within the context. For YHVH is above and within all and He formed the entire universe that we see out of His own Pre-existence, which was before all that now exists, a state which is beyond our comprehension. (Even scientists with their theory of a "Big Bang" cannot say how whatever existed, before it supposedly "banged," was created.)

> "You shall know And you shall believe me and you shall understand that I am He, before Me not he was formed *Al* (All) and after me not he shall become. I (even) I YHWH and besides me there is no savior." Isa. 43:10 There is, was and ever shall be only one Pre-Existent All, whom Jesus knew from his own name (which means "Yah saves[30]") that the only salvation came from oneness with YHVH the All One. See;
>
> <http://www.scripture4all.org>
>
> [30]<http://biblefocus.net/theology/Yeshua/index.html>

Another of YHVH's names deserves recognition in this section, and that is *Al Echad.* With the understanding of *Al* meaning "All" we are now able to see that *Al Echad* means the All One, instead of the awkward and nonsensical meaning, "God One." YHVH is All One, or as it is said in (1 Cor. 15:28) "The One who may be All in all." All One is a designation that has been used by wise teachers of all faiths, repeatedly down through history. For to the holy we are all one, and it is becoming common among many persons, to say and live by the philosophy that we are "all one" and that we are one, in the All One.

The heritage of the Hindu understanding also expresses the sentiment that the Creator is All in all, however, in slightly different words. After giving the names of a number of various deities, the moon, the creator, and the great grandfather (Native Americans also say grandfather) the Bhagavad Gita 11:39-40, gives the famous *vaidika* declaration; "Salutations to thee on every side, Oh All. Infinite in power and prowess, thou pervades all; wherefore thou art all." *Gita Daily Readings.*

<http://www.dailyreadings.com/Aug_22.htm>

> "That all one they may be; as you, Father in me, and I in you, that they in us may be…I in them and You in me that they may be having matured into one." John 17:21 &23

YHVH Himself is frequently called *Al-Elyon*, translated as "God Most High" the word *elyon* being given as an adjective meaning "high" or "lofty. However with the understanding of Al/El as "All" this name of YHVH can now be seen to show Him to be the "All Highest" another example that often the word *Al or El* meaning "All" makes better sense than simply the word "God." Coupled with the word "All," *Al Elyon* thus clearly comes to mean the "All Highest." Aside from the possibility of mere unawareness of the deeper ramifications of the word *Al,* the concept of suggesting that *Al/El* exclusively means mighty or great may be based on a reluctance to recognize the fallibility of organized religion.

It is a shame that scholars following the reintroduction of Hebrew as a spoken language in 1881 did not carry Higgins understanding forward. The inclusion of this understanding helps many of YHVH's titles to have a much deeper meaning. If this common mistake is made out of ignorance it may be simply an example of a lack of understanding on the part of the various translators, and a willingness to submit to group-think rather than rock the boat (sigh) another case of "the blind leading the blind." And the laughable suggestion that it means majesty has only come about since the practice began of kings and queens using the royal "we," there is no indication that the ancient kings spoke in this manner, unless referring to themselves and a council of which *they* were a part.

> "Yahu and Yah were known outside Israel; the forms enter into the composition of foreign proper names; besides, the variation of the name of a certain King of Hammath shows that Ilu is equivalent to Yau, and that Yau is the name of a god. (Much more on the name Yau or Yahu will follow in a later chapter) (Schrader, "Bibl. Bl.," II, p. 42, 56; Sargon, "Cylinder," xxv; Keil, "Fastes," I. 33). Catholic Encyclopedia article on Jehovah (Yahweh) @ <http://www.newadvent.org/cathen/08329a.htm>

This ancient identification of the Al or El with YHVH, derives from the understanding of the service of YHVH's Elohim to YHVH who is "THE ALL," through their oneness with The All, and through the omnipresent spirit of the All-One, YHVH. So in addition to being used as a title the word Al or El eventually came to have a synonymous meaning to the more limited concept of a "god." These "gods" came to be considered as Elohim, separate individuals from the rest of the All Life, and All Space and Time, because it also implied the understanding that the Aleim or Elohim were one with and served *EAL,* "THE ALL." This understanding also clearly requires a willingness to recognize the mistaken understanding of YHVH's pantheon already discussed.

> "YHWH of your Elohim, He God (*Alei*) of the gods (*e-Aleim,* remember "e" means "the") Lord of the lords, the All, the Great..." Deu. 10:17

> "*IEVE Aleikm eua Alei ealeim uadni eadnim Eal Egdl.*" (Notice the word *Eal*, the "e" means "the" and *al* as again shown must indicate the word all. Otherwise, if *al* meant great as often asserted for it, when combined with *egdl* - "the great" (SHD 1419) this becomes the nonsensical phrase "the great the great.")

So in spite of the break in the recognized etymology of the word "all," there is clearly a case for conjecturing that the modern word "all" derived from the Hebrew, Chaldean and Assyrian *"al"* or *"el,"* or *"ilu,"* because of the similarity in spelling and usage. It would be too much of a coincidence to think other wise, since its meaning as "all" came before the accepted etymology of the word "all," with certainly no opportunity for plagiarism on the part of any ancient writers before Moses time.

"And they are sighing sons of Israel from the service and they are crying out and it ascends imploring *Al the Elohim.*" Ex. 2:23 (*Al eAleim,* the emphatic article is found here and therefore it should be translated as came up to *The* Gods or The Aleim/Elohim.) Here we have another verse that makes better sense if the definition of "all" is included in *Al/El.* In this verse the term Aleim is immediately preceded by the Hebrew word for "the" ("e") and before that is the name *Al.* This would traditionally make the phase "imploring mighty the Elohim," or "imploring great the Elohim." It is much clearer when it is instead translated as "imploring all the Elohim," using the new understandings discussed here so far for the words "Al" and "the Elohim."

GOD/KHOD/KHODA/GHAD/GAD/G-D

Webster's New Collegiate Dictionary says the word "god" comes from a German[31] word "got." This word derived from the Teutonic usage that was adopted by Christians in the seventh century. The "heathen" Teutonic peoples in turn received their word from the family of Indo-European languages that got it from languages associated with Sanskrit roots. This usage is to be found for example in the reference to Thor-khod or the khod or god Thor, in *A Tibetan-English Dictionary with Sanskrit Synonyms* by Sarat Chandra Das, it shows that the Teutonic (Germanian) reverence for this god was long preceded by a Sanskrit Thor-god. *The Twentieth Century Dictionary* confirms this pagan origin of the name God where it says, "It was applied to heathen deities; and, later, when the Teutonic peoples were converted to Christianity, the word was elevated to the Christian sense of the meaning." Sarat Chandra Das. *A Tibetan-English Dictionary with Sanskrit Synonyms.* published by Motilal Banarsidass Publ.

<http://books.google.com/books?hl=en&id=EdoKAAAAYAAJ&dq=A+Tibetan-English+Dictionary+with+Sanskrit+Synonyms+Sarat+Chandra+Das&printsec=frontcover&source=web&ots=feXLdXevfk&sig=S7qU1ZWCFUUwi1tj5UbwsUiWjKw>

[31]Since the Germanians are mentioned by Herodotus as one of the tribes of the Persians, their use of "Gott/Got" for God clearly must have some correspondence with the Persian use of "Khoda" for God. The reluctance to recognize this connection is probably because Christian scholars object to any recognition that the Judeo-Christian religion has any connection with that of the Persians. There will be much more on the "wise men" or *Magi* of the Persians who knew of the prediction of the appearance of the star, which they followed as it moved across the sky, at Jesus birth in a later chapter.

The Teutons and their kindred call Him "Gott"; the French call Him "Dieu"; the Spanish "Dios"; the Italians "Dio"; the Portuguese "Deus" which is the Latin word for God. The Greek called

Him *Theos*," the name for "God" used in the Greek NT; the Greeks adopted it from the Persians. *Theos* and the Persian variant "Zeus," derive from the Sanskrit "Dyaus" or Deus meaning, "to shine or give light" (also "day"). *The Catholic Dictionary* art. on "Etymology of the word God" & *Online Etymology Dictionary, Theos.*

<http://www.etymonline.com/index.php?search=zeus&searchmode=none>

<http://www.scripture4all.org/OnlineInterlinear/Greek_Index.htm>

On a related note, from Zeus or Zeus-pater came Jupiter (Deus-god and pater-father; *Dyaus Pitar,* Father Sky, Boyce, Mary. *A History of Zoroastrianism.* p. 23) or the "Father-God" and Jove, the "father of the gods" in Latin mythology, may have come from Jehovih, a variation of Jehovah, pronounced yeh·ho·vē or now Jehovee. (SHD 3069) *Did some Hebrew Christian scholars read the vowels e,o,a of the Tetragram with its consonants YHWH...*)

<http://www.lifespurpose.net/divinename/NameofGod1.htm#A06>

There is clearly a case for similar origins, for the Hebrew word G-d as for the Babylonian word for deity, G-d, since the word God/G-d/Ghad/Gawd was used with the same meaning, by the Assyrians and Babylonians who captured the tribes of Israel. That usage of the name for a deity occurs in the OT, for example with the false "god" Baal sometimes called Baal Peor but also Baalg-d. Miller, Gary C. *Just Who is God?*

<http://www.search-the-scriptures.org/artic-34.htm>

> "And he makes a carving *uls g-d[32]* worshiping it...he burns part and remnant to *Al (or El)* he makes carving (graven image) of *is-gud* to him and he is worshiping and he is praying to him and saying rescue me for you are my *Ali - El*." ([32]this word g-d is translated in KJV as "falling on knees and face," concealing the understanding that g-d = god, but Webster's Revised Unabridged Dictionary gives this exact verse as an example of the OT use of the word "god" translating it as, "He makes a god and worships it." Isa. 44:15&17 Wahiduddins's Web. *Etymology of the Name God.*
>
> <http://dictionary.reference.com/search?q=god > as quoted by;
>
> <http://wahiduddin.net/words/name_god.htm>

The established etymology in *Webster's 1913 Dictionary* gives the origin of the word god, as from the Hindu *hu, huta, khod or khooda* and perhaps the Persian word for god, "*khoda.*" Babylon was in the same area as Persia. The Babylonians were closer to the Sanskrit speaking Hindu culture in distance and time than the Teutonic people of old Germany, so there is no reason to suppose that they may not also have derived *their* Babylonian word g-d from the cultural exchange that took place throughout the Middle East. The Sanskrit root word *hud or huta* has the interpretation of, "what is worshiped by sacrifice" and the followers of Baal definitely subscribed to the practice of both animal and human sacrifice.

The Hebrew word that in fact means God, singular, is *Eloah, Eloih, Eloi or El*. Eloah is the root word recognized by Hebrew scholars to be the singular form of Elohim-the Hebrew word that literally means Gods-plural. The word "God" rather than being one of the original Hebrew words for the Judeo/Christian deity, can thus be traced to "Pagan" usage as far back as the Persian and Babylonian languages (and apparently Sanskrit), as in Baal-god, or gawd/ghad/g-d i.e. Baal-god. (Jud. 8:33, 9:4, 9:46) (SHD 1171)

Most biblical scholars have deliberately not made the association g-d/god even though it is clear that YHVH was never called g-d, gad or god in the Torah. The false "god" Baal-God <u>was</u> called g-d, however, and as mentioned above, that name occurs in the OT mentioning "Baal god" and the city named after him. Jos. 11:17, 12:7, 13:5 (Brown, Diver, Briggs Gesenius Lexicon, SHD 1171)

In the OT (Gen. 30:11) G-d, Ghad or God (SHD 1464) is used to designate the God of Fortune, a Babylonian Deity, the afore mentioned Baal God, this is why it is also synonymous with fortunate or "good," hence our modern understanding; i.e., God is good.

The spelling of the word "god" is identical with the Anglo-Saxon word for "good," and from the forgoing information it can easily be seen that this is because of its association with the meaning "fortunate" or good. It is, however originally from a prime root, meaning; to crowd upon or attack and means to invade, to overcome or to cut. <http://scripturetext.com/genesis/49-19.htm>

Perhaps the tribes of Israel, when taken into captivity, took with them the name "God," it was certainly not one of the original Hebrew divine names in the Torah. When Isaiah condemns the "setting of a table for G-d" i.e. "god," he is rebuking those who practiced, even then, feasting and celebrating the worship of the name G-d instead of YHVH.

> "But you are those who forsake YHWH, who forget my holy mountain, and prepare a table for g-d[33], and that pour drinks for Destiny/*Minni*." Isa. 65:11([33]Strong's #1409) concerning the unrecognized word *g-d,* notice carefully how Strong says it is pronounced: "gawd." This is exactly the same pronunciation as "god."

Gedud (or *g-dud*) a related word from the same root, means a band of raiders. The use of the word God, in the minds of the nations conquered in pursuit of fortune (including the indigenous nations of this continent, now called America) by those using the message of "G-d" as a justification for their acts of conquest, has come to represent just such a band of fortune seeking raiders, in the eyes of those oppressed by that conquest.

> "The Great Spirit knows no boundaries nor will his red children acknowledge any...Once they were a happy race. Now they are made miserable by the white people, who are never contented but are always encroaching...Sell a country! Why not sell the air, the clouds and the great sea (the ocean) as well as the earth? Did not the Great Spirit make them all for the use of all his children?" Tecumseh, Shawnee Chief. *Bartlett's Book of Quotations,* p. 419.

Gen. 49:19 has been translated as "A troop" but it actually says "*g-d g-dud,*" which is "god raiders," and in the previous verse the speaker asks YHVH to save him from these "god raiders." The present materialistic worship of "good" fortune, i.e., G-d/God, rather than *Dabar YHVH* (Gen. 15:1) the *word* and matters, works or prior arrangements of YHVH, continues to this day. (alt. meaning; works, SHD 1697)

36

> "By the word (*dabar*) of YHWH the heavens were made, by the breath (*ruah,* also meaning spirit) of His mouth all their host (were made). (Ps. 33:6)

Sociology has studied individuals who are raised in the wild or in captivity removed from society, without being taught to use words, they have found that these poor blighted souls, have a difficult time ever understanding their culture and socializing in general. Without learning the understanding of the use of words from others we are in a state of ignorance much like an animal. That people raised without human contact fail to ever fully develop important areas like language skills and a self-concept indicates that humans must have received instruction in those areas.

The Elohim, like humanity, also used words and had long since come to understand that their sense of self was composed of and contingent upon words. We will further explore this understanding that when we lose our ability to use words, we lose our very selves and the ability to be logical (a word derived from logos, which along with idea or word actually means reason), explored further in a discussion of Alzheimer's in a later chapter.

> "Upon the *Logos*...Since, therefore, St. John has adopted several other terms which were used by the Gnostics, we must conclude that he derived also the term, Logos, from the same source. If it be further asked, whence did the Gnostics derive this use of the expression, *Word*?...they derived it most probably from the Oriental or Zoroastrian philosophy, from which was borrowed a considerable part of the Manichean (Christian) doctrines. In the Zend-Avesta (attributed to Zarathustra) we meet with a being called "the Word." Higgins, Godfrey. *Anacalypsis* Vol. 1, pp. 120,523,784&792. Note that page numbers of the hard copy do not correspond with the online version. (Later in a discussion of false gods, evidence will be cited, that mentions that Horus - Latin for the Egyptian god Hor - was also known as "the word" made flesh.)

It has been asserted that in Gen. 15 a being called the word of YHVH brought Abraham outside to speak to him. But the literal Hebrew rendering says; "And behold! Word of YHVH (*DBR IEVE*) says to him (Abraham) (4)...And He is bringing forth him toward outside..." (5) It does not specify any being called *logos* or "the word." Now since saying the 'word of YHVH says' can just as well mean to say that Abraham heard the word or voice of YHVH, there is no reason to believe that this is a reference to some other being apart from YHVH himself speaking His own words. It has merely been so read to support various theories concerning the development of the logos as a being other than YHVH in existence in the beginning.

Plutarch provides evidence that labeling someone "the word" was a custom practiced long before this title was ascribed to Yeschu/Joshu/Jesus. "The Horus that Isis bore...is related to have had a charge of illegitimacy brought against him...because he is not pure and without alloy like his father "the word" (Reason), (who exists by himself free from admixture and from passion), but is bastardized by matter, on account of his bodily part. Nevertheless he gains his cause through

37

Hermes, that is "the word" (Reason), bearing witness and proving how nature changing her from after the model of the Intelligible, produces the World…and that Matter being incomplete in itself, was *perfected* by "the word" (Reason[34]), and thus produced the first birth. On which account they tell that this god was lame and lying in darkness, and they name him the "Elder Horus;" for the world did not exist, but as an image as it were, a spectre of the world that was to be. [34]The votaries of Isis…go into the next world carrying with them this "Word," [the revealed Truth.] and nothing else." verse III) Plutarch. *On Isis and Osirus,* LIV.

<http://thriceholy.net/Texts/Isis.html>

> "Indeed, in the Trismegistic literature we find a number of distinctive doctrines of Gnostic Christianity but without the historic Christ; and all these doctrines are seen to have existed for thousands of years previously in direct Egyptian tradition-especially the doctrines of the *Logos*, of the Savior and Virgin Mother, of the second birth and the final union with God. Mead, G. R. S. *Fragments of a Faith Forgotten,* p. 58.

Other even more ridiculous theories are discussed concerning the being called "wisdom" (who is clearly described as feminine previously in Prov. 8:1 and proceeding through the entire chapter), in an attempt to say that this being, that the Bible states is feminine, is somehow to be equated with Jesus. The OT specifically addresses her as feminine in the first verse of Prov. 8 and other places throughout chapter 8, and goes on to discuss her as feminine as well in the first verse of Prov. 9:1. This shows that this being cannot be Jesus; this will be discussed at length in a later section.

Logos is a noun derived from the verb-*lego*, which means to speak intelligently, distinguished from *laleo*-talk esp. without any sense, so with this meaning comes the understanding that a being of "the *logos*" is one who can speak intelligently. Uittenbogaard, Arie. *The name Logos: meaning, origin and etymology.* <http://www.abarim-publications.com/Meaning/Logos.html>

> "If you become rational, (then) the Logos shall unite with thee."

> *The Gospel of Philip.* Verse 120.

> <http://www.metalog.org/files/philip.html>

> "By way of the understanding he achieves a far-reaching emancipation from the shackles of personal hopes and desires, and thereby attains that humble attitude of mind toward the grandeur of reason incarnate in existence, and which, in its profoundest depths, is inaccessible to man. (Einstien, 1930)

Also concerning John's "*Ho Logos*" ("the Word in John 1:1) there is in the *"Targum"* the power of YHVH, to which everything owes its existence, not as in the Massoretic Text, the Elohim. (*Targum,* p. 136-137.) So the "Targums" i.e. "Translations" apparently have identified the power, and the Word (*DBR IEVE*), with YHVH's power. The Hebrews were the first to incorporate vowels into their writing, and the *Shema* (Duet 6:6-9) commands them write and to teach written "words" to their children, especially the understanding of our oneness in YHVH, YHVH Echad.

> "The Brazen Serpent was called the Logos or word by the Chaldee Paraphrast... an emblem of divine wisdom and of the creative energy by which all things were formed...It

is very certain that, in ancient times, the serpent was an object of adoration in almost all nations. Among the Gnostics generally, the serpent was called the Megalistor or Great Builder of the Universe. With the tail in the mouth, Serpents were the ancient emblems of the eternal creator and renovator of the universe." Higgins, Godfrey. *Anacalypsis* Vol. 1, *pp.* 120,523,784&792. Note that the page numbers of the hard copy do not correspond with the online version.

The spiraling serpent variation, *Uroborus*, chosen because the serpent is the only creature that can coil upon itself, is also a symbol for the cycling and recycling of matter. Remember that the twist in the spin of an atom, the twist in DNA and the spinning motion that is the basis of solar systems and galaxies also both involve spiraling patterns. Which is not to say that the serpent (matter) is the Creator of life, as was and still is thought by some, but rather that it is a primal mechanism used by the Great Omni-present Spirit of the Creator.

It is the creative mechanism of matter, not the Creator of life, for in life is growth, metabolism, reaction, pro-creation (reproduction), and responsiveness or spirit (self-motivation and motion; remember that spirited means moved). In matter there is no pro-creation, no ability to react, and no inner metabolism, but simply a growth of the building blocks of the physical universe (physics). All matter living and non-living, in the universe, is therefore the written word of YHVH Elohim, the Great Holy Spirit. ،

In John 1:1 the disciple John says; "In the beginning was the word (*logos*), and the word was with god and the word was god." This understanding of the word of YHVH *Al Emeth*, is open to everyone who hears and understands, and then through faith, works, and surrender of ego, attains to oneness with the will of the Creator for their life. Jesus recognized this state of oneness with the All-One (and His Elohim), when he said "I am in you, you are in me, we are in the Father." John 14:20-21 also see John 17:21

> "In Hellenistic thought the Logos related to the notion that the universe itself is divine, a living being whose soul is God...Christian notions of Jesus as the Logos derive by adoption of Hellenistic ideas within the Jesus sect... This created a fight over the question of Jesus being God or a creation of God. That would be settled at Nicea in 325...The 6th century BC Greek philosopher Heraclitus was the first to use the term Logos...He believed that this force is similar to human reason and that his own thought partook of the divine Logos." Loflin, Lewis. *Judaism Meets Hellenism and the Logos.*
>
> <http://www.sullivan-county.com/id2/jud_logos.htm>

Jesus had through insight, contemplation and meditation, no doubt also come to the enlightenment that his very being was derived from the word of YHVH, *Dabar YHVH*. It was from YHVH's Elohim that humanity, the son's of the Elohim, learned to understand the importance of "the word."

Without the understanding of the word of YHVH, taught to us by the Elohim; we would still be just as an animal that has not been trained. This lack of intelligence can be seen in persons raised in the wild or in those who have lost their intelligence through Alzheimer's. Another reason the Israelites were the chosen of YHVH is because through Moses they were given a written "*Book of the Law"* of Dabar YHVH, to be carried in the Ark of the Covenant (Ex. 40:20, Deu. 31:26).

RIGHTEOUS EARTHLINGS BECOME ELOHIM

"The house of David shall be as Elohim, as the angel of YHWH before them." Zech 12:8

There are many examples that show that mortals ascend through righteousness to eventually become Elohim (Gods), one occurs in Zech. 12:8 "David and the house of David (who were long in the spirit world by Zechariah's time) shall be as Elohim, as messengers (*kmlak* or as-malak) of YHVH..." Abraham is told "you are a prince of Elohim" in Gen. 23:6-7. In Gen. 18:1 three men (Gen. 18:2) who the Bible refers to as YHWH visit Abraham. Apparently in those days when messengers of YHVH were seen it was understood that these messengers were one in YHVH. It should also be noted that the spelling YHVH/Jehovih/IEVE was not used in any cases where a plural number of gods appear speaking as one, Jehovah or IEUE is used instead. See also the section on I AM BECOMING/HE IS BECOMING.

"It is a rare thing that the king requires and there is none that can show it before the king except the Elohim, whose abode of them is not in the flesh." Dan. 2:11

Moses was the first example in the OT where the rank of Elohim was extended to a mortal and it was by order of YHVH. (Ex. 7:1) The OT tells the people; "Elohim and officers, you shall make at all your gates, that YHVH your god has given you, throughout your tribes, and they shall judge the people with just judgment." (Deu. 16:18) In the OT Moses is already called by the title Elohim, even during his lifetime. "See I have made you an Elohim to Pharaoh: and Aaron your brother shall be your prophet." Ex. 7:1

In the following verse the word Elohim was replaced to prevent the understanding that it can also mean a mortal, who is ranked above oneself. Joseph, while serving an Egyptian master who left everything in his hands, replied to his master's wife, when she tried to seduce him; "There is no Elohim in this house above me, and he has not withheld anything from me except you, because you are his wife. So how could I do the Elohim evil and sin against Elohim." Gen. 39:9

"For what nation is so great, who has Elohim so near them?" Deu. 4:7

In Exodus the midwives were commanded to kill the male children but, "The midwives feared the Elohim (*eAleim or ha-Elohim* with the plural predicator "the" remember that "e" = the word "the") and did not as the king of Egypt commanded them, but saved the male children alive. Therefore Elohim dealt well with the midwives and the people multiplied and waxed very strong." Ex. 1:17-20

While many of the relatively modern translators of biblical texts attempt to state that the plural form of the term Elohim refers to the "trinity," it should be remembered that the trinity was a concept developed by Origen of Alexandria, it is nowhere specifically elucidated in the original Hebrew version of the OT. The early form of Trinitarianism was developed by Origen to combat the so-called Gnostic view of a celestial council of Elohim, which was understood by the early church. If there was a trinity from the beginning surely YHVH would have commanded it to be stated explicitly somewhere in Genesis, as the existence of such a trinity would have been of the most fundamental importance to YHVH's establishment of His religion at that time.

The Greeks took up Origen's schema in the later half of the third century but prior to the invention of the Catholic religion the earliest followers recognized the council of the Elohim as the destination of righteous mortals. In the third century, at the behest of the emperor Constantine, the New Testament was compiled, and the Catholic version of Christianity was founded, excluding many gospels and doctrines and much of the previous understanding was thereafter lost. Kelly, *Early Church Doctrines* & Cox, Wade. *The Elect as Elohim.*

<http://www.ccg.org/english/s/p001.html>

& *Plurality of Gods - The Elohim.* <http://www.abovetopsecret.com/forum/thread91529/pg1>

The church adopted a form of Trinitarianism which primarily sought to deny the plurality of the Elohim. The liberties taken with the translations of all the Hebrew names of various divine beings in the translations of the OT is perhaps more than anything what has contributed to the now common misunderstanding that these names all indicate one and the same being. It thus reduces the original story to nonsense in the sight of anyone thinking logically and looking for consistency.

For the serious student the concept of a trinity is inconsistent, incoherent and unfounded in the OT. Origen developed a closed hierarchy of only three elements of the Godhead, a forerunner of Trinitarianism whose sole purpose was to limit the extension of the capacity to be Elohim to three beings and deny it to the elect and the heavenly Host, the *qedosim* or holy ones. No doubt the Elohim must frequently laugh at mortal attempts to conceal the record of their existence, knowing that in the end the truth of their existence and their oneness with YHVH must eventually come out.

> "Sabourin, noting Coppens comment (*ETL*, 1963, pp. 485-500) that the noun *qedosim* designates, in the Masoretic text, the supra-terrestrial Court of YHWH, who are held to be *Elohim* (pp. 102-103), says of this: 'The concept of a heavenly assembly is not a purely literary form , but is an element of the living pattern of Israelite faith.' (p. 75) The pattern and usage of the terms for God is of an extended order. There is no doubt that the meaning was understood whether it was written in Hebrew, or Aramaic, or Chaldee." Cox, Wade. *The Elect as Elohim.*
>
> <http://www.ccg.org/english/s/p001.html>

YHVH is also called *Yahweh-El-Aleim*, translated "the Lord God of gods" (Josh.22:22) however directly translated using all/al/el, it would become, "YHVH All Elohim." Using the traditional translations it becomes the nonsensical Lord God God. Many scholars attempt to refer to verb usage to support the concept of the Elohim as a single individual, but there is no distinct evidence proving that this originally meant one, two or three, rather than any number of Elohim speaking and acting in accord, which would involve the same verb usage. In the next few paragraphs we will examine the understanding that according to Duet 6:4 the ancients knew YHVH is one with His council or congregation of Elohim, and that they are one in Him.

"Listen Israel, YHVH Elohim of us, YHVH (is) One." Deu. 6:4

Oneness is a concept that is difficult for many in organized religions to contemplate, since they are segregationists, with the leaders often living off the contributions of their followers and frequently promoting their own importance by dominating the understanding of the congregation. Rather than living in oneness as Jesus taught them to practice, holding all things in common, they collect tithes. This practice of giving one tenth to the Levite servers under Aaron the priest, was originally because they did the work of butchering animals sacrificed in the tabernacle of the congregation (Lev. 27:32 Tithes will be discussed in depth in a later section.). Do they think that there will be rich and poor or masters and servants in heaven or in the kingdom come? If they do not practice what they preach now, how can they be ready for it when their time comes?

> "And the multitude of them that believed were of one heart and of one soul: neither said any of them that ought of the things which he possessed was his own; but they held all things in common." (Acts 4:32 and Acts 2:44) This is the philosophy taught to the early Christians, rather than the practice of separatism and "tithing" taught by the Levites whose established religious practices were supposed to be changed (Hebrews 7:11-14), by all who truly believed.

There is in the verses quoted here, a great deal of evidence to support the case that the myriad thousands of the Elohim mentioned in Psalms 68 acted, worked and spoke in unity. Duet 6:4 declares, "*Shema Israel, YHVH Aleinu, YHVH echad!*" literally translated "Listen Israel, YHVH Elohim of us[35], YHVH (is) One." Deu. 6:4 ([35]*elohenu* ccg.org/english/s/p147.html)

This verse alone disputes the concept of a trinity, for YHVH is oneness with all, not separate and three, for *echad* is Hebrew for the number one, and is used as such many times throughout the OT. The first definition of (SHD 258), says that it means more properly; united, which, however, still gives the same concept of oneness.

<http://www.eliyah.com/cgi-bin/strongs.cgi?file=hebrewlexicon&isindex=258>

The famous Armstrongian phrase "Uniplural" is an invented grammatical category which confuses and divides. Some Binitarians and Trinitarians propose that the Hebrew word for one (*echad*) the numeral one, is really a "compound one." This may be a clever device to confuse logical thought or perhaps it demonstrates the confusion of the speaker himself. *Echad* occurs some 960 times in the Hebrew Bible, and it is the numeral "one." Used as a numeral adjective it can modify a noun. "One day," "one person," etc. but it still always indicates one.

> "YHWH He is becoming (*UEIE IEVE*) king over all the earth, in that day, YHWH, He shall become One (*Achad/Echad*) and His name One." Zech. 14:9

Hagar saw the angel of YHVH and referred to him inter-changeably as *Al Roi* (*ro'iy* see, SHD

7200 & 7210) the All Seeing, and YHWH, "the one speaking to her," implying that YHVH is a multiplicity yet present in one of His angels. However, only one of His numbers was present and spoke to her through that angel. (Gen. 22:1-12) And when an angel appears to Samson's parents they refer to him as Elohim (Jud. 13:19-22) showing that an Elohim is a high raised angel, yet YHVH is present in all His Elohim, thus "YHVH is One in the Elohim."

The scribes made many changes to the Torah, at least some of which they recorded, even after the time of the recovery of a copy of the law by Hilikiah and the Levites, which they brought to King Josiah. Ezra later interpreted this copy to the Israelites when they came out of exile in Babylon. Their other efforts to put their own spin on the original story may be seen by examining the liberties taken with interpretations of the Hebrew words discussed throughout this book.

The use of the term Elohim occurs 3,350 times in the Bible. There is nothing about YHVH having a council or congregation of Elohim that does not allow for an acceptance of monotheism, with this council working in oneness under YHVH. The movement to assert their definition of monotheism that caused the scribes to change the references to YHVH Elohim, to Adonai Elohim, also meant they had to rewrite many verses to suit their limited interpretation of monotheism and their own records, in the Massorah, provide a record of it.

> "Jewish religious authorities, concerned that the growing worship of angels would be a threat to the belief in one God, excised works like those of the Books of Enoch and the Book of Jubilees from canonical literature. These books are now part of what is known as Apocrypha and Pseudepigrapha." Article, *The Sons of God.*
>
> <http://echoes.devin.com/watchers/sons-of-god.html>

This unfortunately excluded the understanding that YHVH's Elohim were not false gods. Heaven only knows how many writings or passages may have been lost altogether, but thankfully the scribes were not successful in completely eradicating all traces of YHVH's Council of Elohim.

> "For both he that sanctifies and they who are sanctified are all one." Heb. 2:11 (*enos pantes*-they are of one, or *ek heis pas*-out of one all)

Jews and Christians have long disputed over the interpretation of "*YHVH Elohim, YHVH echad,*" (Deu. 6:4) with Jews presenting the understanding that *echad* indicates one, and Christians pointing to the plurality of the word Elohim to say it included Jesus. Now with the understanding of who the Elohim are, it can finally be clear how YHVH (a singular term) can declare Himself to be the Elohim (a plural term) and then it can be seen that they are both correct, as YHVH is one with all.

It is this verse known as "the *Schema,*" to which Jesus refers when asked which commandment was the greatest, in Mark 12:28-29. Which, written as it was originally, and as he would have read it in Hebrew said, "Hear, O Israel! YHVH Elohim is One." rather than "Hear, O Israel; the Lord God is one god." (which make little sense) It remains however for most earthlings to make themselves one with YHVH and subject to His will as Jesus did, (1 Cor. 15:28) and therefore become one with YHVH and His Elohim, who have always watched over us.

43

> "And YHWH He is becoming (*UEIE IEVE*) king over all the earth; on that day YHWH will become one and his name One (*Achad*)." Zech 14:9

Jehovah is the Jewish national name for God, often combined with the names of subordinate beings, that Strong's states to be derived from *hayah* (SHD 1961). Yahovih (or Jehovih) is Yahovah of Hosts. This distinction is preserved in the terms Jehovah (SHD 3068) and Jehovih (SHD 3069). Jehovih (Yahovih) is always rendered *Elohim* when spoken and Jehovah (Yahovah) is always rendered as *Adonai*. Apparently since the *Adonaim* or lords is a title of lesser distinction, one below the distinction of Elohim or gods, in this way the Jews after the time of the Sopherim, sought to protect the transcendent monotheism of Yahovih, Yahovah of the Hosts, above of all the Elohim.

> "The BDB Lexicon states that the Hebrew spelling "יֱהֹוִה" [e.g. Yehovih] occurs 305 times in *the Masoretic Text." The Tetragrammaton in the Bible – Definition.*
>
> <http://www.truthonthenet.com/tetragrammaton.htm>
>
> "Those who want to revocalize Jehovah into Yihweh or Yahweh should also change the names Joseph in Yosiph, Judah in Yehodeh, etc…Therefore, as the famous grammarian W. Gesenius acknowledged, according to the theophoric names, that the name of God could be easily vocalized *Iehouah." Do the Etymologies Found in the Bible Allow Us to Find a Primeval Vocalization?*
>
> <http://www.lifespurpose.net/divinename/NameofGod2.htm>

The substitution of the names Adonai Elohim is traditionally understood to have been so as to prevent speaking the sacred name YHVH, arising from a misunderstanding of the commandment to not take His name in vain or curse YHVH as in Lev. 24:11. Rather, this was an injunction to prevent it becoming a frivolous epithet, like crying out yahoo or hayah etc. when excited or cursing in His name, it was not meant to prevent the use of His name all together. In this way His name is only called out in seriousness, alerting His council of Elohim to give attention to a serious matter.

> "I YHVH Elohim of you...You shall have no other Elohim before me…Not you shall take up the name of YHVH (*IEVE*) Elohim of you for futility (*ishua* KJV, in vain)." Ex. 20:3 & 7"

The instances of the alterations of YHVH to Adonai (by the Sopherim, the scribes) in 134 places are at appendix 32 of the Companion Bible. YHVH is translated as LORD in the NIV and most other English Bibles, using all capital letters, and as *ADONAI* in the Complete Jewish Bible, the instances where the title Adonai occurred was translated as Lord. However, Adonai cannot be considered synonymous with YHVH and this is shown by the fact that there can be multiple *Adonai*, or *Adonim* (*eadnim*) or lords (Ps. 136:3, Isa. 26:13, I Cor. 8:5, Tim. 6:15 etc.).

44

"YHWH to lord of me (*l-adni*) sit! to right hand of me until I shall set your enemies as a stool for your feet." Ps. 110:1

Now the fact that YHVH speaks to this Adonai as His lord, asking him to sit at His right hand, shows that YHVH and Adonai are not one and the same being. The fact that there are multiple lords as in "My lord of the lords" (*ladni eadnim*) Ps. 136:3, shows that this is one of His heavenly hosts ranked below YHVH, for *ladni* is "Lord of Me" or "My lord," in the second case "My lord of lords." This Psalms gives us the descending ranks below YHVH for it begins by giving thanks to YHVH, then to His god of gods (*lalei ealeim*) and then His lord of lords (*ladni eadnim*).

"I speak of things which I have made touching on the king...you love righteousness and hate wickedness and so He anointed you Elohim, Elohim of (you)[36] (anointing) oil of elation *from partners of you*." Ps. 45:1&6-7 ([36]*Aleim Aleik,* God of gods)

Note that this king/Elohim was chosen from amongst other Elohim who were like himself. It follows that they are all humanoid, since humans were made in the image of the Elohim and these Elohim have appeared in human form to mortals throughout the Bible.

"YHWH of your Elohim, He God (*Alei*) of the gods (*e-Aleim,* remember "e" means "the") Lord of the lords, the All the Great..." Deu. 10:17

"*IEVE Aleikm eua Alei ealeim uadni eadnim eal egdi.*"

The same logic used in the question of the term Adonai, can also be applied to the question of the applicability of the title *Eloi/Elei* (or *Eloah* or any other singular spelling variation) to refer to YHVH. *Eloi/Alei* (or *Eloah* etc.). It is not always used as precisely synonymous with the infinite Pre-existent One, YHVH, who is All, (1 Cor. 15:28) since Elohim anointed one of their partners as *Elei* over themselves, a Council or Congregation of Elohim. The distinction between YHVH and *Eloi* can also be shown by the fact that there can be multiple *Eloi/Elei*, that is, Elohim. In both cases, *Eloi* and *Adonai*, recall that the "*im*" ending pluralizes and there can be only one Pre-Existent All-One.

Therefore Yahovih (Jehovih) is the Supreme Pre-existent One, who no one sees (esp.) in human form (Ex. 33:20; John 1:18 & 5:37) and who is All in all (except those who reject oneness), the Great Holy Spirit of All. So while YHVH reigns over the Elohim and is one with them, the name YHVH is sometimes but not always used as synonymous with "Eloi" or "El," who can also be the chief (having a human-like appearance) god of the council of Elohim. (the god over the council of Elohim, or God of gods, *Aleim Aleik*

"Al Elohim[37] is YHWH, Al Elohim is YHWH." Jos. 22:22 ([37]that is "All of the Elohim is YHVH," thus Al of Elohim means, head of a plurality, YHVH who is All in all His Elohim (1 Cor. 15:28) is Al or El, remember the spellings are synonymous, YHVH *is* therefore the only Omnipresent being who can be one with "All of the Elohim")

YHVH ranks above, and is worshiped by Eloi, the Elohim and any of their Adonim/Lords. All of the Elohim and Adonim are known to descend in human form (Gen. 19:2) to earth to carry out the will of YHVH's council of Elohim among mortals. The name Yahovah (Jehovah) was used to refer to the Elohim of Israel, a lesser application than Yahovih, the Supreme light of the Holy Spirit to All the Elohim of the Kosmos. However both of these words can be translated from YHVH/*IEVE.*

I AM BECOMING/HE IS BECOMING

"And He is appearing (a) messenger of YHWH to him…and He is saying, YHWH sees the humiliation of my people…I saw the oppression… and I am descending to rescue him…(Moses) what name of Him shall I say to them…And He is saying Elohim to Moses, 'I Am, what I Am'[38]…thus you shall say to the sons of Israel the "I Am" sent me to you" Ex. 3:2&14

[38]One possible translation of "I Am that I Am" is also "I Am Becoming." (*iei* – 'he is becoming' is from the same root as *aeie* - 'I Am' another of YHVH's names; meaning 'I am or I am becoming see Ex. 3:2&14 scripture4all.org) Literally *"AEIE ashr AEIE..."* (According to Strong's concordance 1961, this expression "I AM" {Heb. "hayah or havah"[39]} means "to be or become.") For examples of its usage see Genesis 1:3, 1:5, 2:7 (became), 4:14 (come, as in "come to pass"), Genesis 11:3 (had), and Genesis 15:1 (came) etc. *Complete Jewish Bible,* copyright © 1998 by David H. Stern. Pub. Jewish New Testament Publications, Inc. www. Dist. by Messianic Jewish Resources.

[39]"The verbal form of "EYEH" is the third person singular masculine imperfect[40] of the verb "HAYAH." This verb "HAYAH" does not mean "to be." It is more nearly understood by the verb "to become" in English though we cannot totally exclude the idea of "being."..The word "EHYEH" is in this "imperfect" form of the verb. "EHYEH" is just as rightly translated by our future tense as by our present tense. Therefore it is just as correct to translate it by "I shall become whom I shall become," as by the phrase "I am becoming whom I am becoming."" (Knight, George A. F. *A Christian Theology of the Old Testament,* pp. 40-41, "God known in His Self-Revelation")

[40]The Hebrew language is very "verb oriented." Much importance is placed on the understanding of their usage. Unlike Greek (or English) though, verbs are not considered as past, present or future tenses but rather perfect or imperfect (a complete or incomplete action). The name YHVH may have originally been derived from the old Semitic root *he-vah-he*[41] *(havah or hayah)* meaning "to be" or "to become." *Behind the Name – Yahweh.* ([41]When pronouncing the letters 'hehvavheh' the sound is phonetically very close to Yahovih (SHD 3069 pronounced yeh·ho·vē or Jehovee) though often rendered 'hayah' the word may have originally been pronounced much closer to 'hehvavheh' see also the Sanskrit word meaning 'to be' *Ahuva* page 152 MHJ) <http://www.behindthename.com/php/view.php?name=yahweh>

"Yahovah (He causes to be) is a title given to all delegates of Yahovah of Hosts or Yahovah of Heaven (Yehovih see SHD 3069). The Bible records Yahovah as being used by three angels at the same time in dealing with Abraham, Lot and Sodom, whereupon

Yahovah rained down fire from Yahovah in heaven (cf. Genesis chapters 18 and 19). Yahovih (SHD 3069) is the only word applied to the One True God Eloah and is read by Jews as Elohim. Yahovah (SHD 3068) is applied to other beings, as well as Yahovah of Hosts and is read as Adonai in those cases. Yahovah was changed to Adonai in 134 places by the Sopherim for this reason (cf. also Bullingers Appendix 32 to the *Companion Bible* for the lists)." Cox, Wade. FAQ Series 1: *The Nature of God.*

< http://www.logon.org/english/S/P003.html>

YHVH and YHWH are generally considered interchangeable, (except where the compound name is YHVH Elohim, where Jehovih/YHVH was always used by the Sopherim). When quoting verses that one might desire to check in <scripture4all.org> for the sake of consistency with the spelling used in that site, the spelling of YHWH has been retained in these quotes. But it is the position of this book that (based on the Middle Eastern the cultural heritage shared with the Sanskrit, ahuva - to be) the letter 'v' is a better and more appropriate transliteration of the Hebrew letter 'vav' than 'w' so the Creator's name is elsewhere usually spelled YHVH. This might be said in modern times as Yehovih or Jehovih.

> The verse quoted before also bears considering in the context of this discussion on He is Becoming/I am becoming. "And "YHWH He is becoming" ("*UEIE IEVE*"; *vav heh yod heh - yod heh vav heh*) king over all the earth; on that day YHWH will become one and his name One (*Achad*)." Zech 14:9 This verse actually uses the compound title of YHVH accompanied by the phrase "He is Becoming," a variation of the meaning of YHVH's name as defined by Ex. 3:2&14.

The 1919 Peake's commentary with over 60 contributors gives us the following information. These were such as professors of Bible languages and professors of Biblical exegesis etc. This commentary says, with reference to Exodus 3:14, "I will be that I will be" is supported by Robertson Smith, Davidson, Driver, M'Neile, and others. "I will be" is actually *aei*, and is used as such in Hos. 13:10, it has, however, been changed to "where?," concealing this understanding. The definition, "I will become," brings out the implications both of the root and tense of the verb havah/hayah. The root denotes becoming rather than being, and the tense (imperfect) marks uncompleted process or activity." (Harford, Rev. George. M.A. Hon. Canon of Liverpool, *Peake's Commentary on the Bible*, 1919 p. 172)

Charles Gianotti (1985. "The Meaning of the Divine Name" Bibliotheca Sacra 39 January-March) claims that all examples of 1. p. s. of HYH (HVH) refers to the future, except possibly two. When Bible translations use the present rendering "I am what I am," the translators deviate from the way they translate 1 p. s. of HYH elsewhere.

YHVH is and always was one with His Elohim. It is thus that YHVH, the "I Am Becoming," could if He so chose, declare both that, "I Am becoming Gods; as He also says I am becoming (plants) for food (Gen. 1:29); I am becoming animals (1:24); I Am becoming humans (2:7); AND I Am becoming Oneness," YHVH Elohim, YHVH Echad. (Deu. 6:4)

When the correct Hebrew names are used it can be seen that this understanding was present in

47

the ancients, since with the Hebrew words in place, 1 Kings 18:39 says; "YHWH He (is) the Elohim! YHWH He (is) the Elohim!" (lit.; *IEVE eua e-aleim,, IEVE eua e-aleim* remember 'e' in Hebrew = the word 'the') Word for word this literally says YHVH *the* gods! NOT, YHVH is "the God." (Because in the term *e-aleim*, the "e" stands for the word "the" and the "im" ending pluralizes) This verse very clearly explains that YHVH, and only YHVH, is one with the Elohim.

It is important to understand the phrases, "I Am Becoming" and/or "He Is Becoming." The single word *"AEIE"* that is translated incorrectly as the phrases, "I Am" or "I Shall Be" from Ex. 3:14, *clearly* contains within it the root word *"IEI"*- implying "become" rather than "be." *IEI* has been translated in the very first verses of the OT (Gen. 1:3), as the phrase, "he is becoming," yet this has been given without the understanding that these first verses of the OT invoke the presence of *AEIE-IEVE*, or that is, YHVH as He is known by His title "He is becoming." (Notice that by not capitalizing the phrase the current translation eliminates the understanding that this is actually a reference to YHVH/AEIE the "I am Becoming.")

In Exodus 3:14 YHVH's messenger says; "say to the sons of Israel the "I Am Becoming" sent me," this phrase translated as, "I am," is well established as YHVH's name. This makes the two words *IEVE* (YHVH) and *AEIE,* with their similar spellings, synonyms for one another. This gives us the definition of YHVH, which said definition is often said to have been lost in prehistoric times.

Now, therefore, to accompany the word Elohim with "He is Becoming" (Elohim *IEI*) as is done throughout the creation story, starting in Gen 1:3, when the Elohim are speaking in oneness with the Creator, and then making a record of their presence (Gen. 2:3-4) shows that YHVH was always present with the Elohim since this is also obviously a variation of "I Am Becoming." The tense *IEI*, is thus simply the basis of *AEIE*, making all three of these words related to our understanding of YHVH, and all with the same definition of "becoming" contained within them.

The variation *IEI* repeatedly accompanies the name Elohim, almost from the beginning of the Genesis creation story, such as in the phrase *"Aleim IEI Aur UIEI Aur"* found in Gen.1:3. "Elohim He shall become light and He is becoming light." (*iei* from the same root as *aeie* - 'I Am' another of YHVH's names; meaning 'to be', or I am becoming – *aeie ashr aeie* Ex. 3:2&14) That word "*IEI*," has been given as "he shall become" and it seems to have been accepted to not be a variant of the word *IEVE or YHVH,* or at least it is not translated as such.

According to the instructions given in Ex 3:14, the OT shows that YHVH/*IEVE,* speaking through His Elohim, defined Himself to Moses as the *AEIE*, or the "I Am Becoming." Therefore to say *IEI*, or "He is becoming," could be the Elohim's invocation of YHVH's presence and thus His power to create. This shows that the Creator as *AEIE*, *"the I Am becoming"* was present from the beginning with His Elohim, since *IEI* is from the same root as *AEIE.*

It lacks elegance to say that one word is, word for word, three words, even though sometimes it is not possible to find one word that fits. If, however, one includes this recognized definition of YHVH from Ex. 3:2&14 *AEIE*, "I am becoming," as synonymous with *IEI* - "He is becoming" (the name used by the Elohim in the creation story), while reading the first chapter of Genesis, then it is obvious that this term *IEI*, "He is Becoming" in fact refers to YHVH and accompanies the word Elohim from the very beginning of Genesis. So even the fundamentalists need not

48

worry if the term Elohim is finally given its rightful meaning for YHVH/*IEVE or AEIE* was with them even in the creation story.

If one were to seek a single word for *IEI or AEIE*, rather than three, it is necessary to find one that means "He-shall-become." The meaning "He-shall-Become" also implies "He shall create from Himself." With *"IEI"* as a basis of *"IEVE,"* it fits quite nicely to give this word as another variation of YHVH, since another name for YHVH that implies "creating," is "Creator."

> "IEVE (YHVH) He helped me, IE (Yah or Jah translated as "the Lord") is my strength, and melody of *"IE UIEI"* (Yah He is Becoming) to me for salvation." Ps.118:14 (see also v. 18&19)

"IE" is a recognized abbreviation of *"IEVE,"* even often translated the same as YHVH or IEVE, in English it is rendered Ya or Yah. (Isa. 12:2, 26:4, 38:11, Ps. 68:4) So it is also obviously related to *"IEVE"* in that both words contain the same root *"IE"* and since it is so frequently coupled with the name Elohim in the phrase *"Aleim IEI"* (Elohim IEI) meaning; Elohim I am becoming, a relationship to the phrase, *Aleim IEVE,* Elohim I Am Becoming, and to the word *"IEVE"* (YHVH) also seems obvious.

YHVH/*"IEVE"* is also coupled in the same way that *"IEI"* is, with the name Elohim and while it may conjointly have the meaning, "He is becoming" it is suggested that as a single word it would more closely be interpreted and defined, word for word, with a meaning somewhat more synonymous with "Creator," making the term, *Elohim IEI* mean the Creator's Elohim, exactly synonymous with *Elohim IEVE,* or that is, YHVH's Elohim.

> "You are my witnesses, says YHWH...before me was no "Al" (or El i.e, All) and after me not "He shall become" (*Ieie).* I even I YHWH and apart from me there is no *Ieie*[42]." Isa. 43:10 [42]"He is becoming," given by some as savior but translated as, "other" by KJV SHD 3467 salvation.

There are no doubt some others who have attempted to make the connection between *IEVE/AEIE YHVH* and *IEI* (He is becoming) but organized religion constitutes a powerful voice, and when the connection cannot be agreed upon the fallback position is that the definition of YHVH/*IEVE* was lost in the distant past. It is, however, still there; in the spelling, in the definition given in Ex. 3:2&14 and for the diligent open-minded student, it can be rediscovered. YHVH means "I Am Becoming" for nothing can come into existence that is not of Him. There is much, however, that is far removed from Him in their minds, by way of the darkness of ego and ignorance, lost from His Light and therefore from enlightenment concerning His Oneness.

> "The Zohar says that the Elohim used this word to form the world." Article on Yah, Yaho, *Encyclopedic Theosophical Glossary,* Ya-Yz, Theosophical Press.

> <http://www.theosociety.org/pasadena/etgloss/ya-yz.htm>

The Hebrew letters transliterated as IE in the online lexicon at <http://www.scripture4all.org>, are further translated into English as Ya, Yah, Yaho etc. The repetitive vibrating sound *IEIEIEIEIE,* is movement and rest, a waveform, as in "Elohim vibrating." (*mrchphth* Gen. 1:2) A wave form perhaps similar to this, was spoken by the myriads of Elohim, "and He is saying[43] Elohim *IEI."*

49

(^{43}*ulamr* Gen. 1:3) So on a related note (all puns intended) sounded in this way by the countless Elohim, this root of YHVH's (*IEVE*) other name *AEIE* (I AM), could be considered as another variation of *YHVH*.

> "And He is blessing Elohim in the seventh time^{44} (*bium*) ...He ceases from all of work *which He creates Elohim to make* these genealogical annals in the time (of) YHVH Elohim making the earth and its heavenly place." Gen.2:3-4 (^{44}KJV translated as day)

For the thousands of Elohim to speak His name in unity, would be a source of energy (called vibrating in Gen. 1:2 or as in physics the definition of "work" is to transfer energy to an object). This would do the work of "separating" and stratifying matter into darkness and light and the various levels and densities in the creation story, just as shaking a bowl of dirt will bring the larger pebbles to the surface. In one of the texts from the Nag Hammadi library, Jesus tells his followers that the sign of the Father is within them, then he says; "And when they ask; what is the sign of the Father within you, you tell them it is *movement and rest*." (Gospel of Thomas 50)

In biblical texts we constantly meet with the expression THE Elohim (*e-aleim – ha elohim* or "The" *Aleim*), but in no instance do we meet with the expression THE YHVH. Imagine how silly and inappropriate it would sound if some one referred to me, for example, as "THE Martha." It would be equally illogical for YHVH to call himself by the very same name (*Elohim*) which he uses to address many of His created beings, except in a context (such as when it is explained as in the Shema), that He is one with His Elohim. Indeed it would be absurd to speak of a singular being as THE YHVH or to use the word "the" in any context except speaking of a multiple number of individuals or in conjunction with a title.

If anyone doubts that the church can be wrong, look again at their treatment of Galileo. (for taking the stance that the earth orbits around the sun, rather than the sun around the earth, as was held by the church) It took the church all this time to admit their mistake, and only recently did the church formally apologize for their treatment of Galileo.

Just as the stubborn stance of the church with Galileo was an attempt to egotistically avoid believing that our earth was not the center of the universe, the convoluted interpretations of the word Elohim by organized religion, is an attempt (albeit perhaps unconscious) to avoid understanding what the ancients knew all along, that is, humans were NOT the first sentient humanoid (Elohim-like) beings whom YHVH had created!

They all want to believe that earth and humans are of the first and central most importance in the universe. Any effort to avoid correcting the usage of the term Elohim as synonymous with YHVH, among those who possess even a glimmer of understanding concerning it, just as much as that incident, will be to continue to try to protect organized religion from the discomfort of acknowledging fallibility. Any continuation of this miss-interpretation, by not telling their followers that our earth and ourselves are only equal in the Creator's eyes with His other worlds and His other created beings and not of the central most importance in all creation; is (just as much as the torment inflicted on Galileo was to avoid admitting we were not the center of the solar system), to avoid admitting that we are not the first and only humanoid (Elohim-like) created beings. Ah, the frail egos of mere mortal earthlings.

"For whom in the heavens, shall be ranked with YHWH, who among the sons of the Elohim is like YHWH? *Al/El* (all[45]) being in terror of the council of the holy ones." Ps. 89:6 ([45]remember from the section on The All, that *al/el* can also mean 'all,' so *Al/El* is not always equivalent to YHVH. Were that so it would here mean that El-YHVH is in terror of His council, rather here it means that *all* the sons of the Elohim were in terror of YHVH's council of holy ones.)

When the OT is read with the understanding of the plurality of the Hebrew word Elohim, the following verses state that YHVH's Elohim came to earth, participated in its (re)generation and inter-bred with humans; and thanks to that cross breeding we became "Homo sapiens sapiens" i.e. sapient beings unlike the animals. In the NT, Jude (the brother of Jesus) describes them as "angels, having left their first estate in heaven" (Jude 1:6)

"…in Plato's *Euthydemus*, Socrates refers to the ancient gods as his *"lords and ancestors,"* while Euhemerus (c.300 BC) was another Greek philosopher who argued that "Ancestor Worship" was the primary source of religion." Goodgame, Peter. *The Spirit World and Civilization.* <http://www.redmoonrising.com/Giza/SpiritCiv5.htm>

Unlike the other animals that live in a state of ignorance of the power of the written word, we then, from our Elohim ancestors, acquired the many brain areas that allow the capacity to read and write and learn symbolic calculations. (like algebra etc.) The deeper levels of symbolic meanings are understood only by beings that can use written language and calculate, not just recognize commands as some animals can. This acquisition of the many improvements to our brains happened all at once, something the process of natural selection could never have achieved instantaneously, since it would have required millions of years for each new brain area to mutate and then be given preference by the hypothesized process of natural selection. (Problems with the 'theory' of natural selection and the many fossils, which appear suddenly in the fossil record with multiple changes, will be discussed in depth further on.)

The word "adam" in Hebrew has the meaning of; mankind, (lit. "dustling"), red dust i.e., earth therefore, earthling. (SHD 119, 120, 122, 127) Biblical texts repeatedly refer to humans as THE Adam, even in later books of the OT. As has been stated previously, using the word "the" makes it a phrase signifying a multiplicity. Only in chapter five of Genesis...does the Bible drop the "THE." It is as absurd to speak of an individual man as "the Adam" as it would be to say "the Sam" or "the Bob" but it is completely logical to use the word "the" when speaking of a race of beings, for example to say: the English or the Chinese. (The Hebrew and Chaldee Dictionary section, of the "James Strong Exhaustive Concordance of the Bible," 8 # 120)

"Male and female He created them and He is blessing them and He is calling the name of them Adam." Gen. 5:2 (notice it says "them" plural)

Besides the above text, Genesis states that the race of Adam (i.e. the Adamic race) were already male and female in Gen. 1:27; BEFORE the metaphorical story of the creation of the woman (*Ashe*, meaning; life giver SHD 2332) in Gen. 2:23. These females appeared before and are distinct from the female known as Eve, especially created later in Gen. 2:21-23, discussed further on in this book.

> "And He is saying Elohim we shall make human in image of *us* (note the plural pronoun)...in image of Elohim He creates him male and female..." Gen. 1:26-27

This reference to making the Adam like themselves, refers not to the creation of the life force, or spirit, in the humans, rather it refers to their *pro-creation* of the human race, and therefore to our resemblance to themselves, and to the process of then "making" the Adam over, so as to learn wisdom and educating them to progress in becoming in the image of sentient beings like themselves, i.e. godlike pro-creators of what we can observe for ourselves, is now a self-aware species capable of learning a multitude of skills, skills that no other animal even comes close to approximating.

The Adam had become capable of exercising judicial discernment; this is a quality that the other animals do not naturally exhibit. Only recently have some of the higher primates (like Koko the gorilla) been taught to use signs that something is "good" and this ability was not an inborn capacity, it is one that had to be taught to them by other sentient beings (humans) capable of judicial discernment, just as our ancestors were taught by the Elohim. Likewise these experimental primate subjects show some limited self-awareness and have acquired the ability to understand words and know themselves by a name, this is also something that we, as they, had to be taught.

> "And (the) Elohim said, behold, the Adam has become as one of *us* (again plural) knowing good and evil." Genesis 3:22

The "grasping" of the understanding good and evil is found in the metaphor of "grasping" or "taking" the fruit from the tree of the knowledge of good and evil. This tree is then coupled with the "Tree of the living ones" (the Adam, earthlings) in Gen. 3:22, and because each involves the outgrowth of branches of offspring grown from participating in acts of procreation. Through the inter-breeding that took place between the "tree of the living ones" (*chiia* also *echiim* Ecc. 9:9:4) and the sons of Elohim, "the tree of the knowledge of good and evil," this act bound them to us. Through their love for us they must labor here (where Satan rules through fear of death), away from the dimension of eternal life. This is why we often see their star-ships watching over us their descendants, away from their eternal life in spirit, laboring to enlighten humans, in a corporeal world where death exists.

> "Let us (again plural) go down and there confound their language." Gen. 11:7

When the Elohim said "the Adam has become as one of *us*" they were clearly speaking to each other. If Elohim referred to a singular being, why would a singular god speak to himself and why would he refer to himself as "us"? While it can be said "God" was talking to himself, there would be no need as He is omniscient (all-knowing).

> "I heard the voice of YHVH saying Whom shall I send and who will go for us?" Isa. 6:8

In the last two thousand years there has been a concerted effort to posit that God was speaking to the "Trinity" or to Jesus, but the OT and Genesis makes no mention of Jesus by name, just as there is no mention of the concept of the "Trinity," this is a recent and modern interpretation, fabricated from various bits and pieces then constructed into a now widely accepted modern concept, never once referred to in biblical texts of the OT or elsewhere, before the last two thousand years. Would not an omniscient God have proudly called his son by name if he were already there with him, especially thus proving His omniscience? Was it because Jesus was created later, at the time of his birth? The NT refers to Jesus as the Son of Man (*ben adam*) or the Son of God, nowhere in the Old Testament does it refer to Jesus as God or even God the Son.

THE WATCHERS

> "My god (*Eloah*) in whom is the spirit of the holy gods (*Elohim*)...And I saw in the visions of my head upon my bed, and, behold, a "watcher" (*oir*) and a holy one came down from heaven." Dan. 4:9,13; also 5:11.

This verse shows that at least some of the watchers were in association with the holy ones, not all were evil, as some would have it. Of note also are many references in religious literature including this one from an Orphic or Pythagorean initiation rite. "Of earth and starry Heaven child am I, my race is of the heavens." (Mead, G. R. S. *Did Jesus Live 100 BC*, p. 384) The Elohim are also sometimes referred to in other Hebrew literature and various records from the ancient Middle East as "the Watchers," in Hebrew the *Zophim*, from the same root as eyes, or as the "*Ur*" of Sumerian and Babylonian literature. They were also known as the *Elahhin*, plural of *Elahh*, the equivalent of Elohim in Chaldean. Cox. Wade. *FAQ Bible Study Old Testament (No. 57).* <http://www.ccg.org/english/s/p057.html>

> "The Watchers were a specific race of divine beings known in Hebrew as *nun resh 'ayin*, "irin" (*resh 'ayin, 'ir* in singular, however another possible meaning of *ayin* will be discussed further on), meaning "those who watch" or "those who are awake," which is translated into Greek as *egregoris* or grigori, meaning "watchers." Collins, Andrew, *From the Ashes of Angels - The Forbidden Legacy of a Fallen Race* (1996) p. 3.

> "Ptah and the other gods were called, in Egyptian, *Ntr* - "Guardian, Watcher" Zechariah Sitchen, *The Wars of Gods and Men.*

The Book of Jubilees (known in early times as the *Apocalypse of Moses)* was allegedly written down by Moses at Mt. Sinai. Scholars though, believe it was most likely composed in the second century BC, and thus can be referenced to reflect some religious thinking from around that time. The following quote is to be found in *The Book of Jubliees* "For in his days the angels of the Lord descended upon earth - those who are named Watchers - that they should instruct the children of men, that they should do judgment and uprightness upon the earth."

> "During the fabled *First Time,* Zep Tepi, when the gods ruled...the *Urshu,* a category of lesser divinities whose title meant "the Watchers."" Graham Hancock, *Fingerprints of the*

Gods.

The human inter-breeding with beings from elsewhere in the Universe is also mentioned in other Hebrew data, for example the Book of Enoch. The Book of Enoch (probably a second century or so BCE forgery, since it contains linguistic anachronisms that place it much later than a book written by the grandson of Adam {before the time of Abraham}, however it still attests to common themes understood by Jews of the second or third century) gives us another reference;

> "*Book of Enoch*" 6:1"And it came to pass when the children of men had multiplied that in those days were born unto (2) them beautiful and comely daughters. And the angels, the children of the heaven, saw and lusted after them, and said to one another: 'Come, let us choose us wives from among the children of men (3) and beget us children.' & 15:2 ...say to the Watchers of heaven, who have sent thee to intercede for them: "You should intercede" for men, and not men (3) for you: Wherefore have ye left the high, holy, and eternal heaven, and lain with women, and defiled yourselves with the daughters of men and taken to yourselves wives, and done like the children (4) of earth, and begotten giants (as your) sons? And though ye were holy, spiritual, living the eternal life, you have defiled yourselves with the blood of women, and have begotten (children) with the blood of flesh, and, as the children of men, have lusted after flesh and blood as those also do who die (5) and perish...(6) But you were formerly (7) spiritual, living the eternal life, and immortal for all generations of the world." Charles, R.H. *The Book of Enoch.* <http://www.heaven.net.nz/writings/thebookofenoch.htm>

The Dead Sea scrolls also mentions the watchers, suggesting that they are spirits or angels. This mention seems to imply that not all spirits or angels who watch us are good apparently some are evil, and try to win us over to do evil. This is perhaps one reason why Jesus said; "lead us not into temptation, but deliver us from evil." (Matt. 6:13)

> "I saw Watchers in my vision, the dream vision. Two men were fighting over me...and holding a great contest over me. I asked them, 'Who are you, that you are thus empowered over me?'... (One) of them was terrifying in his appearance...in his visage like a viper...This (Watcher) so is he? He answered me..." King of Evil."" *Testament of Amram* (4Q535, Manuscript B)

Chapter Two

EARTHLINGS[1] AND THE SERPENT BRAIN

[1]SHD 119, 120, 122, 127 Adam means red dust, soil or earth, therefore Adam is literally; earthling.

THE SERPENT BRAIN

To understand the story of the serpent we must consider that in the ancient world the prevalence of the symbol of the serpent stood for a concept that is no longer familiar to us. In addition the previous information on the serpent as a symbol of corporeality, the serpent symbol and metaphor may perhaps be best understood by first describing something that has become known through biology. We (and other mammals) all have a "serpent brain" or "reptile brain" that lies within the neo-mammalian brain or limbic nerve system. The limbic brain is the base of our e-motions (the feelings that move us); it lies below the neo-cortex, where we "think", project into the future, imagine consequences, and empathize; that is, where we picture what another is feeling. It is the neo-cortex that distinguishes us, and our abilities derived from its use, from the other mammals, and it is what makes us truly "human."

The reptile or "serpent brain," however, controls territorialism, aggression, appetite, fear and the pro-creational drive (lust) to which the *ashe* succumbed and it is these drives governed by the serpent brain that lead to war, violence, and crimes of lust. The drives arising from the "serpent brain" are all material or corporeal, not intellectual, analytical or spiritual, and it reacts and is motivated at the same fierce level that reptiles are motivated.

In ancient times reptiles (sometimes called *tanniyn*/dragons, Gen. 1:21; *behemoths*, meaning incredibly large Job 40:15-24; and *leviathon* Job chapter 41, Psalm 104:25,26 and Isaiah 27:1) were generally grouped together as various types of "serpents," or *tanniyn*, many of the biblical references to dragons have now, however, been changed to read jackals. If these references and various rock carvings from around the world are taken at face value it would appear that there were some few remnants of the dinosaurs/dragons living concurrently with humans. It is entirely possible that these few remnants of the dinosaurs left very few fossils since only one in many millions of animals results in fossilization. Orr, James, M.A., D.D. *Bible Dragons!*

<http://www.accuracyingenesis.com/dragon.html>

& *Dinosaurs and the Bible.* <http://www.clarifyingchristianity.com/dinos.shtml>

According to the Bible, after the time of the temptation of Ashe/Eve, the serpent was to crawl on its belly. (Gen. 3:14) This may signify that the only remaining reptiles were ones that slithered or crawled with their bellies dragging the ground. For all those who walked with their bodies suspended above the ground, their time came to become extinct, perhaps so as to protect humans from the huge dinosaurs, who would have easily destroyed us.

The reptile or "serpent" brain deals with the material world at the most basic levels of existence and survival, individually and as a species. Warriors, and the collective consciousness of all worldly adversaries operating from the reptile brain, the *al enchsh,* or the Al^2 Serpent (Gen3:2) are Satan, a word which literally means, to attack, accuse, or to be an adversary. (SHD 7853) This imagery can help us understand the original "great dragon" metaphor John mentions in Revelations. (12:7) (^{2}remember that *Al/El* can also mean 'all')

Some individuals so ruled begin to actually take on a menacing or threatening, habitually mean appearance, down turned mouths in haggard unloving faces and glaring or sunken eyes that never smile even when the mouth does. Reptilian satanic figures, with hateful faces dressed in red, with hooves, horns and tails, are projections of some of these images stored in racial memory, leftover from the age of reptiles. These images stimulate our own reptile brain, to release adrenaline, engendering fear which in turn drives the survival mechanisms of fight or flight. All the talk of reptilian aliens, however, is nonsense, because reptiles do not have the necessary areas of the brain that would allow them to build and pilot a spacecraft, these are again more fear driven imaginations, stimulated by the reptile brain.

The Elohim, knowing as they did that all life is related, were aware, however, that that the heritage of the serpent or reptile brain, might lead some to give in to temptation. (So they warned those among themselves, who had little experience with these corporeal drives, not to partake of the "tree of the living ones." (Gen. 3:22) The tree of the living ones, (distinct form the tree of the knowledge of good and evil) is the out growth of life that arose from surrendering to the pro-creational drive to mate with the "living ones," the race of adam. The "tree of the knowledge of good and evil," is our genetic complement received from the Elohim and the sharing of the genes "to make intelligent" (Gen. 3:6 rendered "wise" in KJV). In partaking of the "tree of the living ones" the Elohim through their love for us, became bound to labor with us, their offspring, in the dimension of corporeal death, where through the fear of death, Satan, the collective consciousness of the serpent brain, rules as *al enchsh,* or the All Serpent.

When a child is placed in any fearful situation, the serpent brain takes over and they develop less than mature coping mechanisms. These people when grown appear, to mature un-violated adults, to be displaying characteristics sometimes labeled "insane." This is because these impulses are fear and impulse driven, rather than logically planned out. They may be based on shame and fear of discovery, fear of not getting what is (imagined to be) deserved, or fear of being alone, insignificant or non-existent (called boredom) but always when the fear arises, it is habitually coped with through habitual behavior patterns. These habits were formed when that person was not thinking maturely, and these behaviors are then carried forward out of habit.

These habits in turn weaken the life force. When portions of the brain are dying, it allows for a slight degree of stimulation from the spiritual dimension (as in the case with alcohol, drugs and the stimulation of acid forming foods, high in phosphoric acid or sulfuric acid, discussed further in a later chapter) it therefore also allows lower un-enlightened spirits to further these obsessions, through thought forms suggesting re-surrender and enjoyment of the sensations associated with whatever weakness that mortal is prone to.

If one is to rise above these obsessions it is necessary to encourage development of the strength to face and recognize this primal fear, without being moved to find any escape, through pleasure (addictions) power (control) possessions (hoarding wealth) attention-seeking (fame, lust) etc. Until then it will continue to be true of us what Jesus said, "Forgive them for they know not what they do." (Luke 23:34)

Whenever there has been any form of abuse, by the family or outsiders, children are at risk of becoming obsessed with habitual reactions driven by the serpent brain. When a child's life is so miserable that s/he would rather turn off their feelings completely than face their fear of further irrational abuse (when they express their feelings), there is the risk that empathetic skills will be arrested. In order to mature, and rise above the habits and addictions that develop to avoid facing this misery, it is necessary to finally face the fear that arises when facing the possibility of irrationality in others.

Contemplating the lack of fairness and love in the world leads to various attempts to control and manipulate others and avoid responsibility for ones own happiness and wellbeing. When surrendering control to and acknowledging a higher power, the individual must, even in the face of what may feel like overwhelming fear, make a rational decision to turn away (the meaning of repent) from any further participation in also surrendering to indulgences of the serpent brain. This requires faith that in choosing to join forces with those ruled by love and reason (logic derived from logos), they will be guided and protected by those governed by the supreme intelligence of the universe, YHVH, who is one with all those who choose oneness with Him.

When rage attacks block out memory of an event (a phenomena seen in many psychopathic individuals) it is an indication that the serpent or reptile brain has been in control. (This can be because of fear of offense to the ego {self}, loss of control or of physical harm.) While the reptile brain is in control it suppresses rational thinking and also thereafter the storage of memory. Remember that, because of the emphasis society places on the importance of the ego, the fear of a slight, or the desire for gain or power for ego's sake, is more frequently the drive to commit murder and mayhem than the actual fear of loss of physical well being.

It is these drives which we must master, and understanding them, then turn away from the drive to promote self interest and self will and ego (self). (Repent literally means "turn away," so when one truly repents he literally goes a different direction not simply says he believes something or other.) We must rise above these drives to further the self interests of ego, if humanity is to ever have a system come about on earth that (like that of those advanced heavenly beings, who act and exist in the harmony of oneness, and who still watch over us) that is, the kingdom come on earth as it is in the heavens.

It is not enough to just hunt down psychopaths after they are produced; we must also learn how to prevent the formation of this psychopathology. For when we desire to hate and kill them we participate in, encourage and condone the same attitudes involved in their psychopathology (they too think they have a right to judge and punish wrongdoers). Psychopathology is involved to some degree in all cluster B personality disorders (Anti-social, Narcissistic, Borderline and Histrionic). We must intervene with children before they are twisted by an abusive world or through neglect allowed to go unguided spiritually when they begin to descend on the path toward evil. To do this we must unite for the protection of these vulnerable and innocent victims while they are still lovable, and malleable. This must happen before they are subjected to the various forms of abuse and unloving neglect that contribute to and exacerbate these disorders, after which they lose their innocence and cease being lovable. It may not be possible to "cure" a psychopath, but by addressing the protection of the innocent babies (including abuses in the foster care system[3] where children frequently are taken from loving parents when their only crime is poverty, which, incidentally, then costs the taxpayer more than welfare). By supplying loving guidance, when they are at the crossroads of spiritual and moral crises, we can help prevent the formation of new psychopaths.

[3]<http://nasga.wordpress.com/category/cps/>

LUCIFER

Isa. 14:12 "How Art Thou Fallen From Heaven, O Lucifer, Son of the Morning."

In contrast to Satan (the adversary, the collective consciousness of the serpent brain) the word translated "Lucifer" actually appears only ONE time in the OT, in the above verse in Isaiah, and it appears nowhere in the NT. Lucifer is a Latin name, in Roman astronomy Lucifer was the name given to the morning star (Venus). The name derives from the Latin term *lucem ferre*, bringer, or bearer, of light. Early Christian scribes, writing in Latin, as was used by the church, interpreted the verse to mean a fallen angel.

However, Isa. 14:4 says that when Israel is restored they will "take up this taunt against (Lucifer) the *king of Babylon*..." Verse 12 above of Isa. 14, is a part of this taunting song, about an evil Babylonian king, who persecuted the Israelites mercilessly, The OT does not mention Satan at all in this song against this king, or say anywhere, that this king of Babylon was Satan.

The scholars authorized by King James I to translate the Bible into English used versions from Jerome's Latin Vulgate. St. Jerome in the fourth century had translated the Hebraic "*heleyl ben shachar*" which can be literally translated "shining one, son of dawn" as Lucifer, not in itself incorrect. However Jerome's equation of Lucifer with Satan was an arbitrary decision not based on any prior teachings about Satan. The term used in the Greek Septuagint version of Isa. 14:12 is *Eo(u)s phoros*, morning star/Dawn god of light. Mithra "the bull slayer" was also known as the god of the dawn light. Beck, Roger. *Mithraism.*

<http://www.cais-soas.com/CAIS/Religions/iranian/Mithraism/mithraism.htm>

<http://scripture4all.org/OnlineInterlinear/OTpdf/isa14.pdf>

Ancient Hebrew speaking people never believed that Lucifer was a name of Satan and modern Jews still do not believe in Lucifer as "Satan." Satan means resist, as an adversary, SHD 7853, (the opposite of non-resisters i.e. pacifists). War is Satan personified, the collective spirit of adversaries. Lucifer was not equated with Satan until after Jerome, in the Middle Ages, it was later interpretations from which the confusion arose. Christians now generally believe that Satan, the Devil and Lucifer all mean the same individual and that he was created at or near the beginning and refer to the Isaiah story of this evil Babylonian king to support the idea that he was cast down from heaven.

"How you have fallen from the heavens, O *Heleel* (the Shining One) son of the morning, you have been cut down to the ground, you who have laid low the nations! For you have said in your heart; Let me go up to the heavens, let me raise my throne above the stars of El, and let me sit in the mount of meeting on the sides of the north..." Isa. 14:12-13

To see what is meant by "the sides of the north?" we can refer to Psalm 48:2, "Beautiful for situation, the joy of the whole earth, is Mount Zion, on the sides of the north, the city of the great king." So this Babylonian king Lucifer had desired to have control of Jerusalem. In verse 19 he was to be "cast out of (his) grave" As a mortal he could be buried, an immortal demonic being could not have been confined in a grave.

Verse 16 says..." Is this the man that made the earth to tremble?" So Lucifer was A MAN, a mortal king. No immortal angel would be bothered by death, only a mortal man could be "thrust through with a sword." Isa. 14:12-19,21 Verses 18-20, tell of his end and compares it with the other Kings of the nations who were laid down in the grave in glory, rather than in disrepute as he was, because he had slain his own people.

Mormons claim that the Book of Mormon is an ancient record written beginning in about 600 BC, and that ancient author supposedly copied Isaiah in Isaiah's original words. However, if Joseph Smith's claim to translate the supposed "ancient record" were accurate he would not have included the confused King James Version of the Lucifer verse in the Book of Mormon. The LDS Doctrine & Covenants compounds the error in 76:26 when it also affirms that "Lucifer" means Satan. The story in a third Mormon scripture, "The Pearl of Great Price" describes a war in heaven based on Joseph Smith's incorrect interpretation of the word "Lucifer" (which only appears in Isaiah and, is itself a satirical proverb, prophesying the death and disgrace of a tyrant king of Babylon, possibly King Nebuchadnezzar, Sargon II, Sennacherib, or other subsequent Assyrian rulers). Assembly of YHWH, Cascade. *Lucifer.*

<http://www.assemblyoftrueisrael.com/Documents/Lucifer.htm> &

<http://www.lds-mormon.com/lucifer.shtml> quoting Robinson, John J. A Pilgrim's Path..

INCREASED PAIN IN PREGNANCY FROM BABIES WITH LARGER BRAINS

"When men began to multiply on the face of the earth, and daughters were born to them, the "*ben Elohim*" (sons of the Elohim) saw that the daughters of the Adam (remember that Adam is a Hebrew word that also means humans, SHD 119, 120, 122, 127) were good; and they took for themselves women from all whom they chose." Gen. 6:1-2

The metaphor, of Eve when interpreted, is that females, *al eashe* (Gen. 3:1-4) or 'all woman' of the race of "Adam" were seduced by "the serpent." (Remember *al/el* can also mean 'all' and notice that the word *eashe* begins with 'e' or 'the' and so means "all the woman," conversely, to argue that *al/El* means 'god' is actually to interpret this phrase to mean 'god the woman', something the mainstream patriarchs would never accept.") Only later in Gen. 3:20 does *eadm,* 'the adam' name *ashthu,* 'his woman,' whom he called *chue*/Eve. Instead of mating with the primitive "Adam" of her own race, *al eashe* came to worship and desire the Elohim. Her desire was to partake of the "tree of the knowledge of good and evil" (Gen. 3:22). Or that is, a desire to have offspring with the Elohim, who possessed "the tree of the knowledge of good and evil and become as 'gods' the ones (plural) knowing good and evil." (Gen. 3:5 "and your eyes shall be opened and you shall become as Elohim, ones {plural} knowing good and evil."). The blame for her desire was then placed on the urges of the serpent brain. It was these females, spoken of in Gen. 6:1-2, with whom some of the less discerning sons of the Elohim (*ben ha Elohim*) bore offspring, thankfully or we would not be here.

"No curse comes without its cause." Prov. 26:2

The reason the pain of pregnancy was increased, in Gen. 3:16, is because females then had to begin giving birth to babies with heads having extra large brain capacities for the newly introduced areas of the brain. This occurred without a chance for the pelvic regions to have time to adapt to the increased size. It was not a punishment per se, but rather a consequence.

"To the woman (*eashe*) He says I shall increase your pain (grief) in pregnancy, in grief you shall bear sons and man of you, running about you, he shall rule over you." (Gen. 3:16) This last is transcribed as "thy desire shall be to thy husband and he shall rule over you."

Because of a woman's craving for her husband he is able to dominate her. Women have an especially large challenge in facing their fears of being alone, unprotected, etc. because they tend to be physically weaker. Whether male or female the answer is the same, stop fighting (remember fight or flight is a reptile brain function) and try to logically make a plan to escape the abuse and addiction to lust.

The Hebrew word in Gen. 3:20 that is actually translated as Eve is *Chava, or Chavah* (SHD 2332 & 2331) it appears related to the root *hawa* or *hava (havah)* or *avvah* (SHD 2865, 5753, 183 & 185) which also means bow down or worship, prostrate oneself or lust. The craving for her husband, which women then began to exhibit was in turn because having her pelvis stretched out of shape by babies with large brains,[4] it decreased her capacity to achieve orgasm, which promotes ovulation and thus ends her time of estrus. Succumbing to this increase in desire among women allows men to dominate women to this day and it is this desire that women in abusive situations must learn to control if they wish to avoid the abuse.

[4]"Cro-Magnon...brain capacity ranged from 1590 to 1715 cubic centimeters, as compared with our 1400. Were they from another planet?" Landsburg, A. & S. *In Search of Ancient Mysteries,* p.165.

"Homo-sapiens...became extinct looking much the same as they always did." Stephen J. Gould, *Evolution Explosion Not Ascent.*

"After about 38,000 years ago all other human types were replaced world wide by skeletally modern Homo-sapiens sapiens." *Cambridge Encyclopedia of Archaeology,* p. 86.

Humans were suddenly able to draw and made strange symbols on the walls of caves, they could make elaborate tools and personal items. These half-breed humans were exponentially different in their capacity for intelligence, especially compared to pre-*Homo sapiens* like, "*Australopithecus africanus* (or *Sahelanthropus* both tool less vegetarians) and *Homo erectus* (a crude tool maker) who became extinct looking much the same as they always did." ("Evolution Explosion Not Ascent" by Stephen J. Gould. "There is no direct evidence for gradualism within any hominid taxon (class, genus or species)...Each species disappears looking much as it did at its origin." Stephen Gould and Niles Eldredge, *Paleobiology*.

<http://www.jqjacobs.net/anthro/paleo/scavenging.html>

& The Evolution of Man. *Australopithecus robustus*.

<http://www.park.org/Canada/Museum/man/robustus1.html>

"There is a gap of over a million years (in the geological record) between *Australopithecus afarensis* and the first *Homo*...there is a scant 5,000 years (from 40,000 to 35,000 years ago) between the time of the disappearance of the Neanderthals and the official European debut of Homo-sapiens sapiens....(quoting) Steven M. Stanley in *The New Evolutionary Timetable* 'Out of nowhere, our sharp chin, weak brow (no thick brow ridges), high vaulted forehead (also thin skull, diminished teeth, less ponderous jaw, smaller eye orbits, streamlined pelvis, & redesigned vocal tract MHJ) appear in the fossil record.''...A natural miracle took place: Within a critical period of 5,000 years-just 1/7 of 1 percent of the time that has elapsed since the first – known australopithecine's day – we get more significant evolutionary change than in the other 99 6/7 percent of that time; we get a veritable explosion of change [with no transitional species discovered for each of these changes]...discoveries in Borneo, So. Africa, Australia, and the Americas ...fix much earlier dates for Homo-sapiens sapiens debut, showing he was alive and well long before the Neanderthals even came into being...[quoting] G. Phillip Rightmire "The idea fully modern humans appeared only 35,000 to 40,000 years ago is certainly subject to quite drastic change."...Australian archaeologists believe that dates will reach over 60,000 years ago. Pages 132,144,184,186,198&207 "The Genesis Mystery" by Jeffery Goodman Ph.D. [quoting] Michael Cremo and Richard Thompson in their "Forbidden Archeology"...suggest the present acceptable sequence for...*homo-sapiens sapiens* [less than 100,000 years ago]." Page 40 "Red Earth, White Lies" by Vine Deloria Jr.

"There is a stretch of nearly 200,000 years (starting 300,000 years ago) from which no definite Homo erectus fossils are known. ...Where did Cro-Magnon Man, the first of our own Homo-Sapiens species, come from 35,000 years ago? Not from erectus, too great a jump...Not from Neanderthal, a quite different species. Then from where? From the starmen." Flindt & Binder, *Mankind Child of the Stars*, p. 87&94.

"The Origin of Form Was Abrupt Not Gradual. Stuart Newman's now got a seductive theory about the origin of form of all 35 or so animal phyla--"it happened abruptly" not gradually, roughly 600 million years ago via a "pattern language" --which serves as the centerpiece of the "Extended Synthesis."...In this picture you can see there's no real gradualism. Things get formed because of the interaction of gene products and cells and physical mechanisms. You get a whole variety of different forms. Some of the forms survive and some of them don't. But there are no intermediates between one form and another form. *It didn't happen gradually. It happened abruptly.*" (Mazur, 2008) <http://archive.archaeology.org/online/interviews/newman.html>

61

> "And there were giants[5] in the earth in those days and also after that. <u>SO</u> the sons of the Elohim came to all daughters (*al bnuth* remember *Al/El* can mean 'all') of the Adam (*eadm* remember "e" means "the") and they bore the masters who were the mortals of renown eons ago." (⁵ *Nephilim*) Gen. 6:4

<u>Not</u> that the Nephilim were descended from the sons of the Elohim, as many have assumed this verse to say. This is because the KJV says "and also after that, the same were the sons of the Elohim," and uses the term "same," while the Hebrew version never describes them as being "the same" kind of beings, and it has no word anywhere in that verse that means "the same."

Rather it says; "there were Nephilim in those days, <u>SO</u> the sons of the Elohim came to the daughters of Adam and they bore the masters who were the mortals of renown eons ago" That is, the Elohim and the daughters of the Adam gave birth to the masters of mortals SO they could *protect* the humans from the Nephilim/Neanderthals.

> "The Neanderthals had a very short stay on earth appearing 100,000 to 70,000 years ago and vanishing around 35,000 years ago." Goodman, Jeffrey. Ph.D. *The Genesis Mystery*, p.137. In the Museum of Prehistory in Rome, there is an Etruscan silver bowl on which may be seen, among very realistic appearing human hunters on horses, the figure of a large, ape-man-like creature who they are apparently trying to kill. Cremo & Thompson, *The Hidden History of the Human Race*, p. 216.

Even given the above mistranslation some other authors have made the Nephilim/Neanderthal connection. Others have pointed to archaeological evidence from Israel that shows Neanderthals and modern humans existed in the same time periods, with humans sometimes showing up before Neanderthals. Neanderthals and Nephilim share many points in common including; they were both exterminated when humans showed up on the scene and may have been a hybrid race with humans. Even though Neanderthals sometimes had larger brains than humans their ability to make tools, art, etc., were much less skilled. *The Watchers – Nephilim*

<http://www.bibliotecapleyades.net/vida_alien/alien_watchers.htm>

& *The Return of the Nephilim* <http://thereturnofthenephilim.blogspot.com/>

However, it is the abundance of neuro-transmitters, number of connections (humans maintain 100x more connections than most vertebrates) and the development of specific brain areas (called lobes) that comprise intelligence, not size, otherwise elephants would be smarter than humans. Einstein's brain was studied and found to have larger parietal lobes (on the sides near the ears) with more glial cells that produce acetylcholine. There is also some reason to believe that it is the total surface area that affects intelligence, not size. In other words how wrinkled the brain is plays a part, by increasing surface area. (Witelson S.F., Kigar D.L., Harvey T., art. The Exceptional Brain of Albert Einstein, *The Lancet,* 1999l 353: 2149-53) (Diamond M.C., Scheibel A.B., Murphy G.M. Jr., Harvey T., art. On the Brain of Albert Einstein, *Exp Neurol,* 1985, Apr; 88(1): 198-204) *Cortical Folding and Intelligence.*

<http://www.serendip.brynmawr.edu/bb/kinser/Int4.html>

& Ball, Johnathan. *The Question of Non-Human Intelligence.*

<http://www.serendip.brynmawr.edu/bb/neuro/neuro98/202s98-paper2/Ball2.html>

Newly identified remains from Vindija in Croatia, which date to between 42,000 and 28,000 years ago, are more delicate than "classic" Neanderthals. One controversial explanation is that these Neanderthals were interbreeding with modern humans in the region. Details of the research appear in the Journal of Human Evolution. BBC News. *Late Neanderthals More Like Us.*

<http://news.bbc.co.uk/2/hi/science/nature/3346455.stm>

<http://news.bbc.co.uk/1/hi/sci/tech/3346455.stm>

> "A human skull from a Romanian bear cave is shaking up ideas about ancient sex. The *Homo sapiens* skull has a distinctive feature previously found only in Neandertals, providing further evidence of interbreeding between the two species, according to a new study." Handwerk, Brian. *Odd Skull Boosts Human, Neandertal Interbreeding Theory.*
>
> <http://news.nationalgeographic.com/news/2007/08/070802-neanderthals.html>

While scientists interpreting data from fossils theorize a split in "human" ancestors and Neanderthals as much as 350,000 years ago, DNA research suggests that interbreeding still occurred 35,000 years ago. Modern "human" DNA found in Neanderthal genes is consistent with the idea of interbreeding. "This past fall a genetic study suggested that the two species split 400,000 years ago. But days later a bone study suggested that they mated much more recently than that. The newly analyzed skull, reported online this week in the journal *Proceedings of the National Academy of Sciences,* adds to the heated discussion." Roach, John. *Neandertals, Modern Humans May Have Interbred, Skull Study Suggests.*

<http://news.nationalgeographic.com/news/2007/01/070116-neanderthals.html>

CAIN AND ABEL

The sons of the Nephilim/Neanderthals who had, very far back, inter-bred with much earlier humans, while possessing some limited intelligence, still carried the mark of Cain on their forehead (protruding brow ridges). It was thus that the pure line, of the 'sons of the Elohim,' were able to instantly identify and avoid them. This reason is given in Gen. 4:15, "a sign so others will not kill Cain," knowing that he was simply, like a dumb animal, to be avoided but not persecuted for his brutishness. "...the evolutionist authors of "In Search of Neanderthal Man" make the following fascinating and perhaps significant comment regarding the Neanderthal's massive double-arched eyebrow ridge: "Perhaps it provided a signal, even a threat, to others." CreationFoundation.co.uk. *The Missing Link and the Mark of Cain.*

<http://www.creationfoundation.co.uk/#/blog/4566408064/Neanderthal-Enigma-Solved-at-Last/2917148>

The story of Cain and Able is another that requires closer examination. It clearly does not make sense for YHVH to give every herb, seed, and fruit for food in Gen. 1:29, and contrarily be displeased with an offering of it. In addition to the possibility that the story of Cain and Abel was at some point transcribed incorrectly, it definitely should be noticed that it actually does not say that Cain was a "tiller of the ground," it says he was a "servant of the ground," *obd eadme*. The very same words used to describe Cain, *Obd adme* - ground servant (remember the "e" simply means "the") is translated as a husbandman, keeping cattle, in Zech. 13:5. Bible scholars cannot have it both ways either it means a tiller or a husbandman. In fairness it should be noted that just as the word farmer could mean someone growing crops or raising animals this term may also have had duel meanings.

However, it should also be noted that *Obd, abad, awbad* (SHD 5647) can just as well be interpreted as someone practicing animal husbandry, as the interpretation given "tiller of the earth," so at the very least the story is open to interpretation. Clearly the Levite scribes hundreds of years after Moses, who strongly advocated animal sacrifice, would have been unlikely to interpret it in such a way as to make their practice look unacceptable. This interpretation would support the Levite stance in favor of animal sacrifice, in their ongoing conflict with the prophets, who condemned animal sacrifice. (Jos. 22:10-29; Jer. 5:30-31 & 7:14-15 & 7:22-23; Ps. 4:6; Hos. 6:6 twice quoted in. Matt. 9:13&12:7; Pro. 21:3 & 23:20; Isa. 66:17; Dan 1:8-20; Hos. 14:3; Acts 7:42; Rom. 14:1-2; Heb. 10:1-4) Quotes from many of the biblical prophets who condemned the Levite position advocating animal sacrifice will be explored in depth in a later chapter.

> "Woe to you, scribes and Pharisees, hypocrites![6] ([6] the ancient Greek word for actors) For you clean the outside of the cup and the plate, but inside they are full of rapacity and self indulgence." (Matt. 23:25) Rapacity (from the Greek *harpage/harpyia* or like a harpy) is a word that implies a ravenous or voracious appetite, i.e., living on prey as does a harpy, which is a raptor, a bird of prey.

> <http://www.scripture4all.org/OnlineInterlinear/Greek_Index.htm>

Other variations on the shepherd vs. farmer story circulated in Sumerian mythology. In the Myth of *Emish and Enten,* two gods, one of farming and one of shepherding quarrel and have their case judged by Enlil, who sides with the farmer. In the myth of *Cattle and Grain,* Lahar a cattle god and Ashnan a grain goddess also quarrel but the end of the story has not survived. The myth of *Inanna Prefers the Farmer* has Inanna rejecting the shepherd and favoring the farmer. Goodgame, Peter. *The Spirit World and Civilization.*

<http://www.redmoonrising.com/Giza/SpiritCiv5.htm>

So there is every possibility that this verse about Cain has been misinterpreted, perhaps deliberately by the Levite scribes whose rapacious appetites were a clear motive to prefer the translation we have now and refute the effectiveness of any non-animal sacrifice brought by farmers. The verses above show there were ongoing disputes by various prophets inside and outside the Bible (among the Essenes for example) which contended against the stance of the Levite scribes. Those interjections reflect the efforts of the Levites to promote the belief that people *had* to bring them animals to slaughter in the temple, if they wanted their sins to be forgiven.

A "tiller of the ground" is *obd admthu,* as in Prov. 12:11 and a plowman or farmer is *churah* in Amos 9:13 and farmer is *akr* in Jer. 51:23. The word *thchrah,* "you shall plow," a word clearly related to *churah,* is used in Deu. 22:10, showing that this name for a plowman or farmer was well understood at the time the story of Cain in Genesis was originally written down along with the other books of the Torah. So there was a definitive word available to use, if it meant to specify a plowman or a farmer meaning "grower," instead of a word that can also be interpreted as someone practicing animal husbandry. The definitive word for a plowman was not used, so the assumption that Cain was a "tiller of the earth is extremely questionable. It would be the same today, if someone were called a farmer, it would be hard to tell if "farmer" meant someone raising livestock or someone growing crops.

The sons of the Nephilim/Neanderthal were human cross-breeds, who made burrows for themselves in the ground and lived in the earth, in caves and burrows, digging in the earth for roots and grubs. Thus they ate the *m-phri* (of the *eadme*-ground) this phrase has been translated fruit, as from a tree. But fruit from a tree is previously, in Gen. 3:2, called *m-phri otz.*

The word *phri* or *priy* (SHD 6529) is also very close in spelling to the Hebrew word for dig; *phar* or *para* (SHD 2658, & 6544 dig or uncover) with merely a change of vowel points, which were not present in ancient Hebrew, it could have created quite a different meaning. The ground yields fallen wormy fruit, roots, grubs, worms and bugs, which many primates and primitive savages are still known to eat, just as no doubt, the Neanderthal/Nephilim did as well, when they had nothing else.

This would have been considered vile by the Elohim, whose goal to make the Adam like themselves, would clearly have been thwarted by such practices. That the eating of bugs was a considered a problem by the Elohim is evidenced by the fact that they explained to primitive man, in the food laws (Lev. 11:22) that they were not allowed to eat unclean bugs. The Levitican laws allowed them, however, to continue consuming locusts etc. as clean, labeling other bugs as abominations. The custom of eating locusts was still practiced in John the Baptist's time, as he was said to eat locusts and honey in Mark 2:6.

> "Who also eat the flesh of my people...and chop them into pieces, as for the pot, and as flesh within the cauldron. " Micah 3:1-4

The Nephilim/Neanderthal and their half-breed descendants were also not averse to eating other primates just as some of the great apes will (occasionally) eat smaller monkeys. "Gory evidence uncovered in France reveals that the early humans in the region ate one another." BBC News. *Neanderthals Were Cannibals.* <http://news.bbc.co.uk/1/hi/sci/tech/462048.stm> "Starvation and cannibalism were part of everyday life for a population of Neanderthals living in northern Spain 43,000 years ago, a study suggests." BBC News. *Hungry Ancients 'Turned Cannibal'* <http://news.bbc.co.uk/2/hi/science/nature/6209554.stm>

> "Archeological analysis of faunal remains and of lithic and bone tools has suggested that hunting of medium to large mammals was a major element of Neanderthal subsistence. Plant foods were almost invisible in the archeological record..." Richards, Pettitt, Trinkaus, Smith, Paunović, and Karavanić *Neanderthal Diet at Vindija and Neanderthal Predation.* <http://www.pnas.org/cgi/content/full/120178997v1>

The Bible describes the Israelites as being smaller than the Canaanite descendants of the Nephilim. Because of their bloodthirstiness and willingness to also eat human flesh, according to the Bible some of the Israelites attempted to wipe out the Canaanites living in their vicinity. (Jos. 11:21-22) In modern times depending on the purity of their bloodline, we call these skeletons Neanderthals or a Homo Sapiens/Neanderthal mix. There have been reports of skeletons that appear half human/half Neanderthal.

Analysis of the skeletal remains of a four-year-old boy, found in Portugal, has revealed that he may be a Neanderthal/Cro-Magnon hybrid. Paul Rincon with BBC News Online science staff reports that newly identified remains from Vindija in Croatia, are more delicate than "classic" Neanderthals. One controversial explanation is that these Neanderthals were interbreeding with modern humans in the region. BBC News. *Late Neanderthals More Like Us.* <http://news.bbc.co.uk/2/hi/science/nature/3346455.stm>

> "And there we saw the giants (*nephilim*) the sons of *Anak, (*or *Anakim/Anunnaki[7])* which come of the *Nephilim."* Num.13:33 ([7]SHD 6061, the Sumerian Annunaki {depicted as half human} aka *anakim* in the OT, were known as giants, another name for the Canaanites.)

These descendants of the giants were known by many different names and the Canaanites were among those descended from them. "The people are strong that dwell in that land...and moreover we saw the children of Anak there...The Amalekites...the Hittites...and the Jebusites...and the Amorites...and the Canaanites dwell by the sea and by the coast of Jordan..." Num. 13:28-9 Dating homo floresiensis As for dating of the site, a mean of 67,000 years ago is the result of uranium-series dating of two cervid teeth in the same stratigraphic unit as the metatarsal. This method requires the application of a model of uranium absorption over the time since the teeth were deposited. This model is too complicated to describe here; the authors go through several scenarios and conclude that despite the possibility of inaccuracies, the remains are very unlikely to have been deposited as recently as 40,000 years (the approximate age represented by occupation of Niah Cave, Borneo). I have no reason to doubt the dating.

http://johnhawks.net/weblog/fossils/flores/

> "The Emim dwelt therein in times past, great and tall as the Anakim, who were also accounted giants (*Rephaim*) as the Anakim; but the Moabites called them Emim." Deu. 2:10-11

Many have pointed out that the Neanderthal were often shorter than modern humans, so they could not have been "giants." But in addition to the possibility of occasional mutations of extremely large Neanderthals, it should also be noted that many fossils attributed to pre-humans and early man (Homo) were much more diminutive than at present. ("Lucy" 3-4," "Abel" {*S. Tchadensis*} 3," various Hominids 4'8"-6'8," including Arlington man from No. Am. 5'2," *H. Georgicus* 4'11," *A. Afarensis* 3'6"-5," *H. Hablis* 4', etc.) Homo Erectus and earlier species were often around three feet tall. Recent discoveries (in 2004 called the "year of the hobbit") in Malaysia have revealed the skeletons of modern humans, *Homo floresiensis,* who were all under three feet tall. *Early Man: Lucy.* <http://www.bestbiblescience.org/emlu.htm>

Hominid Species <http://www.talkorigins.org/faqs/homs/species.html>

& Mayell, Hillary. *Hobbit-Like Human Ancestor Found in Asia.*

<http://news.nationalgeographic.com/news/2004/10/1027_041027_homo_floresiensis.html>

> Dating homo floresiensis "…archaeological evidence suggests *H. floresiensis* lived at Liang Bua from at least 95,000 to 13,000 years ago." <http://australianmuseum.net.au/Homo-floresiensis>

THE LITTLE PEOPLE

> "And there we saw the Nephilim sons of Anak from the Nephilim and we are becoming in eyes of us as grasshoppers and so we were in eyes of them." Num. 13:33

> "Now, in man it has likewise been observed that the stature of early man is often near the upper limits of pygmy stature whereas we overtop them considerably." Shapiro, H. L. *Pick From the Past.*

> <http://www.naturalhistorymag.com/picks-from-the-past/151691/man-500000-years-from-now?page=4>

Because inter-breeding with the sons or daughters of Anak resulted in offspring who were more animalistic, the chosen people were forbidden to take wives from the daughters of Canaan (just as Abraham was directed). For even if the females were docile, the grown male children could be beast-like, big, hairy and vicious. (Esau-meaning hairy, was such a child of such heritage and named to reflect it, SHD 6215) The Neanderthal were the *Anak,* descendants of the *Nephilim* - giants (Gen. 6:4) the half human offspring of the Adam, who had in much earlier times bred outside of the "chosen race," and back with the original primitive humans thus producing mutant monstrosities.

> "You shall not take a wife from the daughters of Canaan." Gen. 28:1

There are numerous depictions of "little people" or dwarfs in subjection and servitude to the Egyptians. These were in ancient Egypt known as *nmiu*, differentiated from the *dng*; who were the African pygmies. (Time/Life, *Egypt land of the Pharaohs,* p. 46&58) A study which analyzed funerary remains and depictions of dwarfs (by Chahira Kozma, a pediatrician at Georgetown Univ. Hospital in Wash. D.C.), published in the Jan. 2006 issue of the *American Journal of Medical Genetics,* gives us this information; "Dwarfism is thought to have been common in ancient Egypt, with some scholars suggesting it might have been a result of inter-breeding...An Egyptian manual of advice for life of around 1100 BCE, known as "the Instructions" enjoins: "Do not jeer at a blind man nor tease a dwarf." *Dwarves Were Respected in Ancient Egypt: Study.*

<http://www.world-science.net/othernews/othernews-nfrm/051227_egyptdwarf.htm>

These "Egyptian Commandments" which closely parallel the Ten Commandments, also found in the Book of the Dead, counsel one not to covet the wife or property of a neighbor, nor commit murder and not to ridicule the "little people." Kozma says the earliest biological evidence of dwarfs in ancient Egypt dates to the Baderian period, 4500 BCE, and several skeletons from the "Old Kingdom" period of 2700 to 2190 BCE. Desborough, Brian. *Who Were the Israelites?* <http://www.briansbetterworld.com/articles/whoweretheisraelites.html>

& Dwarves Were Respected in Ancient Egypt: Study.

<http://www.world-science.net/othernews/othernews-nfrm/051227_egyptdwarf.htm>

"Egypt is a major source of information on achondroplasia. (Achondroplasic dwarfs are quite different from normally proportioned pituitary dwarfs, who are deficient in growth hormone.) In the Old Kingdom (2700-2190 BCE)...Several achieved important status and had lavish burial places close to the pyramids...Some of their names were Seneb, Pereniankh, Khnumhotpe, and Djeder. There were at least two dwarf gods, Ptah and Bes. The god Ptah was associated with regeneration and rejuvenation." Kosma C. *Dwarfs in Ancient Egypt.* Am. J. Med. Genet. A. 2005 Dec 27. <http://doi.wiley.com/10.1002/ajmg.a.31068>

Not all of these little people are depicted as dwarfs; some have normally proportioned limbs for their size, just reduced overall in size. Depictions of little people and dwarfs abound on tombs, vases, and statues showing them as personal attendants, overseers of linen, animal tenders, jewelers, dancers, and entertainers. According to Kosma she found these dwarfs and little people depicted on in at least 50 tombs. Following are some sites where it is possible to view images of these ancient "little people."

<http://www.gutenberg.org/files/14400/14400-h/14400-h.htm>

(194, bread maker & 195, dwarf Nemhotep)

<http://www.clendening.kumc.edu/dc/rm/a_106p.jpg>

(dwarf, Choun-hotep)

<http://www.guardians.net/sca/congress2000/congress_2000_pt2.htm>

(dwarf Per-ni-ankhu, Dynasty 4)

<http://www.greatdreams.com/thebes/ramiii.htm>

(three "little people" conquered by an Egyptian)

<http://www.abdn.ac.uk/virtualmuseum/index.php?page=object_detail&prefix=ABDUA&n...>

(the famous Imhotep)

<http://sarabe3.tripod.com/israeliteimages.html>

<http://www.iranian.com/Arts/2005/September/Poetic/Images/p.jpg>

(Hinnells, John. *Persian Mythology,* see p. 13 for the rock carving from which this drawing was copied) <http://www.gutenberg.org/files/16653/16653-h/16653-h.htm>

Legends of little people show up in the histories of every culture. There have even been mummies discovered; one 14in. tall called the "Pedro Mountain Mummy" Casper, Wyoming (Readers Digest. *Mysteries of the Unexplained,* p. 40). Skeletons, statues, and miniature tools (From less than 1/4-1/2 in. long! in Lancashire and Devon, England, Egypt, Africa, Australia,

France, Sicily and the Vindhya hills, India) have been found around the world. It would be extremely challenging for large hands to have done the delicate work required to manufacture these tiny stone tools. Readers Digest, *Mysteries of the Unexplained,* p. 43.

"Writers such as Harold Gladwin, E. A. Hooton and Carelton Coon suggested that there are traces of former pygmy populations in America, mainly in the shape of isolated communities of undersized people on the offshore islands...Barry Fell's interest in this problem was aroused in 1980. Fell was engaged on reconstructing the thousands of fragments of crania from sites in east Tennessee, sent to me by Dr. William P. Grigsby and his colleagues. Among the best of the materials they sent me from 600 burials were several fragmented but almost complete crania, with jaws, in which the brain capacity was that of a seven-year-old child (950 cubic cm), yet the teeth showed from their complete development and severe wear that the skulls were from middle-aged individuals. Later Fell received from Dr. Grigsby some complete skulls among which was one unbroken pygmy skull, with the jaws still attached to the facial bones…It looked, therefore, as if a mixed population of several races had lived in the east Tennessee area, and in all probability they would have interbred…American Indians also had a tradition of pygmies (or dwarves), whom they called the Et-nane. Later Fell learned from a colleague that the Shoshone vocabulary also includes a similar word, whose root is nana- and is defined by the compiler of the Shoshone Dictionary as "elf-like people."…Now, when Fell began to analyze the anatomical characteristics of the pygmy skulls from Tennessee, he soon discovered that they matched those of the pygmies of the Philippines, who are also brachycephalic…They must once have been more widely dispersed than our present finds imply. However, since they reached as far east as east Tennessee, and their bones have been found in association with Europoids and inscribed artifacts of Europoid type, such as loom weights and pottery stamps, lettered in ancient Irish (noted as Celtic) and Basque [Fell concluded that there were in fact meetings of the two races…"

<http://www.faculty.ucr.edu/~legneref/bronze/bronze.htm>

There is also another interesting site discussing The Little People of the Cherokee and Native American Lore at the following link <http://www.ilhawaii.net/~stony/lore132.html>

"In Japan we have also evidence of their existence. This country, now inhabited by the Niphonians, or Japanese, as we have come to call them, was previously the home of the Ainu, a white, hairy under-sized race." Edward Tyson. *A Philological Essay Concerning the Pygmies of the Ancients.*

<http://www.gutenberg.org/files/12850/12850-8.txt>

The park at Nemrut Dag was originally a burial mound of king Antiochos I of Kommagene. It is surrounded on the west by colossal statues,…*Zeus Oromasdes* the Graeco-Persian sky god and supreme deity is the largest of the statues. The gods wear Persian headgear, the afore mentioned pointed caps also worn by the little people depicted on the Behistion Rock and legends of little people with white hair are still told among the local people.

The Legend of the White People: "It is remarkable that similar to the Manifestation of the Great Gods in Kommagenian times, the local people have worshiped the manifestation of the so-called white people. On a hot summers evening of July 1987, an old woman named Firat from the village of Eski Kâhta, told me following : "Long ago, before the Prophet ((Zarathustra MHJ), there was a group of soldiers on their way to the town of Malatya. They were passing through the Taurus mountain range. At sunset they wearied. They had very little food. One of the soldiers saw in the distance a light. They went towards the light and came upon a house. The house was inhabited by an old man with white hair together with his daughter and a boy. The soldiers were given food… After the meal, the commander then asked the old man for the hand of his daughter in marriage. The old man did not want, but he was afraid that the soldiers would take his daughter by force. That's why he granted the request and the soldiers left with his daughter. When they arrived at Eski Kâhta, at the same place where the holy house now stands, the girl asked them to stop for a moment. She descended into the dry streambed of a water course. She passed her hand lightly over the dry soil and magically a spring of water bubbled up. That spring still exists. She drank the water and washed herself. Then she asked the earth to open and bury her. Before the soldiers knew what was happening, the earth opened and she disappeared. Since that time it is a holy place and the people built a house on her grave…The old woman told me that her parents have witnessed the appearance of the girl and her friends. She said that they were smaller than normal people and had white hair." *Adiyaman and Nemrut.*

<http://www.enjoyturkey.com/info/sights/adiyaman.htm>)

Webster's online dictionary gives the etymology of elf or *aelf* as having some association with the Latin *alba* meaning, "white." So this name may be a reference to their pale skin and white hair inherited from what various encounters call the "greys" also because of their pale skin. These may be off-world relatives of the little people, ancestral to modern humans. Webster's online "elf." <http://www.merriam-webster.com/dictionary/elf>

> "At Mohenjo-daro (India, excavated in 1922, *The Cambridge Encyclopedia of Archaeology,* p. 24) corpses were of small stature and here the architect confirms the data of the anthropologist-the houses were built for quite small men." Brion, Marcel. *The World of Archaeology; India, China, America,* p.118.

Shem or Shum is a word for land in the Middle East and India. It is also the root of the name of the Semitic peoples (*Eerdman's Bible Dictionary,* p. 923). Among the Shem were some of the "little people" the chosen ones, descended from the Elohim, who can be seen, depicted in servitude to taller people throughout the Middle East. A later chapter will further discuss the descendants of Shem.

> "The people of Israel have NOT separated themselves from the people of the lands, with respect to abominations of the Canaanites etc...so that the holy seed is mixed with the people of those lands." Ezra 9:1-2

In Jer. 48:4-5 the Septuagint reads "unto Zoar" instead of the KJV which reads "her little ones...for in the going down of Horonaim the enemies have heard a cry of destruction." however the discussion goes on in Jer. 48:34 where it says; "Zoar even unto Horonaim" showing that these references are to one and the same people. Evidence will be presented in this section that will demonstrate that this reference to "her little ones" actually refers to the smaller size of the people of Zoar.

"Behold! Please, this city that is near, to flee unto toward there, and it is *mtzor* (little/inferior) I shall escape to there, is it not *mtzor* (inferior/small)? so my soul shall live. (be safe there)...so he called the name of the city *Tzoar/Zoar*. The sun was risen over the earth when Lot came to *Tzoar/Zoar*." Gen. 19:20-23

The word *tzoiri-e* (small SHD 6819), in Jer. 48:34 translated as "little ones" appears to be related to *mtzor*, which in Gen.19:20, is used in the OT to mean "little." This word for "little" is given in the online interlinear Lexicon as meaning, inferior(s) and obviously has a different root from *taf or taphaph* SHD 2945 and 2952, meaning, children. *Zoar* or *Tso'ar, Tsoar*, SHD 6820; which is from SHD 6819, *tsa'ar*, to be small, ignoble: be brought low; this word is obviously related to another word for small, and that word SHD 6686, *Tsaw'ar, or Tsaur* actually means, an Israelite!

> "There Benjamin *tzoir rdm* – inferior or little rulers, chiefs of Judah pelting of them chiefs of Zebulun chiefs, of Naphtali...rebuke you! He scatters people who delight in war." Ps. 68:27,30 This verse appears to refer to the chiefs of Benjamin as small in size! <http://scripture4all.org/OnlineInterlinear/OTpdf/psa68.pdf>

Although not mentioned in the King James Version it can be seen at the link above in Hebrew that this verse is from a psalm to King David, of David and Goliath fame (Isa. 17). Goliath and his people are described elsewhere as giants, but there have never been any confirmed remains of giants in the Middle East. If the most diligent searching has not discovered the fossils of any such race of giants and *has* found remains of small people, then the conclusion logically is that David and his people were much smaller than Goliath's race (Goliath's race would seem closer to normal size modern humans, who acquired genes for taller size through inter-breeding outside of the 'chosen' little people). David, in I Sam. 17:14, is described by the Hebrew word *qatan* (SHD 6996), translated as the youngest but this word can also mean the smallest! <http://scripture4all.org/OnlineInterlinear/OTpdf/1sa17.pdf>

The smaller size of some ancient Israelites could also help explain the change over time of the length of a cubit. A cubit, being originally based on the length of a persons forearm, this length is known to have changed as time went on. (<http://home.teleport.com/~salad/4god/cubit.htm>) It could also help explain why there are two different words both translated as 'youth' in the same sentence about David in I Sam. 17:33. The first *na'ar* (SHD 5288), a reference to David can also have the alternate meaning of 'servant.' Coupled with the evidence in this section on the Little People, it will be seen that Ps. 68:27-30 can be interpreted as a comment on how remarkable it was to see these little chiefs of Judah "pelting the (obviously larger) chiefs of Zebulun and Naphtali." This was apparently an attempt to protect themselves, because they then go on to disparage war and those who "delight in attacking" in the verses following those that mention of the *tzoir rdm*-the little rulers. David was a Bethlehemite a Hebrew word meaning "house of bread[8]" SHD 1022.

<http://www.blueletterbible.org/lang/lexicon/lexicon.cfm?Strongs=H1022&t=KJV>

[8]Bethlehem was as city of the tribe of Judah. Remember from the discussion on II Kings 23:9 that it was Judean priests who were slain by the Levites under Hilikiah (when the Levites seized the priesthood) because the Judean priests would not attend an animal sacrifice; observing Passover with unleavened bread instead.

"Though I am small (*tzoir* SHD 6819) and despised I will not forget Your precepts." Ps.

71

Some of the previous discussion may seem a little farfetched until the following evidence concerning the Behistun (var. Behiston) Rock is taken into consideration. The Behistun Rock has been called the Persian Rosetta stone because it contains inscriptions in three languages, Persian, Susian and Babylonian, first investigated by Sir Henry Rawlinson. Additionally these inscriptions provide an amazing link between the lost tribes of Israel and the Anglo-Saxons! Ancient Assyrian and Babylonian names for Israel were, respectively, Kumri and Ghimri. *The Behistun Rock 519 BC.* <http://www.christianparty.net/behistun.htm>

> "(On) Ptolemy's map of central Scythia...Ptolemy located the Teutons south of the Saxons and north of the (Aggiloi) Anglii (Anglo, later English MHJ). The Teutons were to be swept up in the Anglo-Saxon invasion of Britain. The name Teuton is cognate with Teutarus who was a Scythian...The Saxons represent the Sakae of old meaning Scyths." *Tribal Identifications: Gad.* <http://www.britam.org/gad.html>

The Behistun Rock mentions the Sakae, from whom the Saxons are said to have descended, while in Babylonian these people are called the Ghimri or that is, Israel! Rawlinson stated: "We have reasonable grounds for regarding the Ghimri, or Cimmerians, who first appeared on the confines of Assyria and Media (aka Amaidi) in the seventh century BCE and the Sakae (or Sacae mentioned on the Behistun Rock) nearly two centuries later, as identical with the Beth-Khumree of Samaria, or the Ten tribes (sometimes called the "lost tribes") of the house of Israel." Rawlinson, George. Note in his translation of *History of Herodotus*, Book 7, p. 378.

> "We have seen the Chaldee or Hebrew written language traced to North India, the land of the Sacæ ...of the Scythians; and it may be properly asked, How, in regard to time, my Saxons or Sacæ would be related to them? All difficulties with respect to them, as in any way opposing my system, are at once done away by a passage of Herodotus, who declares that they were two names of the same people. From this I think there can scarcely be any doubt that the Celtæ, the Scythians, and the Saxons, were all tribes of the same people, succeeding one another, with some trifling variations which would naturally arise, in the lapse of time, from the natural tendency which every thing has to change." Higgins, Godfrey. *Anacalypsis,* vol. 2 p.166 & 273. Note that the page numbering of the online version @ Google books, does not correspond with the page numbering of the hard copy.

While these references may at first seem a little obscure, the point of including them is to show that the Israelites, recognized as the Kumri and Ghimri, were in the Babylonian language known as the Sacae or Saxons. The Saxon legends are replete with stories of the "little people," but these legends have been abandoned as myths. However, when all the following evidence is considered, it may eventually become known that they should be reconsidered as another link to our lost history.

> "It should be made clear that the terms 'Cimmerian' (Ghimri) and Scythian' were interchangeable: in Akkadian the name Iskuzai (Asguzai) occurs only exceptionally. Gimirrai (Gamir) was the normal designation for 'Cimmerians' as well as 'Scythians' in Akkadian." On the "Black Obelisk" King Jehu of Israel (son and heir to King Omri of the Northern kingdom of Israel), is wearing the pointed cap of the Saka/Scythian style just as

is the last captive on the Behistun Rock, which is titled above him "Sku(n)kha, the Scythian." <http://www.en.wikipedia.org/wiki/Ten_Lost_Tribes> Citing Maurits Nanning van Loon. *Urartian Art. Its Distinctive Traits in the Light of New Excavations*, Istanbul, 1966. p. 16

These pointed caps (often red in color) are exactly how the "little people" were often depicted in old illustrated stories about them throughout Europe and the British Isles. (The Behiston Rock 519 BC <http://christianparty.net/behistun.htm>) There is still another ancient rock carving depiction, of the one of the "little people" with a pointed cap, amongst a slaughter of a tribe of these "little people" on the stele of Naram. Image: Stele Naram Sim Louvre Sb4.jpg @ <http://www.en.wikipedia.org/wiki/Image:Stele_Naram_Sim_Louvre_Sb4.jpg>

There are numerous photos of this carving on the Behistun Rock available online, and it clearly shows that <u>these grown "Israelite" men (with full beards), were of much shorter stature than their captors, only coming up to their waists!</u> The mention of the Ghimri/Israelites on the Behistun Rock illustrates that these ancient Israelites were a people who were small in stature. If these people migrated to Europe and the British Isles it is not surprising to find so many stories there of "the little people," depicted just as they are on the Behiston Rock, as little bearded men with pointed caps, and now seen imitated everywhere as garden gnome[9] statues with red hats. *The Behiston Rock 519 BC.* <http://www.christianparty.net/behistun.htm> & *Could There Have Been a Race of Little People that Once Occupied Our Lands?*

<http://www.burlingtonnews.net/littlepeople.html>

[9]Paracelsus, gives us the name *pigmaei* or *gnomi* (perhaps from *gamir or ghimri?* MHJ} see the Online Etymology Dictionary – Gnome, dwarf-like earth-dwelling spirit," 1712, from Fr. gnome, from L. gnomus, used 16c. in a treatise by Paracelsus, who gave the name pigmaei or gnomi to elemental earth beings, possibly from Gk. *genomos* [10] "earth-dweller." A less-likely suggestion is that Paracelsus based it on the homonym that means "intelligence" (preserved in <u>gnomic</u>). Popular in children's literature 19c. as a name for red-capped Ger. and Swiss folklore dwarfs. Garden figurines first imported to England late 1860s from Germany."

[10]<http://www.etymonline.com/index.php?term=gnome>

> "The tall Celts, when they arrived, saw the small people disappear in a mysterious way, and, without stopping to investigate, imagined they had become invisible. If they had had the courage or the patience to investigate, they would have found that they had passed into their souterrain (i.e., subterranean; a grotto or cavern under ground)…There may be many souterrains whose entrance has been choked up, and of which no record has been preserved…one discovered at Stranocum; another…from Newberry…has been made in a circular portion…A gallery opens out…in some places not more than three feet six inches high…The remains of ancient cave-dwellers point to a primitive race of small size inhabiting Europe…(concerning) skeletons discovered at Spy in Belgium…Professor Fraipont, who examined them anatomically, "came to the conclusion that the Spy men belonged to a race of small stature…they manufactured flint implements after the type know as Mousterien and were contemporary with the Mammoth." *Ulster Folklore.* <http://www.oldandsold.com/books/ulster-folklore/ulster-folklore-1.shtml>

Orkney's "Tomb of the Eagles", the Skara Brae village, and Mayes Howe, in Britain, are just three relics of buildings from prehistoric days which have entryways that are much too small for humans the height of modern man. Most modern historians have yet to consider that these entryways were designed for smaller people, ascribing them to a desire to force invaders to kneel down, making them more vulnerable, but it may yet be seen that a smaller people built them.

> "*DAOINE SIDHE* (theena shee) # 454: The people of the Sidhe or hollow hills. The inhabitants of the "Otherworld" who, like the Fairies, live behind the world of men but sometimes co-exist peacefully with them. There is a long tradition that the ancient gods and heroes entered the sidhe and lived there…The Daoine Sidhe are the fairy people of Ireland, generally supposed to be the dwindled gods of the early inhabitants of Ireland, the Tuatha Da Danann, who became first the Fenian heroes and then the fairies. Other names are, however, given them for safety's sake, the 'Wee folks', 'the People of That Town', 'the Gentry', 'the Good People, or other euphemistic names. A good account of these Irish fairies is given by Yeats in the first few pages of his Irish Fairy And Folk Tales…(and by Lady Wilde in Ancient Legends Of Ireland Vol. I). They are supposed to be those of the Fallen Angels, too good for Hell: 'Some fell to earth, and dwelt there, long before man was created, as the first gods of the earth. Others fell into the sea.' # 100 - 454 - 711 - 728 – 756." *Encyclopedia of the Celts*.

> <http://www.summerlands.com/crossroads/library/ENCYCLOPEDIA%20OF%20THE%20CELTS/Encyclopedia%20of%20the%20Celts%20%20D%27Aulnoy%20-%20Dywel.htm>

> "Prof. Kollmann, of Basle, has described a group of Neolithic pigmies as having existed at Schaffhausen. The adult interments consisted of the remains of full-grown European types and of small-sized people. These two races were found interred side by side under precisely similar conditions, from which he concludes that they lived peaceably together, notwithstanding racial difference. Their stature (about three feet six inches) may be compared with that of the Veddahs in Ceylon. Prof. Kollmann believes that they were a distinct species of mankind." Tyson, Edward. *A Philological Essay Concerning the Pygmies of the Ancients*. <http://www.gutenberg.org/files/12850/12850-8.txt>

As mentioned previously, Gen. 6:4 tells us that there were giants in those days. "<u>SO</u> the sons of the Elohim came to the daughters of humans and they bore the masters who were the mortals of renown eons ago." These great men of old, with their combination of larger size along with greater intelligence from the Elohim, had greater creativity and greater spiritual abilities than the Adam (the race of humans with whom the Elohim interbred), not however, greater than their Elohim progenitors. The olden masters of mortals were bred SO as to provide protection and leadership for the peaceful and vulnerable "little people" of Israel, the *Tzuar* (SHD 6686 see also 6810 & 6819 meaning little), who were ancestral to the diminutive Israelites seen on the Behistun Rock.

> "For you are a holy people unto YHWH Elohim of you, YHWH Elohim of you has chosen you to be a special people unto Himself…that "<u>you the little one</u>" (*e* = the + *mot* or *ma'at*[11] SHD 4592 littleness [11]*mat kaldu* was aka the Chaldeans, more on them later

<http://www.1911encyclopedia.org/Chaldaea>) from all the peoples that from love of YHWH (*ath*/with) you ...He brought forth YHWH *ath*/with you in hand steadfast and He is ransoming you from house of servants from hand of Pharaoh, King of Egypt." Deu. 7:1-7

As mentioned above, in 2004, called "The Year of the Hobbit, "the existence of many generations of little people (*Homo floresiensis*), less than three feet tall, was conclusively shown to have at one time lived in Malaysia, where their skeletons were discovered on the Island of Flores. These little people were found, not to be the consequence of dwarfism, but rather a race of little people, existing throughout many generations, and proportioned appropriately for their size.

> "Thousands of human bones belonging to numerous individuals have been discovered in the Pacific island nation of Palau...The smaller, older bones represent people who were 3 to 4 feet (94 to 120 centimeters) tall and weighed between 70 and 90 pounds (32 and 41 kilograms), according to the paper." Roach, John. For National Geographic Magazine. *Ancient Bones of Small Humans Discovered in Palau.*

> <http://news.nationalgeographic.com/news/2008/03/080310-palau-bones.html? email=Inside21Mar08>

The importance of the "little people" on the Pacific Islands will become more obvious when we explore evidence of the ruins of a sunken continent, lost at the time of the Great Flood, and recently re-discovered beneath the Pacific Ocean off Okinawa. For the "little people" were descended from the Elohim, and it may eventually be proven that this contributed to a genetic component that occasionally results in what is now known as dwarfism.

<http://www.google.com/search?hl=en&q=underwater+pyramids+japan>

The Nova documentary "Alien From Earth" reports at length on *Homo floresiensis* and also provides information on four small-sized adults discovered at a medieval monastery in Dmanisi, Republic of Georgia. <http://www.pbs.org/wgbh/nova/teachers/programs/3515_hobbit.html>

It may be, perhaps, that we have the Neanderthal/Nephilim, the sons of Anak, to thank for our present height, but along with height, we also acquired some of their barbaric, primitive, bloodthirsty and warlike urges, and lost much of our spiritual sight, i.e. our psychic and "magical" abilities (including healing), inherited through the "little people" from the sons of the Elohim who married the daughters of the Adam (Gen. 6:1-2). The genetic markers for these abilities should be rediscovered and encouraged in future generations.

FORENSIC EVIDENCE

In addition to the ancient written evidence it is also little known that there is modern forensic evidence suggesting humanity originally came from the inter-breeding of two different types of humans; one having earthly primate DNA and the other NOT having this DNA found in all higher primates!. This evidence is found in our DNA. Individuals with Rh negative blood type demonstrate the same kinds of problems in producing offspring that is seen in attempts to interbreed two similar yet genetically incompatible members of the same species, animals who do not naturally interbreed or naturally have the ability to bear offspring.

One example is the horse and the donkey; another is the tiger and lion. When a female of these species tries to carry a fetus fathered by a close yet somewhat incompatible mate from another species, the fetus, when conception is even possible, often miscarries as the result of the antibodies of the mother's bloodstream fighting what her immune system recognizes as an alien invading antigen. In this case the foreign blood type of the fetus is recognized as an antigen, to which the mother's blood reacts by producing antibodies.

> "During pregnancy, Rh-negative is the only one of these blood groups that can cause a problem. It turns out that an Rh-negative mother can make antibodies (part of her immune system's response to invaders)." Greenfield, Marjorie M.D. *Rh Negative Implications for Pregnancy.*

> <http://www.vloggerheads.com/group/RhesusFactor/forum/topics/rhesus-negative-blood>

This is exactly what happens when Rh negative mothers conceive an Rh positive child. Rh is an abbreviation for Rhesus negative, named after a cross-reacting protein first found in rhesus monkeys. It has since been discovered that ALL the higher primates and humans share this trait, EXCEPT for the pervasive strain of Rh negative humans! Because the Rh factor is a recessive gene many Rh positive people can carry this gene and never know it, until they mate with someone who also has this recessive gene and they produce an Rh neg. child. The presence of Rh negative humans indicates that at some point there were two similar yet genetically different species of humans, who have only since been somewhat successful at interbreeding. Boyer, Patty. *Blood Types in Connection to the Alien Phenomenon.*

<http://www.spiritconnectionstore.com/blood-types-alien-connection.htm>

<http://www.google.com/search?hl=en&q=+rhnegative+alien>

Rh pos. babies, with Rh. neg. mothers, often have difficulty the first few days after birth, as the result of the dead blood cells in their bloodstream, which gives their skin a yellowish tinge, called jaundice. Individuals with Rh neg. blood type also often suffer a variety of disease symptoms when they consume the high protein diet prevalent in modern society (more on this in a later chapter).

> "To avoid complications from a blood transfusion, recipients must be sure a donor's blood matches their own, meaning two main factors must agree: the blood group (A, B or 0) and the Rhesus factor, either positive or negative. Both are antigens expressed on the surface of red blood cells--and if they are different, they can invoke an immune attack. About 85 percent of the population is Rhesus-positive...Until now, no one knew the function of the Rhesus factor, which was named after a cross-reacting protein in rhesus monkeys. In today's issue of Nature Genetics, however, scientists from Belgium, France and Italy report that one of its components, RhAG, transports ammonium ions through the cell membrane...In humans, ammonium (from amino acids found in protein, MHJ) is mainly a waste product and becomes toxic at high blood concentrations...Furthermore, RhAG was able to provide transportation in the opposite direction: it pumped toxic methylammonium as well as excess ammonium out of the cells...Whatever its exact role,

76

the new results may help scientists to understand Rhesus-deficiency syndrome, a disease in which either RhCE or RhAG are mutated." Karow, Julia. *A Role for the Rhesus Factor.* <http://www.scientificamerican.com/article.cfm?chanID=sa003&articleID=000D1546-E506-1C67-B882809EC588ED9F>

Interestingly, Rh antigens had long been recognized for their role in transfusion-incompatible immune reactions and hemolytic disease of newborn babies. Although they have been biochemically characterized, a clear physiological role could not be assigned. While ammonia is a base (alkaline), ammonium is an acid, when ammonium builds up in the blood, it disrupts the acid/alkaline balance of the normally neutral bloodstream, which then attempts to neutralize itself by bonding with alkaline reserves from minerals like calcium, magnesium, potassium, etc. throughout the body.

The loss of these reserves in turn lead to muscle tension and cramping (including cramping of the heart muscle aka heart attack) osteoporosis, acid indigestion, skin irritations, tooth decay, nervous disorders including anxiety resulting from an inability to relax, etc. As high levels of ammonium can be cytotoxic, cytoplasmic ammonium has to be kept low. Ludewig, von Wirén, Rentsch, & Frommer. *Rhesus factors and ammonium: a function in efflux?*

<http://www.pubmedcentral.nih.gov/articlerender.fcgi?artid=138916>

Our DNA itself also provides a certain type of forensic evidence, since it constitutes a code or language in itself. Some theories suggest that it is the chemicals themselves, which organize the information in DNA, but this equivalent to saying that it is the ink on the paper that causes a book to be written in a <u>logical and orderly manner</u>. DNA is consistent and orderly, order is the result of some innate wisdom, chaos is the result of random chance, and the movement of inorganic matter is always toward disorder and entropy.

That the universe organizes itself is evidence that the universe itself is alive and intelligent. It is capable of levels of organization and order far beyond anything we will ever achieve or even comprehend for that matter. (Consider the brain for example, no computer can come close to matching all its functions.) Even the smallest living single celled creature[12] has 1.3 million base pairs, creating enough information in its DNA to fill a book. ([12]the microbe SAR 11 who's combined weight exceeds that of all the fish in the oceans. *Bigger Isn't Always Better.*

<http://www.astrobio.net/pressrelease/1689/bigger-isnt-always-better>

"'Humbling' was the prevalent adjective used by the scientific teams and the media to describe the principal finding – that the human genome contains not the anticipated 100,000 - 140,000 genes (the stretches of DNA that direct the production of amino-acids and proteins) but only some 30,000 ± little more than double the 13,601 genes of a fruit fly and barely fifty percent more than the roundworm's 19,098. What a comedown from the pinnacle of the genomic Tree of Life!... It was here, in tracing the vertical evolutionary record contained in the human and the other analyzed genomes, that the scientists ran into an enigma. The "head-scratching discovery by the public consortium," as Science termed it, was that the human genome contains 223 genes that do not have the required predecessors on the genomic evolutionary tree... In other words: At a relatively recent time as Evolution goes, modern humans acquired an extra 223 genes not through gradual evolution, not vertically on the Tree of Life, but horizontally, as a sideways insertion of genetic material from bacteria…"

<http://www.bibliotecapleyades.net/sumer_anunnaki/anunnaki/anu_6.htm>

Now the statement about the genetic material being from bacteria is an assumption, it could also be from viruses, and these reflect a possibility growing in popularity, in the theory of Panspermia[13]. The possibility that viruses abound throughout interstellar space suggest that the Universe itself is alive everywhere and the Great Holy Spirit is its soul and person. This is also suggested by one name of the Creator, YHVH *Al Olum* (which means world without end (elsewhere also worlds), SHD 5769, 5865, 5957, forever & 361 *eylam meaning* space) discussed in depth previously in the section on The All Mighty. [13]see *Evolution from Space.* Hoyle and Wickramasinghe.

EVOLUTION

For those who do not yet entertain doubts about the theory of evolution, or life from matter, and natural selection, it may be important to reconsider the following evidence. In "Evolution A Theory In Crisis" Michael Denton recounts; "The inability of unguided trial and error to reach anything but the most trivial of ends in almost every field of interest obviously raises doubts as to its validity in the biological realm. Such doubts were recently raised by a number of mathematicians and engineers at an international symposium entitled "Mathematical Challenges to the Neo-Darwinian Interpretation of Evolution" The space of all possible amino acid sequences is unimaginably large and consequently sequences which must obey particular restrictions which can be defined, ...(they) are bound to be fantastically rare. Even short unique sequences just ten amino acids long only occur by chance in about 10^{13} average sized proteins; unique sequences 20 amino acids long once in about 10^{39} proteins! As it can easily be shown that no more than 10^{40} possible proteins could have existed on earth since its formation, this means that, if protein functions reside in sequences any less probable than 10^{40}, it becomes increasingly unlikely that any functional proteins could ever have been discovered by chance on earth." Denton, Michael. *Evolution a Theory in Crisis*, p. 314-323.

Recently, Hoyle and Wickramasinghe in *Evolution from Space* (a theory that the universe seeds life everywhere; Panspermia) provided a similar estimate of the possibility of life originating by chance, assuming functional proteins to have a probability of $10^{-20:12}$ "By itself, this probability could be faced, because one must contemplate not just a single shot at obtaining the enzyme, but a very large number of trials such as are supposed to have occurred in an organic soup early in the history of the Earth. The trouble is that there are about 2000 enzymes, and the chance of obtaining them all in a random trial is only one part in $(10^{20})^{2000} = 10^{40,000}$ an outrageously small probability that could not be faced even if the whole universe consisted of organic soup."

"A metaphor by Fred Hoyle has become famous because it vividly conveys the magnitude of the problem: That a living organism emerged by chance from a prebiotic soup is about as likely as that "a tornado sweeping through a junkyard might assemble a Boing 747 from the materials therein." Johnson, Phillip. *Darwin on Trial*, p. 104.

According to the recent documentary "Comets Prophets of Doom" presented by the History Channel, life formed on earth almost as soon as it cooled, so the possibility of life occurring by chance in so short a time (in the cosmic scene) becomes even more miraculous. For this and other reasons more and more scientists are beginning to consider the possibility of life originating on earth from some outside source like comets or interstellar dust. This would be in accord with the mention of seeding in Gen. 1:11. "And He (YHWH) is saying Elohim she shall be verdant (*th-dsha* - green SHD 1877) the earth (*eartz*) verdure <u>seeding</u> seed tree of fruit making fruit to species of him whose seed of him in him on the land and He is becoming so." The "newly" discovered scientific name for this process of seeding is Panspermia, or life from space, discussed more in a later section.

> "Reconstructions of an evolutionary tree branching from a single ancestor have hinged on evidence that sub-Saharan Africans have accumulated more variations in their genetic make-up than any other geographic group. According to the theory they therefore have existed as a relatively separate population for a longer time...The alternative perspective on these same genetic data, however, favors the multi-regional picture of human evolution. It holds that genetic variation within and among groups arises from low but consistent levels of interbreeding...Proponents of this view argue that Africa's greater genetic diversity arose because more (intermingled) people inhabited Africa than any other continent during the rise of H. Sapiens, not because the African population is older." *Science News* Vol.155 2/6/99, pp. 88-89.

The "Cambrian Explosion" of all the different phyla of life forms (from vertebrates down to the simplest of life forms), during the Cambrian period, without precursor fossils in the Pre-Cambrian, is what Stephen Gould has called "the trade secret of paleontology." (Denton, Michael. *Evolution: A Theory in Crisis,* p. 194) Gould's theory, of "punctuated equilibrium," in evolution was formulated to account for their abrupt appearance, without "natural selection" (which is the foundational principle of the theory of evolution), playing any significant role in the actual origin of new species. The fossils of these creatures have shown that they remained unchanged in a state of stasis throughout their existence, in some cases millions of years, then suddenly go extinct sometimes in mass extinctions along with many other life forms and disappear from the geological record. *Paleobiology & Evolution Explosion Not Ascent* by Stephen J. Gould and Niles Eldredge.

Gould goes on to state; "One outstanding fact of the fossil record that many of you may not be aware of; that <u>since the so called Cambrian explosion</u>...during which essentially all the anatomical designs of modern multicellular life made their appearance in the fossil record, <u>no new Phyla of animals have entered the fossil record</u>." Stephen Gould, From a speech at SMU, Harvard, Oct. 2, 1990.

> "Most of the classic evolutionary lineages...have long since lost their scientific respectability, and in spite of the plethora of paleontological information we now have available, there seems to be little to put in their place." (Ager, Derek. *The Nature of the Stratigraphical Record* p. 32-33) One prime example, the frequently quoted Archaeopteryx, touted as in the ancestral lineage to birds; recent evidence shows that they were NOT ancestral to modern birds; "Fossil remains claimed to be of two crow sized birds 75 million years older than Archaeopteryx have been found...a paleontologist at

Texas Tech University, who found the fossils, says they have advanced avian features... (this) tends to confirm what many paleontologists have long suspected, that Archaeopteryx is not on the direct line to modern birds." *Nature* Vol. 322, 1986, p. 677.

Whenever the subject of the lack of transitional fossils is discussed, Archaeopteryx is always touted as a transitional fossil between dinosaurs and modern birds. But the presence of fully formed birds predating Archaeopteryx destroys this position, for there were already birds in existence when Archaeopteryx arrived on the scene.

"The known contrast between the almost un-fossiliferous Precambrian and the highly fossiliferous Cambrian, far from being less striking than in Darwin's time (Simpson, 1960), has been accentuated by the progress of geology...Many recent authors have avoided the full force of the problem by under-rating the magnitude of the contrast. An evident anxiety to preclude any causes of an extra-scientific or even extra-terrestrial nature has led them to underestimate both the sudden appearance and the "advanced" character of the Cambrian fauna." Cowen and Lipps, *Controversies in Earth Sciences,* p. 273.

Colin Patterson, British Museum of Natural History on page 100 of his book, *Darwin's Enigma,* has this to say concerning Gould's theory of punctuated equilibrium, "Well, it seems to me that they have accepted that the fossil record doesn't give them the support they would value so they searched around to find another model and found one...When you haven't got the evidence, you make up a story that will fit the lack of evidence."

JESUS/YESCHUA/YESCHU/JESU/JOSHU

In 1415 the Church of Rome took steps to destroy two books containing Jewish records of "Rabbi[14] Yeschu (Jesus)." Benedict XIII condemned a secret Latin treatise "*Mar Yesu.*" (The term Yesu was also used in Druidism as one of the Druid trinity). Bushby, Tony. *What was the Church Trying to Hide?* [14]The title Rabbi is used at least 14 times in the NT, to address Jesus including; Matt. 26:45,49; John 1:49, 3:2, 6:25 & Mark 11:21, 14:45.

<http://www.bibliotecapleyades.net/biblianazar/esp_biblianazar_5.htm>

"Everyone knows that the Evangeliums (Gospels) were written by neither Yesu nor his apostles, but long after their time by some unknown persons, who...headed their narratives with the names of the apostles." Fauste, Third Century Manichean Christian, confirmed by the *Catholic Encyclopedia,* vol. 6, Sept. 1, 1909, pp. 135-137.

Justin Martyr has confirmed the policy of the Rabbinical authorities, who under their constitution were required to record the condemnation and execution of the one known to them as "Rabbi" Yeschu/Yesu/Jesus. As it was the Jewish Sanhedrin elders who pronounced the death sentence (Matt. 26:57) on "Rabbi Yeschu," such a public act had to be officially recorded upon the Sanhedrin dockets. These records resulted in later stories (written in Greek) of the original Hebrew versions of the execution. *Dialogue*, Oxford trans. 1861, vol. 2, p. 42.

A copy of the story was made by Rabbi Ebron, for the Essene movement, called the *Gospel of the Hebrews*. (the Es-enes, meaning spiritualists as in *es-piritus,* MHJ) When the Church father Jerome read and translated this Gospel (late 400 AD) he wrote to a friend "In the evangel which the Nazarenes and the (also possibly Nazarene) Ebronites (aka Ebionites) use, which recently I translated from Hebrew into Greek, and which is called by most persons the genuine Gospel of Matthew...the Jews have the truth." Jerome added that it was written in the Chaldaic language but with Hebrew letters. And St. Epiphanius wrote; "the Ebronites number among their sect all the surviving relatives of Jesus." Hieronymus, *Commen. to Matthew,* bk.ii, ch. 13.

Later Pope Alexander VI ordered all copies of the *Talmud* destroyed, with the Spanish Inquisitor Torquemada responsible for the elimination of 6000 volumes at Salamanca alone. According to G. R. S. Mead, "The *Talmud* declared categorically that Jesus had lived a century earlier than the date assigned to him by evangelists, and that instead of his being crucified in Jerusalem he was stoned[15] at Lud." Mead, G. R. S. *Did Jesus Live 100 Years BC,* pp. 135-138, 177, 256, 334, 335, 408 & 410.

[15]Tertullian, Bishop of Carthage, in about 197-198 AD, also spoke of his death by stoning. Jewish history has it that *after* stoning his body was hanged on a stake. The word stake, not cross was used in early church documents, the church itself confirmed that "there is no proof of the use of a cross until much later" (than the sixth century MHJ). *Adv. Judeaus,* C.IX, last paragraph & *Acts of the Apostles & New Catholic Encyclopedia,* vol. 4, p. 475.

> "And we are witness of all things which he did both in the land of the Jews, and in Jerusalem; whom they slew and hanged on a tree." Acts 10:13

The word cross was at least in some cases substituted for the word stake or pole in rewriting the Christian texts for example 1 Peter 2:24 see link below for the Greek text. The decision to use the crucifix was ratified by the Sixth Ecumenical Council in 680 AD. (Canon 82) The decree stated that "the figure of a man fastened to a cross be now adopted," the new logos was confirmed by Pope Hadrian I (772-95). Seymour, W.W. *Crosses in Tradition,* N.Y. 1898 & Draper, *Origin of Religious Belief,* p. 252. <http://scripture4all.org/OnlineInterlinear/NTpdf/1pe2.pdf>

> "Christ has redeemed us from the curse of the law, being made a curse for us: for it is written; Cursed is every one that hangs on a tree." Gal. 3:13

Crucifixion of living persons was not practiced among the Jewish elders who condemned Yeschu/Jesus. Capital punishment among them consisted of being stoned to death. After stoning the victim's body was *then* hung on a stake, a pole or a tree. (*Cath. Encyc.,* loc. cit.) "The symbolism was transferred from the cults and had to be legitimized." New Advent. *Archeology of the Cross and the Crucifix.* <http://www.newadvent.org/cathen/04517a.htm>

& Cox, Wade. *The Cross: Its Origin and Significance* (No. 39)

<http://www.ccg.org/english/s/p039.html>

In 1891 Dr. Gustaf H. Dalman...printed a critical text of all the passages censured by the Catholic church in the middle ages, in the *Talmud* (meaning "study") which are said to refer to Jesus. He points out that the Hebrew or Aramaic form "*Jeschu*" or perhaps more correctly "*Yeschu*," is a genuine Jewish name," (i.e., Joshu in English - derived from the Hebrew, *yod-shin-waw* with no *aleph* or "a" to make it into Joshu<u>a</u>; meaning Jehovah saves or Jehovah/Jehovih savior) and not a nickname invented in despite by the Jews, as charged against them by Christian writers, to escape writing the form *Jeshua (Joshua, Jehoshua)* which Christians maintain was the proper Hebrew name of Jesus." Mead, G. R. S. *Did Jesus Live 100 Years BC*, pp. 135-138, 177, 256, 334, 335, 408 &410.

Eunomis, a presbyter in attendance at the Council of Nicaea, left a record stating that the name Yesu (Joshu) was discussed at the Council. (*Acta Concilii Niceni*, Colon 1618) G. R. S. Mead also quotes from; *The Palestinian Gemara...* "He (*Yeschu*) was brought before the court of Justice and stoned." (quoted from) the "*Toldoth Jeschu ha-Notzri*" or History of Jeschu the Nazarene." G. R. S. Mead, *Did Jesus Live 100 Years BC*, pp. 135-138, 177, 256, 334, 335, 408 & 410.

While it may be demonstrated that the version given by the church and organized religion has been subject to mishandling, this does not detract from any respect for the one who inspired the stories in the NT or from the philosophical and spiritual truths he tried to teach. This includes his attempts to teach us that we are gods, for which they killed him, after twisting it to say he claimed to be god. (John 10:34) It is certainly not his fault the later compilers of the NT also included so many myths from other preexistent religions.

Besides the numerous references in the OT, (in which Yeschu/Joshu/Jesus was obviously well learned as he frequently quoted them), the understanding of our descent from the Elohim/Gods is also elaborated upon in the "*Book of Ieou.*" (aka *Iesus/Jesus,* in this Gnostic manuscript, which accredited scholar G.R.S. Mead and others attribute to the Gnostic Christian Valentinus, in the first century CE)

> "The life of the Father is this; that you receive your soul from the "race of understanding" (mind) and that it ceases to be earthly and becomes understanding through that which I say to you...to send the earth to heaven is that he who hears the word of gnosis (Coptic; *knoste*-knowing) has ceased to have the understanding (mind) of a man of earth, but has become a man of heaven, his understanding has ceased to be earthly...by means of the hidden mysteries which show the way to the chosen race." The speaker *Valentinus* is recording statements attributed to Yeschu/Joshu/Jesus. ("Book of Ieou," 40-44)

> <http://www.gnosis.org/library/1ieo.htm>

That verse has the same meaning as to be in the world but not of it, expressed in these NT verses also attributed to Yeschu/Joshu/Jesus; "Do not love the things of the world. If anyone loves the (things of the) world, the love of the Father is not in him. For all that is in the world, the lust of the flesh, the lust of the eyes, and the pride of life, is not of the Father but is of the world. And the world is passing away, and the lust of it; but he who does the will of God abides forever." (1 John 2:15)

> "Pure and undefiled religion before God and the Father is this: to visit orphans and widows in their trouble, and to keep oneself unspotted from the world." (James 1:27)

> "They are not of the world, just as I am not of the world." (John 17:14)

> "Some have attained the Sovereignty of the Heavens laughing, and they came forth

[rejoicing from the world]…If he disdains (the world) and scorns it as a game, he shall come forth laughing." (Ph 96; hyperllinear) Translation and Notes by Paterson Brown. *The Gospel of Philip.* verse 103. <http://www.metalog.org/files/philip.html>

"Those who say that the Lord first died and then arose, are confused. For first he arose and (then) he died. If someone first acquires the resurrection, he will not die; (as) God lives, that one was (is) going to…While we are in this world it is appropriate for us to be born in the resurrection, so that if we are divested of the flesh we shall find our selves in the repose (and) not wander in the transition." *The Gospel of Philip.* verse 22 & 68. <http://www.metalog.org/files/philip.html>

The Coptic (Greek/Egyptian) word *rexit* translated as Christ, in the Bruce Codex Schmidt translation of, *The Book of Ieou,* p. 270-271, seems to be related to the Egyptian word for knowledge from (*rkh*; know) and YHVH is known in Hebrew as *YHVH El Da' at* (translated YHVH god of knowledge). Budge, Wallis. *Egyptian Language,* p. 165&194.

<http://www.thekeep.org/~kunoichi/kunoichi/themestream/glyphs_2b.html>

Yeschu/Joshu/Jesus knew from his own name that YHVH saves, or that is, YHVH offers salvation to all His children who practice oneness in Him, as proclaimed in Isa. 43:10. "I (even) I YHVH and besides me there is no savior." Also see Psalms 9:14 "Show me favor O YHWH…that I may be joyful in your salvation." Surrender to the collective consciousness of oneness, which is YHVH Echad, as Yeschu/Joshu/Jesus did, (John 17:21) is the only salvation from Satan, the adversary. The collective consciousness of adversaries, i.e. warriors, is Satan, the prince of evil, ruling the worldly people.

"Do not learn the way of the Gentiles; Do not be dismayed at the signs of heaven, For the Gentiles are dismayed at them." Jer. 10:2

Yeschu/Joshu/Jesus had also gained the understanding (of who the Elohim were) through direct visitation, for example, when contacted by the spirits of Moses and Elijah (Mark 9:4) who had long since joined forces with the Elohim and the hosts of heaven, far above and beyond the lower and chaotic spirit world of this earth. Because Ecclesiastes 9:5 says the "dead know nothing" some believe this means the spirits of the dead. Whereas in fact it must mean the dead body knows nothing, for the spirits of Moses and Elijah obviously knew perfectly well how to communicate when they reappeared after their death to visit Jesus. (Luke 9:30) It is also important to remember that knowledge of the spirit world occurred the world over, before and after the Judeo/Christian religions.

CONSTANTINE, CHRISTIANITY AND THE NEW TESTAMENT

"But we see Jesus, who was made a little lower than the angels, for the suffering of death." Heb. 2:9 See <http://www.scripture4all.org>

Yeschu/Joshu/Jesus, who spoke Aramaic, did not write or authorize any material himself, it was the decision of Constantine's council of bishops, in the third century, as to which accounts of his life and other manuscripts would be included in the NT. "For as much as *many* have taken in hand to set forth in order a declaration of those things which are most surely believed among us." (Mark 1:1) In 251 AD the number of Presbyters (roving orators or priests) with their different writings had dramatically increased. According to Presbyter Albius Theodoret (circa 255 AD) there were "more than two hundred" variant gospels of the NT in use in his time.

> "The event that triggered the compilation of the New Testament (in Greek in the third century) was the conversion of Constantine, he called the first council of bishops in Nicea in 325 CE." In a letter ...the emperor (Constantine) confessed he would feel secure "Only when I see all venerating the most holy God in the proper cult of the catholic religion. (" *Katholikos*; universal, from Greek, *kata* in respect to & *holos* whole; Thorndike Dictionary, 149) (Constantine and Councils: Christian, "Encyclopedia of Religion" 70-71&125) To resolve the latter, he summoned a universal council...to meet at Nicaea...in 325 AD... The *first* attempt to gather a body of bishops... Constantine commissioned the 318 bishops ...to settle the controversy ...of the ...full divinity of Jesus." Article on Constantine and Councils: Christian, *Encyclopedia of Religion*, pp. 70-71 & 125.

It is clear that the bishops of the Nicean council were mere human beings and not infallible or perfect (not being omniscient, as no human is divine) in their choices as to which manuscripts were included or excluded. For instance the Gospel of Peter, now condemned as Gnostic, was read regularly in the earliest Christian assemblies, the Gospels of Thomas, Philip and Mary etc. found at Nag Hammadi and elsewhere were also excluded. The number of times the NT castigates the Jews, seems to attest to the improbability of those areas of the manuscripts having been written, without alteration, by the early followers of Jesus, since they were all Jews themselves.

At the time of Constantine the ancient world was a mix of various different religions and cults that existed all over the Roman Empire, derived from even as far away as China and India. Constantine included an image of the "savior" Mithra (known also as a Christ and also said to have been born from a virgin on Dec. 25, long recognized by the ancients millennia before the birth of Jesus as the day of the birth of the sun) on the Triumphal Arch. Mithra's presence on the "Triumphal Arch of Constantine was adopted *after* Constantine's victory)" It was built in 315 by the senate *after* his 'conversion' to Christianity, but there is no image or reference to Jesus the Christ. Monday, Ralph. *Christ, Constantine, Sol Invictus* citing; *The Emperor's State of Grace*, by Charles Freeman, "History Today" 51 (2001) 28 Feb. 2005. Roane State Community College Tennessee Electronic Library. Monday, Ralph. *Christ, Constantine, Sol Invictus: the Unconquerable Sun*

<http://www.themystica.com/mystica/articles/c/christ_constantine_sol_invictus.html>

& Nosotro, Rit. *Constantine The Great.*

<http://www.hyperhistory.net/apwh/bios/b2constantine.htm>

The Egyptian Serapis was also called "The Savior." He was considered by (H)adrian, the Roman emperor (117-138 AD) to be the peculiar god of the Christians... "The worshipers of the Sun-god, Serapis, were also called "Christians," and his disciples "Bishops of Christ..." Those who lived according to the Logos (logic i.e. Platonists) were really Christians." (Clemens

Alexandrinus) Doane, T.W. *Bible Myths and Their Parallels in Other Religions,* p. 194 & 568.

Through surrender of the self will and ego (driven by the serpent brain and the fear it generates) Yeschu/Joshu/Jesus became "one" with the Way, the Truth and the Life. (John 14:6) When he says "no one cometh to the Father except through me" this can be interpreted to mean that salvation is through embracing oneness with him and with each other ("That all one they may be; as you, Father in me, and I in you, that they in us may be (All One)." John 17:21), if we are to attain oneness with the Father. While he had become one with the will of the Creator, Yeschu/Joshu/Jesus clearly recognized that the infinite Creator YHVH is greater than himself because he said; "If you loved Me, you would have rejoiced because I go to the Father, for the Father is greater (*meizon*) than I." (John 14:28) If Yeschu/Joshu/Jesus was precisely synonymous with "God" it obviously would not make sense for "God" to speak of his Father as being greater than himself.

> "Keep this mental attitude in you that was also in Christ Jesus, who although he was existing in God's form, gave no consideration to seizure, namely that he should be equal to God" (Phi. 2:6). This passage was changed in the KJV to create the illusion that Jesus *was* equal to God. It was at some point altered to read instead; "Who being in the form of God, thought it *not* robbery to be equal with God."

The argument often given is that the NT says Jesus created everything in the beginning after God the Father (*Theou* in Greek) created him. But the verse so interpreted actually says that the son is "in the image of *Theou* (God KJV) the unseen before-most brought forth of every creation. That in Him is created the All..." This verse (Col. 1:15-16) has been interpreted to mean that when it says "Him" this is a reference to Jesus, translating it as "first-born" but it is obviously more logical to interpret the infinite Creator, the All, as the "Him" who was the unseen before-most of every creation rather than a man (as Jesus is called in Acts 2:22) in a limited human form, therefore much less than the All. This would make this a reference to the unseen *Theos* as the Creator and that it was a reference to Him, the unseen before-most One, who created the All.

Jesus clarifies further that he can do nothing of his own will or as it is phrased in Greek "Not am able I to be doing from myself...but the will of the One sending me Father." John 5:30 As 1Cor. 15:28 states Jesus is subject to the Father and Heb. 2:9 says Jesus was made lower than the angels these conditions clearly explain his reluctance to seize or claim equality to the *Theos* (God KJV). To study these verses in the more concise Greek wording quoted above go to; <http://www.scripture4all.org>

> "The most careful research cannot discover a scrap of external evidence in the first century that witnesses to the existence of Jesus, much less...the doings which the Gospel writers relate of him. The Gospel story, ...is to be traced to the sketch of an ideal life which was intended for purposes of propaganda, and which could be further explained to those who were ready for more definite instructions...To a certain extent it was based on some of the traditions of the actual historic doings of Jesus, but the historical details were often transformed by the light of the mystery-teaching, and much was added in changed form...allegories and parables and actual mystery-doings were woven into it,...which at the time was regarded by the writer as a modest effort at simplifying the spiritual truths of the inner life, by putting them forward in the form of what we should now call a "historic

romance…" he especially did not wish to have it mistaken for the actual historical account of the life of the real Jeschu." Mead, G. R. S. *Did Jesus Live 100 Years BC,* pp. 421,422&423.

If one examines the Catholic Old Testament a different number of books will be found (46 or 47) seven or eight more than in the Protestant Bible (39). The extra books are referred to as the Apocryphal (hidden) or Deuterocanonical books (Second canon). How can the books contained in either one be the only correct "inspired word of God" if they do not agree with each other?

The OT as it has come down in Greek from the Jews of Alexandria also differs in many respects from the Hebrew Scriptures, including different books and the order of the books it contains. In Matt. 5:18, where Yeschu/Joshu/Jesus says, "one jot or tittle shall not pass from the law til all be fulfilled" he uses the HEBREW terms, jot and tittle. This indicates the law he referred to was written in Hebrew, so it was the Ten Commandments or laws that he considered to be intact, <u>not the Greek New Testament compiled by Constantine's bishops, which was not yet in existence at the time he made that statement.</u> Hall, Prentice. *The New Jerome Bible Commentary*, 1990 p. 641.

> "Add nothing to his words, that He not reprove you, and that you may not be proved a liar." Prov. 30:6 & Deu. 4:2

The extra books, *"The Apocrypha,"* are speculated to have never been part of the original OT. Prior to the discovery of the Dead Sea Scrolls the oldest texts of the OT were the *"Leningrad Codex"* (1009 written on the MSS) and the *"Aleppo Codex"* (undated approx. a century older). The OT covers a multitude of authors and more than a thousand-year span, the original copies of some starting from after the time of Moses.

I have addressed some of the apparent changes since the time of those Codices, however it would take a skilled team of Hebrew scholars to address the countless differences between those codices and Hebrew interlinear texts available now. Even at a glance it is clear that they certainly do not read the same, word for word, as the Hebrew text available in the online site mentioned at the beginning of this book. (http://www.scripture4all.org) Heaven only knows what more there is to be discovered if we had word for word interlinear concordances available to us of those codices, and what more was lost or concealed in the past that will never be recovered.

Is it any wonder that the church scholars kept all the Dead Sea manuscripts (that they were charged with studying and translating for the public) unpublished for over thirty years, until after copies of all of them were leaked by a secular party? The discovery of these Hebrew versions of the OT in the Dead Sea Scrolls demonstrates that the "infallible" declaration of the Council of Trent in 1546, was clearly false. (http://biblelight.net)

> "And there are to be no lesser powers between you and Me." Ex. 20:3

While none of us is divine and therefore suited to force their interpretation of the words upon any other, as all have that right to do that for themselves, it is certainly the right of all to have access to all the evidence and then interpret it for themselves. This has been previously made unavailable through the insistence of main stream organized religion upon promoting the Trinitarian version.

"For there must also be heresies among you that they which are approved may be made manifest among you." 1 Cor. 11:19

We were never meant to worship the Bible anyway, since it can be and obviously has been altered by man. One obvious example is in substituting the word God for YHVH, since there can be no argument that the word "God" was <u>never</u> used to mean YHVH in the earliest OT times! We were meant to seek the truth and worship the Great Holy Spirit of Oneness, YHVH Echad.

"YHWH looked down from heaven upon the children of men, to see if there were any acting intelligently, inquiring of *ath* Elohim." Ps. 14:2 (Strong's gives the meaning of the word Hebrew word "*ath*" as; "to assent, properly <u>to come</u>" (SHD 225&226) however it is used elsewhere in the OT as "with" for example; Gen. 5:22. This would then mean we are meant to inquire or consult "with" the Elohim.

The doubt generated by the errors of the church, the contradictions in the modern Bible and the lack of oneness demonstrated during the persecutions and inquisitions by the church, have now led many away from faith and oneness. When the whole truth is known it can clear up this skepticism and lead back to oneness, faith and peace, which should certainly be the goal of any true religion teaching of YHVH the All One. Anyone who is fighting over religion has missed the point.

To pass beyond the fear for self that is generated by the serpent brain, requires a leap of faith, to begin having faith that, rather than self will and ego (or for that matter money or possessions etc.) the Supreme Intelligence of the Universal Mind of our Creator, will sustain us (with His own spirit, present in all organic life), and guide us home to Himself after death.

Because of the advanced abilities of YHVH's Elohim they have the ability to intervene on the behalf of those who stand for the oneness of the kingdom of heaven come to earth, and influence the minds of those around them making a way for them even when they are in their darkest hour. With all this understanding in place the following verse begins to make sense; "I tell you the truth, anyone who has faith in me will do what I have been doing. He will do even greater (*meizona*) things than these, because I am going to the Father." John 14:12

It is only with the cooperation of the Elohim that humans will finally be able to do greater things than Yeschu/Joshu/Jesus, because through our becoming one with their unity of mind they have the ability to not only affect the outcome of human thinking (with what we might call psychic powers, like telepathy, psycho-kinesis, etc.) and everything that results from it, but also many other advanced powers, like faith healing (nowadays called the placebo effect) controlling the weather etc. or other things that we would call miracles. Their oneness with YHVH allows the Elohim to manifest themselves, other living things and their "chariots" physically, when it is YHVH's will. It is from this ability to reconstruct a living body for a spirit that resurrection from the dead is possible.

We can also become a part of the way, the truth and the life, when, through oneness with the truth, and through our alignment with it, we find the enlightenment that is oneness in truth; the ego can do nothing of lasting value, yet the living spirit of the Creator and His will preserves us and allows for even greater miracles to come and then takes us home to oneness in Himself. "If anyone loves me, he will obey my teaching. My Father will love him, and WE will come to him and make *our* home with him." John 14:23

Another name for YHVH is *Al Emet* (Ps. 31:5) the All[16] Truth or All Faithful. The truth of our acts exist forever within the Universal Mind of the Creator, and our being, along with all truth known (all truth that is known in the minds of the Elohim, ourselves, and all other sentient beings) all have continuity through the existence of the spirit of the Universal Being, YHVH. Without Oneness of mind, in our understanding of the concept of symbolic knowledge we could not communicate, because it is only through the shared commonality of language, words, and symbols that we can communicate at all. Mind is communication at its essence for without communication knowledge alone means nothing. Thus All Knowledge and All Truth is one in YHVH as He is *Al Emet* and as we learned earlier He is *Al De'ot,* the All Knowledge. (1 Sam. 2:3) Parsons, John J. *The Hebrew Names of God.* [16]remember from the section on The All, the word Al or El can also mean "all")

<http://www.hebrew4christians.com/Names_of_G-d/El/el.html>

Our spirit, that which moves us, is and always was part of the Great Holy Spirit of the Creator. It is in regaining oneness with the will of the All One, that the truth of all that has been is everlasting. In the light of oneness with YHVH and all those who, in oneness, embrace the light of All Truth, all untruths are revealed to be but darkness or ignorance. And all truth belongs to the Creator for He is one with, and embraces all true knowledge of His creations and His creatures.

YESCHU THE NAZAREAN-ESSENE

"That it might be fulfilled which was spoken by the prophets, he shall be called a Nazarene[17]." Matt. 2:23

[17]Nowhere in Jewish prophetic literature is there any prophecy predicting a Nazarene messiah, what IS foretold in the OT is the appearance of a *Nazarite* (Judges 13:5-7), one who takes a vow to separate[18] themselves from worldly indulgences, abstaining from various forms of impurity. (Num. 6) [18]The word *nazarite* is derived from *nazar* or *nazir* meaning separate or consecrated. (SHD 5144

"Among the Jews, wrote Flavius Josephus in *The Jewish War*, "there are three schools of thought, whose adherents are called Pharisees, Sadducees, and Essenes respectively...If we read the New Testament without knowing the accounts of Josephus, Philo, and the Dead Sea Scrolls, it would never occur to us that a sect like the Essenes existed side by side with the Pharisees and Sadducees." Lehmann, Johannes. *Rabbi J.,* p. 97.

"The whole Jewish community...was divided into three parties, the Pharisees, the Sadducees and the Essenes...every Jew had to belong to one of these sects...he (the biblical Jesus) frequently rebuked the Scribes, Pharisees and Sadducees, he never denounced the Essenes." Ginsberg, Christian. *The Essenes and the Kabbalah,* p. 24.

Josephus explains further that the Essenes were divided into two separate orders, he speaks of an order of marrying Essenes; "Moreover, there is another order of Essenes who agree with the rest as to their way of living and customs and laws but differ from them in the point of marriage." (*Wars of the Jews"* Flavius Josephus) Philo says that Moses instituted the order of the Essenes, and Josephus says that they existed "ever since the ancient times of the fathers." *Between the Testaments.* <www.byhisgrace.cc/cim/Gallery/history.html>

The ancient Christian historian Epiphanius, in his *Panarion,* writes of seven Jewish sects in all; "Sadducees, Scribes, Pharisees, Hemerobaptists, Ossaeans, Nazarean and Herodians." *Panarion* 1:19. Epiphanius links the Hemerobaptists with the Scribes and Pharisees; and the Ossaeans (var. sp. of Essene) with the Nazarean. From this it may be deduced that the two Essene branches, spoken of by Josephus, were the Ossaeans and Nazareans.

Josephus writes primarily of the Ossaeans (aka Essenes) telling us that they "adopt the children of others at a tender age in order to instruct them." However, Philo speaks of the Theraputae (from whence the word therapist derives), who were known as an Egyptian branch of the Nazarean Essenes, quoting Philo's first account; "They do not offer animal sacrifice, judging it more fitting to render their minds truly holy...Their lifestyle is communal." *Ten Gnostic Commandments.* <http://www.essenes.net/intro.htm> *Ancient Historians and the Essenes.* <http://www.essene.com/History/AncientHistoriansAndEssenes.html>

The Dead Sea Scrolls, dated 200-70 BC contain a version of the Beatitudes, attributed to the Jesus of the NT, supposedly born the first year AD. This questions the claim of supporters of modern biblical texts to be the one and only inspired and inerrant word of an All-Knowing God. An All-Knowing God would not plagiarize, then be untruthful about who said it, either that or get the name and birth date of His son wrong, *if* the scrolls written at least 70 years before the year one AD, contain material by Jesus-Yeschu. To read the Dead Sea Scrolls Beatitudes see; Eisenman & Wise, *The Dead Sea Scrolls Uncovered,* p. 175.

> "The scholar who would "exercise caution" in identifying the sect(s) (in the area) of Qumran with the Essenes places himself in an astonishing position: he must suggest seriously that two major parties formed communistic (holding all things in common) religious communities in the same district of the desert of the Dead Sea and lived together in effect for two centuries, holding similar bizarre views, performing similar or rather identical lustrations (baptisms) ritual meals, and ceremonies. He must suppose that one (Christians) carefully described by classical authors, disappeared without leaving building remains or even potsherds behind: the other, systematically ignored by classical authors, left extensive ruins, and indeed a great library." Charlesworth, James. *Jesus and the Dead Sea Scrolls,* p. 3.

According to Epiphanius, the name Christians was given to those who had been called Jessaioi or Essaioi, that is, to the Essenes and Therapeuts. (de Bunsen, Ernest. *The Angel Messiah of the Buddhists, Essenes and Christians,* p. 373.) Allegro says "The Essenes of the Dead Sea Scrolls called themselves the 'men of the New Covenant'[19], or New Testament' and prepared themselves under their teacher 'Joshua'" (one spelling of the Hebrew name translated from the Greek into Jesus in English) to enter the new era. Allegro, John. *The Dead Sea Scrolls and the Christian Myth,* p. 49. John Allegro has edited some of the most important of the Essene documents, King Hussein appointed him honorary advisor on the Dead Sea Scrolls.

[19]The Latin word 'testament' means covenant. The introductory page of the Revised Standard Version of the King James Bible (1971) describes the Christian writings of today as "The New Covenant, commonly called the New Testament."

> "The heavens and the earth will obey His Messiah. He will release the captives, make the blind see, and raise up the downtrodden. Then he will heal the sick, resurrect the dead, and to the poor announce glad tidings." From the Dead Sea Scrolls text known as 4Q521, quoting; Pellegrino, Charles. *Return to Sodom and Gomorrah,* p. 323.

> "The Teacher of Righteousness...according to the "Dead Sea Scrolls" ...preached penitence, poverty, humility, love of one's neighbor, chastity ...the observance ...of the whole Law...He was the Messiah, redeemer of the world...the object of the hostility of the priests...He pronounced judgment on Jerusalem for having put him to death...and at the end of time, he will be the supreme judge. Rather a lot of similarities to Jesus not to have had the same historical source for both stories. Shanks, Herchel. *Understanding the Dead Sea Scrolls,* p. 64&182.

While it does not diminish from any possible evidence on the Essenes, it should be noted that locating the Essenes at Qumran may be partially or wholly inaccurate. "Dr Hirschfeld, of the Hebrew University, recently invited reporters to see 25 spartan stone cubicles above *En Gedi* (35 kilometers south of Qumran) which he suggested had been the Essene settlement rather than the Qumran location...Dr. Hirschfeld bases his opinion that *Ein Gedi* was the original site of the Essenes on a passage from Pliny.

> "Lying below the Essenes was formerly the town of Engedi (infra hos Engada), second only to Jerusalem in the fertility of its land...Next comes Masada...This is the limit of Judea." Pliny the Elder (23 C.E. - 79 C.E.). Moreover, the excavation turned up no evidence of animal bones -- suggesting vegetarianism, which would have been highly unusual at the time." (The Essenes are well known to have been vegetarians.) Ilene Prusher 'Archaeologist says new site casts doubt on Essenes' role', newsday.com." *Discoveries by the Dead Sea, The Essene Controversy.*

> <https://groups.google.com/forum/?fromgroups=#!topic/bit.listserv.christia/Q56NvlCBCw4>

Alvar Elleguard (*Jesus: One Hundred Years Before Christ*) has suggested that the main prototype for the stories of Jesus in the New Testament was the Teacher of Righteousness mentioned in the Dead Sea Scrolls. The Dead Sea Scrolls contain many examples that demonstrate the fact that there was not one single authoritative text of scriptural writings in ancient times, but rather many different versions of the same hand-copied (and sometimes, therefore, frequently altered) texts that circulated among the Palestinian Jews of the time. The scribes and church scholars while attempting to make sense of the various writings often gave their own understanding of the text, which is perhaps the best any of us can do. However, it is only right that we have as much of the original words and meanings available to us as possible, rather than being compelled to blindly accept the censored version that has resulted from the many reinterpretations (by the church scholars and scribes), that occurred throughout history. And while all one can do is give their best interpretation of ancient texts, it is critical that motives of self interest do not move one to distort the meaning, this has happened repeatedly, as the evidence will show.

Chapter Three

GENESIS REVISITED

"B-rashith bara Elohim ath e'smim uath eartz." Gen. 1:1

BY WISDOM

Even though the traditional interpretation would never consider the presence of the Elohim with YHVH during creation, with the understanding of who YHVH's Elohim are we can reconsider their role in the creation story as it appears in the remaining texts. This chapter will consider the Hebrew version of Genesis, in the light of what we have learned about YHVH Elohim (YHVH Lord of the Gods or YHVH's gods depending on the context). Genesis is called the first book of Moses; the original, however, is long since crumbled to dust. The Bible tells us that the present version is based on a copy that was 'found' by the Levites, who then took over the priesthood through murder and enforced their interpretation under threat of death. Thus the chain of evidence cannot be substantiated to ensure that their 'copy' actually represents Moses original intentions. Even then the story of creation would have first been written down in the time of Moses; and this was ages after the time of the creation of the world or even the creation of Adam. This is perhaps one reason that the Psalms (songs) devote more references to the relationship between YHVH and His council Elohim than the rest of the OT; some psalms were no doubt sung and passed down orally since or even before Moses time.

But even after taking all that into account it still can be demonstrated that the interpretation we have been given, that is, the most recent versions in mainstream orthodoxy are also inaccurate. So with some clearer definitions and the following corrections it would seem that the creation story could include some of the following interpretations along with the recognition of the role played by YHVH's Elohim.

"B-rashith bara Elohim ath e'smim uath eartz." (The first verse of Genesis in Hebrew)

"The Bahir: Book of Illumination," says that "The word "beginning" (*rashith[1]*) is nothing other than Wisdom. That the first two words (for they are properly two words *b-rashith; b* or *bayt/beit* is; in, on, with, etc. (*Hebrew Language: Root Words.* <http://www.jewfaq.org/root.htm>) and *rashith (7225)* from the same root as *ro'sh*-SHD 7218) mean by-wisdom, is verified by the official, accredited and admitted authority of the Jewish religion (by virtue of its being possibly the oldest scholastic study of the OT and therefore closer to the original interpretations, as it was understood by ancient Hebrew writers and scholars of the OT). That authority, the *Jerusalem Targum,* gives *b-rashith* as "by wisdom." (Higgins 73,77,78,79,80&785) [1]Remember also that Prov. 8:1-30 mentions a feminine being called "wisdom" as having been with YHVH in the beginning.

The word *bara*, has the meaning exclusively neither of creating from nothing, nor of first forming, or giving the first or new form to matter, but to a renewal of form; so its literal meaning

91

can be, "regenerate" as well as "create." The Genesis creation story begins by describing chaos in the dark, vacant place that was to become the earth, followed by separating (stratifying) the substances in chaos and darkness, so that the first light could penetrate. (Higgins 73,77,78,79,80&785)

> "For Behold, I create new heavens and a new earth; and the former shall not be remembered, nor come into mind." Isa. 65:17

Isaiah's understanding shows that even in his time it was understood that other heavenly places could be created along with other earths, so the interpretation of *bara* meaning regenerated as applying to the 'creation' of the 'heavenly place' of the solar system is substantiated by the Bible itself. Other meanings of the word *bara*, include; choose, cut down, and dispatch. (SHD 1254) Scholars have puzzled over this dual use of *bara* to mean both create and cut (trees). Shortly we will explore why Genesis does not discuss the creation of the stars, then it will be seen that the Creation story actually means that the heavenly place was 'cut out' to create a new area of space for the earth, sun and moon, and the new solar system to be formed. (Incidentally one Hebrew word for Creator is a plural form of the word "*bara.*" (*buria-k*) Ecc. 12:1 This verse was changed to read creator singular in the KJV, it may refer to the Elohim. A plural word for Creator is also seen in Isaiah 54:5.)

> "The earth she became chaos and void and darkness on the surface of submerged chaos...And He is saying; Elohim He shall become light and He is becoming light...And He is seeing Elohim come and assent, the light that (is) good and He is separating (The myriads thousands of?) Elohim, between the light and between the darkness." Gen.1:2-4

In Genesis 1:2 it says that at that time the earth (or dust or dirt) was *tohu* (aka *theu/teu* chaotic motion) and *vohu* (aka *ubeu* or *bohu,* i.e. void or what science might call a vacuum). Matter is always in motion at some level, because (so far anyway) it is not possible to reach absolute zero. The existence of matter and the energy that comprises it are interchangeable concepts, thus motion and matter are two aspects of existence (translated as chaos and void; alternately motion and rest). Now in order for there to be chaos, there must be something that is in a state of chaos. This was present in the random "motion" of the (dark) interstellar dust cloud that formed the proto-stellar cloud, intermingled and dispersed throughout the space[2] in this area of the universe. ([2]the void or vacant vacuum, *vohu*)

This "earth" (SHD 776 also means soil or dust) that Genesis speaks of was not the spherical ball of dirt or earth as we know it, remember it was still formless and void. Since earth also means dirt or dust, in the beginning there was already space and dust, for YHVH Elohim to work with throughout the universe when planets or sun-planets are created. The "earth" that Genesis 1:1 speaks of was earth as in dirt or dust, not "The Earth" as the round planet we now know.

According to the Bible *Tohu* and *Vohu,* chaotic dust and the vacuum were therefore, already in existence before our planet, "the earth," was created. Since there is no mention of their creation, showing up in the second verse of the Bible, this shows that according to the Bible they existed as co-eternal creations of YHVH Elohim. They are in fact YHVH's physical presence, the universe, matter and space, throughout which His spirit pervades all space and rules all motion and therefore all matter and life. This is why it says in Gen. 1:3 "He shall become light." YHVH's body, the matter of the universe, becomes light whenever through the presence of motion (the *ruah ha'kodesh* or holy wind/breath/spirit, created by the *ruah Elohim* Gen. 1:2), it begins to radiate."

As for the re-generation of the material from which the earth and solar system were made (as opposed to the creation of life by the Creator) it is now well known by science that the proto-stellar clouds from which stars form, like the one from which the solar system formed, are not comprised of new material, but rather they result from inter-stellar dust that had existed for long stretches of time, which then being gathered up, over time this debris finally condenses into the sun, the earth and the other planets. The light first became present Gen. 1:3 on the earth (i.e, the dust and water, etc.) that would eventually form the planet earth, as the proto-stellar cloud condensed, separated, and settled into solid bodies that "become light" (i.e. begin to radiate light and heat - infrared light).

Strong's gives the meaning of the word Hebrew word "*ath*" as; "to assent, properly to come" yet the interlinear version (scripture4all.org) elsewhere uses *ath* as the word "with." (#225&226) Apparently Gen. 1:1 would read literally that the "Elohim assent and come to the place where the earth was to be regenerated by wisdom." With the understanding in place of the understanding of 'ath' Gen. 1:4 would also literally read; "And He is seeing Elohim come and assent that the light was good..." Who were they assenting with if not with YHVH and where did they come from if they are not one time mortals from other worlds?

The context (The text of Genesis) demonstrates that this is not the beginning of all creation because there were already created beings- for instance the angels, messengers (and the Elohim), and dwelling places for them to exist, before the creation of the earth. The two words called in the first chapter of Genesis, the heavens, *e'smim*, also means to fix, to enact, or place.

That is to say; *e-smim*, the placements or locations in the heavens (from the root *shem*; the idea of definite or conspicuous position, to dispose (SHD 8034 & 7760); note also that this word is compounded with the dual or plural *"im"* ending making it literally; "the places" for the earth, sun, and moon, etc. In Gen. 2:4 it mentions the earth, and the heavenly place it was to be created *in*, literally; "these genealogical annals of *esmim* and the earth IN to be created them." (Higgins)

Given all this, word for word literally, Gen. 1:1 means "By wisdom (*b-rashith*), regenerated (*bara*), gods (*Elohim*), assent and come (*ath*) to the places (*e'smim* or places in the heavens) and earth (*uath eartz*, the root of our word earth)." The Elohim participated in this work as highly advanced, yet still angelic servants, of YHVH the most high All-One, who alone, however, is the Great Holy Spirit of all life and who alone can breathe life into His creatures. (*Ruach ha Kadesh* i.e. Holy breath, wind or air)

> "And He is making Elohim, TWO of the luminaries, the great ones. The luminary, the great for ruling the day and the luminary, the small, for ruling of the night and the stars." Gen. 1:16

Notice that Gen. 1:16 it states that at the time of the forming of the earth, the sun, and the moon, the Genesis creation story *does not* say that the stars were formed at that time, but only that the moon, one of the two luminaries created at that time, was to be "ruling over the night and the stars" that is; it was to shine over them at night (ruling over them because it was brighter than the stars).

This point, along with the idea of "days" is one that prevents science and the modern interpretation of Judeo/Christian religions from being able to come any where near having a meeting of the minds and moving toward oneness. Unlike the version that has been given in the KJV, a literal interpretation of the Hebrew version of Genesis never says that the creation of the universe and the stars took place at the time of the creation of the sun, the earth and the moon and their heavenly places. It only says that the moon was made to rule over the stars at night, as a lesser luminary than the sun by day.

It has only been assumed that Genesis places the creation first and the creation of the sun and moon later on the 4th day. As opposed to the formation of the earth in the first *ium*, the understanding that the sun and moon were first made to illuminate the day and the night during the fourth *"ium,"* may have been confounded to mean this 'fourth *ium*' was the time of their actual formation. It is possible that it was originally understood that this was when they first began to shine and perhaps it is only modern humans who now read it incorrectly. If they were obscured from illuminating the day and the night on earth prior to the fourth *ium*, by dust in the proto-stellar cloud, the story at this point (the fourth *ium*) may only refer to the time when they were first made to illuminate the earth.

The creation story clearly does not say "In the beginning "God" - singular and alone created the heavens and the earth." But until the advent of science fiction, the possibility of beings advanced enough to help with the regeneration of the material, that comprised the solar system was beyond the contemplation of the minds of most earthlings.

Paradoxically the first verse of the Bible uses *bara* so even if it were phrased in the familiar way it could be read, "In the beginning Elohim *create* the heavenly places and earth." It need not have a plural verb since words like council or assembly can be accompanied by a singular verb when they act in accord as one. If the noun translated as God singular is placed in the translation it reads "God create" whereas it should be "God creates" or "God created." However, if this singular verb, create, is used with the understanding given here it easily becomes a coherent sentence. "By wisdom Elohim create (regenerate) heavenly placement and/with the earth." In other words through their advanced knowledge, i.e. "wisdom," YHVH's Elohim participate in the process of regenerating the interstellar dust into proto-stellar systems and planets made of earth or dirt.

Perhaps by vibrating (*mrchphth* Gen.1:2) the entropy of the chaos, they set things in motion, adding the energy that then results in the vortex of the solar system. It is still not understood by science what gravity is, only how it works, and then it does not work predictably when considered at sizes like galaxies. Remember that, according to physics, a body at rest tends to remain at rest (just as the asteroid belt maintains its equilibrium today), were mere gravitational forces from matter responsible for planetary formation, the asteroid belt should be observed to presently be gathering itself together into one place and forming a larger body. Lee, Chris. Modifying Gravity—An Update On The State Of Modified Theories Of Gravity.

<http://arstechnica.com/science/2007/03/modifying-gravity-an-update-on-the-state-of-modified-theories-of-gravity/>

This may imply that rather than it being a dead process, "create" instead of "created" past tense, YHVH and His Elohim are a living presence responsible for initiating and maintaining the forces that continue to hold our material existence together. Additionally as they go forward creating new solar systems, adding to the visible "solar" system cells in the universe, this would also cause an appearance of expansion. At any rate formative growth processes should certainly be taken as a possible alternative account when considering why the universe is expanding, an explosion is not the only thing that expands, so does anything that is alive and growing.

> "O YHWH...When I consider your heavens, the work of your fingers, the moon and stars, which you *ordained*." Ps. 8:3

When YHVH ordained His Elohim to do so they "vibrated a wind" across the chaos in, Gen. 1:2 (*"uruch aleim mrchphth"*) it began to form vortices and patterns just as dragging your hand through a basin of water makes whirlpools. These whirlpools stratified and condensed into the sun and the solar system, which also contained more vortices to form planets. This process, of planetary formation, only looks permanent to us, because our time frame is so limited, but our solar system will eventually lose heat and die or it will expand, engulfing the planets, then collapse and eventually explode debris back into space to again be recycled into "new" proto-stellar clouds.

And remember, however, while the Elohim participated in the work of forming the proto-stellar cloud and in the "pro-creation" of the human race, they did not breathe the breath of life into the Adam, the Bible clearly states that YHVH did, just as "He is becoming" all living things. The Bible clearly states in Gen. 2:7 that YHVH did and the Elohim assent (*ath*) in Gen. 1:27. (*Ath* means with or assent, so the Elohim approved of the creation of beings formed in their humanoid image.)

So considering everything presented here it is now possible to see that the story becomes completely different when organized religion is allowed to exclude the record of the involvement of YHVH's Elohim in the creation story and biblical history. More than any other, it has most likely been for this reason (to exclude the record of YHVH's Elohim from the creation story) that the confusion has arisen concerning the word Elohim.

It was necessary to completely obscure the possibly plural meaning of Elohim, rather than face the possibility that there were gods/elohim who existed from before the beginning serving YHVH, since it would also be necessary to conjecture that there were other worlds from which they came and organized religion was not prepared to face the possibility that we are not the center of the universe, nor the first humanoids, nor the beginning of the created universe.

THE CREATION STORY, ACCORDING TO *GENESIS*

> Gen. 1:1-5 *"B-rashith bara Elohim ath e'smim uath eartz."* By wisdom, the Elohim regenerate the heavenly place and the earth. (1) Vibrating the chaos (interstellar dust) and the void (space). (2) Separating between light and darkness (stratifying). (4) End of first *ium*[3] - time. (5)

[3] *Ium,/iom/yown,* SHD 3117, from an unused root meaning to be hot, cannot here mean a period of daylight since Gen. 1:5 says the first *ium* already included darkness and light. AND it was not

until the fourth *ium* (by this account following the separation of the proto-stellar cloud), that the light of the sun was first able to shine on earth, making a period of "daylight." Since a 24 hour day as we know it is contingent upon a period of daylight from sunshine, followed by darkness, it is obvious that as well as the meaning of a "day" derived from a root meaning to be "hot," *ium* must also mean a period of warmth or radiating energy i.e., infared light. This would allow *ium* to be translated as a period or time of light.

First *ium*, time of light; "Separating the "dark, vacant chaos" of the proto stellar dust (eartz) cloud, into the still formless layers or regions (belts similar to the asteroid belt) that were to become planet earth, stratifying this belt into separate regions or layers, including that of water, "vibrating over the surface of the waters" thus separating it to be used later.

He is separating Elohim, between the light and between the darkness." So perhaps when He (YHVH) separated the (myriads thousands of) Elohim, all of the work they performed during this separation (stratification) caused the matter of various bodies to begin to radiate, allowing the first light to shine. Everything was previously enveloped in the darkness of the proto-stellar cloud. Some matter, forming into molten young planets, comets and the sun gave off light, while other matter not condensing into bodies remained cold and dark just as the asteroids are still dark to this day. Comets however do radiate, they demonstrate the presence of some physical work[4] in progress. Gen. 1:1-5 ([4]in physics work = the amount of energy transferred by a force)

> Gen. 1:6-8 Creating atmosphere from water, and separating the water (6) separating the water which would become "the water under" (the oceans etc.) from the belt or sphere[5] which was to become "the water on," i.e., the atmosphere (7) end of second time. (8) [5]Dan Watson and colleagues believe they are the first to see a short lived stage of proto-planetary disk formation, and the manner in which a planetary system's supply of water arrives. Material signaled by the infrared spectrum of water vapor can best be explained by material falling from the proto-star's envelope. Results such as these will help astronomers learn about the earliest stages of our solar system. (The cooling effect of this water on the early molten state of the planet has yet to be considered when calculating the age of the earth, MHJ) *Supersonic 'Rain' Falls on Newborn Star.*
>
> <http://www.physorg.com/news107613104.html>

Second *ium*, time of light; Separating the atmosphere i.e. the gases and the water above the earth (i.e, the atmosphere) from the water below; that which would form the oceans. "And He is calling Elohim to light day...And He is making Elohim, the atmosphere and He is separating between the waters which from *under* the atmosphere and between the waters which from *on* to atmosphere...And He is calling Elohim to atmosphere..." Who was calling the Elohim if not YHVH? Gen. 1:6-8

> Gen. 1:9-13 Causing the oceans to flow to one place, leaving dry land (Pangaea?) (9) named dry land, *libshe* and seas, *imim* (10) making green scum and seeding the plant and tree seeds (aka Panspermia) (11) bringing forth different species of plants and seeds (12) end of third time. (13)

Third *ium*, time of light; Separating the water, "*to one place,*" that is, away from the original continent "Pangaea" (from which all the continents later split up) "they shall flow together the waters from under the heavens to place one…He is calling Elohim to dry earth" literally *"ulgra Elohim libshe eartz."*

Then seeding *"mzrio"* the earth (by some process similar to Panspermia, See *Evolution from Space* by world-renowned physicist Sir Fred Hoyle) so it would be eventually become covered with verdant (*verde*-green) life and species of plants. Note that it says; "She is bringing forth verdure (*dsha*)" During this time, <u>before</u> the atmosphere was cleared revealing the sun and moon, which comes about later in the fourth *"ium,"* green scum and primitive plants were apparently already capable of growing with the dim light filtering through the, apparently still completely overcast, cloud cover. Gen.1:9-13

> Gen. 1:14-19 Separating the atmosphere revealing two luminaries, using them to assign days, years, and to give light on earth (14) they become luminaries in atmosphere to give light (15) making the great luminary (the sun) for ruling the day and the small luminary (the moon) for ruling the night and the stars. (16) giving them for light on earth (17) to rule day and night, and separate between light and darkness (18) end of forth time. (19)

Forth *ium*, time of light; (Gen. 1:1) Separating or clearing the atmosphere; "and to separate between the light and between the darkness" thus making (it possible for) the sun to become a luminary by day and for the moon to become a luminary by night, "ruling over the stars" or that is, shining over the (already in existence) stars. Note that in NO place does the OT speak of the creation of the stars. Gen. 1:14-19 So this verse cannot possibly mean the time of the creation of the sun and moon as there was already day and night; and there were already green plants growing on earth which require sunlight.

> Gen. 1:20-23 Creating living things in the waters and in the atmosphere (20) then creating the *ethninm* - monsters "the great ones" (dinosaurs) and all "flyers of wings" (21) giving them His blessing (22) end of fifth time. (23)

Fifth *ium*, time of light; The first flyers (20) in the atmosphere are not described as having wings, these things may have been microorganisms or other floating lifeforms. in the atmosphere, and in the waters, the later ones "flyer of wing" (21) are clearly specified as having wings, these could include bugs, pterodactyls, and the ancient birds mentioned previously in the section on Evolution. After these first living things came the time of the creation of monsters, "*ethninm*" in the oceans (giant reptiles etc.) "they roam the waters" and then the "flyer of wing". This era is known in paleontology as the Cambrian Explosion, because in the Cambrian era all the major phyla appear *without* evidence of any precursor fossils in the Pre-Cambrian. Gen. 1:20-23

> Gen. 1:24-31 Bringing forth land animals and all the soul of all the living (all the different phyla) (24) making different species of land animals (25) making humans in the image of the Elohim (as the Elohim say "in likeness of *us*" plural) holding sway above all creatures (26) creating humans in the image of the Elohim, male *and* female (27) giving them His blessing to subdue the earth (28) giving them herbs, seeds, and fruit to eat for food (29) likewise giving herbs for animals "which in him soul of living" the flying *ouph* (fowls SHD 5776 as opposed to *ayit*, SHD 5861, birds of prey) and *rumsh* on the land (perhaps from SHD 6192 *aram*, gather together, or SHD 7462 graze, *ra'ah + seh*, flock, SHD 7716, i.e., grazing herd animals) (30) end of sixth time. (31)

Sixth *ium*, time of light; After the creatures of the fifth *ium* "He is becoming land animals" (*chith*) and "all the soul of the living," that is all the different phyla of life, including vertebrates; "animal of the land-*eartz* (perhaps meaning mammals since there were already reptiles /monsters)...AND moving animal(s) of the ground. The spelling here is "*e-adme*" Remember "e" = the word "the," so "moving animals of the-*adame*" so possibly , adam-like primates of the type who move across the ground (as opposed to primates living in the trees), so perhaps Australopithecus, Africanus or Sahelanthropus etc. (all tool-less vegetarians)

Only after the creation of these land animals and *e-adme* (the primates?) does YHVH then make the Adam (*e-adm*); the Homo species with arching rounded skulls for larger brains) having the same image or appearance as the Elohim, i.e. humanoid. "we shall make "*adm*" in image of us...male and female he creates *them*." (the Homo sapiens; Later when the sons of the Elohim interbreed with the females of the *adm*, "Cro-Magnon, *Homo sapiens sapiens*, appears on the scene, with even larger brains.)

Then he tells humans what they are to eat; "Behold I give to you all (seeds and fruit) He is becoming for you for food." (remember YHVH becomes all living things) The green herbs for the animals mentioned in verse 30 may refer to the vegetarian animals kept by humans, like chickens, turkeys, cows, sheep, etc *with living souls*. (since this possessing of a soul is not mentioned concerning the reptiles/*ethninm*/monsters) Gen. 1: 24-31

> Gen. 2:1-3 Finishing the work of the Elohim (1) ceasing work in the seventh time. (2) "And He is blessing Elohim in *ium* seventh...He ceases from all of work which He creates Elohim to make these genealogical annals in *ium* to make. (3) These genealogical annals of the heavens and the earth *in to be created them*, in *ium* to make YHVH Elohim the earth and heavens (4)." Gen.2:3-4

Seventh *ium*, time of light; "He is finishing, Elohim in "*ium* the seventh work of him..." the Elohim are ceasing from planet forming tasks preparatory to the creation of all living things by the Holy Spirit of YHVH. This is not to say that YHVH cannot do this Himself and/or did not do so on other worlds, but rather that the Elohim do this work because they enjoy seeing a new world come forth with glorious new life, created by YHVH.

> "And He is answering, YHWH...where were you when I laid the foundations of the earth...and the morning stars jubilated together and all the sons of the Elohim shouted for joy?" Job 38:1-7

In this seventh *ium* YHVH ceases from creating new life forms "and He is blessing Elohim" for their work, this sentence alone shows that the "He" mentioned throughout the first verses of Genesis, can be interpreted as someone different from the Elohim whom *He* blesses in 2:3. "He ceases from all of work of Him *which* He creates Elohim to make" So YHVH creates the Elohim, and us like them eventually, to help do this planet forming work. Gen. 2:1-3

So given all the conditions if the literal fundamentalist's version were taken, there could still be no way for *ium* to mean a 24 hour period of daylight and dark. If one is to try to say the sun was created on the fourth day, there could not have been 24 hour periods of daylight and dark before that. The sun was created after there were already plants on the earth??? Come on. In the third *ium*, the plants had already begun yielding seeds and fruit, a process which obviously does not occur in one twenty four hour day, as trees must mature many years before they bear fruit. Strong's 3117 states that *ium-yowm* can be used figuratively to denote a space of time, therefore a period or an age.

As a result of oscillation, the proto-stellar cloud was periodically bringing debris into the vicinity of the earth, darkening the light available to it, each of these periods had warmer-lighter and a cooler-darker phases, just as there are ice ages or dark ages with warmer-lighter phases between them down through time even up to in the present. There are still times in recorded history during which the sun shines only dimly for long periods and many records of ice ages occurring periodically. See *Yowm*, from the unused root meaning be hot. (SHD 3117) Note also the similarity to the Greek *aeon* or *aion* from whence we derive the word eon.

None of which is to say that there was not also opportunity for error during all the time of transmission after Moses' original efforts to create the Record of Testimony in his own time. Additionally, Hebrew became a dead language for a period of time (Revived as a spoken language by Elizer Ben-Yehuda starting in 1881, his efforts resulted in a dictionary to help other modern Jews once again learn to speak Hebrew) during which it was no longer spoken, so pronunciation must always be in question, and along with it, the possibility that two words with the same spelling existed and held similar or even distinctly different meanings. Since there are no Hebrew dictionaries from Moses time and prior, it is important to remember that there is every possibility that that the word *ium* may have been understood in more than one way depending upon the context.

After the seventh *ium* "He is forming the adam (note the plural predicator 'the'), '*uiitzr IEVE Elohim ath eadmn ophr mn eadme*' literally "He is forming YHWH, Elohim with or assent, the adam from eadme." That is YHVH continues "forming" or developing, the already male and female Adam, previously created as males and females in Gen. 1: 24-31, continuing the process of trans*forming* the dust of the earth into more of the adam/earthlings. (through their consumption of plant life, containing the minerals or dust of the earth combined with light from the sun through photosynthesis), see also Gen. 1: 24-31. He then plants a garden and places the Adam in the garden of Eden, an original paradise on the pristine new earth. The Adamic race or earthlings then learn to name all the animals. Gen. 2:7

After the creation of the male and female adam in Gen. 1: 24-31 and further developing or forming them Gen. 2:7, then YHVH's Elohim "causes to fall...stupor on the Adam" apparently while under some kind of anesthesia, they take from the Adamic race "angular organs" (possibly bone marrow containing DNA?) and are "closing flesh under *her*" (perhaps inserting it into an egg and cloning?) creating a special type of woman-*ashe,* so special that the males of the Adamic race would thereafter be enticed to follow them, "he (*Adm*) shall forsake man father of him and mother of him and he clings in woman of him and they become one flesh" He forsakes his family of origin and clings to this special form of woman (*ashe*) forming a nuclear family and thus began practicing monogamy, rather than the tribal inter-breeding seen in other primates. Gen. 2:21-24

After the females of the Adamic race acquired this special form, given to them in Gen. 2:21-22, the woman-*ashe* (only later is woman called *chue*-Eve in Gen. 3:20) succumb to a strong desire to partake of the "the tree of the knowledge of good and evil" having been enticed by the serpent brain to believe that in doing so they can become "intelligent" (*leshkil*) like the Elohim, whom they adore, as the very Gods they were. "...and you become as Elohim...and she is seeing...and coveted the tree to make intelligent." Gen. 3:5-6

According to the Bible it was these specially created females that the Elohim then found so appealing and amenable, that is, "good," that the Elohim pro-created offspring with them from whom the human race descended. As mentioned previously the further account of their inter-breeding appears in Genesis 6:1-2. "When men began to multiply on the face of the earth, and daughters were born to them, the "*ben Elohim*" (sons of the Elohim) saw that the daughters of the Adam were good; and they took for themselves women (womb-man) from all whom they chose."

Human females in general have superior skills (some quite large differences) in verbal communication. (while males generally do better in math or spatial skills, R. J. Coley, 2001) For example girls talk sooner and advance in early reading and writing skills far ahead of boys, this trend begins to even out after puberty. They are born with this verbal acuity in place because females are the ones who must teach the babies to talk, which anyone who has heard a new mother babbling to an unheeding newborn knows that they naturally love to do.

It is an inborn genetically inherited quality, this special capacity to teach the children, which, coupled with lower levels of the aggression causing testosterone, allow them to be amenable helpful companions and accelerate human development in communication skills. The traits may be the result of some special manipulation of female DNA creating an especially appealing new 'Eve' type of woman. This is generally true however girls exposed to unusually high levels of androgens in the womb...score significantly higher on tests of spatial ability. (Resnick, 1986)

With this distinction arises the understanding that there are two different kinds of intelligence, left brain skills, very good at spatial or mechanical (technological) building skills and keeping count of earthly wealth and the other very good at communicating, teaching and other right brain skills. Without both the human race could not have built and amassed the knowledge and resources that so clearly sets us apart from the animal kingdom.

With the domination of 'masculine' ideology and the concurrent focus on left brain functions, however, our society including the females themselves, have been programmed to believe that the only worth or value lies in technological building skills and keeping account of what is accumulated. (this is why the largest skyscrapers in every city are always the banks, not schools) Even females often only value themselves in as much as they are able to be pleasing to males.

But the necessity of communicating effectively and through that skill re-establishing our oneness is not to be overlooked for it is these right brain holistic ways of thinking that sees the big picture, and the big picture is not looking so pretty. In the interest of amassing and keeping count of "wealth" we are destroying our environment, to say nothing of the destruction of each other in the endless wars of our world. We are driven by the belief that in order to glorify the ego, we must be continually on the go, or attempting to demand that the world's focus of attention (esp. the media) should bring the spotlight onto us in some way. The inability to be alone (and refrain from burning fossil fuels to get someplace), has been lost because of our anxiety to prove ourselves in the eyes of the world, and endlessly burning fuel to always be on the go is the cause of global warming.

This in turn is because our sense of happiness with our selves has been lost. The accumulated hatred and resentment built up from abusive megalomaniacs in our society is passed on through abusive and neglectful parenting. It is poured into the children, allowing abusive parents to vent their frustration with their lives and feelings of inadequacy or indulge themselves with various addictions and sexual abuse. This arises when there is no understanding of the value of the right brain skills and practice of patiently teaching our offspring and no value placed on integrity and respect for the truth.

We need to correct this trend, and refocus on the importance of good right brain skills in mothers (which by giving attention at the right time, i.e. as young babies and little children, builds a healthy sense of self in the child). This must be done rather than viewing females as saleable objects; if not the increasing trend of producing evermore "psychopaths" will continue (*psycho-spirit*, breath, & *pathos*-suffering).

A healthy sense of self manifests as happiness with one's sense of self, without the endlessly ego driven need for attention, gratification or the desire to dominate others. The desire to dominate can manifest in controlling behavior, from the world's power mongers, through sexual predators, child abusers and all the way down to the seemingly insignificant habit of verbally putting others down to try to make oneself feel better. These and other addictions are used to alleviate anxiety arising from dissatisfaction with ones self and ones life.

We as a society must come to realize that it is better to prevent the creation of psychopaths than to capture the "bad guys" after they are created. We must break this cycle, and stop producing "bad guys" i.e. the males, as well as the female psychopaths who then help breed the next generation of abused children. These children grow up with greatly increased chances of becoming psychopaths themselves. No, mothers or parents, are not all to blame, outside influences can also trigger psychopathology, but when patiently loving, instructive and attentive, a good mother (with a father who is a positive supportive male role model) can go a long way toward preventing those outside influences from taking root.

EL SHADDAI, RUACH HA KODESH, SHEKINAH, THE MOTHER

> "The spirit of Al/El she made me, and the breath of Shaddai she is keeping me alive." Job 33:4

The meaning of *Shaddai* may be from the unused verb signifying moisten, pour, *shad* means breast or bosom, Gen. 49:25. (SHD 7699) If as many have suggested *Shaddai* refers to the feminine aspect of the Creator as our sustainer/provider, this clearly accounts for the feminine pronouns used in the above verse when translated word for word from Hebrew. With the understanding that *Al/El* also means "all" it can be seen that " *Al/El Shaddai*" comes to mean " the "All[6] Sustainer," providence, the bosom or nurturing aspect of YHVH. (see also Gen. 17:1, 28:3, 35:11, 43:14, 48:3, Ex. 6:3, Num. 24:6, Ruth 1:20, Job, Ps. 22:10, 68:15, 91:1, Ez. 1:24, 10:5, 23:21). ([6]remember from the section on The All, the word Al or El can also mean "all") Parsons, John J. *The Hebrew Names of God.* <http://www.hebrew4christians.com/Names_of_G-d/El/el.html>

101

"And YHWH spoke to Moses and said to him: I am YHWH. I appeared to Abraham, to Isaac, and to Jacob, as *Al* or *El Shaddai*, but by my name YHWH, I was not known to them. Ex. 6:2-3

"And He is appearing YHWH to Abram and He is saying to him, I (am) *Al/El Shaddai*." Gen. 17:1

"In the days when we were Hebrews we were orphaned, having only our Mother (the Spirit[7]). Yet when we became Messianics, the Father[8] came to be with the Mother for us. *The Gospel of Philip.* verse 6. <http://www.metalog.org/files/philip.html>

[7]El Shaddai (first used in Gen. 17:2), the All Sustenance (from *shad*-breast[9]); remember also that the noun "ruach" in the phrase Holy Spirit - "*ruach hakodesh*" also denotes a sanctified *feminine* breath or wind (SHD 7307). As oneness with All, YHVH would naturally contain both masculine and feminine qualities. (see Gen. 1:27) The Qabbalists called the Holy Spirit ("*Ruach ha-kadosh*") Immah (Ama, aka Amun in Prov. 8) the Mother. (Myer, Isaac. "*The Qabbalah*" p. 182) [9]<http://www.hebrew4christians.com/Names_of_G-d/El/el.html>

[8]"The Father' and 'the Son' are single names, 'the Sacred Spirit' is a double name. For (the Father and the Son) are everywhere— above and below, secretly and manifestly. The Sacred Spirit is in the revealed, she is below, she is in the hidden, she is above."(hyperlink Ph 74c; the Father is above and hidden, the Son is below and revealed, the Sacred Spirit is both above and below, both hidden and manifest…) *The Gospel of Philip.* verse 37.

<http://www.metalog.org/files/philip.html>

"Some say that Miriam (Mary) was impregnated by the Holy Spirit. They are confused, they know not what they say. Whenever was a female impregnated by a female?" *The Gospel of Philip.* verse 18 <http://www.metalog.org/files/philip.html>

Remember also that the root of the Greek word for "spirit" (*pneuma*) means "wind" or "breath." "For Paul it was the spirit of God that animated life and that was seen in the analogy of the wind (*ruach*) and thought to be similar to the breath (*nephesh*) that God breathed into Adam at the dawn of creation)." Spong, John Shelby. *Liberating the Gospels*, p. 222.

"Amongst the Eastern Church communities there is none more clear about the feminine aspect of the Holy Spirit as the corpus of the Coptic-Gnostics. One such document records that Jesus says, 'Even so did my mother, the Holy Spirit, take me by one of my hairs and carry me away to the great mountain Tabor...'" J. J. Hurtak, Ph.D., *The Holy Spirit: The Feminine Aspect of the Godhead.*

<http://www.pistissophia.org/The_Holy_Spirit/the_holy_spirit.html>

"Within Judaism, the *Shekinah*[10] (or "visible" cloud of the Presence appearing in passages when speaking of YHVH dwelling in the Tabernacle or among the Israelites) is a feminine word, thought to be YHVH's feminine aspect; therefore they called the (Holy) Spirit the "mother." ([10]from SHD 7935 dwell) *The Gospel of the Hebrews.* Extracts and Commentary Taken from *Gospel Parallels*, Ed. Throckmorton, Burton H. Jr.

<http://www.essene.com/Gospels/Hebrews.htm>

& The name of God in Judaism. <http://www.nationmaster.com/encyclopedia/The-name-of-God-in-Judaism>

It has however been unthinkable by the modern patriarchs of organized religion, with their insistence on the importance of a masculinized "God" (which modern word, unlike the name YHVH, assigns a gender, thus conveniently eliminating the feminine or "goddess" aspect) to recognize YHVH's inclusion of feminine attributes and call the Holy Spirit "the Mother" as many other ancient religions did.

Chava or *chui* are transliterations of the Hebrew word "Eve" it contains the root *havah,- hvh,* life giver, and this root is also to be found within the related word YHVH. Another feminine name for the deity is *"El Rachum,"* *rechem* meaning womb. (Deu. 4:31) Mother earth, a corporeal body, part of the corporeal universe, can conceive from panspermia processes (just like a large ovum), and bring forth life from YHVH's holy spirit, precisely because she is contained within the infinite omnipresent All-One, YHVH, whose corporeal body is the universe.

It is for this reason that, in the Hebrew words of the Genesis creation story, it repeatedly states of YHVH, acting in the presence of His Elohim that "He is Becoming" all the things and creatures of His creation (remember that "He is Becoming" may be a variation of "I am Becoming" which is one English rendering of YHVH's name "I Am" MHJ).

> "He is becoming the light...He is calling Elohim to light day...and He is saying; Elohim, He shall become atmosphere...He shall become the separation between the waters...He is becoming earth and she is bringing forth...And seed of Him, in Him on the land and He is becoming so," Further on; "He is becoming the luminaries...(the sun and the moon, allowing them to "become" luminaries through the processes of all the work, by the Elohim, of separating the chaos into layers then formed into planetary bodies)...and He is saying; Elohim, she shall bring forth, the earth, soul of living...moving animal and life of land to species of her (the earth) and He is becoming so.... And He is forming YHVH Elohim the human from soil from the ground, and He is blowing in nostrils of him breath of lives and He is Becoming the human to soul living." Gen.1:3-24 & 2:7

He creates out of His very substance, for all things are His and are contained in YHVH our Living Universe and Home of de-Light, His corporeal body is the universe and His holy spirit "becomes" manifest in all His living things. The importance of this understanding lies in the distinction between "He is becoming" (*uiei*) and the word with which it has been replaced "create or creating."

Without the understanding that our universe is the sacred body for the spirit and supreme intelligence of YHVH, (the unified oneness of all truth in one person), we place the Creator off in some heaven separated from all His living things. Then we confidently feel unafraid to destroy that which we believe He created for us to rule over, or just believe there is no spirituality at all. But when it is seen that every living thing contains the sacred spirit of YHVH and shares in some measure of the totality that is His intelligence, *Al Da'at* (All Knowledge), then there is no justification for destroying any thing, unless it is truly necessary for survival.

> "Does not wisdom cry? And understanding put forth her voice? She stands on the top of high places, by the wayside of the paths." Prov. 8:1 (see scripture4all.org)

Wisdom in chapters eight and nine of Proverbs (see especially 8:1-3 & 9:1-3) is repeatedly personified as a feminine being, who was with YHVH in the beginning. (Prov. 8:30) How anyone can interpret these references to Wisdom, a feminine being, to mean Yeschu/Joshu/Jesus is beyond me, we all see what we want to see I suppose. Gary Anderson in his article, *The Interpretation of Genesis 1:1 in the Targums,* in the *Catholic Biblical Quarterly,* 52 (1990) notes that the *Targum Neofiti* says, "This tradition understood the phrase *bere-sheith* to mean; with/by means of (Dame) Wisdom," God (Elohim) created...This is reference is found in *Targum Neofiti.*

> "She stands at the top of the high places, beside the way on the paths. She cries at the gates...Hear for I will speak of excellent things; and the opening of my lips shall be right things. For my mouth shall speak truth;...Receive my instruction...For wisdom is better than rubies and all things that may be desired are not to be compared to it. I wisdom dwell with prudence...I love them that love me...My fruit is better than gold...YHWH possessed me in the beginning of His way, before His works of old. I was set up from the beginning, or before ever the earth was...When He prepared the heavens I was there...Then I was by Him, AMUN and I was daily His delight...and my delights were with the sons of men...Blessed is the man that hears me...For whoso finds me, finds life, and shall obtain favor of YHWH." Prov. 8:2-35

> "Yet wisdom is barren [without a son] hence [she] is called [the Mother]...they themselves being found by the sacred spirit, [the True Mother who] multiplies her sons." *The Gospel of Philip.* verse 40. <http://www.metalog.org/files/philip.html>

OM, AUM, AMEN, AMUN, EAL ENAMN

In the above verse in Proverbs 8:30, the word *Amun* has been translated as "foster," however, it is actually a variation of *Aman-amn* SHD 539, which name is added to a list of YHVH's titles, *e-al namn* in Deu. 7:9. Translating this word as foster in many places has effectively prevented any consideration that these references have any relationship to the "hidden" Amun of the Egyptians or any relationship to the words Amen and Aum or Om. This word, SHD 539, also has the meaning of "truth" which would align with the feminine being called Wisdom throughout Prov. 8. The fact that Proverbs 8 and 9 (where the word *Amun* occurs) repeatedly refers to a *feminine* entity, brings us to our next comparison of related words throughout the ancient Middle East.

Om is often said to be the root word of Amen. Om is another sound that creates a wave pattern, as in; "in the beginning was the word" which means a primal sound or "vibration." Said by the Hindu religion to be that which all other names and forms arise from and to which we all return. Om, the Egyptian and Arabic word for mother, or Am (*Aum*) is mother in Hebrew (also *ima*). It is considered to be the sacred sound or name of the deity, the mother of words and of the breath and/or "the first word" of the universe, in Hindu and religions written in Sanskrit. "The Aum of India, as might well be expected, is found in Persia under the name of Hom." (for example *Ahunavada* 60 @ The Religion of Ahura Mazda. <http://www.zoroaster.com/>

"The word *am* (*alef mem*) in the Hebrew not only signifies might strength power firmness solidity truth but it means also mother as in Genesis ii 24 and love whence the Latin Amo mamma." Higgins, Godfrey. *Anacalypsis,* Vol. 1. 1992 reprint, p. 110, 128 & 131 (note page numbers from the online version do not correspond to those of the hard copy) It is found in names for mother the world over (mom, mum, ama, mama, ma, mother, mater, madre, mere, ma'dar, etc.) and it is the sound an infant makes while nursing, as adults we say yum or mmm-good. Jakobson, Roman. *Why "Mama" and "Papa"?* 1959.

> "The word for "mother" is similar in so many languages and even groups of languages that there seems to be little doubt that it evolved in such a fashion; for we find it with a -m- sound in a great many different parts of the world: in Hebrew it is ima, in Arabic it is umm, in Chinese it is *mu*, while in almost all Indo-European languages it is derived from the Vedic *mâtr*, which in Hindi and Gujarati becomes *ma³ mã*, in Italian and Spanish *madre*, in German mutter, in Russian *h] nv mâty*, in French *mère*, and in the mouths of children—in most European countries at least—mamma, mummy, maman, mom, mum, ma and so on." Mehta, Ardeshir. *Zarathushtra,* p.7. Online ebook @: <http://www.scribd.com/doc/53415779/Zarathushtra-Ardeshir-Mehta>

Om, like Amen means the Divine *Aum* which manifests as all that is. *Amma* is mother in Sanskrit, a compound often used in the names of female goddesses. A related Hebrew word "Amen," has frequently been compared to the Egyptian word "Amun" (*imn*-"whose name is hidden" van den Dungen, Wim. *Amun, the Great God : Hidden, One and Millions.* <http://www.maat.sofiatopia.org/amun.htm>). and a common origin has often been suggested. A word that appears to be related, Aman, shows up in one of YHVH's names, Al Hanne'aman or *eAl namn,* (Deu. 7:9; pleasant SHD 5273 & 5276; although sometimes given as SHD 529 530) which coupled with the concept "All"[11] becomes the All Pleasant, (though given as All Faithful or All Truth). The root "aman" should also perhaps be studied for a possible connection to ama-mother, as to nurse, support or nourish, SHD 539 or SHD 520. ([11]remember from the section on The All, the word Al/El can also mean "all") Parsons, John J. *The Hebrew Names of God.* <http://www.hebrew4christians.com/Names_of_G-d/El/el.html>

It can thus be seen that the Sanskrit Aum/Om influenced not only the Hebrew thinking but also Egyptian thinking as the Egyptian word for mother - Om and the Hidden Egyptian deity Ammon. Amen (h-men), Aum (Om), Ammon. <http://wandren.wordpress.com/2007/10/21/amen-ah-men-aum-om-ammon/>

This idea of substituting another name for an unspoken name of the supreme coincides precisely with the Hebrew practice of keeping the formal pronunciation of YHVH hidden. It may be that this practice among Egyptians derived from their association with the Hebrew who were free to give them the name Aum or Amen, but kept hidden the name of YHVH. It would be quite logical that the ancient Hebrews would end a prayer (that opened calling upon the Father) by using a name for the Mother-Aum, just as Hindus do, thus misleading the Egyptians as to the name of their Father God, YHVH.

<http://www.wikipedia.org/wiki/Om>

& *Hinduism Glossary.*

<http://www.hinduism.about.com/library/weekly/extra/bl-glossary-a.htm>

The Egyptian worship of Amun in the Old Kingdom was as a Hidden primordial deity, a great one, who existed, before creation came into being, along with "Nun" the father of the gods; who was the primordial ocean itself. Amun is referred to in Egyptian as the "Hidden, the One Alone, whose body are Millions,"..."O You, the Great God, Whose Name is Unknown" and "Enduring *in* All things." The Primordial Amun, later became Amun-Re, the sun, "living flame who came forth from Nun," which then in turn became one title of pharaohs, as the central or "sun" king. (Assmann. *The Papyrus Leiden* 3292, 1995, p. 128,133)

<http://www.sofiatopia.org/maat/amun.htm>

Perhaps this similarity arose and became incorporated into the Egyptian theology in prehistoric times when the Hebrew tradition was still only a verbal one. YHVH foresaw that the self driven chaos of Egyptian society would generate an immense number of deities, with followers all believing that promoting their particular philosophy was a way to salvation in the afterlife. He commanded the faithful to keep secret His name, first given to them in prehistoric times, so it would not be lost in the confusion or twisted just as Amen/Aum/Om, the prayer closing mention of the Mother-sustainer was mistakenly transformed, by the Egyptians, into a masculine supreme deity whose meaning and image was "hidden" from them. But the reference to Amun in the OT cannot be mistaken if the entire eighth chapter of Proverbs is read with the Hebrew words present for comparison.

> "It is said in Prov. 8:22 YHWH possessed me wisdom *rasit,* but not *b rasit* which it ought to be to justify our vulgar translation which is The Lord possessed me IN the beginning. The particle (which is) the sign of the ablative case is wanting, but it is interpolated in our translation to justify the rendering, because it would be nonsense to say the Lord possessed me the beginning." Higgins, Godfrey. *Anacalypsis,* p. 134, 255, 764, 228 Note the online page numbering it is not the same as the hard copy.

FALSE GODS VS. YHVH'S ELOHIM

> "Thus you shall say unto them; The Elohim that have *not* made heavens and the earth, even they shall perish from the earth, and from under these heavens." Jer. 10:11

This verse, where the Bible mentions the Elohim, shows that the false gods were not necessarily all inanimate idols, some were capable of being spoken to and understanding. Unlike these false gods, however, YHVH's Elohim were never called to by name, so as to avoid the worship of any individual, and also to show that their unity in YHVH was the source of their power, so they were always simply referred to as YHVH Elohim, or that is, YHVH's gods.

> "Not he shall become to you other Elohim before my face!" Ex. 20:2

> ("Thou shalt have no other gods before me!" KJV)

Why would YHVH need to worry if false gods were all just inanimate idols? Apparently these false Elohim communicated with earthlings, just as YHVH's Elohim did, in attempts to win followers into their religions and spiritual domains. Just as various teachers, prophets and gurus (which means teacher) still try to establish themselves in recent times as authorities. They do so by creating new denominations, dividing religion, in a bid to acquire power over the minds of earthlings and seek to entice followers (and revenue) among those seeking to follow a less than ethical and loving way of living in oneness, in their pursuit of the fulfillment of some self driven desire for power and glory. Instead let us all reclaim our understanding of the beginnings of religion when it was still one under YHVH's infinite order throughout His universe.

These followers of earthly religions and their "gods" eventually end up trapped in the lower spiritual realms near earth or even in hells peopled by dark evil spirits in chaos, (known as demons) possessing or "reincarnating" in mortals in an attempt to enjoy some earthly addiction. This happens when a lack of connection with YHVH's Elohim cuts them off from traversing the Heavens in the chariots of the Elohim (now often called starships or UFOs when sighted) with other godlike companions who give up everything to serve YHVH and work for all.

According to the Bible Abraham was tested by the request of an Elohim to sacrifice his son Isaac, then YHVH's messenger from on high in the heavens counsels him, "You must not be stretching forth your hand to the lad, and you must not be doing aught to him." Gen. 22:1-12 That the Elohim who ordered the sacrifice was a false Elohim (mistakenly taken to be 'God'), attempting to mislead Abraham, is shown by the following statutes one from Deu. 12:31 "You shall not do so to YHVH Elohim of you, every abhorrence of which YHVH hates, that they do for their (false) Elohim, moreover they are burning their sons and daughters in fire to their Elohim." And the next concerning false priests claiming to be representatives of a temple of YHVH (see Jer. 7:8&21-23) who later also tried to justify the practice of sacrificing children to YHVH. (2 Kings 17:16-17) The references to these false priests include; "They set their abominations in the house which is called by My name, defiling it. And they have built the high place of Topheth in the ravine of Ben Hinnom to burn their sons and daughters in fire, *which not I instructed* nor which came into my heart." Jer. 7:3

Without distinguishing which parts of the OT resulted from the efforts of these false priests and scribes, in the "house called by YHVH's name" it is not possible to correctly understand the OT, and distinguish that parts of it were included by them to mislead followers. Consequently everyone thereafter is subject to falling into the same trap, that is, unless there is serious study rather than blind acceptance that every word of the Bible was guided by YHVH, they fail to understand that a little knowledge is a dangerous thing and a grain of truth can sometimes be used to deceive.

While it is important that we rediscover the written evidence of YHVH's council of Elohim, this is not to say that there were not also many false self-assuming earth gods and goddesses who were NOT true servants of YHVH, who are also mentioned in biblical texts including the before mentioned; Baal-Ghad in; Judges 2:11-13, Chemosh Judges 11:24 ; 1Kings 18:18; 2Kings 10:28; Jer. 7:9; Apis Jer. 46:15; Milcom Jer; 49:1-3; Dagon aka Oannes in; Judges 16:23; Molech; 2Kings 23:1. Tammuz is a title meaning "the True Son" (Hooke, S.H. *Babylonian and Assyrian Religion*, p. 22. Tammuz was also known as Usir/Asari/Asher. (Inman, Thomas M.D., *Ancient Pagan and Modern Christian Symbolism*, p. 12) Assyria was named after Ashur or Assur (see Ashur *"Encyclopedia of Religion*, p. 461), and the chief race of Norse gods was the Aesir.

"A parallelism can be established between the story of Marduck, also called Asari (Arnott, W. Muss. *Dictionary of Assyrian Language* Vol. 2, p. 587) and Osiris...the myth of Osiris so far as the incidents of the death and resurrection are concerned, is parallel to the myth of Marduk or Asari, who is equated in the late period to Ashur. If myth and ritual in this particular coincided in Egypt and Assyria, there is a *prima facie* case for assuming that a common origin must be sought for in both myth and ritual in the two countries." Smith, Sidney. *Early History of Assyria*, p. 125.

The original Egyptian spelling of the Egyptian God Asher is Ausar or Asar. (Budge, Wallis. *Egyptian Language*, p. 52) This is the correct Egyptian spelling of the Greek transliteration, Osiris. (Jordan, Michael. *Myths of the World*, p. 236) He was known also as the son of God-Nimrod husband of Ishtar/Semiramis. Ezek. 8:14; Jer. 32:35

While some may find it a strange coincidence that there were so many saviors who were resurrected, when seen from the vantage point of their time it is no coincidence. The Church fathers made sure to incorporate the resurrection story into the NT precisely because it was so popular among the general populace (for a long time prior to the time), when the decision was made by the council of bishops of Nicea to include them in the books of the NT.

EASTER

Ashtaroth appears in 1Kings 11:5,33; Exodus 34:13; Deu. 7:5; 12:2-4; 16:2. Ashtareth/Ashtaroth/Asherah, is also known also as Astarte/Eostre/Easter/Ishtar aka Isis, the original Egyptian spelling was *st* or *ast*. (Isis of Egypt, was Ishtar, Astarte or Ashtaroth in Assyria. (Jordan, M. *Encyclopedia of Gods*, p. 29-30) "The Greeks altered the pronunciation to yield the now familiar Isis." Monaghar, Patricia. *The Book of Goddesses and Heroines*, p. 177.

> "They praise the virgin with hymns in the Arab language and call her Chaamu-that is, Core, or virgin-in Arabic. 22,11 "The Panarion of Epiphanius of Salamis," translated by Frank Williams. An ancient name for Isis is Meri,...Mary." Monaghar, P. *The Book of Goddesses and Heroines*, p. 235.

It is from Ashtaroth/Istar/Easter that we derive the modern springtime holiday of resurrection, Easter. This spring festival was held for thousands of years, prior to the birth of Yeschu/Joshu/Jesus, to celebrate the resurrection of Asher/Ausar/Osiris, whose birth was celebrated on December twenty fifth.

> "One of the most persistent themes in the world's mythologies is that of death and resurrection....There is incontrovertible evidence that more or less identical themes to those central to the Christian story were known to audiences in the ancient Near East, at least two thousand years before the birth of Christ." Jordan, Michael. *Myths of the World*, p. 223.

> "Saviors unnumbered have died for the sins of man and by the hands of man ...Among those connected historically or allegorically with a crucifixion are Prometheus, Adonis, Apollo, Atys, Bacchus, Buddha, Christna, Horus, Indra, Ixion, Mithras, Osiris, Pythagoras, Quetzalcoatl, Semiramis and Jupiter." Hall, Manly P. *The Secret Teachings of All Ages*, p. clxxxiii.

Osiris-Ashur and Isis-Ashtaroth played the role in the New Year festival Dec. 25 of the dying god of the old year, resurrected in the earth mother, with the return of light and life, new growth of vegetation etc. that came with the return of the sun from the underworld. Gray, John. *Near Eastern Mythology* p. 25-58; Burney, Charles. *The Ancient Near East* p.158. & Casson, Lionel. *Ancient Egypt,* p. 184.

THE KRST

The name *Krst* was inscribed on the Palermo stone, now in the Palermo museum, deposited in the tomb of a pharaoh more than a thousand years before the New Testament was written. "Horus was known as the Gracious Child, the Fisher, the Lamb, the lily, the word made flesh, the Krst, the word made truth, he came to fulfill the law." Bishop Theodoret, in the fifth century, confirmed that Jesus was not one of the "Krist" though others of his time were. Drake, W. Raymond. *Gods and Spacemen in the Ancient East, pp.* 126-7, quoting, Gerald Massey, *The Egyptian Book of the Dead and the Mysteries of Amenti.* Bushby, Tony. *The Bible Fraud,* 2001, p. 58. & Bryant, Jacob. *Facts and Speculation on the Origin and History of the Christian Church,* London, 1793.

As mentioned before it does not in any way detract from respect for Yeschu/Joshu/Jesus that so many of the preexistent myths were adopted when compiling the books of the NT. Three centuries after his death it is easy to imagine that Constantine's bishops must have had in their (hand-written) stories many which had become confused with the other stories of various Kristes and Saviors which abounded in those times.

If anyone is in doubt about the arbitrary inclusion in the New Testament, of the most popular myths of ancient times, consider the following evidence. In Egyptian mythology a being known as The Virgin Meri, or the Immaculate Holy Isis (Greek for the Egyptian Ast-Astaroth), has titles which include; Queen of Heaven, Lady of Love. She conceived of God (that is of the god, Osiris, Greek for the Egyptian Asher) she was known as the Mother of God, Hor/Horus, who was known as "the alone begotten Son of the Lord," he sits in heaven on the right hand of God, Lord of the earth. This god of the Egyptians was born again and now is one with God. Does any of this sound familiar?

Citations include; Drake, W. Raymond. *Gods and Spacemen in the Ancient East,* p. 126-7, quoting; Massey, Gerald. *The Egyptian Book of the Dead and the Mysteries of Amenti;* Drohan, Francis Burke. *Jesus Who? The Greatest Mystery Never Told,* pp. 83,84,89&95. Allegro, John. *Dead Sea Scrolls and the Christian Myth,* p. 156; Monaghar, Patricia. *The Book of Goddesses and Heroines,* p.109&235; Grey, John. *Near Eastern Mythology,* p. 31-32; Friedrich, Johannes. *Extinct Languages,* p. 161; Mead, G.R.S. *Did Jesus Live 100 years BC?,* p. 410-411; Mead, G.R.S. *Fragments of a Faith Forgotten,* p. 58 ; Sloane, T.W. *Bible Myths and Their Parallels in Other Religions,* p.364.

Isis brought forth her child, Hor/Horus, on a bed of reeds, after being unable to find accommodations in the town of Teb. As a child, when Horus is lost, he is found by his mother in the temple, teaching the priests. God the Savior, Osiris, known to be born at the winter solstice

(Dec. 25) was resurrected in the spring at Easter, thousands of years before the birth of Yeschu/Joshu/Jesus." (ibid.)

Respecting the celebration we call Easter,-the festival in fact of the Goddess Eostre or the Sidonian Asteroth or Astarte...The whole of the ancient Gentile and Druidical ceremonies of Easter or the Saxon Goddess Ostrt, or Eostre {from whence we get the words "east" and "estrus"} of the Germans, is yet continued over all the Christian world. This festival began with a week's indulgence in all kinds of sports (and feasting), called the carne-vale, or the taking a farewell to animal food, because it was followed by a fast of 40 days." Higgins, Godfrey. Vol. 2 *Anacalypsis,* p. 58-59.

The Egyptian demotic form of the ankh (symbol of life and resurrection) was a crucifix, before the New Testament story of Christ was ever written. (Friedrich, Johannes. *Extinct Languages,* p. 160) The ankh appears to be employed by the divinities to awaken the dead to a new life. The 12th dynasty bas-relief shows the goddess Anukit holding the ankh to the nostrils of pharaoh Usertesen III. The handled cross thus signifies resurrection and precedes the Christian cross symbolizing the same.

> "The crucifix-style cross used by the Christian Church was an ancient Egyptian hieroglyph...meaning – savior." Knight, Christopher & R. Lomas. *The Hiram Key.* p. 24-242

Bishop Augustine, dedicated himself as "a servant of Isis, not Mary." The divine motherhood of Mary was first decided at the third Council of the Church at Ephesus in 431 AD. The proposal that she be posthumously accorded the status of Mother of God, was resisted by Nestorius the Patriarch of Constantinople, and his followers, he said; "Let no one call Mary the mother of God...for Mary was but human." (Augustine, *City of God,* & Edward Gibbon, *History of the Decline and Fall of the Roman Empire,* 1994 ed. p. 986.

CHRISTMAS

> "Do not be dismayed at the signs of heavens, as the nations are from them. The statutes of the people are vain, he that cuts a tree from the woods, the deed of the craftsman and axe. He makes it lovely with silver and gold nailing it in place..." Jer. 10:3-4

According to Godfrey Higgins, Tertullian, Jerome, and other fathers of the church, informed us, that the Gentiles celebrated, on the 25th of December, the birth of the God Sol, under the name of Adonis. In Persia he was Mithra; in Egypt, Phoenicia and Biblis, Adonis. The Persians called the night of December 24th, the Night of Light. At the first moment after midnight of 24th of December, all the nations of the earth, by common consent, celebrated the accouchement of the Queen of Heaven, of the Celestial Virgin of the sphere, and the birth of the God Sol, the infant Orus {Horus} the God of the Day. The Chaldean name of the sun is <u>*Chris*</u> (Horus is previously mentioned to have been called *krst* and like the sun also meant machinator, meaning the material light or plastic formative power. Higgins, Godfrey. Vol. 2 *Anacalypsis,* pp. 587,758 Vol. 1 98,99,102.

He presents further evidence that the Egyptians celebrated the birth of the son of Isis on the 25 of December, Osiris was born on the 25th of December and on the 25th of March, exactly three months from his birth his resurrection from the dead was celebrated. On the same day, in Persia the triumph of the Good over the Evil principle took place, the triumph of the victory of Light over Darkness, of Oromasdes {Ormazd/Hormazd} over Ahriman the spirit of evil. At the same time in Egypt, Phrygia, Syria, were celebrated the deaths and resurrections of Osiris, Atys, and Adonis. "The identity (not the similarity merely) of the systems of Christianity and the systems of the ancient Persians, and other worshipers of the God Sol, must be admitted, indeed cannot be denied." Higgins, Godfrey. Vol. 2 *Anacalypsis,* pp. 587, 758; Vol. 1 - 98, 99, 102.

Higgins goes on to tell us that Josephus gives the name of the Essenes as Esseni, Epiphanius, the Bishop of Salamis changed Essaei into Issaei. Was it that Epiphanius knew of an ancient tradition which declared that Jesus himself had been an Essene, and that the Church Fathers wished to safeguard the doctrinal tradition stereotyped by the ecumenical decisions at Nicaea. The very early Codex Marcianus 125, has enabled us to correct much of this "emendation" by the church, the following is one of the censured passages;

> "(quoting Epiphanius) The Savior was born...on the sixth day of January after 13 days of the winter solstice...This day (of the solstice) the Greeks...celebrate on the 25th day of December, ...called Saturnalia among the Romans, Kronia...(by the Greeks), among the Egyptians (or the Alexandrians)... Kikellia,...after they have kept all-night vigil...they descend with lights into an underground crypt, and carry up a wooden image...with the seal of a cross made in gold on its forehead, and on either hand two similar seals, and on both knees (feet?) two others...And if they are asked the meaning of this mystery, they answer and say: "Today at this hour the Maiden (Kore - meaning virgin[13]), ...the Virgin, gave birth to the aeon...Dusares (Ausares-Osiris, see Mercatante, Anthony. *Who's Who in Egyptian Mythology,* p. 17) that is, Alone-begotten (*monogenes*) of the Lord." ...Here we have a definite statement that one of the most widespread mystic festivals of the ancients was connected with a rite of resurrection. The temple of Kore is the temple of Isis, who is called in Trismegistic literature the World Maiden." Mead, G. R. S. *Did Jesus Live 100 Years BC,* pp. 104,135-138,177,256,334,335,408 &410.

[13]"They praise the virgin with hymns in the Arab language and call her Chaamu-that is, Core, or virgin-in Arabic." An ancient name for Isis is Meri, pronounced the same as Mary. It is easy to see why some early Christians were anxious to adopt the Christmas myth as their own, it must have seemed predestined since Yeschu/Joshu/Jesus mother's name was so similar." Frank Williams, translation of; *The Panarion of Epiphanius of Salamis*, p. 22,11. Monaghar, P. *The Book of Goddesses and Heroines*, p. 235.

> "December 25th seems to have been chosen on account of the Roman custom of keeping this day as the festival of Sol Invictus - i.e. the rebirth of the sun; it was judged fitting to substitute for the pagan feast a Christian one commemorating the birth of the true Sun of the world and Redeemer of mankind." *Pagan Sun Worship and Catholicism Celebrating The Birth of the Sun.*

<http://www.aloha.net/~mikesch/xmas.htm>

Hanukkah occupies an intermediate position between the Jewish seasonal festivals and the occasional rituals, namely, the Feast of Dedication. The reason for describing it as occupying an intermediate position is based, first on its date, since it falls at the time of the winter solstice. Also known as the feast of Lights, there appears to have been a festival in Canaan, of a dedicatory nature, containing the main features of the New year ritual. Such a ritual might well have constituted the archetype for the dedicatory rituals in Canaan, and the dedication of Solomon's temple may have presented features, now obliterated by the editorial process, borrowed from the Canaanite archetype. Hooke, S. H. *The Origins of Early Semitic Ritual,* p. 60.

Chapter Four

THE CHARIOTS OF THE ELOHIM-STARSHIP CARRIERS[1]

"The vehicle (given as chariot SHD 4817 but which actually in this case is *rkb* SHD 7392-3 a much more generic word meaning a ride or vehicle) of Elohim are tens of thousands of thousands, *shnan* (repeated i.e. times tens of thousands of thousands more) Adonai (my Lord) is in them." Ps. 68:17 [1](to ride or carry[2] ; chariot, car, cart and carrier all derive from the same root word "carry." Thorndike Barnhart Comprehensive Desk Dictionary")

[2] Carry in Hebrew is *cabab* (SHD 5437 &5445) a primitive root; meaning to revolve, surround.

THE RIDES OF THE ELOHIM

This chapter will include information on many of the most famous verses that describe the vehicles traversing the skies, that are discussed in the Bible. The Hebrew word *Merkabah*, actually means "to ride" (just as modern slang calls a car someone's 'ride'); it has been interpreted as "chariot," "throne chariot" or "cloud chariot," it has cognates in Ugaritic and several other Semitic languages. It refers to these chariots or carriers of the gods or to the throne chariot of the one Eloah [3] leading the rest of YHVH's Elohim, the central carrier/chariot. ([3] Not to be confused with YHVH, The Infinite and Omnipresent One who is All in all His Elohim, 1 Cor. 15:28, *YHVH Al Olam*, the Great Holy Spirit of the Living Universe.)

It is used in Ezekiel 1:4-26, and Ezekiel chapter ten describes in detail a man, clothed in linen, who after marking all the righteous men, goes in between the wheels of the Cherubim; after he goes out again, the Cherubim rise up shedding light over the courtyard below while rising over the house, and making such a great rushing noise, that it could be heard beyond the courtyard. (Ez. 10:4-5)

There are too many references within the book of Ezekiel to mention them all but if the reader is not already familiar with them it is worth anyone's time to read Ezekiel. "And their appearance and their work was as it were a wheel within a wheel...and they were full of eyes like burning coals of fire." This description resembles modern accounts of round disk-shaped objects ringed by lights. (Ezek. 1:5-28, 9:3, 10,1-, 11:22)

Cherubim were placed at the entrance of paradise, guarding it after the Adam were expelled from the garden of Eden. In Genesis (3:24) they are described as having two whirling swords ("the ones turning themselves") a description that might resemble propellers of some sort. Therefore, because of the swords, the Cherubim have been described as the first created objects or artifacts in the universe. In light of the interpretation of the Creation story given in this book that would of course mean they were the first artificial or mechanical objects seen on *this* planet. (Tanne debe Eliyahu R., i. beginning) Jewishencyclopecia.com *Cherubim.*

<http://www.jewishencyclopedia.com/view.jsp?artid=434&letter=C&search=Cherubim>

The online Jewish Encyclopedia site above says that "In the early days of Israel's history the cherubim became the divine chariot." However, because the cherubim stationed at the Garden of Eden had whirling swords, it is possible to view them as artificial or mechanical objects from the very beginning of Genesis.

It may be that those reading about and transcribing the text, as opposed to the original picture intended, were not able to grasp the picture completely, and changed the text to agree with their own understanding, thus over time anthropomorphized the "chariots of the cherubim." The ancient religions were prone to anthropomorphizing any object they did not understand into "gods" etc. for example turning the sun, moon, stars, wind, etc. into gods.

There are many references to the chariots of the Elohim in Hebrew data in, I Chr. 28:18, they are referred to as; "The chariots of the cherubim, that spread out their wings, and covered the Ark of the Covenant of YHVH." That they are described as "chariots" shows that they were not winged human-like creatures, but rather vehicles, capable of carrying beings. Higgins work in this area bears repeating at this point.

> "The text of Isaiah, if correctly translated, means, that above the throne stood winged serpents; for seraph, translated, is serpent. It is only written, in our translation, in the Hebrew word *seraph* to disguise the word serpent, which our priests did not like...Serpents are constantly seen on the Egyptian monuments...The word Cherub originally meant, and yet sometimes means, serpent... It is a compound word, formed of kr, circle and aub, serpent: in short, a circled or circular serpent or serpent with its tail in its mouth-krub. It was probably the first sacred emblem ever used, whence all such emblematical figures came to be called Cherubs; and this accounts for learned men having made them out to be of many different figures." Higgins, Godfrey. Vol. 1 *Anacalypsis*, p.120, 523, 784 & 792. Note that the page numbers of the hard copy are different from the online version @ google books. For further definitions see also the following reference link.@ Etymology online under Seraphim.

> <http://www.etymonline.com/index.php?search=seraphim&searchmode=none>

> *Seraphim* are mentioned by Isaiah as being on either side of the throne chariot of the Elohim. The "Online Etymology Dictionary" also makes an association between the Seraphim (SHD 8313 & 8314) which also can mean fiery flying serpents, and Cherubim, saying, "the word seems to have some etymological sense of flying."

Isaiah discusses what we might now call rocket ships, because of their long arrow like shape, with tails of fire at the aft. This "serpent" imagery could easily have been an archaic interpretation of Isaiah's original attempt to depict a rocket, with two sets of wings to the fore and two to the aft, and the upright tail at the foot (seen as wings covering the feet) just as our space shuttle has for stability.

> "In the year that King Uziah died I saw Adonai sitting upon the throne and his train filled the temple. Above it stood the seraphim; each had six wing, with two he covered his face, and with two he covered his feet, and with two he did fly." Isa. 6:1-2

"Arise, your light has come and the glory of YHWH, He is radiant upon you...Who are these who fly along like thick clouds (*kob*)?" Isa.60:1-8

Ezekiel and many other accounts throughout the Bible begin with a description of the appearance of a cloud, often large and dark, full of flashing lights, within are various glittering or metallic objects, and thunder and lightning. A variety of clouds followed the Israelites for forty years throughout the wilderness. The number of cloud references throughout the OT are too many to quote them all but anyone can find them by doing a search for cloud on; <http://www.ebible.com/>

"The glory of YHWH settled on Mt. Sinai. For six days the cloud covered the mountain, and on the seventh day YHWH called to Moses from within the cloud. " Ex. 24:16

Lenticular clouds often form above mountain tops, and according to the OT it was a cloud that formed above Mt. Sinai up into which Moses went, to receive the Ten Commandments. Within Judaism, the *Shekina*[4] (or "visible" cloud of the Presence) is so called because it is, at times, the visible dwelling place of YHVH Elohim. ([4]from SHD 7935 dwell) Remember that it was a pillar of cloud, *omud eonn* (Deu. 31:15 also called in Hebrew *tiymarah* SHD 8490) that preceded the Israelites by day (Ex. 13:21-22); their instructions were to stay when it covered the tabernacle and the altar, and travel onward when it rose up. (Ex. 40:38) (Num.9:21)

"I am going to come to you in a dense cloud, so that the people will hear me speaking to you and will always believe you." Ex. 19:9

Not everyone has spiritual abilities, sometimes called psychic sight or clairvoyance. So YHVH Elohim sometimes uses clouds as a sign to guide those who became His chosen (because they chose Him by revering all life and practicing oneness). These visible signs from YHVH Elohim include pillars of whirling columns of cloud, lenticular clouds, dramatic dark clouds full of various colors of lights, and clouds with any specific shape having meaning, such as human-like, or of recognizable symbols, etc.

"YHVH Elohim you are exceedingly great, clothed in splendor and honor. Wrapped in *aur* (light[5])...the One placing thick cloud chariot (*rkubu*) going on wings of wind. The One making the *ruach* (spirit or wind) His messenger, and His ministers a flaming fire." Ps. 104:1-3 [5]Note that the Hebrew word for "light" is masculine while the Hebrew word for "spirit" is feminine. *The Gospel of Philip.* verse 30.

<http://www.metalog.org/files/philip.html>

Given the prevalence of lenticular clouds seen in religious paintings down through the ages (see for examples; UFOs *In Earth's History.* <http://www.crystalinks.com/ufohistory.html>) the cloud imagery combined with round hollow, smoking, flying objects, possibly enveloped in a cloud, calls to mind many descriptions of UFOs reported in modern times. Following are some URLs having especially dramatic pictures.

<http://www.greatdreams.com/circles.gif> <http://www.ufocasebook.com/diazlarge.jpg>

<http://www.flatrock.org.nz/topics/photographs/squarely_in_wellington.htm>

<http://www.jach.hawaii.edu/UKIRT/public/images/telescope/lent_cloud2.jpg>

> "And He is descending, YHWH in cloud and He is stationing himself there and calling in the name of YHWH." Ex. 34:5

If YHVH and His Elohim are beings of pure light or energy, it is reasonable to suppose that, just as any object carrying a charge will do, their presence would attract a cloud. This phenomena can be seen occasionally around the tails of jet planes, were a lenticular cloud forms behind the jet, looking as though the lenticular cloud is standing on edge and the jet is coming out of its center. Some photos of these phenomena can be seen at the links below.

<http://users.hfx.eastlink.ca/~sryan/flying.html>
<http://www.arachnoid.com/alaska2005/air_water.html>

Remember also that according to the OT it was a flying smoking furnace (*thnur oshn*) that came down to Abraham during his sacrifice in (Gen. 15:17) (see also SHD 3565) This Hebrew phrase, "*thnur oshn,*" is very similar to the following place name *Kr - ashan, Kor- oshn or Khor-oshan.* (SHD 3565) *Kowr`Ashan* kore aw-shawn' from (SHD 3564 and 6227); meaning furnace of smoke; Cor-Ashan, a place in Palestine:--Chor-ashan (Qotayba b. was Moslem governor of Khorasan, in 73/712, (first mentioned in the *Avesta,* attributed to Zarathustra). *Afrighid Dynasty.* <http://www.iranicaonline.org/articles/afrighid-dynasty>

Khwarezm, also known as Chorasmia, bordered Khorasan on the north. "Many Scholars believe Khwarezm to be what ancient Avestic texts refer to as "*Ariyaneh Waeje*" or "Aryan/Iran vij." These sources claim that Old Urgench, which was the capital of ancient Khwarezm for many years, was actually "Ourva" the eighth land of Ahura Mazda mentioned in the Pahlavi text of the [5]Vendidad. Wikipedia, article on Khwarezm at; <http://www.en.wikipedia.org/wiki/Khwarezm> citing Musa Javan. Bastan, Tarikh-i Ijtima'i Iran-i. *The Social History of Iran,* 1961, p. 24.

C. E. Bosworth believes the first part of the name Chorasmia to be made up of a root meaning "the sun" and the last part of a root meaning "earth" (i.e., land, MHJ). Wikipedia. *Khwarezm.* citing Bosworth, C. E. *Encyclopedia of Islam,* Vol. IV, 1978. p. 1061.

<http://en.wikipedia.org/wiki/Wwiki/Khwarezm>

[5]This would be in very close accord with the understanding of the root Aur/Hor/Or meaning light in Hebrew and many other ancient languages, more on these words for light in a following section on YHVH's Light/Aur/Hor/Or.

> "And to them which were in Hormah, and to them which were in Chor-ashan..." I Sam. 30:30 (Note that both of these place names employ the root Hor, Chor or Khor, i.e. sun or sunlight, therefore this could easily be considered as a cognate of *Aur* or light in Hebrew. MHJ) Kaviani, Khodadad, *Zartosht & Zoroastrianism, Season Calandar.*

> <http://www.rozanehmagazine.com/allariclesII/akhodiMJ02.html>

Let us consider the first part of this place name, *Kr* this is the same as the first part of the word cherub - *kr-ub*. The image of a flying smoking furnace fits very well with many modern sightings, especially when it is remembered that these furnaces were *round* vessels. If this *kr,* is one half of the meaning of *krub* or Cherub, then combined with *ub/oob/awb/uwb*, a dark cloud SHD 5743 etc., we have the imagery of a round flying vessel, smoking or obscured in a cloud.

THE CHARIOTS OF THE CHERUBIM

> "The chariots of the cherubim that spread out their wings, and covered the Ark of the Covenant of YHWH." Chr. 28:18

The word Cherub, according to the online Strong's Hebrew Lexicon, is "of uncertain derivation." (SHD 3742) As well as Higgins analysis seems to fit with the flying association between Cherubim and Seraphim, it may be that through association with imagery from the Egyptian and Middle Eastern religious symbols, "cherubim" came to be synonymous with "flying serpents" sometimes depicted in Egypt carrying a human on their back and later still evolved into winged humanoids. West, John Anthony. *Serpent in the Sky.* (cover picture)

<http://books.google.com/books/about/The_Serpent_in_the_Sky.html?id=0S1qpP7By9IC>

& Ryan, Patrick C. *The Animals of Creation.*

<http://www.mega.nu/protolanguage/proto-religion/animals-of-creation.htm>

However, it may be that, earlier than all this, the original meaning was closer to the round flying smoking furnace surrounded by cloud, that are described in the writings about Abraham (Gen. 15:17) and this may account for in the mention of the smoking limekiln analogy in the story of the visitation to Mt. Sinai. (Ex. 19:18)

> "What do angels and cabbages have in common? Well they both share the Hebrew word *kruv*, Jastrow...says they share a common root...the shared etymology "round" Balashon – Hebrew Language Detective. *Kruv.* <http://www.balashon.com/2007/07/kruv.html>

So the following breakdowns of the word "cherub" warrant some further consideration; (SHD 3564) *kuwr koor* from an unused root meaning; a pot or furnace (as if excavated):--furnace. (SHD 37340) *kor kore* from the same as 3564; properly, a deep *round* vessel. Remember also that carry, the meaning of chariot, *rkb* (SHD 5437&5445) in Hebrew is *cabab* (SHD 5437) a primitive root; which also means to revolve, surround.

Combine those definitions for the first part of *krub, kr,* with those for the last part of the word cherub, *ub;* (SHD 5743) *`uwb oob* a primitive root; to be dense or dark, i.e. to becloud:--cover with a cloud; (SHD 5645) *`ab awb* (masculine and feminine); from (SHD 574); properly, an envelope, i.e. darkness (or density II Chr. 4:17) specifically, a (scud) cloud; (thick) cloud. Here we have a round, perhaps dark cloud, like the lenticular clouds so frequently identified with modern UFOs.

> "You came near and stood at the foot of the mountain while it blazed with fire to the very heavens, with black clouds and deep darkness." Deu. 4:11 (to see a picture of such a cloud go to <http://www.ufocasebook.com/diazlarge.jpg>)

> "He made darkness his secret place: His pavilions round about Him were dark waters and

thick clouds of the skies." Ps. 18:11

"Clouds and darkness are around about Him: righteousness and judgment are the habitation of His throne." Ps. 97:2

The Catholic Encyclopedia discusses the word cherub in section I "In Philology" mentioning that, "A similar metathesis and play upon sound undoubtedly exists between *Kerub* and *Rakab*, "to ride" and *Merkaba,* "chariot."" Notice the similarity of the Hebrew spelling of chariot *mrkb,* and cherub *kr-ub* (also *rkb* SHD 7392 ride) it seems reasonable to suggest that there was an association in the minds of the ancients since these cherubs and chariots have been used inter-changeably as in Chr. 28:18.

"The chariots of the cherubim that spread out their wings, and covered the Ark of the Covenant of YHWH." I Chr. 28:18

While the Cherubim on the ark are described in later parts of the OT (I Kings 6:23-28; 8:6-7; II Chr. 3:7 & 10-13) as having their wings meet to touch each others, those in Solomon's temple are described as having their wings outstretched (after the manner of airplanes or the space shuttle).

"After that he took the Testimony and put it into the Ark." Ex. 40:20 "Take this scroll[6] of the law, and put "in the side" (inside) of the Ark of the Covenant of YHVH Elohim, that it be there as a testimony." Deu. 31:26 [6]This verse specifically mentions a "scroll" not the same as the stone tablets of the Ten Commandments.

The mercy seat was placed atop the ark of the testimony, inside of which the written record was kept. Since written records were kept inside the Ark of the Covenant, it is hard to understand how anyone could imagine this ark to be a radio or a battery as has been illogically suggested by some. (Although there *is* a written reference in the OT to Moses making a burning serpent on a pole in Num. 21:8, so that the Israelites could see serpents and not get bitten "the ones being bitten, he sees him and he lives..." this may refer to a copy of what appears to be lights displayed on many walls of Egyptian temples, called in the OT, *Nehustan*, conversely it may only be some kind of brass or copper, oil burning lamp.) Its destruction is described in II Kings 18:4. Dörnenburg, Frank. *Electric Lights in Egypt?*

<http://www.world-mysteries.com/sar_lights_fd1.htm>

"And you shall make two cherubim of gold, of beaten work shall you make them, in the two ends of the mercy seat." Ex. 25:18

This seat is described as having two cherubim, one on either end, and according to the OT Moses sat between them to consult with YHVH and His Elohim. As pointed out before their is every possibility that the word *cherub* only later came to mean an angel or a chubby baby with wings. The cherub on the ark may be fiery winged "serpents" that is, long and cigar shaped, or round, circular, smoking, flying objects but either way they are definitely referred to as the chariots of the cherubim in I Chr. 28:18. The circular serpents are described elsewhere, outside of the Bible, as having their tail in their mouth. That they were not humanoid is further shown by the fact that according to the OT Moses was told to make the cherubim on the ark after a pattern that he was shown while he was up on the mountain, receiving the law. (The Ten Commandments)

"And you shall make one cherub on one end and one cherub on the other end, even of the mercy seat shall you make the cherubim on the two ends thereof...And I will meet with you and I will commune with you from above the mercy seat, which (is) upon the ark of the testimony...(then discussing everything he was to make) And see that you make them after the *pattern,* which was showed you on the mountain." Ex. 25:18&40

This verse shows that they were not angels or babies with wings, for humans or babies would not be described as a pattern, the Elohim would have said have said something to the effect that he was to make them look human-like with wings, if that were the true definition of a cherubim. The phrase "who sittest upon the Cherubim" occurs in, Sam. 4:4, II Sam. 6:2, II Kings 19, Isa. 37:37, Ps. 79:2 &98:1. If the definition of flying youths or babies were accurate this would create a most undignified image of an anthropomorphized YHVH or Eloah sitting upon another person. Surely since they are the more powerful beings they would not need lesser beings to carry them around.

I Samuel 4:4 calls the ark by two different names; "So the people sent to Shiloh and carried from there the Ark of the Covenant of YHVH of hosts, *who is sitting upon the chariots*. And the two sons of Eli, were there with the Ark of the Covenant of the Elohim namely, Hophni and Phinehas...And when the Ark of the Covenant of YHVH came into the camp, all the people shouted with a great shout...And when the Philistines heard...they were afraid, for they said;...who shall deliver us out of the hand of the Elohim, *the noble ones,* these are the Elohim who smote the Egyptians." Now the fact that they referred to the Elohim, calling them the noble ones, plural, shows that even the Philistines knew that YHVH, in Himself, comprised the unity of all His Elohim.

> "And He rode upon a cherub and He is flying and He is swooping on wings of wind. He is setting darkness concealing Him round about a booth of darkness of thick clouds.
>
> "From the brightness in front of Him thick clouds passed hail and embers of fire." II Sam. 22:11
>
> "Behold there appeared a chariot of fire...and Elijah was taken to heaven in a whirlwind." II Kings 2:1
>
> "Then I turned , and lifted up my eyes, and looked and beheld a flying roll[7]. And he said unto me, what do you see? And I answered, I see a flying roll: the length of it is twenty cubits, and the breadth of it ten cubits." Zech. 5:1 [7](*mgle* SHD 4039 *mgillah* a volume, or that is like a scroll, long and cylindrical, as is also reported by some in UFO sightings MHJ)
>
> "It was exalted in the chariots of the Spirit, and the name went forth in the midst of them." Enoch 69:2

In the Dead Sea Scrolls there is also a beautiful passage, referring to a sighting by the Essenes; "The Cherubim praise the vision of the Throne-chariot above the celestial sphere, and they extol the radiance of the fiery firmament beneath the throne of His glory. And the Holy Angels come and go between the whirling wheels, like a fiery vision of most holy spirits; and around them stream rivulets of molten fire, like incandescent bronze, a radiance of many brilliant colors, of exquisite hues gloriously mingled, the Spirits of the living God move in constant accord with the glory of the Wonderful Chariot." The Dead Sea Scrolls were discovered in 1947. (Allegro, 99)

119

The cherubim are also described by Ezekiel as having "chariots" in or on which they rode. "It was Ezekiel who saw the glorious vision, which was showed him upon the chariot of the cherubim." (Sirach 49:8) If a cherub was originally known as a round cloud or disk-shaped object with wings, then rather than winged youths or even the winged griffins speculated by other authors, the cherubim/chariots of the Elohim seem closer to a well known image (called by many names throughout the ancient Middle East); that image is the famous "winged disk" which YHVH mentions as a sign of righteousness in Mal. 4:2. "But unto you that fear of my name shall the Sun (*shmsh* SHD 8121 & 8122) of righteousness arise with healing in his wings." Mal. 4:2 (the one speaking in this verse is YHVH of hosts, see Mal. 4:1) The following verse also mentions their wings." And He rode upon a cherub and did fly: yea, he did fly upon the wings of the wind-*ruach*." Ps. 18:10

Chapter Five

THE STAR THAT TRAVELED ACROSS THE SKY

"Now when Yeschu/Joshu/Jesus was born in Bethlehem of Judaea, in the days of Herod the king, behold there came magos (magi, wise men) from the east, to Jerusalem. Saying; Where is he that is born, King of the Jews? For we saw his star in the east and have come to do him obeisance...When he (Herod) had heard these things...he demanded to know where the Christ should be born. And they said unto him, in Bethlehem of Judaea: "for thus it is written by *the prophet*..." They departed and lo the star, which they saw in the east, *went and stood* over where the young child was. When they saw the star, they rejoiced with exceeding great joy...And being warned of God in a dream that they should not return to Herod, they departed to their own country." Matt. 2:1—12

THE STAR THAT THE ZARATHUSTRIAN MAGI FOLLOWED

This chapter will discuss in depth the history behind the prophet who predicted the appearance of a star at the birth of the expected messiah. Now clearly a real star does not move and certainly not in proximity to some wise men here below who were following it to see where it would lead them. What was it that distinguished these magi as wise men? Was it among other things, that they had been told to expect such an event by a prophet, and if so by what prophet? One obviously important enough to be simply called *the prophet*, as though he were well known to everyone, yet there is no such prophet or prophecy mentioned in the Bible.

Rather than being frightened of such an occurrence, these men were obviously wise enough to know that such a vision was a sign and go and discover its portent. From where did they acquire that wisdom? There is no such prophecy by any prophet in the Bible, yet these wise men knew of some prophet that had foretold such an event and they were obviously under the protection of the Creator since He warned them to depart so as to escape Herod.

This prophecy must certainly, in the view of Christians, lend this mysterious "prophet" some credence and an aura of acceptability, considering how important this event, the birth of Yeschu/Joshu/Jesus was to become to that religion. The three wise men were Magi (*magos*, in Greek, from the *Avestan* word *maga* or *magha*, and from where we derive the word magic[1]) who understood the traditions and followed the teachings of Zoroaster/Zarathustra, the prophet who had foretold just such an event. *Wise Men and Women Still Seek Him Today.*

<http://www.farsinet.com/wisemen/magi.html>

<http://www.scripture4all.org/OnlineInterlinear/Greek_Index.htm>

> "Zoroaster (the name is the Greek transliteration of the Persian Zarathustra, perhaps from Zarath-burning and Ushtra-light, Chatterjee, Jatindra Mohon M. A., *Ethical Conceptions of the Gathas,* p. 7)...the first of the prophets of the world's major religions (is) older than

Moses, Buddha or Confucius." Hinnells, John. *Persian Mythology*, p. 9.

[1] *Earliest Reference Describes Christ as 'Magician'.* "A bowl, dating to between the late 2nd century B.C. and the early 1st century A.D., is engraved with what may be the world's first known reference to Christ. The engraving reads, 'DIA CHRSTOU O GOISTAIS,' which has been interpreted to mean either, 'by Christ the magician' or, 'the magician by Christ.'" (<http://www.nbcnews.com/id/26972493/ns/technology_and_science-science/t/earliest-reference-describes-christ-magician/>) Magos, Magi, Magus, Magavan[2] from Old Persian, a priest of Zarathustra (Zoroaster). The Bible gives us the direction, East and the legend states that the magi-wise men were from Persia (Iran) - Balthasar, Melchior, Caspar - thus being priests of the Zarathustra religion, the mages. (ibid. <http://www.farsinet.com/wisemen/magi.html>) (Assyrian scholars now inform us that they have found the hoary, primitive original of it, of magic, magi and imago, etc. It is from an old Akkadian[3] word, "*imga,*" meaning wise, holy, and learned, and was used as the distinguishing title of their wisest sages, priests, and philosophers, who, as may be supposed, gradually formed a peculiar caste, which merged into the ruling priestly order. Henry O. Wagner/Belle M. Wagner/Thomas H. Burgoyne. *The Light of Egypt, Volume II.* <http://www.fullbooks.com/The-Light-of-Egypt-Volume-II3.html>) [3]Remember Akkadian is a Semitic/Shemitic cuneiform language from about 2400 BCE, adapted from the oldest written language, Sumerian, also cuneiform.

<http://www.orinst.ox.ac.uk/eanes/akkadian_language.html>

[2]"A man or woman who had been saved[4] is a *magavan* (as a member of a Zarathustrian community, a *Maghahya*)... (and) regardless of race, sex, or social status, is the religious equal of every other." [4]Zarathustra was the first in written history to be known as a savior, called in that language, *saosyant.* Rivilo, Oliver P. *The Origins of Christianity.* <http://www.revilo-oliver.com/rpo/RPO_NewChrist/chap9.htm>

> "The apocryphal *Arabic Gospel of the Infancy*, 7:1 says in its account of the Magi that they came to Jerusalem according the prediction of Zoroaster.'" <http://opensiuc.lib.siu.edu/cgi/viewcontent.cgi?article=1904&context=ocj>

> "Magi came from the East to Jerusalem in conformity with *the prophecy of Zoroaster*, and they had with them gifts, gold, frankincense, and myrhh, and they worshiped him (the babe)." (from the *Euangelium Infantiae,* which is to be found in the *Codex Apocryphus Novi Testamenti*[5] edited by Ioannes Carolus Tbilo {Lipsiae, 1832} Vol. I, p.71) [5]A collection of apocryphal writings excluded from the contents of the New Testament. Oliver, Revilo P. *The Origins of Christianity.*
> < http://www.revilo-oliver.com/rpo/RPO_NewChrist/chap9.htm>

> "There is a...famous prophecy[6] of Zeradusht (Zoroaster/Zarathustra) who declared that in the latter day a virgin should conceive and bear a son, and that a star should appear blazing at noon-day...The *Chreestian* (sic) religion...evidently existed from the earliest time; and Jesus Christ was nothing but the ninth *Avatar* coming in his proper order." Higgins, Godfrey. *Anacalypsis,* Vol. 1 p. 190,573 and Vol. 2 p. 368.

> [6]"We worship the guardian spirit of the holy maid (virgin means maid,

Jedhri, who is called the all-conquering, for she will bring him forth who will destroy the malice of the demons and of men." *Sacred book of Zoroaster*

<http://lists.ibiblio.org/pipermail/corpus-paul/20050119/005196.html>

Thus the origins of religions in the Middle East cannot be understood without studying the religion of Zarathustra, the prophet of the oldest monotheistic religion of the area. By association and by his prediction of this important event, the starting point for Christianity, clearly Zarathustra should be recognized and embraced by Christians as having an involvement in the earliest foundation of their religion. For by his prophecy of the birth of Yeschu/Joshu/Jesus he participated in and was motivated by forces emanating from the Creator, albeit called by another name (*Ormazd*[7]) in Zarathustra's time and language.

[7]Historians often use the Zarathustrian name for deity - *Ormazd/Ormuzd/Hormazd* and Ahura mazda synonymously but it will be shown (in a later section on YAHUWAH/YAHU/AHU, that Ahu/Ahura[8] was used to mean lord in Old Persian or Avestan) and that *Ormazd* with the prefix "Or," actually contains a reference to Light (meaning the opposite of darkness or ignorance *Aur or Hor* in Hebrew SHD 215 more in the section following on YHVH's Light); both are coupled with *Mazda*- Wise or Intelligent, therefore *Ormazd* is the Living Intelligent Light, the All Knowing[9] YHVH ([9]*Al Da'at YHVH* as seen in 1 Sam. 2:3). *Madda* in Hebrew, SHD 4093, means intelligence or consciousness: -- knowledge, science, thought; in Sanskrit *Medha*, also means intelligence. (A.V.W. Jackson 1892 had interpreted Mazda instead as a substantive, corresponding with the Vedic feminine noun *medha* "mental vigor, perceptive power, wisdom" and he accordingly rendered Ahura Mazda's name as 'Lord Wisdom'…")

<http://books.google.com/books?id=F3gfAAAAIAAJ&q=mazda#v=snippet&q=mazda&f=false>

[8]"In the Gathas, "*ahura*" is used in four ways. First, it is used to describe *Ahura Mazda*. Second it is used to refer to the aspects of divinity (just as is Elohim, MHJ) (unspecified *amesha spentas*) which are metaphorically called "lords" (Y30.9, Y31.4). Third it is used to describe God's mastery (or lordship) over the divine aspects. Fourth, the words *ahura* (Y29.2 and Y31.10) and *ahu* (Y29.6) are used to refer to the person who is to be pastor of the good vision on this earth. And Zarathustra was chosen for this task (Y29.8)." McIntyre, Dina G. *The Talisman.*

<http://www.zoroastrian.org.uk/vohuman/Article/The%20Talisman.htm>

"This is the number of angels: in all they number three hundred sixty-five. They all worked together until they completed each limb of the psychical and material body. There were other angels over the remaining passions, and I have not told you about them. If you want to know about them, the information is recorded in the Book of Zoroaster." - from *The Secret Book of John* ("The Teaching of the Savior") Nag Hammadi Codex II. Although the surviving edition of "The Teaching of the Savior" dates from the fourth century CE (as part of the gnostic Nag Hammadi library), it indicates a continuing tradition rooted in Zoroastrianism...The influence of Zoroastrian belief is particularly evident in the pseudepigraphical book of 1 Enoch and Jubilees as well as a number of other texts in <u>Dead Sea Scrolls</u>.

<http://gnosis.org/naghamm/apocjn-davies.html>

In Sanskrit, a related language to both Hebrew and Old Persian, *ahara* means; breath, just as *ruach or ruah* (SHD 7306) in Hebrew also means YHVH's "holy breath" wind or spirit, however just as YHVH was pre-existent to His breath in going forth (within the *uruch Elohim or aleim ruch* Gen. 1:2; 6:1), so is *Hormazda/Ormazd* pre-existent to His breath/*ahara or ahura mazda* which is another name for YHVH's chosen El/Al or Eloah of Elohim(God of Gods). Since these words *ahura/ruah* when spoken are phonetically so similar it seems obvious that *ruah/ruach* (breath) should be considered as a possible cognate of *ahura/ahara* (breath). *Sanskri, Tamil and Pahlavi Dictionaries.* <http://webapps.uni-koeln.de/tamil/>

With all this understanding included in our study of the origin of these related names, and after studying the next section on YHVH's Light we will be able to then consider Ormazd (the Wise Light) as an prehistoric name for the Creator and Ahura as an ancient name for His Elohim. And after examining biblical references to YHVH as "Light" (also in the next section) it will become clear that the only difference is that of language, not meaning. The Hebrew *ruah-spirit-wind-breath* can be seen to be a cognate of the Persian/Sanskrit *Ahura-Asura-Asu-breath*, this theme will be developed again further on in a section discussing the mention of Ahura in the extremely ancient *Rig Veda*.

> "By the word of YHWH the heavens were made and by the breath of his mouth all the hosts (were made)." Ps. 33:6

Zarathustra's prophecy is also preserved in the writings of Salomon, Bishop of Basra, and Theodore bar Konai: "Zoroaster said to his favorite disciples; 'At the end of time and at the final dissolution, a child shall be conceived in the womb of a virgin...They will take him and crucify him upon a tree, and heaven and earth shall sit in mourning for his sake...He will come with the armies of light, and be borne aloft on white clouds...He shall descend from my family, <u>for I am he and he is I: he is in me and I am in him</u>." Oliver, Revilo P. *The Origins of Christianity.*

> "I am in you, you are in me, we are in the Father." John 14:20 (And we shall see further on in the *Chaldean Oracles* that the Chaldean followers of Zarathustra also taught of the Creator as the Father.)

The wise men or magi (also called in Dan. 1:20, *eashphim*), the followers of Zarathustra, had been expecting the appearance of just such a "star" for a long time, and knew that the event was important enough to seek out the location of the star. Who else after reading this far in all these various insights into the "hidden mysteries" would not also be wise enough to now understand what they were seeing if they witnessed such a "star-ship" moving about in the sky? For now when one sees those mysterious lights of various brilliant colors, in the sky, doing things no aircraft can do (not to be confused with hoaxed photos of solid metallic objects) it may now be understood that the spirits of the "watchers," YHVH's Elohim are with us, watching over us and guiding us, as they have from the beginning.

The first century writer, Philo, compared the Essenes with the Persian Magi and also with the Indian Yogis. Others have also connected the Druids with "the Magi of the old Persians." (Macey, Albert G. *Encyclopedia of Freemasonry,* 1917, p. 258) According to Diodorus of Sicily in *Bibliotheca Historica,* the cult of the Magussaeans was a combination of heretical Zoroastrianism and the Babylonian astrology of the Chaldeans (who were originally called in the Bible *Kasdim.* Gen. 11:32; the *Kasdiym* were from "*Arpakhsadiym*" of *Arpachsad,* who was an ancestor of Abraham, only later on were they called Chaldeans. more on them further on).

YHVH'S LIGHT/AUR/HOR/OR

"The people going in darkness, they see *Aur,* light of the great ones dwelling in the land of the shadow of death, <u>Aur</u> (light SHD 215) *He* is bright over them. Is. 9:2 This verse shows that YHWH was also called *Aur,* for who else is the "Light" of the great ones dwelling in the land of death, and who is referred to as "He"? *Aur* here means light just as it can be found in the Persian name of the Creator, *Or-mazd.* This name does not make reference to physical light, which is merely emblematical of the light of the Creator, who is *Al Emeth and Al De'ot (Al Deoth)* the Light of All Truth and All Knowledge. "The expression 'God of Knowledge' in the Qumran text has been seen as a reflection of Ahura Mazda's name, Lord of Wisdom, cleverly Judaized as *el deoth (al da'at* – now data), a title borrowed from 1 Sam. 2:3" Myers, Peter. *The Influence of Zoroastrian Religion on Judaism,* p.423.

<http://www.derafsh-kaviyani.com/english/influenceofzoroastrian.pdf>

One of YHVH's names is *YHVH Ori,* as found in Ps. 27:1, meaning "YHVH Light of me." And Yeschu/Joshu/Jesus recognized *Aur/Hor,* the "Light" of the Holy Spirit (*ruah/ahura hakodesh*) as synonymous with the YHVH, the Father, because he said for example, "I am in you, you are in me, and we are in the Father." (John 14:20) and "Then spake Jesus again unto them, saying, I am the light of the world." (John 8:12) So the Christian religion surely cannot deny that Yeschu/Joshu/Jesus embraced "the Light" as emblematic of the divine. However this ancient word for the Creator refers to the light of spirit, mind, and intelligent thought, not the material light of the universe, which is secondary, a material creation arising from the Light of the Creator.

"As the appearance of the bow in the cloud in the day of rain, so was the appearance of the brightness round about the appearance of the likeness of the glory of YHWH." Ez. 1:28

"YHWH A*ur-i* (my Light) and my salvation." Ps. 27:1

"For the fruit of the Light (*Aur*) consists in all goodness, righteousness and truth." Eph. 5:9

"YHWH He shall become to you *l Aur* (for light) for eon." Isa. 60:20

"Rejoice not over me because I fall, I will rise, or if I am sitting in darkness, YHWH will be a light (*aur*) to me." Micah 7:8

"Al (El) YHWH He shall enlighten *(u-iar)* us. With boughs in hand, join in the festal procession." Ps. 118:27 (changed to "bind the festal sacrifice" in some texts, again probably by the Levites to support their practice of animal sacrifice)

"Every good gift and every perfect gratuity comes down from above, from the Father of the Lights (Gr. *Pater ho phos*)..." James 1:17

The Dead Sea scrolls give us this passage on the "light of life," excluded from the Masoretic text. "After he has suffered, he will see the Light of life and be satisfied. By his knowledge My righteous servant will justify many and he will bear their iniquities." Isa. 53:11 No doubt this reference to the "Light of life" was changed by the Levite scribes since it could be interpreted to be in conflict with their philosophy of animal sacrifice. Apparently, however, they were not able to effectively excise all such inferences because they left in such references as Ps. 42:8 which, when studied in Hebrew, reveals YHVH's true Light.

Ps. 42:8 explains to us that another of YHVH's names is *YHVH Al Chaiyai,* or *YHVH Al Chayim* (SHD 2419 is Chiy'el, The All[10] Living YHVH). That this is so can also be seen in Jos. 3:10 which at <http://www.scripture4all.org> can be seen to *actually* say in Hebrew; "In this you shall know that *Al Chi - All[10] Life is within you.*" ([10]Remember from the section on The All that *Al or El* can also mean all.) Parsons, John J. *The Hebrew Names of God.*

<http://www.hebrew4christians.com/Names_of_G-d/El/el.html>

"Once the whole world the people as one to *Enlil[11]* in one tongue gave voice. Then did the *En* (lord)...change the speech of their mouths, he having set up contention in it, in the human speech that had been one." ([11]*En*-Lord, *lil*-sky, also perhaps related to the Assyrian word *ilu* which corresponds to the Hebrew word *El or Al* God) SHD 410, some authors think it is perhaps also related to the Assyrian word for bright, *ellu,* related to *halal* SHD 1984. Sumerian Epic *Enmerkar and the Lord of Aratta (*c. 2000 BCE) quoted by Peter Goodgame, *The Spirit World and Civilization.*

<http://www.redmoonrising.com/Giza/SpiritCiv5.htm>

This is obviously referring to the same story as the tower of Bab-el, see Gen. 11:9. It is this confusion of languages that has led to so many misunderstandings among the different religions. But remember that the Bible also says that, in time, religions will come to see that all those who worship the Creator by different names are however really still All One. "YHWH He is becoming (*UEIE IEVE*) king over all the earth, in that day, YHWH, He shall become One (*Achad/Echad*) and His name One." Zech. 14:9

Light in Hebrew or Aramaic is "*Or,*" "*Hor,*" or "*Aur*"; in Amoritic-'*R,* in Ugaritic-'*ar,* in Akkadian (including Babylonian) -*urr,* in Phoenician-*aur.* A Chinese word for the sun is; `*R* and in Sanskrit the sun is called *Aru.* The commonality of these words shows that in the most ancient times the words for light and sun had some common phonetics and meanings. These would have been derived from languages originating before the events depicted in the stories of the confusion of languages. This confusion of languages is also discussed in the epic *Enmerkar and the Lord of Aratta* . (references to these words include #215 *Hebrew-Aramaic Dictionary, The New American Standard Exhaustive Concordance of the Bible,* Huffmon, H.B. *Amorite Personal Names in the Mari Texts,* p.169; Higgins, Godfrey. Vol. 1 *Anacalypsis,* p.587; & Chen, Janey. *A Practical English-Chinese Pronouncing Dictionary,* p. 394. *Sanskri, Tamil and Pahlavi Dictionaries.* <http://webapps.uni-koeln.de/tamil/>

Khor in the Zarathustrian teachings means sun or sunlight. After examining the foregoing information on cognates of the Hebrew word *Aur,* it should now become clear to the seeker of knowledge concerning ancient etymological cognates of YHVH / Aur, that *Khor* is another symbol of the light, *Aur/Or/Hor* etc. This understanding degenerated among the ignorant into worship of the emblem (the sun) instead of the light of all intelligence, YHVH. The sun is merely the physical symbol of an originally spiritual concept. It was known that everyone shares in YHVH's light, since the Father is the Great Holy Spirit who is All in all who embrace oneness. (1 Cor. 15:28) YHVH is the infinite *Aur* (light) of All-Knowledge (*Omniscient*), YHVH *Al Da'at* (All Knowledge), known to Zarathustra's followers as Ormazd – the Light Wise. Kaviani, Khodadad. *Zartosht & Zoroastrianism, Season Calandar.*

<http://www.rozanehmagazine.com/allariclesII/akhodiMJ02.html>

> "And the Light shines in the darkness and the darkness comprehended it not." John 1:5

The name *Garduneh-e Khorshid,* also contains in its structure this word *khor.* The *Garduneh-e Khorshid* is an ancient symbol that represents the revolving sun, fire, infinity, or continuing recreation, it is found in the center of the winged disk of many ancient cultures. This ancient symbol of the Creator's creative light was unfortunately commandeered by Hitler's violent regime and called a swastika, so it now has negative connotations attached. Some meanings of the winged sun will be explored in a following section. Concerning the rest of the phrase, *Khorshid* or *Khorshidi,* it seems the history of this word should be analyzed in connection with another of YHVH's known names said to be used in Abraham's time, Shaddai (*shidi*). In Ex. 6:2-3, it is said that this name was used by followers of YHVH *before* the Hebrew name YHVH was given to them by Moses. Thus any people using the name *Shidi* as those ancestral to the Hebrew people the Chaldeans/ *Kasdiym,* existing before the Hebrew language, yet still according to Gen. 9:26 the Elohim of Shem (from before the time of Noah) were still among YHVH's blessed, although these people were speaking a different language and using a different name for YHVH. *Religious Sungazing.*

<http://scripture4all.org/OnlineInterlinear/OTpdf/gen9.pdf>

<http://sunlight.orgfree.com/history_of_sun_gazing.htm>

> "And YHWH spoke to Moses and said to him: I am YHWH. I appeared to Abraham, to Isaac, and to Jacob, as *Al or El Shaddai*, but by my name YHWH, I was not known to them. Ex. 6:2-3

The citations mentioned above on *Or/Hor/Aur* are among the earliest written languages. In Sumerian, the earliest known written phonetic language (Simons, Geoff. *Iraq; from Sumer to Saddam,* p.115-117); the word; *uru* means luminous and *u* light and *ar or ra* in Sumerian (*Ra* also alternates in Egyptian with *Hor*[12] as an Egyptian name for the sun or the god of the sun) meaning to shine or blaze. (*uru* in Shumerian became *alu* in Akkadian which became *ir* in Hebrew. Rohl, David. *Legend the Genesis of Civilization.* P. 185.)

> "Orus (Horus) I repeat, is nothing but the Hebrew word *aur,* ilux, light – the very light so often spoken of by St. John, in the first chapter of his gospel." Higgins, Godfrey. *Anacalypsis vol. I,* p. 312.

127

[12]Horus is the Latin form of the Egyptian sun-god *Hor* (*Hru/Hor/Horus* in Egyptian also has the meaning of god of the day[13] and or therefore also a reference to the light of day or daylight). Horowitz, Anthony. *Myths and Mythology,* p. 253. ([13]*Zeus aka Zeus Oromasdes* was also known as the god of the day, or god of the burning sky-*Zeus Aitherios,* more on Zeus in the next section. Cook, Arthur Bernard. *Zeus A Study in Ancient Religion.* p. 740

<http://www.phoenixandturtle.net/excerptmill/Cook2.htm>).

Hor (the Egyptian hieroglyphic was a hawk) was already known in the most prehistoric of Egyptian inscriptions, only later this name was changed to (the Greek form) Horus. Hor was, "Originally distinct from Horus, the son of Isis and Osiris[14], inevitably the two gods were confused." Fairman, H.W. *The Triumph of Horus,* p.128.

> [14]"The god's name *Wsir...*was written at first with the sign for a throne, followed by the sign for an eye;...Among the many meanings suggested is one cognate of *Ashur,* implying a Syrian origin..." *The Ancient Gods Speak - A guide to Egyptian Religion,* edited by Redford, Donald B. 2002, p. 304.

> "*Asar-luhi* is his foremost name which *Anu* (*An* is the Sumerian word for "heaven" and is the name of the sky god who is the prime mover in creation, and the distant supreme leader of the gods...He is the Father of all the gods...") gave him...*Asar* bestower of the cultivated land who establishes its boundaries the creator of grain and herbs who causes vegetation to sprout forth. *Babylonian Creation Epic,* quoted by Peter Goodgame, *The Spirit World and Civilization* <http://www.redmoonrising.com/Giza/SpiritCiv5.htm>

THEOS/DIOS/DEUS/ZEUS

It is well known by scholars, although perhaps not by many Christians (those not versed in the original Greek words used in the writing of the NT), that *Theos* is the word used for God throughout the Greek NT. Now we know Yeschu/Joshu/Jesus was of course referring to YHVH Elohim when he quoted Ps. 82:6 in John 10:34 "I said ye are Gods/Elohim." The Elohim are referred to in the NT as the host of heaven (*stratia ho ouranos,* Acts 7:42). The biblical adoption of the word *Theos* (from the same source as *Dios/Deus/Zeus,* i.e. the Sanskrit *Dyaus*[15]) demonstrates the fact that the Greek word *Theos* (if even used by Yeschu/Joshu/Jesus, who spoke Aramaic) was used by him as synonymous with YHVH Elohim. ([15]see *Catholic Encyclopedia* article. on "Etymology of the word God") Furthermore the following quote from Herodotus gives us information that clearly shows that another variant of *Theos/Dios/Deus,* that is Zeus (aka *Zeus Oromasdes* and *Zeus Ouranios*) was also used by the Magi when referring to the whole circle of the host of Heaven, as one being, YHVH Elohim. Cook, Arthur Bernard. *Zeus A Study in Ancient Religion,* p. 740.

<http://www.phoenixandturtle.net/excerptmill/Cook2.htm>
<http://www.scripture4all.org/OnlineInterlinear/Greek_Index.htm>

"As to the usages of the Persians, I know them to be these. It is not their custom to make and set up statues and temples and altars, but those who make such they deem foolish, as I suppose, because they never believed the gods, as do the Greeks, to be in the likeness of men; but they call the whole circle of heaven Zeus (i.e. *Theos/Dios/Deus/Dyaus* etc. aka *Zeus Oromasdes[16]*), and to *Him* they offer sacrifice on the highest peaks of the mountains." Herodotos (I, 131) That they called the whole circle 'Him' shows two things, the divinity was revered as a person and two He was not in the form of a man. This is just as the NT says *Theos/Deus/Zeus* is the All in all and YHVH *Olam* (i.e., space[17]) also has no image. 1 Cor. 15:28.

[16]The *Encyclopedia Britannica* equates *Zeus Oromasdes* with *Jupiter[18] Dolichenus* in its article on the later, stating; ... "under Achaemenidian rule (6th-4th century BCE) he was identified with the Persian god Ahura Mazda, thus becoming a god of the universe..." One of the first, if not the first to equate the Greek and Persian god *Zeus* as *Oromasdes* (Ormazd) as one and the same being was king Mithridates who erected steles at Nimrod/Nimrud/Nimrut giving both the Greek and Persian names for a variety of gods: 1. *Apollo/Mithras*; 2. *Artagnes/Herakles* (Hercules); 3. *Zeus/Oromasdes*; 4. *Hera/Teleia* & 5. *Helios/Hermes. Adiyaman and Nemrut.*

<http://www.enjoyturkey.com/info/sights/adiyaman.htm>

[17] http://www.hebrew4christians.com/Names_of_G-d/El/el.html

[18]Deuspiter i.e, *Zeuspiter,* Sky Father - *Piter/Pater* is the well recognized Indo-European or Sanskrit root of father; in Egypt the Father Creator God was known as "*Ptah-Nun, the Father who begat Atum* (is Atum Adam? MHJ);...*Ptah* the Great, that is the heart and tongue of the *Ennead* (perhaps adopted from the Sumerian pantheon of Gods, *An or En* - meaning lord in Sumerian, i.e., a council of lords, MHJ); *Ptah* who gave birth to the Gods... (from a Memphite text cited by David Rohl in *Legend the Genesis of Civilization.* p. 347) By the time of Alexander the Great *Amun[19]* was also associated with Zeus." This mention of the Memphite text is quoted by Peter Goodgame, *The Spirit World and Civilization.*

<http://www.redmoonrising.com/Giza/SpiritCiv5.htm>

According to Cross, Ptah is often called *the lord (or one) of eternity,* he suggests that this identification of El with Ptah lead to the epithet *'olam* "eternal" being applied to El so early and so consistently. Cross, Frank Moore (1973). *Canaanite Myth and Hebrew Epic* (1973, p. 19) Cambridge, Mass.: Harvard University Press. <http://en.wikipedia.org/wiki/El_(god)>

[19]Amun, the *sacred wisdom* is mentioned in Prov. 8:30, the knowledge of whom has been effectively concealed, all this time, by translating *Amun* as the word foster, yet it should now be clear to objective review that Amun is the divine feminine being called wisdom or *Amun* of Prov. 8:1. Only the unwillingness to embrace the feminine aspect of the Creator, will prevent the acceptance of this as a much more reasonable explanation, for the ancient wisdom of *Aum* (or *Ama* in Hebrew) is the long hidden mother aspect of the Father god *Ptah/Piter/Pater.* Because the understanding of *Amun* was "hidden" from the Egyptians it eventually became obscure that *Amun* was originally a feminine deity and thus also hidden from posterity.

In 1989, *Nemrut Dag* (on Mt. Nemrud named after Nimrod from the OT, by Christians who later came to live there) was declared a state park. It is surrounded on the west by colossal statues erected by Mithridate's son Antiochos. Professor K. Dormer has traced the genealogy of Antiochos 1, who was born of a Persian father and a Seleucid-Macedonian mother. His findings indicate that Antiochos I of Commagene claimed descent, through his father Mithradates, from

Dareios (Darius) 1 (522-486 BCE) and, through his mother Laodike, from Alexander the Great (356-323 BCE). (ibid. <http://www.enjoyturkey.com/info/sights/adiyaman.htm>)

The park at Nemrut Dag was originally a burial mound of king Antiochos I of Kommagene. It is surrounded on the west by colossal statues, on the east by a fire altar in the shape of a stepped pyramid. Inscriptions identify the statues, which are the same as those above named by Mithradates. *Zeus Oromasdes* the Graeco-Persian sky god and supreme deity is the largest of the statues. The gods wear Persian headgear, the afore mentioned pointed caps also worn by the little people depicted on the Behistion Rock. ibid.

<http://www.enjoyturkey.com/info/sights/adiyaman.htm>)

> "It is generally assumed that he (i.e. Herodotus) calls the supreme deity "Zeus" merely from his Greek instinct. But it is a least possible that he heard in Persia a name for the sky-god which sounded so much like "Zeus," being in fact the same word, that he really believed they used the familiar name." *Syncretism in Religion as Illustrated in the History of Parsism* by Rev. J. H. Moulton (Transactions of the Third International Congress for the History of Religions Oxford 1908 ii. 89 ff) as quoted by Cook, Arthur Bernard. *Zeus A Study in Ancient Religion*
>
> <http://www.phoenixandturtle.net/excerptmill/Cook2.htm>).

The general acceptance and use of the words *Theos* and *ouranos/ouranios*, for YHVH and His heavenly host in the NT shows a clear connection between the *Zeus Oromasdes* and *Zeus Ouranios* of the Magi's teachings (from Zarathustra the prophet who predicted the appearance of the star at Yeschu/Joshu/Jesus birth) and the teachings of Yeschu/Joshu/Jesus found in the NT. And it shows that the word Zeus as known by the Persian Magi, was originally not thought to be in the form of a man-god, but encompassed all the heavenly circle as unified in One sentient being. This is the same conceptualization as spoken of in the NT as The One who is All (1 Cor. 15:28). This is to be seen in their reference to the infinite Supreme being of the Cosmos as <u>Him</u>. And in the section on the *Chaldean Oracles* we will also see that they called the Supreme Being, the Father, long before Yeschu/Joshu/Jesus referred to Him as the Father.

Also as mentioned previously, one of the Jewish names for the Creator, used as far back as Abraham is, *Al/El Oulm or Olam.* (Gen. 21:33, Ps. 90:1-3, 93:2, Isa. 26;4) (World(s) without end, SHD 5769, 5865, 5957, forever & 361 *eylam meaning* space) This name for YHVH means everlasting time and space, the infinite, Living Universe, YHVH's material presence, whose spirit pervades all.

> "And YHWH He rains on Sodom and Gomorrah sulfur and fire from YHWH from heaven." Gen.19:24 (this phrase '*math YHWH mn eShmim*' is translated as "from YHWH from heaven" but it can be seen that the second word "from" - *mn* is not exactly the same as the first "from" - *math,* yet this Bible verse makes it clear that YHWH rains from Himself.

Plato also considered that the world was a living being with intelligence and soul "woven right through from the center to the outermost heaven." Plato, *Timaeus* 36, as quoted by Settegast, Mary. *When Zarathustra Spoke,* 2005, p. 135.

"I worship thee, Oh my great Friend, by singing thy name and going around Mazda." Gatha 51-22, as quoted by Chatterjee, Jatindra Mohon, M. A. *Ethical Conceptions of the Gathas,* p. 123. Because the Ormazdian religion is anti-iconic, it has been suggested that going around Mazda, must mean going around His temple, but with the understanding that we live within the physical manifestation of our Creator and His spirit also lives within us, it can be seen that Zarathustra understood himself to be going around Mazda, singing or as one might say, "going around the Universe, singing."

This meaning is also found in another name for YHVH, *Al Hashamayim* (Ps. 136:26) or *lAl Eshmim,* "All[20] the Heavens," often translated as "God *of* the Heavens" but there is in fact no word "of," in the phrase, YHVH is "All the Heavens." Parsons, John J. *The Hebrew Names of God.* <http://www.hebrew4christians.com/Names_of_G-d/El/el.html> [20]Remember from the section on The All, that *Al or El* can also mean "all."

"The name of the god: *Zervan akarana,* i.e. boundless time, appears in the Avesta though not in the Gathas, but in the later *Yasna* and in the *Vendidad.* Space and time, *Thwasha and Zurvan,* are named together in *Yasna* 72:10 as divine powers. According to Bidez and Cumont, *Thwasha* means "space…"*Eudemos* speaks of a being, 'that some call place, some time and that unites in itself all intelligible things'...*Topos and Chronos,* this pair corresponds exactly to the pair *Thwasha and Zurvan* in the *Avesta...Eudemos* testimony tells us that these views were held by certain Magi as early as the forth century BCE." Van der Waerden, Bartel. *The Birth of Astronomy,* 1974, p. 163.

Rather than Zarathustra being influenced by later Chaldeans, from information in Bartel van der Waerden's, *The Birth of Astronomy (1974)* it would appear that the emphasis the Chaldean/Kasdim put on astronomy/astrology resulted from the influence of the Zoroastrian doctrine that the Sky God/Creator of humans occupied all the heavens (or stars). Waerden says; "Primitive Zodiacal Astrology...is known from texts ascribed to Orpheus and Zoroaster...There are some reasons to assume that this type of astrology was already in use under the Chaldean reign." van der Waerden, Bartel. *The Birth of Astronomy* 1974, p. 128.

After evidence is presented dating Zarathustra to before 3000 BCE it will be seen that apparently some of those in the later Chaldeans had distorted Zarathustra's understanding of mankind's extraterrestrial origins and, as earthlings are prone to do, looked for the cause of our existence in the material universe, studying astronomy and inventing astrological theories. If the Cause for existence were to be found in matter, then the materialists must consider the dimension of mind where thought exists. How big is a thought, can it be measured or weighted? For there is one thing that can be proven to exist that is not material, and that is thought.

Science has tried, but the EEG's and other devices for measuring the electrical emissions from thought, has shown that they extend beyond the brain, even to where they can be "read" as to whether someone is lying, dreaming, meditating, etc. and as to whether that person is happy or sad and other meanings. Imagine how much more they will be able to "read" these emissions that result from brainwaves in the future and who is to say that some sensitive people are not genetically capable of already doing the same? Anthony, Mark. *Mind and Emotion.*

"Matter cannot develop life or consciousness, unless it had the potentiality of them in its nature. No amount of shock from the external environment can extract life out of mere matter." Krishnan, Radha. *Indian Philosophy,* p. 181; cited by Chatterjee, Jatindra Mohon, M. A. *Ethical Conceptions of the Gathas,* p. 220.

"By adapting the structure of the institution of the warrior and superimposing upon it an ethical component, Zarathustra was able to suggest that the real battle was the one against the forces of evil, and the real prize would not be territory, or even men and cattle, but the realization of the good dominion (*khshathra*) of Ahura Mazda." *Zoroastrianism* by Peter Clark

According to J. R. Hinnells, *Zorastrian Savior Imagery and Its Influence on the New Testament* Zarathustra's influence on Christianity has been especially seen in the Savior's[21] defeat of the demons, his gathering of men for the judgment scene (referred to as; "the final turning point of the creation" Yasna 43.4-5); his raising of the dead (Y 30.7); and his administration of the judgment day. (Zarathustra also developed the concept that humans have free will to choose between good and evil. MHJ)

[21]The term Savior was used repeatedly to refer to Zarathustra. Sumerian the earliest known written language contains references in its literature to a savior "*su-tu-tu,*" who this savior is has not been established but it is well known that Zarathustra was the first man in recorded history referred to as a savior (*saosyant*). *Sumerian Proverbs,* p. 414.

THE SHEMSU HOR FOLLOWERS OF LIGHT

"If the Sumerians (or rather 'Shumer' to use the form found in the cuneiform documents) were people of such outstanding literary and cultural importance for the ancient Near Eastern world…why is it that there seems to be little trace of them in the Bible?…a solution to this rather puzzling enigma was suggested over a quarter of a century ago by my teacher and colleague, Arno Poebel,…Poebel's suggestion has found no responsive echo among Orientalists,…It is my conviction, however, that it will stand the test of time and in due course be recognized…If Poebel's hypothesis turns out to be correct, and Shem is identical with Shumer-Sumer, we must assume that the authors of the Bible, or at least some of them, considered the Sumerians to have been the original ancestors of the Hebrew people." Kramer, Samuel N. *The Sumerians.* pp. 297-298.

With the understanding that *Hor/Or/Aur/Ar* meant "Light throughout the ancient Middle East," *Hor* (the hawk symbol on a banner pole) and the *Shemsu Hor,* translated as the entourage or followers of Hor, can actually be seen to mean the *Shem*[22] who followed the "Light" (Hor) of the Creator. The evidence will show that originally the understanding was that this was the Light of Intelligence (in Hebrew this would be said as *Owr/Aur* SHD 215 and *Madda* SHD 4093 combined making *Owr-madda*, in Persian Or-mazd), *not* the sun, which as a symbol was merely emblematical of this concept. Because over time many people took the worship of this Light of the Cosmic Mind to mean the sun, eventually it devolved into sun worship.

[22]Note the word *Shem* (*Shum* or *shem* SHD 8035 in Hebrew means a name, therefore also possibly the name of a people, a nation.) in this name, these were Shemetic or Semetic people

migrating from Shumeria/Shemeria. (Interestingly enough the movie industry for once probably got it right in the movie *The Scorpion King,* when they called this early Egyptian conqueror an Akkadian. (The name Scorpion king was adopted from early Egyptian depictions on the *Mace Head of King Scorpion*) It is well known that the *Shemsu Hor* invaded Egypt before the first kings of the Old Kingdom, they are mentioned in king lists of Manetho, the *Turin Papyrus* and the *Papyrus of Tulli,* as existing prior to the first kings of Egypt. Their (the Shemsu Hor) symbol for Hor, the Hawk, was already present in the very <u>earliest</u> predynastic symbols, in prehistoric times and prior to the beginnings of the Egyptian phonetic writing of hieroglyphic words.

> "The predynastic people are seen to have had narrow skulls with a height measurement exceeding the breadth, a condition common also in Negroes. The reverse is the case in the Dynastic Race, who not only had broader skulls[23] but the height of these skulls, while exceeding that in the Predynastic Race, is still less than the breadth." Goodgame, Peter. *Egypt's Forgotten Origins.* Citing David Rohl. *Legend – the Genesis of Civilization.* [23]Remember from the discussion of Einstein's skull that it was the width of the skull that contained the lobes that distinguished his brain from the average. These genetically inherited lobes came form the interbreeding of the sons of the Elohim with the daughters of the Adam, the earthly humans said by science to have originated in Africa. Goodgame, Peter. *Egypt's Forgotten Origins.*

> <http://www.redmoonrising.com/Giza/EgyptsOrigins4.htm>

> "The sacred place *Djeba* in *Wetjeset-Neter* having been created, the Sanctified Ruler...appeared. He came from the underworld...as a protector, and is said to resemble the *Nefer- her.* (the sanctified[24] falcon- *hr* or *Hor*-Light) {[24]*Nefer* also means beautiful in Egyptian.} This account is to be found on the temple walls at Edfu. Reymond, E. A. E. *Mythical Origin of the Egyptian Temple,* p. 12-22.

The Egyptians themselves adopted the name Horus as the son of Isis and Osiris, he was named after the ancient Horus (Horus the Elder aka *Hor/Or/Aur,* this name was carried by the followers of Hor (*Shemsu Hor*) when they entered Egypt). Evidence of this exists in Egyptian legends as discussed by the ancient historian Plutarch. Plutarch's account explains the eventual confusion of the original and ancient "Hor" with Horus son of Isis. Because of this confusion the ancient Hor came eventually to be also called simply Horus. "The Horus that Isis bore...is related to have had a charge of illegitimacy brought against him...because he is not pure and without alloy like his father "the word" (Reason),...they name *Him* the "Elder Horus;" Plutarch. *On Isis and Osirus,* LIV. <http://thriceholy.net/Texts/Isis.html>

The Hawk symbol of Hor/Horus the Elder also occurs in a pictograph of the Sumerian god *Enki*[25].. *Enki* means *en*-lord, *ki*-earth, a title, *not his name,* additionally *Enlil* (*en-lil-{il/al/el},* *lord of the sky i.e., Al-all*) was the title of the lord of the sky (*lil*-sky or 'all' the heavens). His image is found on a Sumerian cylinder seal (with hieroglyphics that clearly resemble those of the Egyptians) depicting him holding a Hawk on one hand while a stream of water with fish in it flows behind or over him. To see this cylinder seal go to following url. Goodgame, Peter. *The Spirit World and Civilization.* http://www.redmoonrising.com/Giza/SpiritCiv5.htm>

[25]In the Persian tradition Enki was Ahura Mazda, the god of Life <u>and Light</u>, who was also known as *Ohrmazd* (or *Ormuzd,* however, as we have seen *Ormazd* and *Ahura Mazda* are

not actually one and the same)." Gardner, Laurence. *Genesis of the Grail Kings.* p. 133.

<http://books.google.com/books?
id=5subHQf5kToC&pg=PA133&lpg=PA133&dq=enki+ahura&source=web&ots=O0BV
GhgbKf&sig=EDN4y7UcqZRUIH2v8APsaQIDMoU&hl=en>

"*Enki* ("Lord of the Earth") was called *Ea* in Akkadian (*East* Semitic, Akkadian is a Semitic language.) – that is to say in the Babylonian tradition. Scholars have determined that *Ea* was vocalized as 'Eya' So when Moses stood before the burning bush and asked the name of the god of the mountain…The voice of God simply replied '*Eyah asher Eyah*' – 'I am (the one) who is called Eyah' – the name of *Ea* in its *West* Semitic (i.e., Hebrew) form." Goodgame, Peter. *Domination by Deception.*

<http://www.redmoonrising.com/Giza/DomDec6.htm> & David Rohl. *Legend – the Genesis of Civilization.*

The incorporation of the Hawk symbol of Hor/Light from Sumeria thus became the symbol for the allegiance of those *Kasdym*/Chaldean followers of the Light. ("Horus, the sky god, was closely associated at Edfu with the winged sun-disc, *Harakhty…*" Rohl, David. *Legend the Genesis of Civilization.* p.333.) These were the proto-Hebrew and Zarathustrian followers of *Aur/Hor/Or* - Light, when they invaded or migrated into prehistoric Egypt. "The Chaldaean name of the sun is (*hrs*) chris...the solar fire, and like the sun also meant machinator...meaning the material light or plastic formative power..." Higgins, Godfrey. Vol. 1 *Anacalypsis,* p. 587,588. This, it will be seen in a later section (Dating Zarathustra Before Abraham), was a later corruption of Zarathustra's teachings on the "Light" which he taught (as in the name *Ormazd*) to be representative of the All-Highest Light (Intelligence) of the omnipresent Great Holy Spirit.

"The god of the Falcon Tribe, the tribe that invaded and conquered Egypt, was clearly Enki…after Enki's (the Lord of the Earth's) cult center of Eridu was abandoned he re-invented himself within the Falcon Tribe." Goodgame, Peter. *The Spirit World and Civilization.* <http://www.redmoonrising.com/Giza/SpiritCiv5.htm>

"The original of Horus was probably that of a sky god, known as "lord of the sky". The Egyptian word "*her*" (*hor, har*) from which the god's name derived means "the one on high", or "the distant one… As *Behdety,* or 'he of the *behdet,*' Horus was the hawk-winged sun disk which seems to incorporate the idea of the passage of the sun through the sky" Dunn, Jimmy. *Horus, the God of Kings.* <http://www.touregypt.net/featurestories/horus.htm> Also concerning Horus, Peter Goodgame says "In ancient Egypt the priests of the sacred rites were known as *horoskopi*[26]." (ibid. <http://www.redmoonrising.com/Giza/DomDec6.htm>) ([26]the origin of horoscope? MHJ)

Further evidence concerning the Egyptian adoption of the winged disk and other Assyrian and Sumerian symbols, seen to be already in use in Egypt's earliest times, will be discussed in the following section on the Winged Disk. Taken together all this evidence indicates that the "followers of Hor/Light" known as the Shemsu Hor were in existence in the ancient Middle East *before* the founding of the first Egyptian dynasties. They became known as the Shemsu Hor *after* they eventually invaded Egypt, this was *before* the first kings of Egypt's First or Old Dynasty. Arnett, William. Plate XLIV or XLIX *The Predynastic Origin of Egyptian Hieroglyphs.*

"What Petrie found (at Nakada) was conclusive evidence of a group of invaders who were associated with artifacts whose origin was clearly traceable back to Mesopotamia[27] ...Mesopotamian influence is again seen in the Third Dynasty with the creation of the great step-pyramid of Djoser as Saqqara which is recognized as Egypt's first pyramid and obviously modeled after a Sumerian ziggurat." Goodgame, Peter. *Egypt's Forgotten Origins*. <http://www.redmoonrising.com/Giza/EgyptsOrigins4.htm>

[27]The Akkadians[28] (aka Mesopotamia is actually a Greek appellation for the area now known as Iraq). The name comes from "mesopotamios," which means "between the rivers" in Greek; the two rivers are the Tigris and the Euphrates. <www.digonsite.com/glossary/hm.html> Byrnes, Dan. *Religion From the Time of the Ice Ages...* [28]Remember Akkadian is a Semitic Language.

<http://www.danbyrnes.com.au/lostworlds/features/iceage.htm>

After studying the foregoing it seems important to touch again on another of YHVH's names, given in the following as *"UIEI,"* this name occurs in the phrase *"Elohim IEI Aur UIEI Aur,"* found in Gen.1:2 , translated as *"Elohim he shall become light, He is becoming[29] light."* So taking into account all the previous information, it is important to consider this verse in light of information on the prehistoric monotheistic religion now called Zoroastrianism or Mazdaism, which also recognized that the Creator *Aur* or *Or/Hor* was the first or Supreme Light. [29]Remember that "He is Becoming" refers to *UEIE IEVE* "I am Becoming YHVH" (as in Zech 14:9 see http://www.scripture4all.org) - YHVH "I Am Becoming." IEVE/IEUE - I Am Becoming is often rendered "I Am. Ex. 3:2&14

"We shall walk in the *Aur* (light) of YHWH." Isa. 2:5

Scholars have often compared the Hebrew and Zorastrian religions, finding many other beliefs in common and have often suggested that the Hebrew story derived some elements from the earlier prehistoric Zarathustrian religion, recognized by many scholars as the oldest written monotheistic religion. Further on we will go into many of those similarities in an attempt to show continuity in early human understanding of the *Aur* (Light vs. darkness/ignorance) of YHVH's Elohim and their "star" ships, even in prehistoric times, before the Hebrew written language came into existence among the Israelites following Moses.

"Kindness and truth they are preceding faces of you, happy are the people who are shouting YHWH, in the light of your face they shall walk." Ps. 89:15

THE WINGED SUN DISK IN THE BIBLE

"But unto you that fear of my name shall the Sun (*shmsh* SHD 8121 & 8122) of righteousness arise with healing in his wings." Mal. 4:2 (the one speaking in this verse is YHWH of hosts, see Mal. 4:1)

The OT mentions of the winged sun symbol in the above verse. This symbol shows up early in the ancient Middle Eastern culture but is mostly identified with the Egyptians. In speaking of one such depiction of a winged disk from the Louvre Museum, on page 415 in his book *Legend the Genesis of Civilization,* David Rohl says "You might be forgiven for thinking that this is an Egyptian winged sun-disc, however you would be wrong. It comes from the palace of Darius I at Susa. The Persians, Urartians, Hittites and Mesopotamians[30] all employed this striking motif to represent their sky-gods. The winged sun-disc was not an original invention of the Egyptians." (The Mayan heiroglyphs also contain a 'winged wheel cross' and it also means 'sun' in that language, on a completely different continent! MHJ)

> "Rather than developing slowly...it seemed that the civilization of Egypt had emerged all at once and fully formed....remains from the pre-dynastic period dated to around 3600 BC showed no trace of writing, suddenly and inexplicably, the hieroglyphs ...began to appear...in a complete and perfect state. Even the very earliest hieroglyphs were already stylized and conventionalized... absolutely no traces of evolution from simple to more sophisticated styles ...one explanation, ...that Egypt had received its sudden and tremendous cultural boost from some other known civilization of the ancient world - Sumer on the Lower Euphrates in Mesopotamia, being the most likely...a variety of shared building and architectural styles did suggest a link between the two regions." Hancock, G. *The Sign and the Seal,* p. 317.

> [30]"To deny, therefore, that Egyptian and Mesopotamian systems of writing are related amounts to maintaining that Egypt invented independently a complex and not very consistent system at the very moment of being influenced in its art and architecture by Mesopotamia where a precisely similar system had just been developed from a more primitive stage." Frankfort, Henri. *The Birth of Civilization in the Near East.* pp. 100-111.

There were many Middle Eastern peoples whose understanding of the light (of truth or wisdom) of the Creator had deteriorated into the worship of *Shamash* (or the variation *Chemosh*) the sun or sun god. But the above Bible verse seems to indicate that while the Israelites were aware of the flight of the "winged" disk, this symbol was seen as something that appeared to them as a sign, in recognition of righteousness and healthy living. However in ancient Babylon a stylized wheel cross or solar cross also symbolized the sun god Shamash. Search shamash see symbols 28:21; 29:1 & Group 28:22 <http://www.symbols.com/>

It is likely that along with the symbols which became the basis of the Egyptian hieroglyphics, adopted from the ancient Middle East, the Egyptians also adopted the use of the solar cross and the winged disk, more information on the origin of the solar cross will be presented further on. "The wheel or solar cross called a *niwt* occurs (in Egyptian)...as the name of any sacred place which was created in the primeval age." Reymond, E. A. E. *Mythical Origin of the Egyptian Temple,* p. 14. As renowned Egyptologist Dr. Wallis Budge says; "the Egyptians borrowed much of their knowledge of the signs of the Zodiac, together with much else, from the Greeks, who had derived a great deal of the astronomical lore from the Babylonians." Budge, Wallis Ph.D. *The Gods of the Egyptians,* vol. ii. p. 312.

> "The Semitic origin of the Egyptians has been strongly urged on several grounds, especially the remarkable likeness of religious rites. (esp. see the winged disk of the Egyptians and that of Ahura Mazda)...Either Jews and Arabs got their faith and ceremonies from Egypt, or they and the Egyptians obtained them from some common

source. (that would be the Ormazdian religion, MHJ) Assyrian discoveries satisfy us that the Semitic people of the Euphrates were long preceded by a Turanian one. The very alphabet of the Semites,...was borrowed and adapted, in Assyria from Turanians, in Palestine from Egypt." Bonwick, James. *Egyptian Belief and Modern Thought,* p. 431.

If the Egyptians adopted their language from the ancient Middle East, it is very likely that they also adopted certain other symbols, such as those having religious significance. The winged disk and winged sun may be one such example. Some may argue that the kings or pharaohs of the Egyptian "Old Kingdom" date to earlier than the Semitic peoples, however the Egyptian's dates for their early first kingdom do *not* seem to correspond to dates derived from radiocarbon dating processes. There were so many differing factions in Egypt, their own written language eventually became incomprehensible to even themselves, the same may well have happened with their historical dates

> "The plot of the data suggests that the Egyptian historical dates beyond 4,000 years ago may be somewhat too old." Renfrew, Colin. *Before Civilization,* p. 72 quoting; Libby, the inventor of the radiocarbon method. A section following will discuss the possibility that if anything the historical dates would appear to be too recent, not too old, (because contamination from very old interstellar dust contaminates all radiometric tests making dates appear very old) suggesting that it was the records of the Egyptians which are inaccurate.

THE WINGED SYMBOLS OF AHURA MAZDA

> "He (Zarathustra) was the founder of the Magi who were priests of the religion of the Sun or of that Being of whom the Sun was the visible form or emblem." Higgins, Godfrey. *Anacalypsis,* p. 86, note that the page numbering of the online version does not correspond with that of the hard copy. <http://members.tripod.com/~pc93/anacv1b2.htm>

Earlier than its use for Shamash, the winged sun and the solar cross[31] is also well known to be one of the symbols of Ormazd and Ahura Mazda (it later also became a symbol associated with the sun god Mithra whose appearance evolved out of Zarathustra's religion, see the following discussion on Mithraism). According to d'Alviella (*The Migration of Symbols*) the wheel cross is a sun symbol or solar cross and Indian historian Firoze Davar points out that; "The symbol of the Zarathustrian faith is the sun." A winged solar cross appears as early as the 9th century BCE, an image of this winged solar cross, on a stele to Assurnasirpal II at Nimrud (recall that in the Theos/Dios/Deus/Zeus section Mithridate equates Zeus as a name of Oromasdes/Ormazd thus as the head of the pantheon represented at Nimrud this symbol could be equated with Ormazd whose religion is well known to have devolved into sun-worship). The winged cross can be viewed at the wiki on the winged sun. These solar crosses may have evolved into the later *fravashar* or *farafavars,* symbolic of Ahura Mazda Wikipedia. *The Winged Sun.*

<http://www.en.wikipedia.org/wiki/Winged_sun>

[31]The solar cross is associated with Ahura Mazda and the Zarathustrian religion as the center of

the winged disk of Ahura Mazda. Some scholars are finally making the connection between these solar crosses and the Celtic crosses adopted by Christianity. "Scholars speculate that the Celtic Cross developed from the sun cross, solar cross, sun wheel, etc., a pre-Christian symbol found in northwest Europe and Scandinavia -- a cross inside a circle, or a four-spoked wheel. When Christianity came to Ireland and Scotland, Christians extended the bottom spoke of this familiar symbol to remind them of the cross on which their new Savior was crucified." Dr. Ralph F. Wilson. *Celtic Stone Crosses.* <http://www.joyfulheart.com/stpatrick/stone-crosses.htm>

Sumerian pictograph characters from before 3000 BC, which later became cuneiform, include the wheel cross or solar cross among their symbols. (Time/Life, *The Age of God Kings)* "Although the cross is now assumed to be a wholly Christian symbol, it has been used by many cultures in different ages. It was used on Bronze Age Burial artifacts some 4,000 years ago;...by the Buddhists the cross was the axis of the wheel of the Law." Bord, J.&C. *Ancient Mysteries of Britain,* p. 89. "The wheel cross, ...is common on rock carvings and it appears in ancient Egypt, China, pre-Columbian America, and the Near East. ...When the first ideographic writing systems were developed it was included." Linngman, Carl G. *Dictionary of Symbols,* p. 28-31.

Settegast suggests these solar cross symbols, beautifully illustrated in her book as they were found, painted in dark and light colors, on numerous pottery bowls to be representative of the Zarathustrian emphasis on the forces of the Light (wisdom) and Darkness (ignorance). "Outstanding among the ceramic patterns of this period were combinations of cross and circle, often referred to "wheels" or wheeled cross" designs..." (p. 75) She says they were "superior to the later Ubaid pottery and associated with the "conspicuous absence" of arrow and spear heads, of an apparently advanced and peaceful people...The displays of human skulls associated with the Pre-pottery Nomadic B were nowhere in evidence among the early painted pottery cultures." Settegast, Mary. *When Zarathustra Spoke,* 2005, pp. 39 & 87.

> "The same analysts who theorized that the symbols painted on these ceramic surfaces represented encoded ideological information observed that the pottery bearing those symbols was distributed over a very large geographical area." Settegast, Mary. *When Zarathustra Spoke,* 2005, p. 75; citing Tosi, M.; S. Malek; Shahmirzadi; and M. A. Joyenda, 1992. *The Bronze Age in Iran and Afghanistan.*

These fine bowls were apparently ritually used, for they do not appear to have been used for cooking. They represent striking patterns with stark contrasts suggesting the apposition between the forces of the "Light" (wisdom or intelligence) and the forces of darkness (i.e., ignorance and evil), among which the wheeled solar cross predominates, dating to the time of the second "Neolithic Revolution" (5000 BCE). Settegast suggests they may be evidence of "the first" Zarathustra's influence on the development of agricultural settlements in 6000 BCE. Remember that there were many other later Zarathustra's or Zoroaster's, and stories about them, confused with the original Zarathustra's existence down through time. While Settegast does not mention a specific interpretation of the solar cross on this pottery (as symbolic of the All Highest Light - Ormazd) she gives many illustrations of their presence, on pottery of the era in her book, and does suggest their association with Zarathustra's religious teachings. (more on a prehistoric date for this "first Zarathustra" in the section, Dating Zarathustra, following) Mary Settegast, *Plato, Prehistorian* (published 2000)

138

<http://books.google.com/books/about/Plato_prehistorian.html?id=gtCBAAAAMAAJ

&<http://www.symbols.com/> & <http://www.en.wikipedia.org/wiki/winged_sun>

> "The first complex societies arose in a region which may not have had as long a history of habitation as other regions of the Near East...There is no evidence for warfare in the Ubaid period...(and) the temples are evidence of a shared religious ideology."

> <http://www.historicity.org/?cat=6> (Halaf arose first 6500-5500 BCE then Ubaid 5500-4000 BCE)

> <http://www.metmuseum.org/toah/hd/ubai/hd_ubai.htm> & *The Ubaid Period.* (5500-4000 BC) see Halaf link on webpage

The winged disk appears on numerous Bronze Age royal seals (in the Luwian language *Sol Suus*, symbolizing royal power, in Hebrew *suws, soos* or *siys* SHD 7797 means bright). The winged disk symbol also appears from ca. 8th century BCE, on Hebrew seals, one such seal is translated as "possession of Hezekiah, son of Ahaz, king of Juda." Along with the above Bible verse that mentions the winged sun as a "righteous" symbol, this usage demonstrates the Hebrew recognition and acceptance of this symbol as one related to YHVH Elohim. Wikipedia. *Faravahar.* <http://www.answers.com/topic/faravahar>

There are depictions throughout the ancient Middle East showing winged discs and winged *farafavars*. (Symbolic of Ahura Mazda; a related symbol, the solar cross appears even in prehistoric times and appears frequently beginning with the Bronze age c. 3500-2000.) Some look like airplanes, complete with what appear to be landing gear, usually carrying one god[32] yet a number of these flying machines carry three occupants. So the winged solar cross can apparently represent Ahura Mazda or guardian angels from the Zarathustrian religion as well as "*Shamash*" equated with the winged sun in Mal. 4:2.The fact that there is often more than one occupant in the *faravahars*, shows that they were understood to be some sort of vehicle. Another ancient Persian image shows a god riding on a cloud remember there is also a Bible verse describing one such image, Isa.60:1-8. *Religious Sungazing. (many images slow link)*

<http://sunlight.orgfree.com/history_of_sun_gazing.htm>&
<http://www.answers.com/topic/faravahar> &

<http://en.wikipedia.org/wiki/Sun_cross>&

[32]<http://altreligion.about.com/od/symbols/a/faravahar.htm>

Winged disk references include; Rice, Edward. *Babylon next to Nineveh,* p. 75; Sitchin, Zechariah. *Stairway to Heaven,* p. 80; Gershman, Minorsky & Sanghvi, *Persia the Immortal Kingdom,* p. 37; and Von Daniken, Eric. *In Search of Ancient Gods,* p. 26-36; and numerous online images.

MITHRAISM VS. THE CHALDEAN ORACLES

"The Chaldean Sun-god, Mithra, was called the 'Triple' and the trinitarian idea of the

139

Chaldeans was a doctrine of the Akkadians." Blavatsky, H. P. *The Chaldean Legend*, Theosophy, Vol. 52, No. 6, April 1964, p. 175-182.

<http://www.wisdomworld.org/additional/ListOfCollatedArticles/TheChaldeanLegend.html>

According to Grassmann (col.557) "Even more instructive is the series of references to *Trita Aptya...Trita* (aka *Trimurti*) is originally "the third"...probably obliged for his name and worship (i.187.1;i.163.2.3;1.52.5;viii.7.24) to a pre-Vedic point of view, because of which he also occurs often in the Zend." (*Zend-Avesta*, attrib. Zarathustra) D.D. Kosambi, *Combined Methods in Indology and Other Writings* <http://www.alibris.com/booksearch?qwork=9101855>

The existence of this early "trinity" is also confirmed by the *Chaldean Oracles* (aka *Oracula Magica Zoroastris,*1599, etc.) attributed to Zarathustra/Zoroaster. Sapere Aude in his preface to the Oracles states; "Berosus is said to be the first who introduced the writings of the Chaldeans concerning Astronomy and Philosophy among the Greeks." The first heading of the Chaldean/Kasdim Oracles is; "Cause. God." (the second line of the title is the original trinity) "Father. Mind. Fire." *The Chaldean Oracles.* Attributed to Zoroaster.

<http://www.hermetic.com/texts/chaldean.html>

After considering the evidence in the section on Dating Zarathustra older than Abraham it will be seen that the Chaldean/Kasdim trinity was the original holy trinity, after which many others were modeled in an attempt to anthropomorphize the Father (who is All). This was an attempt to change The One, who originally had no image, into a human form so as to make some individual "god" or false Elohim, with a humanoid form, worshipful. Few serious scholars now deny that "Holy Trinities" show up throughout the Middle East and that this pattern was adopted by Constantine's Councils after the third century. Some of the better known are the Babylonian trinity; *Ashtaroth, Baal and Tammuz*[33] ([33]meaning "true son" Hooke, S.H. *Babylonian and Assyria n Religion,* p. 22) *Brahma, Vishnu and Shiva* constituted the *Trimûrti* or Indian Trinity, and the Egyptian trinity of Father Mother and only begotten Son was; *Isis/Ast, Osirus/Asshur,* and *Hor/Horus.*

As mentioned previously in the discussion on "Easter," sometimes it is the father figure who dies and is resurrected, sometimes it is the son who is the resurrected "sun god" but the resurrection stories and "trinities" replay throughout all the ancient Middle East long prior to the time of Jeschu/Yeschu/Jesus. The popularity of resurrection stories was in part because for the uneducated masses it conveniently explained the dipping of the sun down toward the horizon, into the "underworld" coinciding with all of nature "dying" in winter; then rising or being reborn three days after the winter solstice, Dec. 25th, as the sun began its return northward, to be fully resurrected along with all life in spring at Easter. Hence all the fertility symbols, eggs, bunnies, flowers.

According to Eusebius, the Oracles say, in verse 1; "But God is He having the head of the Hawk." This verse does not show up in either of the other ancient collections, Cory seems to have been the first to discover it in the writings of Eusebius. The symbol of the Hawk as Hor/Light shows up in the most ancient hieroglyphics of the Egyptians, and other ancient Middle Eastern religions (Hor and the Shemsu Hor, the Followers of Hor [i.e. Followers of Light MHJ] were <u>already</u> present in the pre-dynastic times and thereafter became incorporated into prehistoric Egyptian hieroglyphs. Hancock and Bauval, *The Message of the Sphinx,* p.192-196; William Arnett, *The Predynastic Origin of Egyptian Hieroglyphs,* Plate XLIV or XLIX.

However, later on after an Egyptian written language developed, Hor became Horus, a Greek derivative just as is Isis and Osiris are Greek variants of their Egyptian names *Ast* and *Ashur.* As mentioned previously the word Hor/Or/Aur appears in all of the most ancient written languages with the meaning of "Light."

The *Chaldean Oracles* tell us in verses 22 & 24 "For not in Matter did the Fire, which is in the first beyond, enclose His active Power, *but in Mind*; for the Framer of the Fiery World is the Mind of mind...and thence a Fiery whirlwind...penetrating the abysses of the Universe" (The Big Bang? MHJ). "The Mind of the Father said all things should be cut into Three ("Father. Mind. Fire.")...The Father mingled every Spirit from this triad...For in each World shineth the Triad, over which the Monad ruleth. The first course (The Great Holy Spirit, MHJ) is Sacred, in the middle place (space, MHJ) courses the sun, in the third the Earth (matter, MHJ) is heated by the internal fire (the molten core, MHJ)." (verses 28, 30, 36) (This Trinity corresponds to; First - Spirit/the Father, Second - Etherea/space/void, and Third - Matter/earth/all the physical or material universe, MHJ) ibid. <http://www.hermetic.com/texts/chaldean.html>

> "Zarathushtra's emphasis on Principles is reflected in the *Gatha*'s stress on strict and uncompromising monotheism—a monotheism so strict, as we have seen, that it did not countenance even other *names* conferred upon the Great Spirit: a lesson his followers seem to have forgotten over the ages, when at a later period they compiled a list of 101 names of Ahura Mazda...it is as clear as can be that the term Ahura Mazda which Zarathushtra selected for the Supreme Being is best translated into English by the expression "Great Spirit" or "Mighty Spirit."" Mehta, Ardeshir. *Zarathushtra,* p. 81. ebook at:
>
> <http://www.dnzt.org/images/BOOKS-PHOTOS/ENGLISH%20BOOKS/Zarathushtra%20-%20ARDESHIR%20%20MEHTA.pdf>
>
> *"Ahya yasa nemangha Ustana jasto rafedhrahya Manyeuhs Mazdao paourvim spentahya.* For this I pray—I call upon Thy Name with hands outstretched—for *Rapture,* Holy Bliss: O Great Spirit, first I pray for this!" *Gatha 28.1* (As translated by Mehta, Ardeshir. *Zarathushtra,* p. 87. ebook @ above url)

Franz Cumont, who founded the study of Mithraism considered the Mysteries of Mithras to have evolved from the *Magussaeans* of Asia Minor, the Hellenized Magi, whose later ideas reflected their magical and astrological beliefs. Lactantius Placidus says the Mithraic cult passed from the Persians to the Phrygians, and from them to the Romans. *Wisemen of the East.*

<http://www.thedyinggod.com/chaldeanmagi/>

The Roman Mithras was identified with the sun "*Deus Sol Invictus Mithras*" (In Rome, Dec. 25 was the day of the rebirth of *Natilis Invictus,* the Invincible Sun), however, the Iranian Mithra was the god of the dawn light. The Iranian Mithra was a god of cattle and pastures, the Roman Mithras was called by Porphyry (40) a "cattle thief." The Roman Mithras, as his mightiest deed, sacrifices a bull, while the earlier Iranian Mithra was a god of righteousness, and this animal sacrifice would have been considered an act of evil: just as it was when Ahriman slew the primal bull of creation. Perhaps the moral of the Ahriman story was that it was originally meant to demonstrate how evil and disease came to mankind through the decision to begin eating meat (as was mentioned of humans developing disease after they left the "Garden of Eden" Gen. 9:2-5). (more on the effects of an unhealthy diet in a later chapter) Porphyry, *On the Cave of the Nymphs*. <http://www.tertullian.org/fathers/porphyry_cave_of_nymphs_02_translation.htm>

& Beck, Roger. *The Religion of the Mithras Cult in the Roman Empire: Mysteries of the Unconquered Sun.* <http://bmcr.brynmawr.edu/2006/2006-12-08.html>

Kaufman Kohler, in the *Jewish Encyclopedia* article on Merkabah mysticism say the rites of Mithraism "bear such a striking resemblance to those by which the Merkabah-riders approached the Deity that there can be little doubt as to the Mithraic origin of the latter." The Mithraic religion is itself one that has been shown to be a corrupted form of the Zarathustrian religion.

<http://www.dnzt.org/images/BOOKS-PHOTOS/ENGLISH%20BOOKS/Zarathushtra%20-%20ARDESHIR%20%20MEHTA.pdf>

"That only is right for any one, which is right for everyone else." Gatha 43-1

Mithra a sun god, was depicted as a bull slayer, this religious invention was a later corruption of Zarathustra's original teaching condemning Ahriman, the spirit of evil, for killing bulls and he expressly forbids the killing of bulls (*Yasna* 29). Mithra's mediation and sacrificial meal was, no doubt, to avoid conforming to the discipline of Zarathustra's commandments against eating meat. If the savior Mithra "mediated" for those desiring to eat flesh, then their ritualization of the meal absolved those in attendance (at least in their own minds) from responsibility for their actions. (as medical science has shown the consequences of an unhealthy diet are not so easily avoided more on this in the chapter on early religious beliefs and intuitions on diet and how it correlates to modern diet and health research) Porphyry, *On the Cave of the Nymphs* 6 and @

<http://www.tertullian.org/fathers/porphyry_cave_of_nymphs_02_translation.htm>

"The Elohim were often mentally aggregated under the generalized term *tseba'oth* (fem. pl. from the root *tsaba'* a host, an army SHD 6635) as in the expression 'host of heaven'." Article on Elohim, *Theosophy Dictionary* online @;

<http://www.experiencefestival.com/a/elohim/id/105136>

The *Chaldean Oracles* also mentions the word, *Sabaoth* or *TzBuat,* meaning hosts, there is also the related word *Shboh.* A similar word found in Hebrew is *Sabbath* (SHD 7673) whose origin goes back even further to pre-Semitic times and cultures. In the Babylonian cuneiform tablets of the *Sabattu* it is described as a day of rest. The Akkadian term *shapattu* refers to the Full moon. The *sa*-heart *bat*-ceasing, *sabat* was observed on the 7th, 14th, 21st, and 28th days of the "month." (month is itself a word derived from "moon"). Thirteen-28 day months divides much better into a 365 year than the Christian 12 month calendar, devised to avoid the number 13 which priests in the Middle Ages did not like. So it is not difficult to conclude that the ancient *sabat* days, on the phases of the moon, were originally put aside for communion with YHVH's holy council; and YHVH Elohim of hosts, is also known also as *YHVH Elohim Sabboath (IEVE Aleim Tzbauth* as in Ps. 80:19). <http://www.hermetic.com/texts/chaldean.html>

Chapter Six

THE CHALDEAN KASDIM FROM BEFORE ABRAHAM

"And Terah took Abram his son and Lot...and they went forth from Ur of the *Kasdim[1]*, to go to Canaan." Gen. 11:31 (in KJV translated as Chaldee)

<http://scripture4all.org/OnlineInterlinear/OTpdf/gen11.pdf>

CHALDEAN/KASDIM ORIGINS OF JUDEO-CHRISTIAN MYSTICISM

[1]This chapter will discuss some of the known history of the Chaldees, called *Kasdiym/Kasdim* in the Bible (Gen. 11:32; Jer. 50:10; 51:24,35 SHD 3778 & 3779). Kasdim, meaning "*Arpakhsadiym*" of *Arpachsad* (who was ancestral to Abraham, the name may also have some association with modern Pakistan, meaning 'the pure') a son of Shem, son of Noah (Gen. 11:12). The name Chaldee/Chaldea comes from the Assyrian/Akkadian term *Kaldu[2]*, used for the territory of Chaldea. (*The Chaldeans* by David Kelly, quoting; *Abraham and the Merchants of Ura* by C. H. Gordon <http://www.cgca.net/coglinks/origin/oon2.1/vol2_1p2.html>)

> [2]"The expressions "Chaldaea r" and "Chaldaeans" are frequently used in the Old Testament as equivalents for "Babylonia" and "Babylonians...(however) The sudden rise of the later Babylonian empire...tended to produce so thorough an amalgamation of the Chaldaeans and Babylonians...considered as two kindred branches of the same original Semite stock, that in the course of time no perceptible differences existed between them...Consequently, the term "Chaldaean" came quite naturally to be used in later days as synonymous with "Babylonian...The early *Kaldi* had seized and held from very ancient times the region of old Sumer," <http://www.1911encyclopedia.org/Chaldaea>

The Chaldeans are mentioned by the first century historian Josephus, in his *Jewish Antiquities*. (1.6.4) According to Shelagh McKenna, since Chaldee means servant of God, it was probably the *Arpachsadite* priests who were referred to as Chaldees. "The Israelite association explains the existence of a Jewish sect called the Essenes, whose members learned Zoroastrian doctrines (including pacifism and vegetarianism MHJ). Jesus was a Essene (of the Nazarean branch, MHJ), and the Zoroastrian magi were deeply involved in the establishment of Christianity." Article *The Magi - A Short History* by Shelagh McKenna

<http://archive.is/A8oH>

> "I bring him Babylon-ward, land of the *Kasdym* (Chaldees)." Ez. 12:13

The priestly caste of the Magi, were nomadic Shamanists who occupied Babylon along with the Persians, the Israelites were exposed to their religion while in Babylon. Darius writes of repairing temples that the *Magus* had destroyed. (Bh. {Pers. Text} i.63-66) Their presence in Babylon is mentioned in the OT by Jeremiah, speaking of *Nergalsharezer Rab Mag*, or that is a Magian Rabbi (Jer. 39:3,13) Rab or Rabbi, meaning Chief Magi. (SHD7248, 7229)

"The ancient Persians believed that the Supreme Being was surrounded with angels, or what they called Aeons or emanations, from the divine substance. This was also the opinion of the Manichean, and of almost all the Gnostic sects of Christians...(treating) Deu. 33.2...M. Veausobre has shown that the Hebrew word *asdt*[3] which the Septuagint translates angels, means effusions, that is emanations, from the divine substance...Thus we see here that the doctrines of the Persians and that of the Jews, and we shall see afterward, of the Gnostic and Manichean Christians, were in reality the same...Nothing can be more absurd than the vulgar translation, which is made from a copy in which the words have been divided by the Masorets. But it was necessary to risk any absurdity, rather than let the fact be discovered that the word meant angels or emanations, which would so strongly tend to confirm the doctrine of the Gnostics, and also prove that the religions of Moses and the Persians were the same...The first religion, therefore, of the Persians, was the worship of the true God, and they continued in it for some time after Abraham was expelled from Chaldaea, having the same faith and worship as Abraham had, except only in those points concerning which he received instruction after his going into Haran and Canaan...Abraham...came from Ur of the Chaldees (...the peninsula of *Saurastra* or of *Sura-stan*, according to Higgins named after Zarathustra). The Pythagoras learned (in the following quote) of the Magi; 'Oromasdes in his body resembles light; in his soul truth.'" Higgins, Godfrey. Vol. 1 *Anacalypsis,* pp.73,76,80,102,235&389.

[3]However, the online translation at <http://www.scripture4all.org> gives the translation of *ashdth* in Deu. 33:2 as; "fiery-edict" so it is clear that the translation continues to be under revision.

"And He is saying YHWH from Sinai He comes and He is radiant, from Seir for them He shines, from mountain of Paran[4], and He arrives from myriads of holy one(s) from right of Him *ashdth* to them." Deu. 33:2 ([4]from the *Juwuri* language, related to the language of Caucasian Persians (*Farsi* or *Paran*) <http://2pic.20m.com/ECJ.html> This mention of the territory of Paran/Persia in the Torah confirms an extremely ancient date for Persia, this concept is discussed in depth in the section on Persia/Parashi/Barashi...etc.

J. Burnet in his *Early Greek Philosophy*, 1958, tells us that early mysticism teachings originated from the Chaldean/Kasdim, spreading via the Aryans and sources he refers to as vaguely Scythian (along with the Medes they occupied Persia ca.1000 BCE) into Europe and east into India. According to *A Compendious Syriac Dictionary,* the name Chaldean refers to an occupation rather than an ethnic background, they were astronomer priests and/or astrologers. (Burnet, J. *Early Greek Philosophy ,* 4th Ed., London, 1958, p. 81 ff)

<http://www.ccg.org/english/s/p235.html> & <p039> Haynes, Edward S. *Early Persia.*

<http://timelines.ws/countries/PERSIA.HTML>

As early as the turn of the 3rd millennium BCE, the neolithic *Kel'teminar* culture flourished in the "Chorasmian" oasis (which I suggest to be adopted from the name Hormazda/Ormazda meaning something like "Hormazdian" or at the very least containing the word *Or/Hor/Khor* meaning light or sun MHJ) Vinogradov, 1968; idem, 1981.

Remains of the Bronze Age *Suyargan* (beginning of the 2nd millennium B.C.E.), Tazabag'yab (middle and late 2nd millennium B.C.E.), and *Amirabad* (10th-8th centuries B.C.E.) cultures have also been identified there (Itina, 1977). What is suggested here is that since the name Chorasmia was first mentioned in the Avesta (Yt. 10:14), attributed to Zarathustra, it makes it very likely that this name reflects the use of the root word Hor/Or/Khor meaning "Light" or "sun" as discussed in the previous section on the words for light in other ancient languages. Benveniste, p. 265-74; Gershevitch, p. 14; Hinz, p, 27; Abaev, p. 320. *Chorasmia.*

<http://www.iranica.com/newsite/articles/v5f5/v5f5a015.html>

> "The Chorasmians ruled the Akes river valley, before it came under the control of the Persians. (Herodotus 3.117) and some scholars have recognized the memory of a brief period of Chorasmian Scythian rule in the southeast Caspian region. This story, together with the mention by Hecateus of Miletus (apud Atheneus, II, p. 70A-B; Jacoby, *Fragmente* I, p. 38) of Chorasmians living "toward the sunrise" from the Parthians, has given rise to a hypothesis about the existence in Pre-Achaemenid times of a powerful kingdom conventionally called "Greater Chorasmia...There has been general agreement that the homeland of the Zoroastrian religion...was located in Chorasmia." Ibid.

<http://www.iranica.com/newsite/articles/v5f5/v5f5a015.html>

The existence of the "Chaldean/Kasdim magi" (remember from p. 113 the holy-*imag* were mentioned in Akkadian cuneiform writings) associated with Zarathustra's religion, is prior to the time of Abraham; this supports dating Zarathustra's life to some time before Abraham. It is reasonable to say well before, because it would have taken time for a Chaldean kingdom to form after Zarathustra's Chaldean Kasdim/magi, spread word of his teachings. Since the history of the Chaldean/Kasdim date back to before Abraham, Zarathustra's influence on the Chaldean/Kasdim magi/priests places his birth before that time, adding further confirmation to the dates for Zarathustra given by Aristotle, Xanthus of Lydia, Eudoxus of Cnidus, Hermippus, Hermodorus, Aristotle, Plutarch, Diogenes Laertius, and Pliny.

If the earlier pre-Abraham Chaldeans/Kasdim were not priests of the same Chaldean/Kasdim religion as the later one (who were known to have been followers of the monotheistic Zarathustrian religion, albeit sometimes in corrupted form) then pray tell, of what religion were they priests, and where is the evidence showing that the Chaldean religion completely changed its tenets in mid course? For if Zarathustra as a "Chaldean" simply appeared as a later prophet of *that* religion then there should be some remnants of that hypothetical "Chaldean" religion and its hypothetical gods to be seen in Zarathustra's teachings, when it is in fact the opposite, remnants of Zarathustra's teachings are to be found in the records of the Chaldean/Kasdim teachings.

For it would be unreasonable to suggest that one man took a preexisting religion and *completely* changed its polytheistic structure to monotheism; to where there was no trace of any such hypothetical Chaldean "gods" remaining. And that he then persuaded the other members of that religion to abandon all the gods and the beliefs of such a proposed pre-existing "Chaldean" religion, while still considering themselves members of such a hypothetically previous religion. If the angelic beings in Zarathustra's teachings, like Spenta Armaiti or the fravashars (guardian angels), were traces of those earlier beliefs, then as guardian angels who was their Creator or God? And why is that religion not named and its gods castigated by Zarathustra if he hypothetically made such efforts toward changing this religion of the Chaldean/Kasdim? It is because his religion did not come later, it came before and the Chaldean Kasdim/magi came later! And these are the same Chaldean/Kasdim mentioned in the OT as already existing in the time of Abraham.

> "The original Magi were one of the six tribes of the Medians (Her. i.101) who were a western branch of the same race." Kosambi, D.D. *Combined Methods in Indology and Other Writings.* <http://www.vidyaonline.org/arvindgupta/ddkindopartone.pdf>

The *Medes* were also known as the *Mada* or *Amadai*, absence of any mention of them in the Avesta would seem to place these writings from the Zarathustrian religion before the Medes of the 9th century BCE. However many of the Medians were Zarathustrians and their language was closely related to Aryan (Old Persian) the same as are many writings of the Zarathustrian religion. It may even be that the *Amadai* were a people whose name makes reference to *Spenta Armaiti*. Spenta Armaiti appears repeatedly in the writings attributed to Zarathustra, and according to Harvey and Slocum in their *Old Iranian Online* site "Spenta Armaiti...had the earth entrusted to her care." The Amesha Spentas a related name, were the "Holy Immortals" or "Bounteous Immortals," the same as were called the Elohim in Hebrew. In the teachings of Zarathustra, in the Yasna 45:4, it says; … "the good working Armaiti is His (God's) daughter. "The Avestan text, however it is translated, makes one thing very clear, Spenta Armaiti is a feminine[5] entity." *Early Persia.*

<http://faculty.winthrop.edu/haynese/syll/notes/331/PERSIA.html>

Angels Appendix. <http://www.heart7.net/spirit/aa.html>

[5]Shapero, Hannah M. G. *Spenta Armaiti: Spirit of Serenity.*

<http://www.pyracantha.com/Z/armaiti.html>

> "Spenta Armaiti is one of the "Holy Immortals." Their position in Gathic theology is extremely high; so very high, indeed, that in many places the *Gatha* seem to address themselves to the Amesha Spentas as if they were living, breathing, conscious entities, not incorporeal Principles attributes of the Divine. At times we find them all addressed together as Mazdao Ahuraongho, "The Mazda Ahuras" (plural), a term which includes the Supreme Being as well. There is virtually no verse in the *Gatha* which does not speak of one or the other of the Amesha Spentas. The *Gatha* are, in a sense, Hymns *specifically addressed* these Eternal Holy Ones." Ardeshir Mehta, *Zarathushtra,* .80-81. ebook @

> <http://homepage.mac.com/ardeshir/Zarathushtra-Ch.1-6,Draft.pdf>

Ormazd creates two mainyus or forces, the *Spenta*[6] or Holy force and the *Angra* or unholy force. From one of the verses of the 30th chapter of the *Yasna,* "*At cha hyat ta hem mainyu jasetem paourvim dazda gaem cha ajyaitim cha.* Now when the two mainyus first came together, they created motion and also inertia or non-movement, i.e. rest." (*Gatha 30.44*) Recall from the previous discussion on "movement and rest," *tohu and vohu,* that these were also terms used in the first verses of Genesis and later discussed by Yeschu/Joshu/Jesus in the Gospel of Thomas verse 50. [6]"Spenta qualifies words other than Manyu, particularly Armaiti or Mazda." Chatterjee, Jatindra Mohon, M. A. *Ethical Conceptions of the Gathas,* p. 100.

> "He is the lord of the moving and the immovable." Gatha 51-12

There are certainly a great many place names in the OT that could well be derived from the Zarathustrian/Ormazdian religion; There is *Zurishaddai/Zarushaddai* (Num. 1:6, 2:12, 7:36, 41 & 10:19) of whom some of the Israelites are numbered as *ben tzurishdi* "sons of Zurishaddai." In Hebrew this is another way of saying a whole race of people, just as *ben elohim*, means sons of the Elohim, i.e. humans. In light of the information on the Zoar/Little people/Sakae in the chapter on Earthlings, it is entirely possible that this family or race of people may have descended from followers of Zarathustra. *Zarushaddai* may have been a tribal name whose spelling became, an ever so slightly altered, reference to members of the Zarathustrian religion (who worshiped the Father/Creator by the name Ormazd).

> "Some scholars are of the opinion that as Zoroastrianism spread, some of the Sakas adopted its teachings." Litvinsky, B. A.; A. Abetekov, and H. Yusupov, *History of Civilization of Central Asia Vol. II*, p. 31.

There is also *Zarethan* a city beside the city of Adam Jos. 3:16 also called, *Zeredathah, Zereth-the-shahar*, Zarephath (toward 1 Kings 17:9). As mentioned in the section on the little people, the word *Tsaur or Tsaw'er.* (SHD 6686) means both small and an Israelite. (some of whom may have come from *Tso'ar/Zoar*, SHD 6820 also meaning small) All of these words Strong's has related to the words for small and little, *tsa'ar* (SHD 6819). There are many references to the city of *Tsoar*/Zoar, a city mentioned as early as Genesis (13:10) as already in existence before Abraham's time.

Zoar-aster was a spelling of Zarathustra used by various ancient historians and the name Zoar is recognized in legends of a savior who was crucified. Zarathustra was by various accounts put to death because of his religious beliefs. Because of this legend, accounts his death may show up in the Orient among Indian priests known as the Bonzes, also in China among priests of the Foists or Poists; because the Bonzes/Buddhists have a legend of the crucifixion of "Zoar of the Bonzes." This would mean the abbreviated name Zoar was used as a form of Zarathustra, in their language and teachings. Holding, James Patrick. *Zoar Losers.*

<http://www.tektonics.org/copycat/zoar.html>

Some biblical references to Zoar include; Gen. 13:10, 14:2 & 8, 19:22,23 & 30, Deu. 34:3, Isa. 15:5. In Jer. 48:4-5 the Septuagint reads "unto Zoar" instead of the KJV "her little ones...for in the going down of Horonaim the enemies have heard a cry of destruction." However the discussion goes on in Jer. 48:34 where it says; "Zoar even unto Horonaim" showing that these references are to the same people, the little people descended from the Elohim. Remember Aur/Hor/Or the Hebrew name for light, is also sometimes used as a variation of the "Or" in Ormazd, just as when it is spelled "Hormazd."

Concerning the reference to "Horonaim," as mentioned previously the word "*Hor*" or "*Or*" or "*Aur*" is the word for light in the most ancient written languages of the Middle East including Hebrew so this will most likely, eventually be confirmed as a reference to a city of the Hormazdians. It is also mentioned in Num. 33:37 that Aaron died on Mt. Hor or that is, "Mt. Light," this mountain, which was already in existence before the Torah was written, was also likely to have been named after the Hormazdian religion.

> "Zoroaster the sage (magi)...called the good power Oromazes (Mazda) and the evil

power Areimanius (Ahriman), and he further declared that among all things perceptible to the senses, Oromazes may best be compared to light, and Areimanius, conversely, to darkness and ignorance, and midway between the two is Mithras; for this reason the Persians gave to Mithras the name of Mediator." (Plutarch, *On Isis and Osiris*) <http://www.pesherofchrist.infinitesoulutions.com/Pagan_neighbors/Isis_Osiris.html>

Zarathustra taught monotheism but some of the later "Magi" had adopted the paganism of Babylon worshiping Bel or Baal. According to Nigosian in *The Zoroastrian Faith,* some had fallen away from Zarathustra's condemnation of animal sacrifice as given in the *Yasna and Gathas,* and had begun to offer sacrifices in the high places just as is mentioned of the Israelites in the OT. (for example II Chr. 33:17, I Kings 14:23, II Kings 23:5, Hosea 4:13) Porphyry reported that some would not eat meat because they had adopted ideas of reincarnation, however reincarnation is not found in orthodox Zoroastrianism.

The Maggussaeans of Asia Minor, in what is now Turkey, were Persian emigrants speaking the language of Aramaic, rather than the *Palahvi* in which Zarathustra's teachings were written. Many were therefore unable to read their own scriptures, and apparently had lost the essence of Zarathustra's teachings. *The Chaldean Magi.*

<http://www.thedyinggod.com/chaldeanmagi/index.html>

Hermippus, who lived about 200 BCE wrote a book on the Magi and believed in the Oriental (Zarathustrianism was considered to be from the 'Orient' MHJ) origin of Greek thought. According to Pliny, he "commented upon two million verses left by Zarathustra...(and) placing Zarathustra five thousand years before the Trojan war" (*Natural History* 30.4) The *Encyclopedia of Religion and Ethics* (ERE) notes that the Magis in India, referred to in the *Bharesya Purana,* and the *Brhat-samhita,* are identified by L. H. Gray as probably Magians. *The Chaldean Magi.*

<http://www.thedyinggod.com/chaldeanma ugaritgi/index.html>

Burnet indicates that the influence on early Greek philosophy occurred *before* the first mention of the Gymnosophists and Magi, by Antigonus of Cerystus, quoted by Diogenes Laertius. Diogenes taught, that the Magi taught, the future resurrection of men to a deathless existence. (Encyclopedia of Religion and Ethics, vol. 4, p. 244) (Burnet, J. *Early Greek Philosophy,* 4th Ed., London, 1958, pp. 81ff, & *Encyclopedia of Religion and Ethics* vol. 4, p. 244, quoted by

<http://www.ccg.org/english/s/B7_1.html >

> "Porphyry asserted that Pythagoras was taught in Babylon by (the Chaldean) Zaratas, a disciple of Zoroaster, and initiated into the highest esoteric mysteries of the Zoroastrians. Aristoxenus, friend and pupil of Aristotle (who had been taught by the Pythagorean, Xenophilos) who came originally from Pythagorean circles, had also maintained that Pythagoras had been a student of Zaratas." *The Chaldean Magi.*

> <http://www.thedyinggod.com/chaldeanmagi/index.html>

The extension of the Mystery religion into Egypt was also to lead to confusion amongst writers, attributing Egyptian influence on the Greek cults, when it was actually the Magian Shaman mysticism which influenced both. (Burnet, J. *Early Greek Philosophy,* 4th Ed., London, 1958, pp. 88 ff)

Greek interest in the 'Oriental' teachings of Zarathustra, resulted in the production of many pseudo-epigraphical works, written in Greek, falsely attributed to Zoroaster and his disciples. These have resulted in many contradictory dates for his existence, but clearly there is evidence showing he lived much earlier than accounts resulting from some of those falsifications would purport. "Bidez and Cumont have sought to demonstrate, in *The Hellenized Magi*, these documents held nothing of orthodox Zoroastrian content."

Ibid. <http://www.thedyinggod.com/chaldeanmagi/index.html>

In Plato's *Euthydemus*, Socrates refers to the ancient gods as his "lords *and* ancestors" showing the same theme as given in the Genesis (6:1-2) account of humanities descent from the gods. Andrew Louth in *The Origin of the Christian Mystical Tradition -From Plato to Denys*, Clarendon Press, Oxford, traces the Greek influence (inherited at least in part from Magian/Zarathustrian input) on the development of Christian mysticism. Some of this influence on Christianity and some references to these hidden mysteries by Yeschu/Joshu/Jesus will be further explored in the section on Hidden Mysteries in a later chapter.

ABRAM OF THE CHALDEE/KASDIM

The mention of Abram leaving from the land of his birth, named as Ur of the Chaldees (the Hebrew word is *Kshdim*) in Genesis, testifies to the existence of the Chaldeans/Kasdim long before the time of Moses (estimated to be roughly 1250-1350 BCE). The argument that the name Chaldean is anachronistic, while true, does not make the Hebrew reference invalid, since Chaldean is not the word used in the Hebrew version, *Kshdim* is, and it is the Hebrew word that is synonymous with the Assyrian-Akkadian Chaldee/*Kaldu*. It was clearly translated as such because in post-exilic times the Chaldeans and the *Kasdim* were understood by scribes to be one and the same.

Abraham's life time, is considered by most scholars to be around 1800-1900 BCE or earlier. Martin Haug, Ph.D., wrote in his book, *The Sacred Language, Writings and Religions of the Parsis,* "The Magi are said to have called their religion *Kesh-i-Ibraham.* (another reference to the name *Kshdim*) They traced their religious books to Abraham, who was believed to have brought them from Heaven." (p. 16)

> "An Islamic tradition handed down by the Persian poets tells how Abraham, not wishing to eat alone, once sought to share his meal with an old man he met in the desert. When the time came to pray, he realized that his guest was a Zoroastrian and wanted to send him away. But an angel restrained Abraham saying, "God has fed this man for a hundred years, how could you refuse him a meal?" (Yann, Richard, *Land of a Thousand and One Courtesies,* Unesco Courie, Feb. 1990, p. 30)
>
> <http://www.encyclopedia.com/doc/1G1-135732896.html>

The Chaldee/Kasdim priests, who later are known to be associated with both the Magi and Zarathustra, are thus mentioned in the OT to have been in existence before the time of Abraham. That they were known as priests shows that they were members of a religion, one that was already in existence *before* the time of Abraham. Jos. 24:2, says; "In the distant past your ancestors lived beyond the Euphrates River, including Terah the father of Abraham and Nac-hor. (perhaps another inclusion of the word Hor/Chor/Or) They worshiped *aleim achrim* (Elohim Achrim)."

This word *Achrim* SHD 310, is translated, by KJV as other or strange gods, however *Achrach akh-rakh* SHD 315, is recognized as a related word, and it is derived from SHD 310 and 251 meaning, after (his) brother: *Achrach*, an Israelite:--*Aharah*. (Note the similarity of *Aharah* to the ancient word *Ahura* MHJ). It will be shown in the following section on Yahuwah/Yahu/Ahu, that the name *Yahu* was in use for the Creator in Persia, at the same time in history that the Jews also said *Yahu*, both meaning 'Lord.') So these *Elohim achrim/aharah* may have been considered 'brother' gods, to the Elohim of the Israelites. Actually as Strong's definition of the name *Achrach* (SHD 310 &315) tells us, their followers were also Israelites, albeit by another tribal name - *Achrach*, one used before the term "Israelite" was coined. They were not so called until after the time of Jacob, Abraham's grandson, who was first nicknamed "Israel" in Gen. 35:10 whereas the Elohim Achrim were in existence in the land of Abraham's ancestors. Gen. 11:31

These sons of "Shem" from whom Abraham descended, spoke another language but the *Chaldean Oracles* show, that the Chaldee/Kasdim still worshiped the Father. *Yahu* meant "the Lord" in their language just as it did to at least some of the ancient Jews. Some of their Elohim were, however, called by other names, in the languages of the far distant past, since the Elohim, whose personal names were perhaps known, may have not yet risen to positions within YHVH's council of Elohim from before Abraham's time.

The Bible, however, still points out to us that YHVH blessed these Elohim of Shem. Gen. 9:26 tells us; (before *Arpachsad* and his people, the *Arpakhsadiym* of Shem, Gen. 11:12, who were the *Ksadim*/Chaldeans, from before the time of Abraham, so, therefore, long before Moses or Joshua) "And He is saying blessed are YHWH('s) Elohim of Shem and Canaan shall become his servant." So even the Elohim of the prehistoric past in the ancient land of Shem, who existed before Hebrew developed as a spoken language, were also YHVH's blessed Elohim.

> "Dr Shuckford gives other reasons to shew that the religions of Abraham and of the Persians were the same. He states that Dr Hyde was of his opinion and thus concludes. The first religion therefore of the Persians was the worship of the true God, and they continued in it for some time after Abraham was expelled Chaldaea, having the same faith and worship as Abraham had except only in those points concerning which he received instruction after going into Haran and into Canaan." Higgins, Godfrey. *Anacalypsis,* p. 84, Note that the page numbering of the online book does not correspond with those of the hard copy.
>
> <http://books.google.com/books?id=zySeQXg5_HIC&pg=PA80&lpg=PA80&dq=Dr+Shuckford+the+religions+of+Abraham+and+of+the+Persians+Higgins,+Godfrey.+Anacalypsis&source=web&ots=-9eWbXwEdu&sig=wAkqO_OrRSovvA0amkyVhO0yozU&hl=en >

It is entirely reasonable that the presence of YHVH and His Elohim were with mankind all along even before Abraham. If the presence of the spiritual guidance of YHVH's council of Elohim is posited from the beginning, then to suggest that in all the time between the time of the Adam and the time of Abraham, humanity was completely destitute of their spiritual guidance, is extremely unthinkable. The Elohim were watching out for humanity all along, albeit called by whatever language was in use at the time. These records were not written down in Hebrew, since the Hebrew language had yet to develop. But the biblical references to the Elohim of Shem as being blessed, serves as a reminder to us that the presence of the Elohim of Shem was beneficent and blessed even in the distant prehistoric past before the time of Israel and before the Hebrew Bible was written.

> "In adoration toward the rising Sun we see that the religion of the Magi had become corrupted by the Arabians and that in order to avoid this very corruption and preserve the worship of one God, which was the great object of Moses, that to which all the forms and ordinances of discipline both of the Magi and Moses were subservient, he established a law. (against bowing to the east, MHJ)" Higgins, Godfrey. *Anacalypsis,* p. 97, Note that the page numbering of the online book does not correspond with those of the hard copy. <http://books.google.com/books?id=zySeQXg5_HIC&pg=PA88&lpg=PA88&dq=the+religion+of+the+Magi+had+become+corrupted+by+the+Arabians&source=web&ots=-9eWbXxG8q&sig=6bhXG0ofHG29oEAOzzQirpIn8Bk&hl=en >

Abraham near the end of his life tells his servant to "go to my country, and to my kindred and take a wife unto my son Isaac...and he arose and went to *Aram-Naharaim* (Mesopotamia), unto the city of Nahor. Which later probably became the kingdom of *Mitanni.* Nahor was in the Balikh valley of Northern Mesopotamia, so the Ur, i.e., city of the Chaldee which is mentioned is located in the northern land where the followers of Zarathustra was known to have lived. (Note also the similarity of the name Ur to the many other place names incorporating Or/Hor/Ur/Aur meaning "light" as in Ormazd.) Harran was located in present day Turkey along a tributary of the Euphrates River. After Abram's family left it says; "they came unto Harran," if he had come from the Ur in southern Mesopotamia, why would he go to northern Mesopotamia on a journey to Canaan? *Where was Abraham's Ur?*

<http://www.bibleandscience.com/bible/books/genesis/ur.htm>

Mitanni nobility, known as *Marya*, were an Indo-Aryan warrior caste, referred to in the Bible as Horites (Gen. 14:6), the Horites worshipped the Indian Mitra[7]/Mithra, who they called "the mediator" (*meson*), between *Hormazes* (Ormazd) and *Areimanius* (Ahriman) the spirit of evil. That the Horites were already in existence at the time of Abram and Lot also demonstrates the presence of the teachings of Zarathustra as predating Abraham, because the Horites followed a degenerated form of Zarathustra's teachings concerning Ormazd. These Horites followed some form of Mithraism, which had fallen away from the peaceful, loving, vegetarian approach Zarathustra taught and actually advocated observing a sacrificial meal as some kind of worship advocated by Mithra.

[7]"...the *dvandvah* expression *mitra-vourunai* is none other than the archaic *'Mithra-Baga'* of the *Avesta...* But while in the *Vedas, Bhaga* is a minor divinity in its own right, in proto-Indo-Iranian times this was an epithet of *Vouruna's...*" Boyce, Mary (2001), *Mithra the King and Varuna the Master,* pp. 239–257. "The Avesta common noun *mithra* demonstrably, however, means something like 'pact, contract, covenant...'" Boyce, Mary. *A History of Zoroastrianism.*

The balance of scholarly opinion has shifted from one of a continuity of Zarathustra's teachings, to instead one of re-invention, metamorphosing through Chaldea, and the Hellenized Magi, the Magusaeans, into later forms which lost much of Zarathustra's purity in the transition. (Plutarch, *On Isis and Osiris (*46-7) see de Jong 1997: pp. 171-7; on Mithra as judge, see Shaked 1980) 6) <http://www.briansbetterworld.com/articles/whoweretheisraelites.html> Beck, Roger. *Mithraism.* <http://www.cais-soas.com/cais/Religions/iranian/Mithraism/mithraism.htm>

This means that Abraham before coming from Ur of the Chaldee/Kasdim, had earlier left behind family among the Mitanni/Horites, but Abraham's family were still under the protection of YHVH's Elohim of the Shem, worshipers of the Light of YHVH, but by the archaic name *Hor* (as in *Hor-mazd*), the Wise Light.

DATING ZARATHUSTRA BEFORE ABRAHAM

"Aristotle[8] put the birth of Zarathustra at 6350 years BC. (Sethna, T.R. *Zarathustra,* p. 2) "Some place him 6,000 years before Plato or Xerxes, some 5,000 years before the Trojan war (Xanthus of Lydia, Eudoxus of Cnidus, Hermippus, Hermodorus, Aristotle, Plutarch, Diogenes Laertius, and Pliny)." article on Zarathustra "*Encyclopedia of Religion*, p. 556. [8]"Aristotle in the first book of his work *On Philosophy* says the magi are more ancient even than the Egyptians." Peter Myers, *The Influence of Zoroastrian Religion on Judaism,* citing *The Works of Aristotle,* trans. into English, ed. Ross, D. p. 7, fragment 6.

"…three manuscripts have survived from this historian (Diogenes Lertius) in one of which the date of Zoroaster's birth is quoted as 600 years before Achamenian Xerex's invasion of Greece. In the other two manuscripts Zoroaster's birthday is quoted as 6000 B.C. which resembles many other ancient Grecian historiographers. Although this mistaken registration of Zoroaster's birthday was repeated by subsequent Greek chronographers, the main source for subsequent quotations was Lertius' third manuscript, whereas in the other two manuscripts he quotes 6,000 B.C. as the prophet's birthday. Meanwhile elsewhere in his book, relating from Hermodoros, Plato's student, the same author (Diogenes Lertius) says Zoroaster was born 5000 years before the battle of Troy. Now considering the fact that at least more than 9 famous Grecian historians (Aristotle, Odoxous, Pollianus, Hermitus, Plutarch, Theopompous, Suidas, Eskoloiyon and Laktantius) have all mentioned Zoroaster's birth as 6000 years before the birth of Christ or 5000 years before the war of Troy or 6000 years before invasion of Greece by Xerxes, it is definite that in his third volume Lertius has dropped a zero from the birthday and this error has led to all this chaos in the history (of Zarathustra)."

http://www.iranchamber.com/religions/articles/zarathushtra_first_monotheist_prophet.php

In "Plato, Prehistorian" by Mary Settegast (published 2000) she suggests a 6500 B.C.E. date for Zarathustra. She writes, "Pliny (Nat Hist. xxx3-4) stated that both Aristotle and Eudoxus believed that Zarathustra lived 6,000 years before the death of Plato. Plutarch (De Isid. 369) claimed that Zarathustra would have been "older than Plato by 6,000" years...In *Timaeus* (26)

Socrates accepts the story of the (seventh millennium birth of Zarathustra) as did Solon before him. Zarathustra's early birth date was repeated by Eudoxus, by an annotator of the "Alcibiades I" attributed to Plato, and using a different standard of measurement, by Plutarch and Hermippus (Pliny, Nat. Hist. XXX.4; Plutarch, "De Isid." 369) Settegast, Mary. *Plato, Prehistorian* (published 2000) p. 10-11.

> "But as respectable as these sources would seem to be, until recently there was not enough archaeological evidence in their favor to overcome the existing viewpoint...The situation is changing rapidly, however, and it now appears that the existing viewpoint is wrong." Settegast, Mary. *Plato, Prehistorian* (published 2000) p. 10-11.

Settegast also digs around in the *Avesta*, comparing the *Gathas* to the *Vendida*, showing how the differing tone in both suggest the teachings of two different Zarathustras at two disparately separate times (that is the 7th millennium BCE and 600 BCE, MHJ) "The language of the Vendidad shows it could not have been composed even in the same millennium as Zarathustra. Suggested translations of this term as 'high priest' and 'greatest or highest Zarathustra' may mean that Zarathustra as well as *Zarathustrotema* was a priestly title, a generic term...(The conclusion could be that the Zoroastrian scriptures subsequent to the Gathas were composed by other people, perhaps holding the Zarathustrian 'title'." MHJ)

Not only do the Gathas appear to be a good deal older linguistically than even the oldest parts of the Younger Avesta, but the same characters who speak and act with immediacy in the Gathic hymns are represented in the Younger Avesta as belonging to a remote past...If the younger Avesta, or some part of it, does belong to a Late Neolithic stage of culture, the Gathas must have been composed earlier...he (Zarathustra) refers to himself in the Gathas[9] as a *zaotar*, a fully qualified priest, as well as a *vaedemna*, one who knows...A much disputed passage in the Avesta (Y.XIX.18) mentions a hierarchy of five leaders, the uppermost of which was evidently known as the *Zarathustrotema*." Settegast, Mary. *Plato, Prehistorian* (published 2000) pp. 213, 214.

[9]It should be observed, however, that in some verses of the Gathas, Zarathustra is referred to in the third person. It seems unlikely that Zarathustra would speak of himself in this manner saying for example; "Oh Ahura, Zarathustra prayed for that Manyu (spirit) which is Spenta[10] most." Gatha 33-12 (or 33-13 @ *The Religion of Ahura Mazda.* <http://www.zoroaster.com/index.htm>) ([10]beneficent spirit, opposite of the *Angra-manyu*- evil spirit) This would seem to indicate that at least parts of the Gatha's were written *about* Zarathustra and not by him. Since the word *Gatha* like the Sanskrit *Gita* means songs, it is extremely likely that these songs, while they may have originated with Zarathustra, were passed down orally, by followers who learned these songs and occasionally sang about Zarathustra, for many eons before the Gathas were actually written down.

> "It was Childe (V. Gordon) who gave the name "Neolithic Revolution" (5000 BC) to the transition from hunter-gatherer to farmer, considered by many scholars to have been the most important single event in human history...even with the limited information at hand, it is possible to speak of a genuine transformation of Iran in the last half of the sixth millennium BC...the numerical increase in permanent settlements was proportionately larger than at any other time in prehistory...why so many, already possessing developed traditions of their own, should have chosen the life of a farmer – and often on land that

required irrigation – remains a mystery to pre-historians." Settegast, Mary. *Plato, Prehistorian* p. 3,9, & 235.

Settegast places the *first* Neolithic revolution around the 10,350 - 7,050 BCE, dates which Graham Hancock mentions as a "*Zep Tepi*" (meaning "first time," quoting David Rohl in *Legend,* followed by the time of the *Shemsu Hor*) of that time, that came with a ready-evolved civilization and she mentions that they appeared to have prior experience in agriculture; according to Settegast, they bore an astonishing diversity of traditions of settled life that were as well established as they were unprecedented. She says these were patently not nomads just turned farmer, but experienced settlers whose techniques had been perfected elsewhere.

<http://www.redmoonrising.com/Giza/SpiritCiv5.htm>

> "Iranian and English archeologists have discovered the Middle East's oldest village which dates back to at least 9800 BC in western Iran. The unique archeological discovery reveals Iran was the main Neolithic center of the Middle East. "The historical site dates back to 9800 BC and evidence suggest inhabitance in the site continued until 7400 BC."

<http://www.presstv.ir/detail.aspx?id=95901&sectionid=3510212>

Settegast goes on to tell us that, almost two thousand years passed (after the first Neolithic revolution) without any significant innovations, and then the civilizing "revolution" almost died, but a second great Neolithic impulse thrust permanent agricultural settlements into the far corners of Iran, out onto the plains of Mesopotamia, and as far west as the Balkan countries, in the last half of the sixth millennium. As Settegast explains, what we have then, are two Neolithic agricultural revolutions from nomad to cities, two major phases in the changeover to settled farming. The first, a late eighth millennium (or 10,000 years ago) eruption of agricultural communities in the Near East. The second, a massive late sixth millennium (8,000 years ago) adoption of settled agricultural life by local populations from Iran to southeast Europe.

> "Orthodox Zoroastrian tradition dates him (Zarathustra) to 628 B.C. but many western scholars find that far too recent a time…Some feel that a second millennium is a more likely setting for Zarathustra. Few would go as far as the Greeks. But…at no later time in Iranian prehistory would the transition from nomad to settler be as abrupt, wide reaching or profound as it was in the middle of the sixth millennium B.C....Midway in the course of history, Zarathustra came to offer (or to remind men of) the opportunity to collaborate in the work of redemption, in the restoration of perfection toward which all creation is striving. At the end of time another *saosyant* (savior) will appear and lead the forces of light in an ordeal by fire…leaving the good unharmed." ibid. p. 222 (Settegast, 2000)

Mary Settegast's opening quote seems worthy of repeating; "The principle scientific advances are known to come not so much from the linear accumulation of new facts but rather from the periodic questioning of our least criticized premises." Settegast, Mary. *When Zarathustra Spoke,* p. 1; quoting Cauvin, Jacques. *The Birth of the Gods and the Origins of Agriculture.*

The efforts, by western scholars mired in concepts established by church scholars, to place Zarathustra at only a few hundred years BCE, ignoring the wisdom of the ancient historians, may reflect in part the power of Catholic teachings of the last two thousand years, more so than the actual historical evidence. In their efforts to place the modern interpretation of Judeo/Christian religions as preeminent to all others, a great deal of evidence that indicates Zarathustra's influence on the Judeo/Christian foundations has been swept aside. For to expose this evidence would be to remind those of the Judeo/Christian religions that long before the time of Moses, when the Bible was first written, Abraham was already long preceded by other ancient followers of YHVH/Yahu/Ahu/Ahura and His Elohim of Shem (whom the OT recognized as blessed Gen. 9:26) from which came *Arpachsad,* (Gen. 11:12) the Kasdim/Chaldean/magi and eventually Abraham.

MENTIONS OF ZARATHUSTRA'S RELIGION IN THE RIGVEDA

"In Sanskrit, *Surya*, son of the sky is also known as *Savitar* (aka avatar, from *sav* enliven, beget etc.) and by the name of *Bhaga*...which is found in the name of the *Bhagavad Gita* (Song of the Blessed One or Divine Song, written down from verbal transmissions, originally sung just as were the Psalms) meaning God, in Iranic[11] it (*Bhagha*) is an epithet of Ormuzd...Whenever there is lack of righteousness, and wrong arises, I (the Deity) emit myself...The avatars...are meant." Hopkins, Edward. *The Religions of India,* p. 389,393 &447.

> [11]"The numerous isoglosses shared by Indic and Iranian languages include the common use of the word *airya* (Old Persian) or *Arya* (Old Indic) when speaking of themselves. (The name of the country "Iran" is derived from this root, as is the now contaminated term Aryan." Settegast, Mary. *When Zarathustra Spoke,* 2005, p. 56 quoting Sims-Williams, *The Iranian Languages* 1998.

> ..."many Vedic images and themes - such as deities, archaic elements of culture, reminiscences of bygone periods - were a great deal older than the formal compositions themselves. If those elements date back as far as the eighth millennium BC, the traditions described in the *Rig Veda* could theoretically represent a continuation of practices...Linguists are still puzzled by the fact that the earliest inscriptional evidence of the Vedic language comes not from India but from northern Iraq." Settegast, Mary. *When Zarathustra Spoke,* 2005, pp. 85-87.

In the *Gathas* (compare this word to the Vedic *Gitas*, both words mean songs) hymns said to be the oldest Zoroastrian material, known as Zarathustra's own words, the terms *Hormazd* and *Ahura Mazda* both occur. These hymns were most likely the songs that were sung, to preserve the words Zarathustra taught his followers, just as Psalms had preserved much of what Moses sang and taught the Israelites to sing according to the OT. (for example Ex. 15:1-2, Deu. 31:22-23) Some songs were among those known as the oral law or oral teachings.

The Jews called their oral heritage the *Mishnah*, the first codification of the Oral Law. The term Mishnah is derived from the Hebrew verb *shanah*, meaning "to repeat" and to recapitulate one's learning, or teaching. Initially the sages used to learn the Oral Law (as is implied by its name) through oral repetition. Robertson, Struan. *Sacred Texts.*

<http://www1.uni-hamburg.de/rz3a035//texts.html>

In line 43-47 of the first Gatha *Ahunavada*, and also in the others, the singer sings the

155

Zoroastrian creed; "I profess *Hormazd*, in accordance with Zarathustra, abstaining from *daevas,* (devils) and act according to the law of Ahura mazda." "*Fravarane Mazdayasno Zarathushtrish Vidaevo Ahurakaesho.*" The understanding of *Or/Hor/Aur* the Light, as synonymous with the Creator (in Hebrew and far into the ancient written history of Middle Eastern cultures) is of central importance. When Ahuramazda is used as synonymous with the Creator Ormazd, it can be seen that this is again is a recurrence of the same problem found in the OT; that is, the problem of confusing a god or messenger, through whom the Creator speaks, with the All Highest Light of All Truth, our Creator, the Great Holy Spirit, The All One. *Gathas.*

<http://www.zoroaster.com/gatha.htm>

The *Rig Veda* and later vedas make mention of many "gods" yet also clarify that; "In all the gods there is only one divinity" *Rig Veda* 55. Many historians have noted the influence of Zarathustra on the Hindu pantheon. "Although there were non-Zorastrian divinities among these gods, the influence of Zoroastrianism was indubitable." Litvinsky, B. A. *History of Civilization of Central Asia Vol. III,* p. 253.

> "In the Rigveda's most linguistically archaic layers, an epithet --*asura*[12] --was attributed to several of the more important gods...by the beginning of the middle compositional period...the term *asura* had been stripped of its elevated meaning...the *devas*[12] , pure and simple became the victors, the ones worthy of worship...Zarathustra sang of a quite similar cosmic struggle, in which the *asuras* -- or rather the *ahuras*, as they were known to him -- appear to have retained their elevated status...Taken in conjunction with the similar usage in the earliest Rigveda, this suggests the Indo-Iranian antiquity of the terms honorific meaning." Scott L. Harvey and Jonathan Slocum, *Old Iranian Online.*

> <://www.utexas.edu/cola/centers/lrc/eieol/aveol-0-X.html>

> [12]"The *Satapatha Brahmana* mentions, the Deavas and Asuras were both from (the time of) Prajapati." Dr. Samar Abbas, Article "History of Iran: Dehiya on the Jat Iranic Identity..."

> <http://www.iranchamber.com/history/articles/iranic_identity_of_mauryas3.php>

Apparently at one time Brahma of the Vedas was originally considered to have been a man, a saintly man but yet a one time mortal. The process of deification of Brahma to the position of Creator would have no doubt taken many eons. Apparently the Bible is not the only religious document that underwent modifications and editing to suit someone's religious ideas and interpretations.

> "It must be remembered that the Brahma of modern times, the God of the ardent theism of some of the best of the later Hindus, had not then (at the time of advent of Buddhism) come into existence; that conception was one effect of the influence of Mohammedan and Christian thought upon Hindu minds. While regarded however as essentially of the same class as all other external spirits (a one time man), Brahma was still regarded as a superior spirit." Davids, T.W. Rhys. *Of the "Buddhist Suttras,"* p. 163.

As mentioned earlier the Gathas were probably songs based on Zarathustra's teachings. Because of the presence of verses speaking about Zarathustra in the third person, they were, therefore, probably not likely written by him, either that or they were altered later. The Gathas as songs originating with Zarathustra, were probably passed down orally for many eons before being written down.

> "Then Brahmâ (the Creator[13] Himself, no less!) bowed down before the Glorious *Hari Medhas* (i.e., Ahura Mazda, if Mehta is correct, MHJ), and learned from him the best of religions, with all its principles and secrets." (*Shânti Parva* 348.30). As quoted by Mehta, Ardeshir. ebook *Zarathushtra,* note 21, p. 61. [13]This reference by Mehta reflects the modern day understanding of the name Brahma as synonymous with the Creator, not the original Brahma a human. Chatterjee, Jatindra Mohon, M. A. *Ethical Conceptions of the Gathas,* p. 438-9. @;

> <http://homepage.mac.com/ardeshir/Zarathushtra-Ch.1-6,Draft.pdf>

> "The long roll of saints mentioned in the Fravardin Yasht, represent the respective *Magha-patis* (lords of the confederation) of the day. The confederation was known as Magha (51-11; 51-16) which is derived from the root to be great. The high Priest of the confederation was known as *Magha-pati* (*pati* seems related to *Pater*/Father so perhaps the Father Magi, MHJ)...A member of the confederation was known as a Maghavan (Gatha, 51-15; 33-7) or Majya[14] (Gatha, 31-17) or simply Maja[14] (30-2)." Chatterjee, Jatindra Mohon M. A. *Ethical Conceptions of the Gathas,* p.140. ([14]varients of magi)

> "When shall I uproot the (worship of an) idol from this Congregation (*maghahya*)?" *Gatha 48.10* (the Gatha's are attributed to Zarathustra) also see Gatha 19:15.

As mentioned previously, later day followers of Zarathustra were known as Magi, members of the *Maghahya,* as in the verse above, which were congregations or communities of these followers of Zarathustra. These communities are mentioned in the oldest of the Vedas, the *Rig Veda* by the name *Maghavat.* These congregations or communities would have taken some time to form, so Zarathustra could not have used an already written *Rig Veda* as the basis for his teachings or plagiarized this name *Maghavat* from the *Rig Veda,* a name peculiar to his communities. This mention of them in the *Rig Veda* shows they were separate communities distinctly mentioned apart from the communities of the followers of the purely Vedic teachings.

> "Even the *Bhavishya Purâna* contains a veiled reference to the Zoroastrians, in that it describes the *Atharva Veda* to be the *Veda* of the Mâghas. As we have seen—and as we shall further elaborate later on—the Magha was the name given by Zarathushtra to the Church he founded for the spread of the Message of Mazda." Mehta, Ardeshir. *Zarathushtra,* p.62. ebook @;

> <http://www.homepage.mac.com/ardeshir/Ch.6-SingleSided-Draft.pdf>

Zarathustra could not have plagiarized the use of the word *Maghavat* from the *Rig Veda.* It is not possible to plagiarize a word that describes communities that did not yet exist and one that would not have had any meaning until *after* the existence of Zarathustra's communities of Magi/Magha, the *Maghavats.* It could be argued that the mention of the name *Ahura* in the *Rig Veda* (addressed in the next section) was a change in spelling inserted at a later date (after being used by Zarathustra, as a substitute for *Asura),* by someone editing the writings of the *Rig Vedas.* But this argument could not be used concerning the mention of the *Maghavats* in the *Rig Veda* verse

157

about Zarathustra's communities of *magha/magi*. Because to insert this name for his communities, in a discussion seeking the welfare of both the communities of the followers of the *Rig Veda* and the *Maghavats*, would have had no meaning to readers of the *Rig Veda*, until *after* the time of the existence of those communities. And further it would have completely obscured the meaning of the verse and the original intentions of that author to have done so.

Therefore this mention of Zarathustra's communities, the *Maghavats* shows that Zarathustrian communities were already in existence at the time of the writing of the *Rig Veda*s. The antiquity of the *Rig Veda*, which it should be emphasized is the oldest of the Vedas, is now dated 3000 BCE. (see following section) It thus places the time of Zarathustra, by this mention of his communities of followers as already formed, at some time before the writing of the *Rig Veda*, thus very far back in prehistoric times; this again gives support to the dates given by the many ancient historians mentioned before (Remember that mention of the magi or *imga* are also found in one of the earliest cuneiform languages – Akkadian, see previous section on The Star that the Zarathustrian Magi Followed). It should be noted that these historians were writing at many separate times and with little connection to each other. The mention of the communities of the *Maghavats* appears in the following verse of the *Rig Veda*;

> "Agni teach us our prayer. Bless the <u>*Maghavats*</u> also. May both the communities be under thy protection. Help us always to weal (i.e. welfare or charity)." *Rigveda 7.1.20* this verse is also quoted by Ardeshir Mehta in his ebook *Zarathushtra* (1999) p. 48. @: <http://www.homepage.mac.com/ardeshir/Ch.6-SingleSided-Draft.pdf>

Had Zarathusta, as a hypothetical Vedic sage (as proposed by some), modeled his religion on the same names for good spirits/gods and evil spirits/devils as found in the Vedas, he would in all likelihood have used whatever definitions of *deavas*/devils and *ahura/asuras*/gods understood at the time of his writing. For if he had lived during the times of the later writings in the Vedas, and incorporated their terminology into his teachings, he would in all probability have incorporated their meanings from that time as well; rather than confusing his disciples with an archaic word with what would, hypothetically, by then have been a negative connotation and one that many would not understand in a positive light. Similarly if he came along after the Veda's were already written, the cognate of *ahura*, that is, *asura*, had by this time devolved out of meaning a deity, and had come to mean quite the opposite so why would he choose a name for deity that would then have been equated with lower spirits and demons, to teach his disciples of as a name for deity? This logically places his existence at or before the time of the earliest writings in the Vedas and mention of the communities of his followers known as *maghavat*s places their existence as already formed before the time of the writing of the *Rig Veda*.

158

Chapter Seven

YAHUWAH/YAHU/AHU

…"the priests of the god *Khnub*…conspired with *Vidranga*, who was administrator here, to destroy the temple of *YAHU* in the fortress of *Yeb*…when Cambyses came to Egypt he found it already constructed. They (the Persians) knocked down all the temples of the Egyptian gods; but no one damaged this temple…Look to your clients and friends here in Egypt. Let a letter be sent from you to them concerning the temple of *Yahu* to construct it in the fortress of Yeb as it was before…if you do this so that this temple is reconstructed…you shall have honor before *Yahu, the God of the Heavens*…" *Petition to Authorize Elephantine Temple Reconstruction* (by the Jews of Elephantine), current location Staatliche Museen, Berlin Germany, Inventory number P13495, Transliteration by K. C. Hanson adapted (2005) from Cowley 1923.

<http://www.kchanson.com/ancdocs/westsem/templeauth.html>

THE JEWISH TEMPLE OF YAHU AT ELEPHANTINE

This chapter will discuss the official letter of petition which was written (in Aramaic) by the Jews of Elephantine, Egypt, in 407 BCE and related evidence concerning the name *Yahu*. *Yahu* is the English transliteration of the Hebrew name (*yod, heh, vav* or *yod vav*) used by the Jewish people of Elephantine. The letter requested help rebuilding their "temple of *Yahu/Yaho,*" destroyed at the end of the fifth century BCE, concerning which they wrote to the governor of Judah (Peters, John Punnel. *The Religion of the Hebrews.* p. 89).

Concerning these manuscripts, the previous reference has this to say "The papyri discovered at Elephantine use *Yahu, not Yahuveh*, evidence of the former as the original form…It may be noted further, that it is in the tribe of Judah (from whom Yeschu/Joshu/Jesus descended MHJ) that names compounded with the divine name *Yah* (for *Yahuvih*) first become prominent…In northern Syria there was a people called *Jaudi*[1] or *Judaeans* and in that region, as shown by the inscriptions from Zingirli and its neighborhood, closely resembles Hebrew. It is possible that this indicates a god *Yahu*…" (The mention in that letter that the temple was not harmed by the invading Persians shows that the Persians also respected *Yahu* as the Supreme ruler of heaven. MHJ)

[1] *Yehu-da* (SHD 3063), meaning praised, contains within it the form *Yehu* so perhaps 'praise *Yehu*.' *Yehuda* or *Judah* is the source of the name Jew. Jew is believed to come from *Yehud* the Persian name for Judea. <http://en.wikipedia.org/wiki/Etymology_of_the_word_Jew> Since *Yadi* in Assyrian terminology meant Judah, the word *Yad*, in Old Persian meaning revere or worship, also appears to be related. Davidy, Yair. *Hebrew Celtic Namesakes.*

<http://www.britam.org/namesakes.html>

"From the striking similarity between the religion of Moses and that of the Persians it is not difficult to see the reason why Cyrus Darius and the Persians restored the temples of Jerusalem and Gerizim when they destroyed the temples of the idolaters in Egypt and other places which in fact they did wherever they came. It appears probable that the temple on Gerizim was built or restored within a few years of the same time with that at Jerusalem and for the same reason <u>because the religion *was* that of the Persians.</u>" Higgins, Godfrey. *Anacalypsis,* p. 86, note that the page number of the online version *does not* correspond to the hard copy. <<u>http://members.tripod.com/~pc93/anacv1b2.htm</u>>

The significance of the Elephantine letter is that it shows that *Yahu* (or *Yaho*), is recognized as an early Jewish form of YHVH/Yahuvih/Yahu/Yah. *Yahu* (also Ahu in Persian) is also recognized to be a later variation of the Persian Ahura, found for example in writings of the Avesta Yasna (historically placed later than the Gatha's).With this connection established between the Zarathustrian name of the Creator in the later times of the Ormazdians and the Hebrew name for the Creator in the earliest times of the Jewish Religion, it can be seen that this name was deliberately chosen by the Elohim of Moses time. It was used in the earliest Hebrew writings as a name of the Creator that had ancient, even pre-historic significance, within the tribes if the Semitic/Shemitic peoples from long before the time invention of the Hebrew language. This ancient variation of YHVH had been known and used by some of His chosen all along. Although according to the Bible *Yahu* or YHVH was not used by Abraham (Ex. 6:2-3) it obviously *WAS* used by other ancient Jewish tribes, since it came to be used as a cognate of YHVH, in the name of this Jewish "temple of *Yahu.*"

> "We know for certain (Taylor cylinder) that the Assyrians pronounced the name *Yahu...*the root means "to breathe" (just as *ruach hakodesh* means breath[2], wind or spirit, MHJ)...in cuneiform the signs used can sometimes be read either *Ahu or Yahu...*" Forlong, James George Roche. *Faiths of Man: A Cyclopaedia of Religions,* Vol. II - E to M, p. 330.

> [2]Mary Boyce in *A History of Zoroastrianism.* pp. 79-80, says "two Avestan words for wind *vayu* and *vata* (are) both from the same root *va* 'blow'…In the Vedas *Vayu,* (is) 'the soul of the gods'…In all living beings *Vayu* (Note the phonetic similarity to *IEVE - yod, heh, vav, heh,* the Hebrew spelling of YHVH, see Gen 2:4 <u>http://www.scripture4all.org</u>), is the life-breath, in the Cosmos He (*Vayu*) is the breath of Life."

The *Catholic Encyclopedia* makes the following argument, in its article on Jehovah; "As to the theory that Jahveh has a Chaldean or and Accadian origin, its foundation is not very solid:...the common or popular name of God is said to have been *Yahu* or Yah,...this contention if true[3] does not prove the Chaldean or Accadian origin of the Hebrew Divine name;...*Yahu* never appears in the Bible...Hommel (Altisrael. Ueberlieferung, 1897, pp. 144, 225) feels certain that he has discovered the Chaldean god Yau..." [3](However the above reference to the *Jewish* temple of *Yahu* clearly shows it to be true, that *Yahu* was a well recognized Persian/Hebrew cognate of YHVH. MHJ) *Article on Jehovah.* <<u>http://www.newadvent.org</u>>

> "Most important of all, however, from a point of view of the history of the religion of the Jews, is what Delitzsch states concerning the name Jahweh (Jehovah). On p. 46 of his first lecture (German edition) he gives half-tone reproductions of three tablets preserved in the British Museum, which according to him, contain three forms of the personal name "Jahweh is God" -*Ya'we-ilu, Yawe-ilu, and Yaum-ilu.* The last of these names we may

dismiss at once, the form being clearly not that of Yahweh, (but rather closer to Aum, 'the Mother is god,' MHJ) but of *Yah*, the Jah of Psalm 114:35 and several other passages. The other two, however, are not so lightly dealt with, notwithstanding the objections of other Assyriologists and Orientalists." (Pinches, Theophilus G. "Appendix." *The Old Testament in the Light of the Historical Records of Assyria and Babylonia.* London. The Society for Promoting Christian Knowledge. 1908. 3rd Revised Edition [2d Edition was 1903] pp. 535-536.) <http://www.bibleorigins.net/YahwehYawUgarit.html>

But then in another section on the name Isaias, the *Catholic Encyclopedia* goes on to say that the name *Yahu does* appear in the Bible, as a part of the name of the prophet Isaias[1]; "The name Isaias signifies "Yahweh is salvation…It assumes two different forms...in II Kings 19:2: II Chr. 26:22; 32:20-32, it is read *Yesha'yahu,...*" Now perhaps they need to check their own references, but the name *Yahu* obviously *does* appear in the Bible in this prophet's name! And while its presence, in the letter from the Jews of Elephantine, may not for some prove that YHVH derived from the Chaldean *Yahu*, it does show that both the Israelites and the Chaldeans used the same name, *Yahu* (as one of multitude of names used by both peoples) for the Creator, and thus shows a commonality in spiritual beliefs, for what is more fundamental to a religion than its name for the Creator? This commonality came to its fruition when the Magi followed the "star," predicted by Zarathustra, according to their beliefs, of a coming savior with whom he was one, through his oneness in the All One. (Just as Yeschu/Joshu/Jesus said; "I am in you, you are in me, we are in the Father." John 14:20) [1]also in the name *Mikhayah* (who is like *Yahu*, Yehu, Yah?) ibid. <http://www.newadvent.org/cathen/08179b.htm>

> "The question remains, however, whether it is Israelitish or was borrowed. Friedrich Delitzsch, in discussing this question, asserts that the Semitic tribes from whom the family of Hammurabi came, and who entered Babylon 2500 , knew and worshiped the god Ya've, Ya'u (*i.e.*, , Yahu; "Babel und Bibel," 5th ed., i. 78 *et seq.*); and Zimmern (in Schrader, "K. A. T." 3d ed., pp. 465-468) reaches the conclusion that "Yahu" or "Yhwh" is found in Babylonian only as the name of a foreign deity, a view with which Delitzsch agrees in his third and final lecture on "Babel und Bibel" (pp. 39, 60, Stuttgart, 1905)...According to Delitzsch (*Wo Lag das Paradies*? 1881), this form was the original one, and was expanded into YHWH." *JewishEncyclopedia.com*

> <http://www.jewishencyclopedia.com/view.jsp?artid=165&letter=T&search=yahu>

The influence of Zarathustra on the Judeo/Christian religion has often been noted, but it is more than just an influence, it is actually essentially the same religion, in spirit and in truth, for it was still the worship of the Father - *Yahu* or YHVH, albeit by another people speaking a different language. The term *Yahu* is used in the Avesta (for example; *Nirangistan,* ritual specifications, verse 54; and *Yasna Sacred Liturgy,* 16:7) of the Zarathustrian religion. The *Journal of the American Oriental Society* also gives the following information on *Yahu;*

> "*yahu,* Avesta *yazu.* This word occurs in vii. 15, 11; but this is a late hymn, and it is the only passage in ii-vii. where the word occurs. Elsewhere it is found in viii. 4, 5; 19. 12; 49. 13; 73. 5; i, 20. 10; 74.5; 79. 4. Excepting 73, all these hymns contain late words, and correspondence with i., x. But after all, the equating of *yazu* with *yahu* is not phonetically certain." Seventeenth Volume of the *Journal of the American Oriental Society,* edited by

Lanman, Charles R. and George R. Moore p.83-84. (This reflects speculation that *yazu* is another variation of *yahu* occurring in the Zarathustrian or Ormazdian religion.)

Two other related names that are used much the same as is YHVH/YAH, are *Ahura/Ahu.* According to the *Theosophy Dictionary* Ahura derives from the root *ahu* conscious life, a meaning also used by 13th century Iranian mystic poet, Rumi. from Article on Yah, Yaho, *Encyclopedic Theosophical Glossary,* Ya-Yz, Theosophical Press

<http://www.theosociety.org/pasadena/etgloss/ya-yz.htm> & *Theosophy Dictionary on Ahu.* <http://www.experiencefestival.com/a/ahu/id/98093>

"In a posthumous work entitled *Vedic Chronology and Vedanga Jyotish* the late B. G. Tilak traces the word Jehovih or Jahve directly to the Vedic literature, he says, "Jehovah is undoubtedly the same word as the Chaldean Yahve, "and then proceeds: - "The word Yahu (Z. yazu), Yahve...occurs several times in the Rigveda;...though Moses may have borrowed it from the Chaldeans yet the Chaldean tongue cannot claim it to originally be their own[5]..." Prasad, Ganga. *The Fountainhead of Religion, A Comparative Study of the Principles of Religion,* p.53.

<http://books.google.com/books?hl=en&id=0QO_zed25R4C&dq=Prasad,+Ganga. +The+Fountainhead+of+Religion, +A+Comparative+Study+of+the+Principles+of+Religion&printsec=frontcover&source= web&ots=IMp58S9kno&sig=OgLX7GQ8E5H_XtyDAoHP3ZfbqAU>

[5]The statement that, "the Chaldeans cannot claim it to originally be their own," was likely made under the common assumption that the *Rig Veda* is older than the Zarathustrian religion. But the evidence in this book shows that the God of Zarathustra's religion and communities of his followers were already known by name at the time of the composition of the oldest of the vedas, the *Rig Veda* and in fact they were written about *in the Rig Veda*. This is shown by the presence in the *Rig Veda* of Zarathusta's name for the deity (Ahura) and by mention of his communities of followers, *Maghavat*s. His religion would have had to already existed for these to have been mentioned in the *Rig Veda*, proving that he lived prior to the time of the writing of the *Rig Veda*, now dated to 3000 BCE.[6]

[6]"The significance of establishing this date (1900 BCE) for the drying up of the Sarasvati River (mentioned in the *Rig Veda* 07.095.01.1-2) is, that it pushes the date for the composition of the *Rig Veda* back to approximately 3,000 BCE[7], as enunciated by the Vedic tradition itself. The late dating of the Vedic literatures by Indologists is based on speculated dates of 1500 BCE for the Aryan Invasion and 1200 BCE for the *Rig Veda*, both now disproved by scientific evidence." Osborn, David. *Scientific Verification of Vedic Knowledge,* article @ Archaeology Online

<http://www.archaeologyonline.net/artifacts/scientific-verif-vedas.html>

[7]"The most popular date for the proper appearance of a distinctive Sumerian civilization (Sumerian[8] is generally accepted as the oldest written language) is about 3500BC... origins of the Sumerian people are still unknown." Byrnes, Dan. *Religion From the Time of the Ice Ages...* <http://www.danbyrnes.com.au/lostworlds/features/iceage.htm> [8]As mentioned previously Akkadian, a cuneiform language derived from Sumerian, contains

162

references to the *imag/magi* so this dates references to these *magicians* back to at least 2400 BCE.

In the *Ahunavar or Ahuna Vairya* (Yatha Ahu Vairyo) of the Ormazdian religion, *Ahu* is translated as 'lord' or God. "Just as is the will of the Lord, so to is that of the spiritual leader owing to his righteousness." *Yatha Ahu Vairyo atha ratush ashat chit hacha.* This is the first line of the *Ahunavar* (Yatha Ahu Vairyo) Avesta & English by the late Dossabhoy S. Framroze available at; <http://www.zoroaster.com/avesta/Ahuanavar.htm> "Just as God (Ahu) is to be adored so is His prophet (Ragu)." Chatterjee, Jatindra Mohon, M. A. *Ethical Conceptions of the Gathas,* p. 60.

> "Ahu: derived from ah, meaning "to be, to exist or to be present," it stands for an outstanding being, a distinctive entity and therefore a person of distinction. The Gathas explain Ahu as the person "who is free from enmity, who helps the living world, who activated the noble, and who can repel the fury of the wrongful (Song 1.2,3)." Thus ahu is a person who holds authority. It is generally rendered as "lord" in English...Ahura: this is the same word as ahu above with suffix-ra added. This is a suffix of action which intensifies and strengthens the word. It means "being, existing, present." When applied to God, it means The Supreme Being, It forms a separable part of a dual name given to God - Ahura Mazda - by Zarathustra. In harmony with other translators and Western tradition, I have rendered it variously as God and Lord." Jafarey, Ali A. *The Gathas, Our Guide* <http://www.zarathushtra.com/z/gatha/The%20Gathas%20-%20AAJ.pdf>

In the foregoing it can be seen that *Ahu* is recognized as another name of a God or Lord (one of the "holy immortals" amesha spenta...called lords in Y30.9, Y31.4,...Zarathustra was chosen as "lord" or pastor, Y 29.8) used as a contraction of Ahura. These Ahu-Ahura, the "lords of creation," the *Mazdao Ahuraongho*, "The Mazda Ahuras" (plural), are collectively one with Ormazd or as would be said in the Judeo/Christian religion, YHVH Elohim. With this understanding it can be seen that Ahura Mazda is the chief "wise lord" or Elohim (or god) serving Ormazd (*Or*-Light *Mazd*-Intelligent/Wise) the infinite Light/*Aur* of YHVH.

This confusion between the Supreme or Master Light and His Wise Lord arose because people forgot the importance of the Omni-present, All Seeing Pre-Existent, Supremely Intelligent Light of the Universal Mind. They focused on the humanoid Ahu/Ahura, just as people did in the OT concerning YHVH's El/Elohim. In the Zarathustrian religion, just as in the Judeo/Christian religion, those finite beings (the Elohim or Ahu) who are one with the Light, and through whom He spoke, thus became confused with the Infinite Light of the Great Holy Spirit. Yet YHVH is more than just a collective, having also personality above and before all His creation.

> "So may we be those that make this world advance, O Mazda and ye other Ahuras, come hither, vouchsafing (to us) admission into your company and Asha, in order that (our) thought may gather together while reason is still shaky." Yasna 30:9 "If Asha[9] is to be invoked and Mazda and the other Ahuras and Ashi and Armaiti, do thou seek for me, O Vohu Manah (1), the mighty Dominion, by the increase of which we might vanquish the Lie." *Avesta: Yasna – Ahunavaiti Gatha* 31:4
>
> <http://www.avesta.org/yasna/y28to34b.htm>

[9]"For Zoroaster there existed both the principle *asa* (*asha*) and Asa (Asha) who was a divinity, one of the seven Bounteous Immortals…who are 'of one mind, of one voice, of one act; whose mind is one, whose voice is one, whose act is one, whose father and ruler is one, the Creator Ahura Mazda.' (Yt. 19.16-18" Boyce, Mary. *A History of Zoroastrianism.* pp. 199-203.

Since the Zarathustrian religion has so much history and other similarities in common with the Judeo-Christian, these similarities in use and structure shows *Ahura-Ahu/Yahu* to just be other ancient variations of *YHVH/Yahuvih/Yahu* used by members of the family of Abraham, who were left behind. This was before *Ahura-Ahu/Yahu* evolved within the Hebrew language into the somewhat unrecognizable cognates of these earlier terminologies. Yet even in those times (referring to the Supreme Intelligent Light *YHVH/Yahuvih-Yahu,* who being the Great Holy Spirit of the All One has no image), and in both religions worship of images was forbidden. Anyone who spends time repeating these names aloud cannot fail to hear their similarities and the evidence presented here provides a history of their evolution into the forms now commonly recognized in the Hebrew language and religions.

Keki R. Bhote discussing Zarathustra's influence on the *Upanishads* writes; "Jawaharlal Nehru, in his landmark book: "The Discovery of India" states categorically that the Gathic Avesta is nearer to Vedas (ancient Sanskrit) than the Vedas are to the later classical Sanskrit." Bhote goes on to quote Burrows, another author as follows; "Linguistically, the Gathas of Sanskrit and the Rg Veda are so close that it is possible to find verses in the Gathas which, simply by phonetic substitution, can be turned into intelligible Vedic Sanskrit." 6 citing T. Burrows, The Sanskrit Language, Faber & Faber, London, 1973. Keki R. Bhote , *The Seminal Contribution of Zarathushtra and His Gathas to the Upanishads* .

<http://www.s-s-z.org/downloads/Gathas%20to%20the%20Upanishads.pdf>

There are Sanskrit variations of *Ahura,* including the same abbreviated name *Ahu,* which in Sanskrit means to invoke, and other words containing this root for example *AhUrya,* meaning one to whom homage is paid (i.e., chieftain *Rig Veda*, i, 69, 4) and *Ahuva* or *A-hvR,* to be invoked. This last is so similar phonetically to the spelling YHVH that it bears pointing out especially that this presence of the "V" may reflect an influence on the spread of the pronunciation Yahovah/Yahovih with a "V" rather than YHWH with a "W," through the Middle Eastern cultural exchanges which were continually going on through trade in that part of the world. *Sanskri, Tamil and Pahlavi Dictionaries.* <http://webapps.uni-koeln.de/tamil/>

YHVH was known by many other names used throughout the OT including the *Al Emet* (All Truth or All Faithful) since He has been among His children and left His footprints since the beginning; it is not surprising that some of His infinite number of names may not have made it into the Bible. Yet since He is All Truth, we must not separate ourselves from oneness with the All One and His other children of ancient Shem by excluding their related names for the Creator albeit occurring outside the Bible.

Use of the name *Ahura* as a name of deity is actually to be found in the Vedas, which shows conclusively that at the time of the composition of this Veda, it was already recognized as a name for deity. Coupled with the rest of the evidence cited here there can be little question that the Indian Aryans of the Vedic period, in composing this verse, already knew of and at least some of them revered the God of the Iranians; *Ahura*. It has already been shown that they had at one time equated this name for the deity as synonymous with the name *Asura*, which they used extensively throughout the Vedas, in earlier times for gods and later on for lesser spirits and demons. The occurrence of the mention of *Ahura* is in the *Sama Veda;*

> "O Ahura, I now dedicate this to thee." *Ahura idam ti paridadami aham.* Quoted from the *Sâma Veda, Mantra Brâhmana 1.6.21* as translated by Mehta, Ardeshir, in his ebook *Zarathushtra* (1999) p. 22.

Other persons mentioned in the Vedas are called worshipers of Ahura. "God inspired Kapila[10] with Knowledge and saw him flourishing. The theory of cosmic Evolution, under the influence of the Gunas, that he expounded, became known as *Samkhya* or Knowledge... (aka *Samkhya* yoga, mentioned in the Zarathustrian Gathas; "Which are the secrets of the *Samkhya*." Gatha 48-3 "Through thy *Samkhya*, Oh Mazda." Gatha 48-12 as quoted by Chatterjee, p. 107) Now Kapila seems to have been a worshiper of Ahura Mazda. Pancha-Sikha whose proficiency in the *Samkhya* system earned him the name of "a second Kapila," has been called a disciple of (Kapila, who is) "the worshiper of Ahura...Santiparva, 218-10. (translated by Chatterjee) "Who (Pancha-Sikha), the foremost disciple of "the worshiper of Ahura," has been supposed to be living forever (in people's memory)." Chatterjee, Jatindra Mohon. M. A. *Ethical Conceptions of the Gathas*, p. 106.

[10]"Anterior to Buddha and mentioned in Buddhist literature and in the Vedas, sometimes under the name Vasudeva (who is also called the father of Krishna, MHJ) or under the name Kapilya, for whose philosophy of numbers the Cabbala was named." Page 338 & 368 "The Hindu Pantheon" by Edward Moor and "Secret Societies" (section on the Cabbala) by Charles Hecklethorn.

> "Mazda is no other than Varuna." *Rig Veda* 4-42-7 p.203 As a matter of fact the name "Varuna" comes 44th. in the list of 101 names of Ahura Mazda as recited by the Parsis in their prayer." Chatterjee, Jatindra Mohon, M. A. *Ethical Conceptions of the Gathas*, p. 204

Now of course the opposite could be argued, as some have, that Zarathustra was a Vedic sage who it would seem by this theory, had plagiarized this single occurrence of the name Ahura from the Vedas. Why would Zarathustra single out a name that occurs only one time, as the Supreme deity of his religion, especially when by that time it would have been understood as a cognate of the Sanskrit word for demons-*asura*? This is not a reasonable assumption, nor one that can be logically supported. If one uses that argument then using any ancient documents to place any dates also falls apart, because any such unsupported argument can always be asserted. We can only go with what we have, and what we have is the pre-existence and understanding of the word Ahura for the deity prior to the writing of the *Sama Veda*.

> "Of course, the subsequent interpolation of new materials in the Vedas was not an easy thing...the purity of the text of the Veda being jealously guarded by the Brahmans, in a way unknown to any other literature of the world." Chatterjee, Jatindra Mohon, M. A. *Ethical Conceptions of the Gathas*, p. 179; quoting Macdonell, *History of Sanskrit Literature*, p. 50.

The fact that the name Ahura only occurs once in the Vedas makes it much more probable that it was a lone archaic term. One that somehow survived linguistic changes and the editing processes, that the Vedas are known to have gone through over time, as the language and beliefs of their original culture changed. The *Chaldean Oracles* attrib. to Zarathustra, and other references make it clear that followers of his religion revered the Father. The Vedas themselves mention some of these changes from an older order that worshiped the Father Ahura Mazda (called in India during those later times, *Varuna*) to a newer order.

> "Many a year have I lived with them; I shall now accept Indra and abjure the Father. Varuna, along with his fire and his Soma (*Haoma*) has retreated. The old regime has changed. I shall accept the new order." *Rig Veda 10.12.4* Mehta, Ardeshir. *Zarathushtra,* p.7. Online ebook @;
>
> <http://homepage.mac.com/ardeshir/Zarathushtra-Ch.1-6,Draft.pdf>

It is highly unlikely that Zarathustra, if he had lived in those times as a Vedic sage, would base an entire religion on this single occurrence of the name Ahura in the Vedas, when the context makes it difficult to determine the exact meaning and then again try to teach it to disciples who, following Zarathustra as a hypothetical Vedic sage, would have been more familiar with the Vedic term *Asura*, used predominately throughout the Vedas, during this later proposed time[11] for Zarathustra's existence. ([11]if he had lived sometime after the writing of the Vedas)

The numerous linguistic similarities of the Vedas and the Gathas show that either Zarathustra plagiarized the Vedas or that they were influenced by his religious teachings. All the evidence presented here cannot logically be accounted for by the first case, so by the process of elimination this leaves the conclusion that Zarathustra's existence, communities (of Magha/magi), and his teachings of Ahura, must have come before the writing of the first of the Vedas, the *Rig Veda* (therefore before 3000 BCE).

> "Sanat-Sujata...all the Vedas tell the same truth. (Udyoga Parva 43:3) but takes good care to repeat, that the Zend is also as good a Veda as any other." (Udyoga Parva 43:51) (p.184) search for Devasura War (p. 193) "Still up to the time of the *Mahabharata*, the tradition of a fifth Veda had not died out, Sanat-Sujata emphasizes its importance." O Kshatriya, Atharva, the Apostle of Organization, sung the Zend Veda. (Referring to the same name used in the Zend Avesta, MHJ) It is not a fact, that those who know the Zend Veda, but have not read the other Vedas...do not know the truth that the others teach." (Udyoga Parva 43:50) For India and Iran had not yet ceased to be one people. Chatterjee, Jatindra Mohon, M. A. *Ethical Conceptions of the Gathas,* pp. 184-194.

Spenta Armati, whose presence permeates the teachings of Zarathustra, is also mentioned in the *Rig Veda*, showing that understanding of her existence was already known at the time of the writing of the *Rig Veda*. "Gracious Agni, to our great joy, bring by the path of Deva-Yana, the great Armati, the celestial Angel, exalted, worshiped with gift of homage and who knows Rita (Asha?)." *Rig Veda* 5-43-5 as quoted by Jatindra Mohon Chatterjee, M. A, *Ethical Conceptions of the Gathas.*

> (Mazda) has made Conscience the father, and active Armaiti his daughter." Gatha 45-4
> "Who is the Creator of the angel of Devotion and Love - Spenta Armaiti?" Gatha 44-11

Because Zarathustra was so well known in ancient times he was often simply referred to in many ancient writings as the "the prophet," just as he was in the NT, so the prevalence of his influence has often been overlooked. But the reference to so many other elements of his religious teachings about Ormazd, Ahuramazda, and the Holy Immortals, shows that often these mentions in the *Rig Veda* of "the prophet" priest, preceptor, or teacher, in the *Bhagavadgita*, and the *Mahabarata*, etc., must now be considered to refer to Zarathustra, when the context makes sense for it to be so understood. For as observed in the *Rig Veda*, "There is One (*Ahuh*), though the sages know them by many names (*Indram, Mitra, Varuna, Agnim, Ahur[12]*)." *Rig Veda* 1.164.46 [12]Ahu/Ahura/Lord

1.164.46a índram mitram varunam agnim <u>ahur</u>

1.164.46b atho divyah sa suparno garutman

1.164.46c ekam sad vipra bahudha vadanti

1.164.46d agn yamam matarisvanam <u>ahuh</u>
Thomson, Karen and Jonathan Slocum. *The Rig Veda, Metrically Restored Text.*

<http://www.utexas.edu/cola/centers/lrc/RV/>

PERSIA/PARASHI/BARAHSHI/PARS/FARS/PARAN

"Although Zoroaster's teachings shape the theology of Darius' utterances, no mark of Avestan influence is to be found in their vocabulary. Persian, not Avestan, religious terms are used, with the word baga (just as in the *Bhaga vad gita* MHJ) "god" appearing instead of the characteristic Zoroastrian *yazata*...Zorastrian missionaries to Persia must have presented their prophet's teachings there in the Persian language...the use of baga as the general term for "god" persisted for many generations in Persia..." Myers, Peter. *The Influence of Zoroastrian Religion on Judaism*, p.122.

<http://users.cyberone.com.au/myers/zoroaster-judaism.html>

In Vedic times Iran was divided into three parts: Parthia, Persia and Media. In India it was called Parshu[13]; in Iran, Parsa or Pars. The Hebrew word for Iran, *Paras*, also derives from the same source. Persia ultimately became the name of the confederation of these three. All three are mentioned in the *Rig Veda. Rig Veda 7.83.1; Rig Veda 8.6.46; Rig Veda 6.27.8; Rig Veda 10.33.3;* This clearly places the time of the writings of the Vedas *after* the development of these early names for the territories that were to become known as Persia. Remember that the information given earlier on the drying up of the Sarasvati River places the writing of the *Rig Veda* earlier than 3,000 BCE.

[13]"In Pânîni's rules of grammar we find the following dictum: "By the addition of a suffix, the word Parshu is changed to Parshava, which means 'The Persians'." *Pânîni 5.3.117* as quoted by Mehta, Ardeshir, in the draft of the first six chapters of his ebook *Zarathushtra* (1999) p. 29. @; <http://www.homepage.mac.com/ardeshir/Ch.6-

However we need to also consider that given the following evidence, the time of the original territories comprising the foundation of Persia, may itself actually be earlier than usually given in history books. Along with the understanding of the evolution of the "gods" of the Vedas, we must also consider how early the beginning states that formed the Persian kingdom may have existed. Because there is no written history remaining of these most prehistoric of times, we are limited to a few references. However the following reference certainly indicates that there was a kingdom of a very similar name that existed in the same territory and preceded the one known to us as Persia.

> "Old Babylonian copies of inscriptions of Sargon (a title meaning; true king) of Akkad (alt. spelled Akkaid, Agade, Haikwad?) (2334-2279) place the formation of the Old Akkadian Empire in the twenty -fourth century BC, however Sargon's successor Rimush (2278-2270 BC) claims to have torn the foundations of *Barahshi* (seemingly an alternate spelling of Parashi-Persia, MHJ) from among the people of Elam. Carter and Stolper, *Elam Surveys of Political History and Archaeology,* p.11-12&231.

This indicates the pre-existence of the country, *Barahshi/Parashi,* well before the time of Sargon and Rimush (2278-2270 BC) for which a new foundation (central seat) was then established, in Akkaid, with Rimush as ruler. The significance of this information is the pre-existence of a land known variously as Persia/Parashi/Barahshi prior to 2270 BC, when it is usually said by history not to have existed until the first millennium BC. "The earliest occurrence of Parsa is found in Assyrian cuneiform records of the ninth century BC in the form of Parsua...but is Parsa an Iranian name or is it a pre-Iranian place-name from which the Persians took their own name and transplanted it to the south as an ethnic name? In favor of the latter we have E. Herzfeld's suggestion (in *Zoroaster and His World* vol.2, p.727-8) that Assyrian Parsua descends from a form of paraphrase of the third millennium BC." Frye, Richard. *The Heritage of Persia,* p. 45.

> "And He is saying YHWH from Sinai He comes and He is radiant, from Seir for them He shines, from mountain of *Paran*[14], and He arrives from myriads of holy one(s) from right of Him *ashdth* to them." Deu. 33:2 [14](the *Jnwuri*/Jewish language is related to the language of Caucasian Persians (*Farsi* or *Paran*)) <http://2pic.20m.com/ECJ.html> This mention of the territory of *Paran*/Persia in the Torah confirms a founding date for Persia as far older than traditionally taught.

After considering all the evidence it is not surprising that the Judeo/Christian scholars have always tried to date Zarathustra as some time after the establishment of their religion because it would not have looked good for their claims to be the first and only religion that worshiped the Creator Yahu/YHVH. But this can no longer be supported, Zarathustra's time and the establishment of his religious teachings of the Creator can generally now be accepted to predate Hebrew writings from the time of Moses.

> "When Moses led the Jews to Palestine out of Egypt, about 1350 BCE he found the atmosphere surcharged with Zoroastrian ideas, and the land interspersed with edicts in praise of Ahura Mazda - as Hommel's discovery of the name *Assara Mazas* in an Assrian record of the middle of the *second millennium* BCE abundantly shows." Chatterjee, Jatindra Mohon. M. A, *Ethical Conceptions of the Gathas,* p. 546; citing Moulton, *Early*

Now some readers may be saying what does all this have to do with starships and lost data on the Chariots of the Elohim. Just this, it is important to establish evidence of these connections, between the ancient "lords" of the Zarathustrian religion and the "lords" of the Judeo/Christian, for those who look for solid historical confirmation. It is not enough to just assert a theory of visitation to mankind (even in prehistoric times), a chain of evidence, to satisfy the scientifically minded, must support it. Obviously whenever one goes far enough back into prehistoric times the remaining evidence is bound to be sketchy. However, hopefully by creating this chain of evidence and accompanying it with word and symbol interpretations, such as the meanings of the winged solar cross, future archaeological discoveries will inspire others to fill in the blanks and flesh out the connections given here.

Because at the time of the compilation of the NT, the decision was made to exclude Zarathustra's name as the prophet who predicted the "star" ship that appeared at the birth of Yeschu/Joshu/Jesus, and therefore the understanding that it was his prediction which was mentioned in the NT, of the appearance of the star that traveled through the skies guiding the Magi; modern Judeo/Christian religions have been left in the dark concerning Zarathustra's importance. No doubt in their efforts to establish a new universal religion (remember Catholic means universal) Constantine's bishops did not want to make reference to an ancient religion that was already established. This might have diminished the authority of their "new" religion and directed followers away from themselves and back toward the ancient religion of Zarathustra.

But the truth is that the highest of all the masters, prophets, teachers, and saviors, including Yeschu/Joshu/Jesus and Zarathustra, have often been guided by, and associated with the appearance of these "starships. They were assisted and guided by the "Lords of creation," the Elohim (or *Ahuraongo* in Persian), whose ships are often now called UFOs. It is important for humanity to again understand that in the prehistoric Zarathustrian religion as well as in the more modern Judeo/Christian religion, the ancient records of these finite "lords" (by any name in any language) who served the Creator (by any name in any language) and by their oneness with Him, often over time came to be confused with the Light of the Infinite Great Holy Spirit Himself. Modern evidence and recent communications from them (YHVH Elohim) is still to be presented in a later chapter and the importance of Zarathustra's time and place in history will thereafter become more obvious when this modern evidence is considered.

Judeo/Christian scholars cling to their theory of the primacy of the Bible as first and foremost monotheistic religion historically, despite mounting evidence against holding such an exclusive attitude against oneness in spirituality, but as Zech. 14:9 tells us; "YHWH will become king over all the earth, in that day, YHWH, He shall become One (Achad/Echad) and His name One." With the understanding that *Yahu* was used, not only by the early Jews in times after Moses, but also by the remnants of the followers of Zarathustra's teachings, it can be seen that both these religions although in different languages, used the same name for the Creator, *Yahu*. Since (based on the Dating Zarathustra section in this book) Zarathustra's teachings were to go on to influence Buddhism, Hinduism, Islam and the Judeo/Christian religions, they with their various names for the Creator are in fact also One with the religion which predicted the birth of a new savior. With this understanding it can be seen that all the various names for the Creator, evolved out of those teachings. The true essence of their teachings are in fact one with all truth from the

Father/Creator. He is *Yahu* in Zarathustra's teachings and He eventually became known as YHVH/Yahu, and was so recognized by descendants of the followers of both Zarathustra and Moses.

THE WORD AND THE FIRE PRIEST

> "Larson notes that Ahuramazda not only had seven archangels, but he also had 'the spirit of Wisdom, His active, creative agency in the universe: a concept startlingly similar to the logos of Zeno the Stoic, Philo Judaeus, and the Fourth Gospel." (John 1:1) Peter Myers, *The Influence of Zoroastrian Religion on Judaism,* citing Martin Larson, *The Religion of the Occident.* <http://users.cyberone.com.au/myers/zoroaster-judaism.html>

As mentioned previously in the section on the Logos "the word" (*logic* or reason) shows up outside of the NT including in the teachings of Zarathustra. This sacred history of "the word" was therefore under consideration long before the phrase was used in the NT. There has been speculation by many scholars that this refers to the word Om/Aum, the name of the Creator's feminine aspect, called wisdom or *Amun,* in Prov. 8 & 9, as discussed earlier in the section on Om/Aum etc.

> "The Sacred Word of Ahuna-Vairya did I, Ahura Mazda, repeat…The Word which was before the Earth, before the Creatures, before the Trees, before "Fire-the-Son-of-Ahura-Mazda,"[15] before the Holy Man, before the Evil Ones, …before all Corporeal Life, before all the Good Creation of Mazda, the Seed of Asha. *Yasna 19* as quoted by Mehta, Ardeshir. *Zarathushtra,* p. 76. ebook @
>
> <http://homepage.mac.com/ardeshir/Zarathushtra-Ch.1-6,Draft.pdf>

[15]This phrase *'Atar (Atar* means fire) *puthro Ahurahe Mazdao,'* "Fire the-son-of-Ahura-Mazda" (*Yasna 19)* is found in the Zoroastrian scriptures outside the Gathas. But it is not found in the Gathas" (Mehta, *Zarathushtra,* p. 75 url ibid.) It would understandably not be found in songs originally taught by him, if this is a reference to Zarathustra himself. For he would be unlikely to refer to himself with a descriptive phrase (which was more likely coined later in describing him).

> "I Laud Agni (fire), the chosen priest, god, minister of sacrifice." 1.1.1 *Rikveda 1:1-50.*
> <http://oaks.nvg.org/rv1.html>

The above phrase; "Fire the-son-of-Ahura-Mazda" (*Yasna 19)* when taken to mean a reference to Zarathustra, accounts for the importance given to the phrase; *'agnim ilé purohitam.'* It is found in the first line of the first book of the oldest Veda, the *Rig Veda,* and is translated variously as; "Fire, thou preceptor (teacher) of Iran." and "I Laud Agni (fire in Sanskrit) the chosen Priest, God, minister of sacrifice."

> "Therefore he shall send YHWH of hosts…And He becomes the Light (*Aur*) of Israel to 'Fire[16] and holy one of Him'…" Isa. 10:17 ([16]fire-*ash* in Hebrew, *atar* in Persian). Taking the foregoing into consideration this could be easily be interpreted as a reference to a "fire priest," which would make the translation; "Therefore he shall send YHWH of

170

hosts…and He becomes *Aur/Or* Light of Israel and to "fire priest holy one of Him." (Equating YHVH with *Aur/Or* just as in Zarathustra's name for the Creator-Ormazd (*Or*-Light, *mazd*-wise) and referring to Zarathustra as 'Fire and holy one of Him')

There are more than fifty translations of the Ahuna-Vairya, following is the gist of many combined;

Just as the Lord (*Ahu*) wills (*vairyo*)..*Yatha ahu vairyo*
the prophet (*ratush*) is chosen by truth (*asha*)....................................,*atha ratush ashat chit hacha,*
the gift of loving mind (*vohu mano* or good mind)............................*Vangheush dazda manangho*
for good deeds in the world..*shyaothananam angheush*
for the wise one (*Mazdai*)...*Mazdai*
the Kingdom is the Lord's (*khshathrem-cha ahurai*)......................................*xshathremcha Ahurai a*
and is for him who is pastor (*vastar*) to the poor.............................*yim drigubyo dadat vastarem.*

Fire was also the most important means of offering sacrifices to YHVH, and thus Mosaic law strictly prescribed that Fire should be kept burning continually on the altar." (Lev. 6:12-13) The practice of offering sacrifices at a communal fire stretches far back into prehistoric time, for it was thus that the community came together, each bringing what they had and sacrificing it for the sake of the common good, and for the welfare of the community. However, Zarathustra strictly forbade animal sacrifice and the eating of their flesh. Verses discussing efforts by the Levite scribes to convert followers to the practice of animal sacrifice, and which practice Yeschu/Joshu/Jesus repudiated (Matt. 9:13&12:7), will be discussed again further on. Also in this subject the quote from Higgins bears repeating, further demonstrating that the religion of Zarathustra was much the same as the religion of early Christians;

> "Upon the *Logos*...Since, therefore, St. John has adopted several other terms which were used by the Gnostics, we must conclude that he derived also the term, Logos, from the same source. If it be further asked, whence did the Gnostics derive this use of the expression, *Word* ?...they derived it most probably from the Oriental or Zoroastrian philosophy, from which was borrowed a considerable part of the Manichean (Christian) doctrines. In the Zend-Avesta (attributed to Zarathustra) we meet with a being called "the Word." Higgins, Godfrey. *Anacalypsis* Vol. 1, pp. 120,523,784&792; Note that page numbering of the hard copy does not correspond to that of the online version.

The Yasna declares: And whosoever in this corporeal life, O Spitama Zarathushtra, doth mentally repeat this Word of Mine, and further mentally repeating it doth mutter it, and further muttering it doth chant it aloud, and further chanting it doth sing its praises—his soul will I, Ahura Mazda, help to cross over the Bridge into the best World, into the Highest World, the World of Truth, the Realm of Eternal Light." Ardeshir Mehta, *Zarathushtra*, .75-76. ebook @

<http://homepage.mac.com/ardeshir/Zarathushtra-Ch.1-6,Draft.pdf>

THE "TURNING POINT" JUDGMENT DAY

"The final turning point of the creation" Yasna 43.4-5

Some only see the coming of judgment day as a Judeo/Christian idea, but the Bible and Yeschu/Joshu/Jesus, whose birth was predicted by Zarathustra's, was clearly influenced by Zarathustra' teachings, including that of the judgment day for the righteous and the sinners. This concept was already expounded in Zarathustra's ancient religion, and was incorporated into the NT when it was compiled because it was a concept commonly understood by Yeschu/Joshu/Jesus and his disciples along with many other people of their time.

> "Herakleitos' judgment by fire probably goes back to Iranian ideas; but it also contains a new element. In the Avesta the (judgment day) fire annihilates only the evil, not the earth and certainly not the whole universe." van der Waerden, Bartel. *The Birth of Astronomy* 1974, p. 135.

Apparently Zarathustra could not only foresee the reappearance of a traveling "star" ship at Yeschu/Joshu/Jesus birth, which the Magi followed across the desert, he could also foresee that the collective consciousness of the serpent brain - Satan, would, because of his desire to make others suffer, would inspire mankind to make his most heinous weapons of war to be a form of fire (bombs). The origin for the name Satan also derives from the Persian *Sheitan/Sheytan,* the evil one, found in writings of the Zarathustrian religion. The *Nirang-i-Gomez malidan,* in the *Avesta* says; "(May) Satan/*Sheytan* be defeated and destroyed, the works and workers or *Ahriman* the accursed (be) destroyed!"

> "It is useless to talk of giving up physical activity, while mental activity cannot be got rid of, without killing the mind, without ceasing to be what we are- for the seat of activity is the mind." Chatterjee, Jatindra Mohon, M. A. *Ethical Conceptions of the Gathas,* p.310.

In Zarathustra's teachings the Creator created two *mainyus* or forces, the Spenta "Peaceful" or "Holy" force and the Angra or "unholy" force (aka *Ahriman*). *Angra Mainyu/Sheytan,* the unholy force. This is, as we would say, Satan the Adversary. The collective consciousness of all adversaries, ruled by Satan the serpent or reptile brain, i.e., all warriors and their leaders, will try by war to possess the earth for themselves, leaving all those pacifists who have withdrawn from desiring the things of the world unharmed. "Those wicked people also who consider the rich man and the rich woman as great, and exhaust themselves for the acquisition of wealth, and deflect the mind of the pious from all that is best, vitiate my perception." (Gatha 32-11) Recall also at this point the similarity with Yeschu/Joshu/Jesus's teachings against loving the things of the world. (1 John 2:15; John 17:14)

> "The important point to notice here, is that the good spirit and his followers struggle in combination, against the powers of evil, and that the final victory depends *on the collaboration of God and man.* This is the only religion in which the work of man is a condition of the victory of God of over evil. Hence the religion of Zarathustra is in a unique sense, the religion of morality. The struggle for good is the duty required by the religion, and this duty can be fulfilled by moral action only." Chatterjee, Jatindra Mohon, M. A. *Ethical Conceptions of the Gathas,* p. 558; quoting Macdonell, *Comparative Religion.* p. 57.

"The Persian word for Heaven (paradise) was also adopted by the Jews and appears in the NT."

(Luke 23:43) (Chatterjee p. 376 citing Markham, *History of Persia,* pp. 66-67) The kingdom of heaven or paradise, often referred to as 'kingdom come,' can only be brought about by our own participation in its establishment. It is unreasonable to suppose that the Father will take people who, still continue on with their pursuit of evil, and place them in a paradisiacal setting, for they would soon turn it back into the chaos we presently have. (Y. 35.6; 41.2; 37.3; 39.2) from Settegast, Mary, *When Zarathustra Spoke,* p.62.

> "And to Thy good Kingdom, O Ahura Mazda! May we attain forever, and a good King be Thou over us. And let each man of us, and so each woman, thus abide, O Thou most beneficent of beings, and for both the worlds!" *Yasna Haptanghaiti.* 41.2 Translated by Mills, L. H. <http://www.avesta.org/yasna/y35to42s.htm>

It is only reasonable that a God who is love would not inflict torture on His own children, who He created or allowed to be created imperfectly; and that He would not have had prophets to teach His children in prehistoric times prior to the Hebrew language and the writing's of the OT. All suffering is the consequence of our own decision to disobey His loving wisdom. "No curse comes without its cause." (Pro. 26:2) When we do not live according to His laws they are accompanied by their own consequences. He is not angry, for our mistakes do Him no harm, rather we harm ourselves when we fail to practice peace or when we fail to live by any of His laws (including avoiding disease through good nutrition discussed in a later chapter). However, in the end while sinners may suffer judgment by this fire, created by their own hands, eventually rather like the Catholic concept of purgatory, even they can eventually be redeemed.

> "And when the frenzy departs from these sinners, then Mazda Himself, with the help of His Loving Mind, makes them understand, and inspires in them His Strength; Ahura (*Yahowah*) Himself instructs those who surrender the Lie into the hands of Righteousness." *Gatha 30.8*

We cannot stop others from fighting by fighting them, if a leader is to maintain a position of moral superiority (a concept posited by many including Gandhi, who refused any monetary gain in the form of a salary and whose position on non-violent protest later became an inspiration for Martin Luther King) they must abstain from fighting and especially from all forms of murder, remembering "Thou shalt not kill." When peace is practiced, and there is recognition that all the earth belongs to the Creator, and to the Creator alone, then and then only is the truth apparent. For the truth is that removing ourselves from worldly desires and conflict, is the best way to insure that we will be among those who will be saved from this judgment by fire.

> "Then forthwith the inflated Devil collapses, while those who are purest in heart are yoked to the cord of the Loving Mind. *Gatha 30.10*

Chapter Eight

THE OLD TESTAMENT FROM EZRA'S TIME

"<u>You must NOT be trusting in words of falsehood</u>, (because they are) saying; the temple of YHWH, the temple of YHWH, the temple of YHWH...thus *he* says; 'YHWH of Hosts, the Elohim of Israel; Add on your sacrifices, and *eat flesh!*' (This passage is a rebuke to the false priests of this false temple which purports to have YHVH saying *eat flesh!;* this is obviously meant ironically indicating that animal sacrifice is a defiling abomination, for the following verse {and a later verse} go on to dispute this falsely contrived position as follows. MHJ) For <u>I spoke</u> <u>*NOT* unto your fathers, nor commanded them in the day that I brought them out of Egypt, on</u> <u>matters of burnt offerings and sacrifices</u>. But rather this thing I instructed them to say; Listen to my voice (conscience MHJ), and I will become your Elohim, and you shall become my people...<u>They set their abominations in the house which is called by My name, defiling it</u>."

Jer. 7:4;21-23;30 <http://scripture4all.org/OnlineInterlinear/OTpdf/jer7.pdf>

THE LYING PEN OF THE LEVITE SCRIBES

"<u>How can you say; We are wise for we have the law of YHWH, when actually the lying</u>[1] <u>pen of the scribes has handled it falsely</u>?" (Jer. 8:8) This verse was altered to read "vain pen" instead of "<u>pen of falsehood</u>" as it stands in Hebrew.

[1]<u>Sheqer</u> SHD 8267 from 8266 <u>lie or falsehood</u> This word for a lie or a falsehood is previously translated in Jer. 7:4 (and elsewhere) as falsehood; if it was used as falsehood in that verse (by the same author, Jeremiah) it shows that he would have also meant it as falsehood in Jer.8:8, but that it was modified to 'vain' by someone at a later date to prevent the understanding that Jeremiah was accusing the scribes of being dishonest in their renderings of the 'law' of the OT.

& <http://scripture4all.org/OnlineInterlinear/OTpdf/jer8.pdf>

This chapter will give some historical evidence on the Levite scribes, the Sopherim. The above verse discussing them in their own time was altered to read "vain pen" instead of "pen of falsehood" as it stands in Hebrew (see http://www.scripture4all.org). It is difficult to say just how far back this misinterpretation began, but this verse in Hebrew clearly demonstrates that, according to Jeremiah, the version we were given from the scribes is at least partly falsehood.

And it once again shows that sometime after Jeremiah the OT was again altered from its original intended meaning. It seem that those very scribes clearly have the most motive for making this change of wording; so in all likelihood it began with the Sopherim. They were the very school of scribes who Jeremiah was castigating, since they were the ones who interpreted Hebrew words (to the illiterate Israelites, many of whom who had lost the ability to speak the Hebrew language while in slavery in Babylon), before Jeremiah and for centuries after he wrote that verse.

Long after the time of Moses and the children of Israel, during the exile of the Israelites in Babylon, many of them had apparently lost their understanding of the original written records of the Exodus, the "*Book of the Law*" and the *Testimony* (Ex. 40:20, Deu. 31:26) carried in the Ark. However among them were those who still listened to YHVH's voice (what we now called conscience) they had no kings and followed the Creator only; "In those days there was no king over Israel: every man did that which was right in his own eyes." Judges 21:25

> "The *nr* (lamp or light) of YHWH is the human breath (*nshmth*) that searches his insides." Prov. 20:27

Many were still choosing to follow the original diet given in the Garden of Eden. "I have given you every herb (plants) yielding seed...and every tree with seed in its fruit, for you for food." Gen. 1:29 (discussed in depth in a later chapter on diet) This is why so many Israelites were grieved to the point of crying when commanded by Ezra and the Levites to kill thousands of animals, kept for milk, butter and wool, for a blood sacrifice to celebrate Passover according to the Levite interpretation.

> "All the people were weeping as they were hearing the words...So the Levites stilled all the people saying, hold your peace, for the day is holy, neither be grieved...*From the days of Joshua son of Nun*[2] *until that day*, the Israelites had not celebrated it like this." Neh. 8:2-11&17

[2]According to the OT Joshua was Moses' minister and governor to the Israelites (Deu. 34:9 & Jos. 1:1) and lived concurrently with Moses. According to the OT he was forty years old when chosen by Moses, to go on a reconnaissance mission. Joshua, as the minister to the Israelites, was not one of the Levites (Num.13:8, 1:10) demonstrating that the title of minister to the Israelites, is *not* synonymous with that of the Levites who served under the priesthood of Aaron and his sons. Aaron and his sons were priests over the Levites, not over the altar of the Israelites, which the Levites were not even allowed to touch. (Num. 18:1-5) The Levites were originally servers in the tabernacle of the congregation, in charge of animal sacrifice (butchering, cooking and serving sacrificed animals) to feed the mixed multitudes.

As the verses from the OT in this chapter will show, the Levites eventually overthrew the true and rightful first priesthood and formed what is called in the OT the "priesthood of the second order." (II Kings 23:3-4) According to their own record they murdered those priests who understood the importance of remembering the "host of heaven" i.e. YHVH's Elohim. This was purportedly because these priests refused to participate in the Levite interpretation of Passover, as requiring the sacrifice of animals for the Passover, and stayed with their brothers in Judah, eating unleavened bread instead.

For this minimal infraction to the Levite's newly presumed authority and because they burned incense to the host of heaven, they were murdered. That such simple offenses resulted in their death shows that it was really the Levites who were evil, and that these priests were murdered just because their refusal to partake of the Levites animal sacrifice was taken as an insult by the Levites who had long coveted the priesthood.

Along with the demise of the first order of the priesthood, the understanding of YHVH's Elohim was lost, because these murderers were from the very same group of Levite scribes whose members later altered the OT and gave their own twist to the term given in the OT, "YHVH Elohim" (YHVH Lord of the gods or YHVH's gods depending on the context), and rendered it as a singular title afterward translated as Lord God[3] instead. ([3]*Adonai Elohim*)

THE LEVITE USURPERS OF THE PRIESTHOOD

"And you shall give the Levites to Aaron and to sons of him...and Aaron and his sons shall give supervision and they (the Levites) shall observe the priesthood of them (Aaron and his sons)." Num. 3:9-10

Except for Aaron, Moses brother, who shared his bloodline, the rest of the Levites were never called priests in the first four books of the OT. According to the Torah Moses repeatedly said that only Aaron and his sons were priests, *over* the Levite servers, not over the altar of the children of Israel which the Levites were not even allowed to touch (Num. 18:32), the children of Israel, however, *were* allowed to use that altar. In the first four books of the Bible, it is said the Levites are servers under the priests Aaron and his sons. One incidence where they were called priests actually says when transliterated directly from Hebrew;

"<u>NOT</u> he shall be for priests, the Levites, all of tribes of Levi portion and allotment with Israel, fire offerings of YHWH and allotment of him they shall eat." Deu. 18:1

<u>http://www.scripture4all.org/OnlineInterlinear/Hebrew_Index.htm</u>

This verse was transliterated from the above Hebrew word for word rendering of it (which can be read at the above site) to its present form as it now reads as follows in the KJV "The priests the Levites, and all the tribe of Levi, shall have no part nor inheritance with Israel: they shall eat the offerings of YHWH made by fire, and His inheritance." Deu.18:1 The Levite scribes were no doubt shocked when they came to this verse. Whether by them or at some later time, it clearly was at some point changed in the OT, concealing this record of Moses decision to exclude them from the priesthood. In fact the OT not only said they were NOT to be priests, but the Levites had actually already once before tried to take over the priesthood while Moses still lived.

"Now Korath...the son of Levi...gathered themselves together against Moses *and* against Aaron, and said unto them; *You take too much upon yourself,* seeing all the congregation are holy, every one of them, and YHWH is among them: wherefore do you lift yourselves above the congregation of YHWH...And Moses said unto Korath, Hear I pray you sons of Levi: Does it seem to be such a small thing, that the Elohim of Israel has separated you from the congregation of Israel, the bring you near unto Himself to do service in the tabernacle of YHWH, and to stand before the congregation to minister unto them? And has He brought you near Him, <u>and all your brothers the Levi with you</u> *And You Seek The Priesthood Also?* For which cause both you and all your company are gathered together *against* YHWH?...And Moses said, Hereby you shall know that YHWH has sent me to do all these works; for I have not done them of my own mind...And the earth opened up her mouth and swallowed them up, and all the men that appertained to Korath, and all their goods." Num. 16:1-32

176

There are no references to the Levites as priests in the first four books of the OT, quite the contrary, and only a few references that *appear* to refer to the Levites as priests in Deuteronomy, the last of the five books ascribed to Moses. One of these verses (Deu. 17:9) can be seen to actually simply list them among various functionaries or officers, along with those of the priesthood (Aaron and his sons) through which the people could bring matters to a judge. So that it is only a question of where one places the punctuation, writing it so as to say, "the priests, the Levites, and unto the judge" or "the priests the Levites, and unto the judge," thus making what was actually their inclusion in a list, of various agents answering to Moses, appear to designate them as priests.

Another example of the possibility of taking a list to mean that the son's of Levi were priests, occurs in Deu. 31:9; "the priests, sons of Levi, the ones carrying the coffer of the covenant of YHWH, and to all of the old ones of Israel."

The second incidence that appears to render them priests (Deu. 17:18) will be addressed in the following pages. Besides these references (occurring toward the end of the Torah) there are only a few more equally ambiguous references like Deu. 21:5, 24:8, 27:9. As mentioned previously there were numerous obvious changes to the book of Deuteronomy, appearing as anachronistic references from a much later time, these will be discussed specifically in a later section on Deuteronomy. Obviously after making these few minor adjustments, additions, and misinterpretations in the latter part of the Torah, the Levite scribes felt they were in a position to completely take over the power of the priesthood and run things according to their own desires.

So according to the OT, the question of the Levites aspiring to become priests had already been addressed by Moses when they had revolted against Moses and Aaron. Only later, in Ezra's time, who apparently was from Aaron's line, at some point, it came to be interpreted that *all* the Levites were priests, and they then succeeded in turning many of the people to the animal sacrifice cult of the Levites.

> "A wonderful and horrible thing is committed in the lands. The prophets prophesy falsely, and the priests bear rule by their means, and my people love to have it so, and what will you do in the end thereof?...Therefore will I do unto this house, which is called by my name, wherein you trust, and unto the place which I gave to you and to your fathers, as I have done to Shiloh. And I will cast you out of my sight." Jer. 5:30-31 & 7:14-15

It is no small coincidence that also around this time many historically known alterations to the OT also took place and were recorded, by the Sopherim, the Levite scribes. This resulted in many contradictions between the prophets and the cult of animal sacrifice instituted by the Levite scribes and false priests. The Bible itself makes it obvious that false priests used these altered interpretations to influence the illiterate Israelites, instructing them that animal sacrifices were necessary to receive healing and forgiveness of sins.

> "For <u>I spoke not unto your fathers, nor commanded them</u> in the day that I brought them out of Egypt, <u>on matters of burnt offerings and sacrifices</u>. But rather this thing I instructed them to say; Listen to my voice (conscience MHJ), and I will become your Elohim, and you shall become my people...They set their abominations in the house which is called by my name, defiling it." Jer. 7:22-23

177

<http://scripture4all.org/OnlineInterlinear/OTpdf/jer7.pdf>

Aaron was the priest over the Levite servers, and his sons were to perform the same function. The understanding of their role as priests over the Levite butchers only, was eventually lost or obliterated over time. The directions for the Levite servers in the book of Leviticus and the instances where the priests and their Levite servers are mentioned in the same sentence were falsely interpreted by the Levite scribes to mean that *they* were priests, whereas according to the OT Moses stated in Deu. 18:1, (*when it is rendered directly from the Hebrew*), that the Levites were NOT to be priests. They later parlayed their role as *servers* in the tabernacle of the congregation, under the priests Aaron and his sons, using this function to eventually portray themselves as priests, to anyone so illiterate as to fail to see the distinction. The transcriptions to conceal their proper role was later used by the Levite scribes to justify the formation of this so-called "priesthood of the second order" which was actually a cult of animal sacrifice in disguise, using YHVH's name without His blessing, as can be seen from the following verse from the NT.

> "They made a calf in those days and led sacrifice to the idol…Turns yet the God (*Theos*) and besides (instead) gives them to be offering divine service to the host of heaven (*stratia ho ouranos,* Old Testament-*tseba'oth*); as it is written in the scroll of the prophets, <u>no slayed ones and sacrifices you offered to Me</u> (God) for forty years in the wilderness, house of Israel." Acts 7:42

<http://scripture4all.org/OnlineInterlinear/NTpdf/act7.pdf>

The story of the current version available to us begins with the discovery of a copy of the "Law of Moses" by Hilikiah, Ezra's great-grandfather, under the reign of King Josiah. After this event the Bible indicates that most of the Israelites became illiterate during their exile in Babylon. This copy was inherited by Levite scribes and priests from before Ezra, and later (re)introduced to the Israelites by Ezra.

> "When they brought the money for (repair of the temple v:10) the House of Jehovah, Hilikiah the priest found a book of the law of YHWH given by Moses. And Hilkiah answered and said to Shaphan the scribe; I have found a book of the law in the house of the YHWH And Hilkiah delivered the book to Shaphan. And Shaphan carried the book back to the king (Josiah). And Shaphan read it before the king...when the king had heard the words of the law, he rent his clothes...(saying) great is YHWH's rage against us because our forefathers did not do according to all that is written in this book...Go inquire of YHWH for me, and for them that are left in Israel and Judah, concerning the words of the book that is found: for great is the wrath of YHWH that is poured out upon us because our fathers have not kept the word of YHWH that is written in this book" II Chr. 34:15-24

The section of the copy of the so-called "Law," being under consideration by Josiah, the Passover sacrifice, is purportedly based on earlier biblical texts. This "copy" is actually not authenticated, and it clearly cannot be established as being precisely and accurately the same as Moses' *Book of the Law.* Previous authors, including possibly earlier Levites may actually have adapted it to suit their own interests.

Yet even these texts (for which continuity from the time of the original writings of Moses cannot be established), *actually* say in Hebrew "Tell the whole community of Israel that on the tenth day of this month each man is to take a lamb for his family, one for each household...(marking) blood...*on the houses which they shall eat him*. (7)...And *they* (are to) eat the flesh on *this* night...not reserving any for morning...And this day shall be a memorial for generations for eons...and *you* shall observe the feast of *unleavened breads[4]*, that in this very day I brought your hosts of you out of the land of Egypt." Ex. 12:3-8, 17

[4]Notice that in verse 7 it refers to "the houses which" were to eat the lambs, *not everyone*. AND it actually says that the memorial observance thereafter is for Moses and all the generations which were to follow, to eat unleavened bread for seven days (Ex. 12:18). This verse is interpreted in KJV as "wherein they *shall* eat it" instead of the word for word interpretation that reads "on the houses *which* they shall eat him in*" in Hebrew.

<http://scripture4all.org/OnlineInterlinear/OTpdf/exo12.pdf>Sacrifice you

The verse previous (6) which has been interpreted to say that "every" one of the assembly shall slay a lamb, in fact says "all of the assembly", which is not specifically *everyone*, but rather a reference to an event that was to take place among all those in the assembly aka the mixed multitude. That this was not everyone, including the children of Israel, can be seen in the directions to Moses and and all the generations which were to follow, to eat unleavened bread to celebrate Passover. That this phrase "all the assembly" was translated to say "every one" shows further meddling with the text, in all probability by Ezra and the Levite scribes (the Sopherim) to promote their animal sacrifice cult.

Notice in verse 17 that the memorial observance thereafter was to be unleavened bread (just as Yeschu/Joshu/Jesus ate only bread and wine at the Last Supper at Passover), NOT that the remembrance of the Passover has be commemorated by continuing to kill and eat lambs. This one particular occurrence of killing the young sheep, is stated to be as a sign to YHVH's angels so they could protect the infants of the assembly (the mixed multitude) who would have died along with the first born of the Egyptians.

Killing the lambs was perhaps also so as to not be held back by the comparatively slow progress of young lambs who would have been left behind to starve (then suffer, die, and go to waste anyway) without the ewes who were to go in haste (according to Ex. 12:11) with the Israelites. So besides being a sign to the angels (Ex. 12:13) this may have been a mercy killing as well as a utilitarian act out of necessity.

> "Sacrifice you, sacrifices of righteousness and trust to YHWH, many ones saying, who shall show us goodness? Lift you over us, light of faces of You, YHWH." Ps. 4:6

After the Exodus the Israelites ate manna, until they began to complain (because some among them had become addicted to eating meat while in Egypt). This protein addiction arises because of the high levels of the destructive acid forming minerals, phosphorous (which can form phosphorus acid) and sulfur (which can form sulfuric acid) and chlorine (which can form hydro-chloric acid), found in flesh foods, but not found in vegetable foods. A healthy body contains minerals in a ratio of 80:20 alkaline to acid; meat has extremely high quantities of acid forming minerals, with pork even higher still in these harmful acids.

Just as pouring sulfuric acid or phosphoric acid over living tissue will destroy it, the damage done by consuming these acids over and above the extremely minimal proportions necessary to health (already minimally present in grains and seeds). These acids thus continually destroy the cells of the body by robbing electrons from healthy cells (a process aka the theory of 'free radicals'), which must then be repaired. This requires much more protein than a body in a state of healthy equilibrium; this intense desire for protein and high levels of stomach acid was called by the ancients "bloodlust."

YHVH Elohim knew how great their hunger was (because of the high levels of stomach acid their previous diet had caused them to have), the OT says that flesh was brought for those who so lusted. However, YHVH told them they would eat it until it came out of their nostrils, and it became loathsome to them (Num. 11:6-34). But the Bible makes it clear that eating flesh was against YHVH's wishes, because it says His anger was hot and then because of their bloodlust He brought a plague on them. "YHWH smote the people with a very great plague." (33)

> "Now our soul is dried away, there is nothing at all besides this manna...Then Moses heard the people weep throughout their families...and the anger of YHWH was kindled greatly: Moses was also displeased...And Moses said unto the Lord...Whence should I have flesh to give all this people? For they weep unto me saying give us flesh to eat...And Moses said...Shall the flocks and herds be slain for them to satisfy them? (obviously a shocking idea to Moses)...And there went forth a wind from YHWH, and brought quails from the sea, and let them fall by the camp...And while the flesh was still between their teeth, before it was chewed, the wrath of YHWH was kindled against the people, and YHWH smote the people with a very great plague...And they called the name of that place *Kibroth Hattaavah*[5]: because of the people that lusted. (⁵SHD 6914 bloodlust for flesh foods)" Num. 11:6-34

"*Kibroth Hattaavah*" has been translated as the place of "longing" in some modern Bibles, probably to avoid offending those who eat meat, but the root '*avah* (SHD 183) shows that the meaning implies lust. Surprisingly this *is* the meaning given in the KJV, showing that their desire for meat was a lust for blood.

> "The function of sacrifice in one of the most misunderstood matters in the Bible. Modern readers take it to mean the unnecessary taking of animal life, or they believe that the person who offered the sacrifice was giving up something of his or her own in order to compensate for some sin or perhaps to win God's favor. In the biblical world, however, the most common type of sacrifice was for meals. The apparent rationale was that if humans wanted to eat meat they had to recognize that they were taking life. They could not regard this as an ordinary act of daily secular life. Friedman, Richard. *Who Wrote the Bible?,* 1987, p. 91-92.

It is not commonly understood nowadays that the ancient ritual practice of animal sacrifice referred to the consumption of animal flesh. But according to the OT they were understood to be one and the same thing by the ancients; a community effort overseen by the servers trained from among the Levites, to at times sustain the poor of the assembly of the mixed multitude by distributing the cooked flesh among these people, to be consumed immediately by all who ate meat (since they had no way to store it).

It was from this occasional necessity that it came to be understood that such an act was a sacrifice, since the owner of the animal relinquished or "sacrificed" his right to sole ownership of the animal, to be then given as meat to everyone in the congregation. Since they had no refrigeration or means to preserve meat, when it was more than enough for one person or family, it had to be consumed immediately or thrown away. This sacrifice was originally done out of necessity, during the forty years (Deu. 1:3) the Israelites and the mixed multitude of other races, wandered without land to till, and distributed by the Levite servers in the tabernacle of the congregation, to everyone in need, to prevent starvation.

According to the OT during the Exodus, Moses speaks of those among the tribes who do eat flesh commanding them on how they must prepare it. "And he sent young men, *of the children of Israel which offered burnt offerings,* and sacrificed peace offerings of oxen to YHWH." (Ex. 24:5) Notice that the directions concerning sacrifice was only for those "of the children of Israel which offered burnt offerings," not all of the Israelites. Those who did *not* eat meat were not bound to perform any of the necessarily hygienic rituals for sacrificing animals, because it only applied to those who did so. Now let us examine some of the laws and instructions for those who did.

THE LEVITICAN HYGIENE LAWS

> "And you shall sequester the sons of Israel from uncleanness to them, so they shall not die from uncleanness to them, defiling them in the tabernacle of Me (the tabernacle of the congregation where Levites sacrificed animals) which is in midst of them." Lev. 15:31

Aaron is garbed in protective armor, especially to perform animal sacrifices for the tabernacle of the congregation, in Ex. 28. It is said that he must wear among other things a breastplate (to protect him while holding the animals head and horns) and a special plate of gold (a helmet) to wear on his head (36) (*Thummim and Urim*) "that Aaron may bear the iniquity of the holy things" (38).

Now this statement demonstrates that the practice involved a necessary *iniquity* (according to Webster's iniquity is a "gross injustice or wickedness"). Because it was a necessary iniquity, for the feeding those who ate meat, while they wandered forty years without the means to grow food, Moses wrote the Levitican laws to insure that it must *only* be done in a holy, pure, or sanctified[6] way. ([6]What we would call hygienic)

> "And you shall bring Aaron and his sons to the door of the tabernacle of the congregation and wash them with water." Ex. 40:12

> "And he shall flay (filet) the burnt offering, and cut it into pieces ...But his inwards and his legs shall he wash in water. Lev. 1:6,9

Almost the entire book of Leviticus goes on concerning animal sacrifice and how it must always be brought to the Levite tabernacle servers and Aaron the priest in charge of them, and handled according to the special Levitican laws written by Moses to protect the mixed multitude from the spread of contagious diseases, called in those times plagues.

Remember also that the story of Cain was one where changes were made to the literal meaning, making it appear to prefer animal sacrifice over vegetable foods. Another change to the OT occurs at the very end of Exodus, in ch. 40:29. This verse speaks of the "offering commanded by YHWH (on the altar)." It has been changed from "ascent or present offerings as YHVH instructed Moses" the change was made to read "meat offering as YHWH instructed Moses," thus making it appear that meat was sacrificed on the altar when it was in fact forbidden in Ex. 30:1&9.

Clearly someone went to a great deal of trouble to change many passages as they read in Hebrew to include references to meat eating and animal sacrifice as they now read in the KJV. In Gen. 24:33 the word meat was inserted changing the meaning. In Gen. 1:29 and Lev. 25:6 the word food was changed to read meat. In Ex. 30:9 assent offering has been changed to meat offering. The description of present offerings (food given as a present to everyone) was frequently changed throughout the OT to read meat offerings, including; Ex. 29:41; Ex. 40:29; Num. 4:16; Num. 6:15; Num. 7:13,19,25,31,37,43,49,55,61,67,73,79,87; Num. 15:4,6,9,24; Num. 18:9; Num. 28:8,9,12,13; and all throughout Num. 29. To see all these changes you can go to:

<http://scripture4all.org/OnlineInterlinear/Hebrew_Index.htm>

These were all changed from present offering, to read "meat offering," even in the instances where the offering clearly refers to bread or non meat foods made from grain etc. This occurs throughout the entire second chapter of Leviticus where it refers to baked goods and bread offerings, clearly made of flour and grain. In Judges 1:7 the word food scraps was changed to meat scraps and in Judges 14:14 the word food, in this case discussing milk, has been changed to read meat. These are evidence of the self-interest that motivated the Levite scribes (and perhaps others later), who changed them, in their advocacy of animal sacrifice and consuming the flesh.

Except for the second chapter, the book of Leviticus consists almost entirely of instructions for handling meat, in the most hygienic way possible (during the Exodus when the Israelites could not grow food), by the Levites servers who are described as having been otherwise disinherited among the children of Israel and kept separate from them.

> "Only you shall not number the tribe of Levi, neither take the sum of them among the children of Israel." Num. 1:49

52% of Ashkenazi Levites are not Semites according to the YDNA models and the current explanations...East European Jews are 25% E3b (which indicates an African/Hamitic origin)...They may have been part of the mixed multitude in the Exodus...We know that the lineages in known Semitic nations are G, I and J...the original Semetic Haplogroup was F and divided into I and J and probably G...this stem (F) determines all the other Haplogroup from F to R...only 10% of tested Ashkenazi Levites are of known direct Jewish/Israelite YDNA. Cox, Wade. *The Genetic Origin of Nations*. <http://ccg.org/English/S/p265.html>

As mentioned much earlier the Levite Aaron, priest over the Levite servers, and his wife Miriam were afflicted with leprosy after eating flesh and mention of this in Num.12:12, while later altered by the Levite Sopherim, is still available to us as recorded in the Massorah. *More Emendations*. <http://www.geocities.com/~hebrew_roots/html/hr-2-3-02.html>

> "The Levites shall pitch (their tents) round about the tabernacle of testimony (where animals were sacrificed) that there be no wrath[7] upon the congregation of the children of

Israel." Num. 1:53 [7]In the form of plagues, from flesh eating bacteria, like leprosy, e. coli, giardia, salmonella and other forms of dysentery etc., which once distributed among those who ate meat, could go on to contaminate everyone.

"And after that when the Levites shall go to do service of the tabernacle of the congregation: *you shall cleanse them*, and offer them for an offering...And I have given the Levites...that there be no plague among the children of Israel, when the children of Israel come near the sanctuary (where the altar was kept, different from the tabernacle of the congregation or testimony, see below)." Num. 8:15,19

The Levites, who were not among the pure-blooded Israelites, were accustomed to flesh foods and therefore were assigned to handle animals to be sacrificed when necessary, in prescribed ways. This was so as to protect the mixed multitude from the worst consequences, thus bringing afflictions upon them and spreading disease organisms carried by flesh foods (called plagues) throughout all the Israelites.

"And the Lord said to Aaron, you and your sons and your father's house with you shall bear the *iniquity* of the sanctuary: and you and your sons with you shall bear the *iniquity* of your priesthood...And they (the Levites) shall keep the charge of all the tabernacle: only they shall NOT come near the *vessels of the sanctuary and the altar*, so that neither you nor they die...And you (Aaron and sons) shall keep the charge of the sanctuary, and the charge of the altar, so that there be no more wrath[8] any more upon the children of Israel." Num. 18:1-5 ([8]in the form of plagues, i.e. the spread of contagious diseases, from meat-eating bacteria and other diseases carried by animals)

The reason the "vessels and the altar of the sanctuary," were not to be touched by the Levite butchers (nor was meat allowed to be offered there, Ex. 30:1&9 "You shall make an altar...You shall offer no meat offering...thereon.") was because plagues could thereby be spread among the vegetarian Israelites, who offered their non-meat offerings using the vessels at the altar of the sanctuary, *NOT* at the tabernacle of the congregation which served meat. As mentioned before the verse later in Exodus (40:29) were it says meat was offered on the altar does not actually say "meat offering" it says "present offering," it was changed at some point to read "meat" in the present version. <http://scripture4all.org/OnlineInterlinear/OTpdf/exo40.pdf>

"I have taken your brethren, the Levites from among the children of Israel: to you they are given as a gift for YHWH, to do the service of the tabernacle of the (general) congregation." Num. 18:6

It can be seen in the verses following that the danger to the children of Israel was because they were not physically adapted to resist exposure to bacterial contamination. Not being regularly exposed to it by eating meat, they had no antibodies built up in their immune systems. The Levites were therefore *originally* only in charge of the "service of the tabernacle of the (general) congregation."

"Neither must the children of Israel[9] henceforth come near the tabernacle of the congregation (where meat was prepared) lest they bear sin and die. (not having any immunity) But the Levite shall do service of the tabernacle of the congregation, and they shall bear their *iniquity*..." Num. 18:22-23 ([9]obviously vegetarians since their altar was

183

considered pure and because they might die if thus contaminated)

"And you (the Levites) shall bear no sin[10] by reason of it, when you have heaved from the best of it: <u>neither shall you pollute *the holy things[11] of the children of Israel*</u>, lest you die." Num. 18:32 ([10]Having regularly been exposed to meat-eating bacteria, the Levites had mostly developed immunity, so they bore no sin, or that is, suffered no consequences, but the spread of contamination could cause a plague that might then affect the rest of the mixed multitude AND the Children of Israel with deadly dysentery.)

<u>http://scripture4all.org/OnlineInterlinear/OTpdf/num18.pdf</u>

[11]The pure vegetarians among the children of Israel prepared their sacrifices to the congregation, of bread, and vegetable foods, with their pure and "holy things," the "vessels of the sanctuary and offered them at that altar" (Num. 18:1-5) The Levite butchers were not allowed to pollute or even come near this altar, so as to avoid contamination, which could cause deadly plagues among those not regularly exposed to such micro-organisms.

If the Levites had actually been priests why else would they be prohibited from touching the "holy things" when the children of Israel were allowed to do so? These more subtle understandings were missed by the Levite scribes turned priests, who edited the manuscripts; one because they refused to see that their lifestyle caused contagious disease called plagues, and two because of the association between meat eating and early onset Alzheimer's, which dimmed their ability to think logically. (the association between Alzheimer's and meat eating is discussed in depth in the following chapter on health and diet)

It was the priesthood who regularly consumed the flesh of sacrificed animals, thus becoming addicted to flesh; this happens because the high acid mineral content in meat breaks down tissue that then requires more protein for rebuilding. Because of the twisted meaning given by the Levites and the scribes to the instructions given to the Israelites by Moses, the Essenes, the Ebionites or Nazarenes, and some of the Gnostics believed that the book of Leviticus had become corrupt or (re)written by an evil angel. Shaw, Michael. *Archives of Systematic Vegetarian Theology.* <u>http://www.all-creatures.org/discuss/svtxbibessene1ms.html</u>

Moses wrote the Levitican laws to teach the Levite servers how to handle the meat, for example, removing blood and fat and certain organs; washing it; keeping it only one or two days after cooking etc., (Lev. 7:15-21 and the entire book of Lev.) so that everything would be kept relatively purified to prevent the spread of contamination to all the people. The Levitican laws were obviously written by Moses with an understanding of these possibly deadly consequences. That he knew how to deal with these things, when there was no means of studying these disease causing micro-organisms scientifically, shows guidance from advanced beings, YHVH's Elohim.

That Leviticus was only the law for priests in charge of the Levites, not the law for all the Israelites is also shown by an account in the OT of Joshua and the Israelites with whom he dwelt. According to the OT Joshua's people found animal sacrifice abhorrent and considered it so bound to lead to moral back-sliding, that they "assembled a host to go up on" the tribes of Reuben, G-d, and the half tribe of Manasseh, who they thought were creating a sacrificial altar in Jos. 22:10-29 (more below). According to the Levitican laws the mixed multitude was forbidden to eat meat at other altars, because the meat would not be properly prepared and could spread plagues among all the people.

That this story is incorrectly interpreted to mean that they went to there to make war is shown by the fact that they *did not* fight, but rather simply talked. The book of Joshua also records that the Israelites proper observed a Passover consisting of parched grain made into unleavened cakes (Jos. 5:10-11). And there is no mention of eating meat or sacrificing animals in the Hebrew transliteration of the book of Joshua. (<http://www.scripture4all.org>).

It might be argued that according to the Bible Joshua was a warrior, and no stranger to bloodshed, but it may be seen that even if these records were not redacted by the Levite scribes, there was perhaps sometimes no other practical recourse when some of the circumstances are considered. The true Israelites were often beset by the Canaanites and the other various tribes descended from the Nephilim-Neanderthals. There was no living with many of these sub-human peoples who were not only vicious, but would even go so far as sacrificing and eating the smaller Israelites, who were not warriors at all. It may be that some of the larger members of Moses' mixed multitude felt themselves to have been forced into defensive positions in protecting the masses and the nonviolent little people. Not only did the willingness of the Canaanites to eat anything spread disease, but also their willingness to practice bestiality and then copulate freely among themselves created STD epidemics, also called plagues among the ancients. Num. 31:15-16

Remember there were also Egyptian slaves or servants, of other races (the mixed multitude Ex. 12:38), who were to go with the Israelites. The original Passover during the Exodus from Egypt, may have been commanded so as to build up the strength of those people, among the Israelites, who along with the mixed multitude, <u>had</u> already been compelled to survive by eating meat while servants to the Egyptians. While not mandated for everyone (Ex. 12:7), this may have been allowed to fortify those individuals who already ate meat, for their trek out of bondage. (Ex. 12:47) This was then interpreted, by the Levite scribes to Josiah and thereafter, as mandated by that one occurrence, to be continually re-enacted as a regular observance at Passover, when unleavened bread was actually ordained .

> "So kill the Passover (lamb) and sanctify yourselves, and prepare your brethren that they may do according to the word of the lord by the hand of Moses. And King Josiah gave to people, of the flock, lambs and kids, all for the Passover offerings...to the number of thirty thousand and six hundred small cattle, and five hundred oxen from the kings possession...And they killed the Passover sacrifice, and the priests sprinkled the blood from their hands, and the Levites flayed (filleted) them." II Chr. 35:7-1

Strangely enough the Levite scribes proudly recount in the OT, their murderous over-throw of the priests who practiced a Passover of unleavened bread and consulted with the "hosts of heaven," YHVH's Elohim (and therefore were in a position to pass down their knowledge of the Elohim). This happened around the beginning of the same time when, through the efforts of the Levite scribes, the changes took place to the references of YHVH Elohim, enforcing the words and worship of the Lord God (begun around the time of Saul) instead. Fortunately for history, the lack of compunction, shown by the Levite scribes, in performing this murderous act and then recording it, has given us a record of the demise of the true priesthood, who understood the power of calling on the hosts of heaven, YHVH Elohim.

THE SECOND PRIESTHOOD

> "And the king (Josiah)...made a covenant...to perform the words of *this* covenant that was written in *this* book...And the king commanded Hilkiah the priest and *the priests of the SECOND* order, to bring forth out of the temple of YHWH all the vessels that were made for Baal, and for the grove, <u>AND</u> for all the *host of heaven*[12] (*tzba eshmim*) and he burned them." II Kings 23:3-4

[12]*YHVH Zeba'oth* or "YHVH of hosts" is in fact one of YHVH's titles. It is used throughout the OT including I Sam. 1:3, Ps. 148:2, & Isaiah 54:5. That the "host of heaven," *were* YHVH's Elohim is shown by other references to them in association with YHVH as in the following verses where they are called by the exact same name, *tzba eshmim*; the hosts of heaven.

> "Praise YHWH, all His heavenly hosts, you his servants who do his will." Ps. 103:21

"Therefore hear the word of YHWH, I saw YHWH sitting on His throne and all the host of the heavens (*tzba eshmim*) standing on His right and His left." I Kings 22:19 This prophet, Micaiah went on to say if his prophecy came true (that the king would fail in battle) it would prove that he was a true prophet, and it indeed came true. Whether or not their prophecies came true, was considered the test of true prophets. (Deu. 18:22) The name *tzba eshmim,* of the host of heaven, is the same as is used in II Chr. 18:18, II Kings 23:5 and elsewhere, Isa. 34:4, etc.

> "Praise Him, all His angels; praise Him all His heavenly hosts." Ps. 148:2

The story of the Levite revolt who formed the SECOND priesthood (destroying the original priesthood who consulted with YHVH's "host of heaven," the Elohim), is also recounted in II Chr. 34:5, though not in the same detail. II Kings goes on to praise king Josiah for overthrowing all the priests who worshiped Baal G-d, and other idols however, the verses following show they then also went on, in their bid for power, to destroy those priests of Judah who burned incense to all the hosts of heaven.

> "And he (King Josiah) put down all the idolatrous priests, whom the kings of Judah[13] had ordained to burn incense...them also that burned incense to Baal, to the sun, and to the moon, and to the constellations (*mazzaloth*-zodiac) AND to all *the host of heaven (tzba eshimim)*...AND he brought the priests *out of the cities of Judah*, and defiled the high places where the priests had burned incense, from Geba to Beersheba, and broke down the high places of the gates that were in the entering of the gates of Joshua, the governor of the city...<u>Nevertheless these priests of the high places came not</u> up to (the newly established) altar (for animal sacrifice) of the Lord in Jerusalem<u>, but they did eat of the unleavened bread among their brethren.</u> (since they were among the Israelites who observed a vegetarian Passover) II Kings 23:5-9

> [13]"The scepter shall not depart from Judah, not the ruler's staff from between his feet, until he comes to whom it belongs; and to him shall be the obedience of the peoples."

186

Gen. 49:8-10. Remember that Yeschu/Joshu/Jesus was from the tribe of Judah (Heb. 7:14,16) and thus came to be called "the king of the Jews."

That these priests *out of the cities of Judah* were observing a Passover shows that they were followers of the "Law of Moses" obeying YHVH's instructions. That they were given the opportunity to come to the Levite Passover (interpreted by the Levites as requiring the sacrifice of lambs) and refused shows that this was the area of the law in which they were judged by the Levites to be in default. Their burning of incense to the "host of heaven" was just an excuse the Levites used to justify murdering them; otherwise they would not have even been given the opportunity to attend the sacrifice of lambs for the Levite Passover (since the Passover was only for Israelites Ex 12:43).

That their Passover consisted of unleavened bread shows that there *were* alternative ways to celebrate Passover other than slaughtering lambs. And their refusal to attend also shows that if they did not want to be involved in a celebration that required eating meat, then they probably did not eat meat at other less important times. For why else would they rather die than attend a free feast?

These two paltry areas of difference, burning incense to the host of heaven and refusing to come and eat the sacrificed animals, justified their murder (along with the priests of Baal and those who burned incense to the sun and moon) in the minds of the Levite animal sacrifice cult. During the next few hundred years these Levite scribes turned priests, were thereafter bound to condemn all those who recognized the importance of YHVH's hosts of heaven, and went on to try to obliterate all references that appeared to discuss to YHVH's Elohim. Which, among other changes were conveniently done by changing many plural references to YHVH Elohim, the host of heaven, to the singular word Adonai or "Lord." They also altered any passages where the names YHVH and Elohim or Adonai were used in such a way that it made it clear these words did not indicate one and the same entity.

This it is established to have been done, because as mentioned elsewhere, they left records of their changes. (found in the Massorah discussed again further on) Fortunately for history, like most murderers they were not successful in twisting all traces of their horrendous crimes, nor all the references to YHVH's Elohim, the hosts of heaven.

"Thus the heavens and the earth were finished, and all the host of them." Gen. 2:1

As mentioned previously the Dead Seas scrolls include a verse concerning the coming to see the importance of "the light of life" in all creatures. The reason for its exclusion is clear, because it is obviously in conflict with the Levites - Massorite heritage of demanding for animals to sacrifice, from the people, in exchange for absolution from sins. "After he has suffered, he will see the light of life and be satisfied. By his knowledge My righteous servant will justify many and he will bear their iniquities." Isa. 53:11

The unwillingness of the priests of Judah, to come and eat the lambs being sacrificed by the Levites, to celebrate Passover, was seen as an insult by the Levite usurpers who had begun to move into positions of power. The unleavened bread-eating priests of *YHVH Zeba'oth,* YHVH of hosts, were then killed for refusing to come to the newly established Levite false temple of YHWH, to partake of the meat Passover, demanded by this animal sacrifice cult, masquerading

187

as the true temple of YHVH. That the Levites freely broke the commandment "Thou shalt not kill" shows that it was *they* who really were the false priests!

> "And he slew all the priests of the high places that were there upon the altars, and burned the men's bones upon them...And the king commanded[14] all the people, saying, 'Keep the Passover unto the Lord your God, as it is written in the book of *this* covenant'...that he might perform the words of the law which were written in the book that Hilkiah the priest found in the house of the Lord. Surely there was not one holden such a Passover from the days of the Judges." II Kings 23:20-22 ([14]why would the people need to be commanded to eat a free meal of meat unless there was some resistance to doing so? This again shows that some Israelites were vegetarians)

II Kings 23 says that Josiah slew or sacrificed ALL the priests of the high places, including those who refused to partake of the sacrificial lambs (eating unleavened bread instead). This shows that along with the false priests of Baal etc. he also slew these priests called in (II Kings 23:9) priests of the high places, who were the priests of the *first order,* priests of YHVH's host of Heaven.

> "You are <u>YHWH: you made the heaven, the heaven of heavens, with all the host</u>...and all the host of heaven worship you." Neh. 9:6

Now given all the other violence recorded in this corrupted version of Moses' law, handed down to us with the editing by the Levite priests, the killing of all the priests as idolatrous might be considered by some as all well and good (except remember, Thou shalt not kill). But King Josiah and the Levite priests also went on to over throw the priests of Judah (who unlike the Levites *were* numbered among the Israelites Num. 2:33). These priests followed YHVH, doing after the manner of the priests who sat on the mercy seat since Moses. This can seen in that they were observing the Passover in remembrance of YHVH Elohim bringing them out of Egypt. So it follows that they burned incense and prayed, just as Moses did, for the aid of YHVH's holy gods (Dan. 4:8 & 5:11 and Jos. 24:19), the "hosts of heaven"!

Richard Elliott Friedman (*Who Wrote the Bible,* 1987) has argued that the Levitical community of Anathoth promoted Josiah's reforms. Solomon drove the Anathoth Levites from power upon his accession, when Abiathar was deposed and exiled to Anathoth. They could not have been contented with this position after having had the honor of carrying the Ark of the Covenant before Solomon. The Bible itself says that the "Law of Moses" was lost during this time and then a copy[15] was "found" by the Levite priest Hilkiah who delivered it to Shaphan the scribe. (II Ki.22:8) ([15]which therefore cannot be proven to be the original of Moses)

All these actions are recorded to have transpired at the time when these Levite scribes conspired together to persuade King Josiah to adopt, and enforce on everyone, their interpretation of the Levitican law (originally only meant for those among the mixed multitude who sacrificed animals). Afterwards this version was passed on from the Levites who found it (in their bid for power ultimately granted to Ezra by King Artaxerxes), to Ezra who was then given power to command ALL the people to eat an animal sacrifice for Passover. (Ezra 7:26 quoted and addressed elsewhere) <u>That they had to be commanded to eat this free feast shows that some Israelites were reluctant to eat animals.</u>

In the very early book of Samuel, who himself built an altar (I Sam. 7:17) and of whom it was said, "YHWH was with him" (I Sam. 3:19), there is also mention of other priests who were not Levites. This again shows that the priesthood was not originally the domain of the Levites. The first three kings, Saul, David, and Solomon all sacrificed at altars in various places and the text does not criticize them for this at all. "David's sons were priests." (II Sam. 8:18) This verse has been changed in the KJV to read "David's son's were chief rulers."

David's sons were from the tribe of Judah and at one time possessed the Ark of the Covenant. In a later reference in I Chr. 18: 17, the Chronicler edited this account to read "David's sons were high officials" showing that this passage was no doubt rewritten by a Levite jealously guarding the status of priest or someone intent on eliminating any references not supporting that view.

> "Therefore says YHWH of hosts...<u>from the prophets of Jerusalem (who killed the prophets of Judah) is pollution going forth unto all the land</u>...Hearken not to the words of the prophets (of Jerusalem)...they are not speaking from the mouth of YHWH...I have not sent these prophets...for you overturned the words of Elohim, living ones, YHWH of hosts, Elohim of us...and I will bring an everlasting reproach upon you, and a perpetual shame which shall not be forgotten." Jer. 23:15-40

Like many murderers they probably thought themselves cleverer than most, figuring they would never be found out. But little did they know that every word they wrote would come under the most microscopic scrutiny, and the minute traces of their deeds would eventually <u>reveal *them to actually* be the false prophets</u>. They no doubt thought they had successfully rationalized their murders, justifying their breaking the commandment "Thou shalt not kill," by claiming idolatry, but they are convicted by their own hand as also responsible for the deaths of the true prophets.

Some may wonder what does a book about *The Lost Data On The Chariots Of The Elohim*, have to do with questions of diet disputes by various factions? Just this, because those who carried the knowledge of YHVH's Elohim, the host of heaven and their chariots of fire, were vegetarian, the Levites, insulted by their refusal to participate in an animal sacrifice at the Levite's newly established altar, purportedly a temple of YHVH, murdered them.

AND along with their destruction, the knowledge of YHVH's Elohim and their teachings of the presence of the heavenly chariots of the Elohim were also lost! Nay! Deliberately destroyed as heretical, to the Levite's limited understanding of monotheism, as they then went on to eliminate all references to YHVH Elohim, substituting "Adonai Elohim" instead. This action in turn may also have had something to do with the increased incidence of Alzheimer's among those who regularly ate the meat of these animal sacrifices, thus limiting their ability to understand the enormity of their actions. (For evidence that animal fat contributes to Alzheimer's see the chapter on diet and Alzheimer's.)

Their take on the story of the Passover (that it required animal sacrifice) was the interpretation that was given to the Exodus story by Ezra and the scribes. Following is a quote from King Artaxerxes' letter giving Ezra the power he coveted, to command the Israelites to partake of this animal sacrifice, calling it '*the law of thy God*'. "And whosoever will not do the law of thy God...let judgment be executed speedily upon him, unto death, or banishment, or confiscation of goods, or imprisonment." Ezra 7:26

That there had to be an injunction by the king, giving this power to Ezra, clearly demonstrates that there was resistance to this practice of animal sacrifice and burnt offerings among the Israelites. And that the commandment "Thou shalt not kill" was again transgressed further demonstrates the falseness of their so-called priesthood.

> "And Ezra the priest brought the law before the congregation...and he read therein...and beside him stood (26 Levite scribes named) and the Levites taught the people to understand...and gave the meaning...*All the people were weeping*[15] as they were hearing the words. (distressed and dismayed to hear of this command to kill these animals for the blood sacrifice and the burnt offerings and that they must then *eat* them) Then he said unto them; Go your way, eat the fat, and drink, and send portions to them for whom nothing was prepared...So the Levites stilled all the people saying, hold your peace, for the day is holy, neither be grieved...*From The Days Of Joshua Son Of Nun Until That Day*, the Israelites had not celebrated it like this." Neh. 8:2-11&17 ([15]Why would they be weeping at being commanded to eat a feast of meat unless they were vegetarians who did not want to kill the animals or eat the meat?)

To see what the children of Israel actually thought of the Levitican practice of killing and eating animal sacrifices, study the following passage. It concerns Joshua, who the OT gives as Moses' minister and governor of the Israelites, when they heard that some of the Israelites had built an altar for animal sacrifice.

> "The children of Reuben...G-d...and the half tribe of Manasseh built there an altar great to see...And when the children of Israel heard of it the whole congregation...'assembled a host to go up on them' (KJV says this means "to go to war" but it seems obvious they merely went to dispute with them, since they talked rather than fought)...And they came unto the children of Reuben...G-d...and Manasseh...saying, Thus say the whole congregation of YHWH; What offense is this?...Is the iniquity of Peor (Baal Peor, Deu. 4:3) too little for us, which we are not cleansed of (the plagues or diseases from this iniquity) to this day, although there was a plague in the congregation of YHWH, that you are turning away from following YHWH in that you have built an altar, that you might revolt against YHWH?...did not Achan commit the same offense of the accursed thing and wrath came against the whole congregation of Israel...Then the children of Reuben...G-d...and Manasseh answered...YHWH, Al of Elohim...knows if it was built in revolt and offense to YHWH...YHWH himself shall see if we built an altar for ascent offerings and present offerings or if we built an altar for *peace offerings*, so the sons of Israel shall not say we have no part in YHWH... We do this to say, tomorrow when they should say to sons of us or future generations, and we say see! The model of the altar of YHWH, *which they made, the father's of us, not for ascent offerings and NOT FOR SACRIFICE*, but as a testimony between us. Far be it from us to revolt from YHWH and turn away this day, to build an altar for ascent offering, for present offerings and for sacrifice." Jos. 22:10-29

This clearly says that the altar of the Israelites was *not* for sacrifices (meat offerings), but only for peace offerings (those requiring no violence). So given all the previous evidence it can be seen that Moses' orders to bring animals to the Levites *in the Tabernacle of the Congregation* was initially only to insure proper bloodletting, and removal of fat, by those who had been taught this practice and its benefits. It was *not* meant to be taken as an order that those who did not eat meat must also bring *their* animals to be sacrificed. The Levites had been taught how to perform this sacrifice properly, during times of hardship, so that uneducated people would not eat meat with the blood and fat still in it. A later chapter will explore in depth the harmful consequences this could cause especially the connection between animal fat and heart disease and Alzheimer's.

This dissertation must of necessity often consist of very subtle indications, everything overt having surely been excised by the Levites or later defenders of a carnivorous diet. Only verses that discuss those areas, which themselves have been misinterpreted or hidden, and have slipped through the efforts of the Levite scribes are being presented here. However, the very fact that there are so many contradictions on this subject shows that there has been editing and revisions. For had YHVH written it Himself He would have been internally consistent and perfect.

It would be possible to use many other verses to make a case in favor of the Levites, and in favor of animal sacrifice. This has been the interpretation given all along since the time of Ezra. So it is therefore unnecessary to mention all the possible verses (which may have been inserted by the Levite usurpers anyway), or by other less than enlightened individuals supporting carnivorous diet, so those verses need not be explored in this text as others have already done this *ad nauseum.*

THE SECOND TEMPLE

There was an effort by the elders of Judah and servants of YHVH Elohim, to rebuild the temple of YHVH. It was effectively thwarted by the Levites because they wanted the benefit of running the so-called temple of YHWH in Jerusalem. They appealed to Darius, the king of Persia. (Ezra 5:8-11) and he forced the elders of Judah to stop building their temple.

The Levites used the record of an old order by King Cyrus of Babylon to manipulate King Darius into establishing *their* authority to build the temple in Jerusalem. AND they instigated this by telling this foreign king that if *that* building were allowed to go forward, "then they (the Judeans, of whom Jesus descended) will not pay toll, tribute, and custom, and so you shall endamage the revenue of the kings." Ezra 4:13-19

The Levites used this threat to induce the king to prevent these elders from building a temple in Judah, siding with a non-Israelite authority AGAINST the priests of Judah. It was at this same time that Ezra was granted power over the Israelites, to command them to submit to the authority of the Levites and participate in an animal sacrifice.

That this miss-interpretation of the record found in the old ruins of the temple, and promoted by Hilikiah and Ezra, commanding the people to kill and eat their animals, was the law of YHVH, is vehemently disputed even at the time of Ezra. In addition to Jeremiah's words this was also done by the prophet Isaiah in his instruction *against* blood sacrifice and the eating of these "burnt offerings."

> "Hear O heavens, and Earth, for YHWH has spoken..., My people transgress me...they do not consider ...they forsake YHWH, they spurned the Holy One of Israel, they are estranged, going backward. From the sole of the foot even unto the head there is no

soundness, but wounds, and putrefying sores...<u>Why? To what purpose is the multitude of your sacrifices unto Me? says YHWH...I delight not in the blood of bullocks, lambs or goats...</u>And when you spread forth your hands, I will hide my eyes...I will not hear: because your hands are full of blood. Wash yourself, purge yourselves; leave off the evil of these doings." Isa. 1:2-16

"Thus says YHWH, heaven is my throne, and the earth is my footstool...For all these things my hand has made...He that kills an ox is as if he had killed a man...burning incense he blesses lawlessness, moreover they choose their own ways and abominations." Isa. 66:1-3

"A righteous man knows compassion for his beasts, wicked ones are cruel. A tiller of the land is satisfied with bread, the man following vain things heartlessly covets the wicked net (trap) of evil men." Prov. 12:10-12

The practice of animal sacrifice is also addressed in Psalms 50:1-15. "YHWH He speaks and He is calling earth...from Zion consummation of loveliness Elohim, He shines, He shall come Elohim of us and must not be silent...gather to Me kind-ones...Elohim of you, I shall not reprove you, upon the sacrifices you make, and your burnt offerings, which are in front of Me continually from you. I shall not take from your houses young bulls or from your folds he goats. To Me belongs every animal of the wildwood and the beasts of a thousand mountains, I know all flying things, and mammals of the field are with Me. If I were famished, would I say to you to have them (habitance) and then from the fullness of her <u>would I eat the flesh of bulls? And drink the blood of he goats?</u> (Rather) Sacrifice to Elohim acclamation and make vows to the Supreme and call Me in days of distress, I shall liberate you and you shall glorify me."

"<u>I desire kindness[16], not sacrifice</u>. And the knowledge of Elohim more than burnt offerings." Hos. 6:6 [16]mercy KJV This verse is twice quoted by Yeschu/Joshu/Jesus. (Matt. 9:13&12:7)

"Turn to YHWH and say to Him, forgive all iniquity and receive us graciously, so we will offer the prayers of our lips instead of calves." Hosea 14:3

"To do justice and judgment is more acceptable to YHWH than sacrifice." Prov. 21:3

"YHWH is good to all and compassionate in all of His doings." Ps. 145:9

The Bible verses cited above demonstrate that the Second Temple, established by the Levite cult of animal sacrifice, was not fully recognized by a variety of Israelite prophets. It had evolved out of all these events, <u>under the auspices of a foreign power (King Darius, following the decree made by King Cyrus of Babylon</u>. And it further demonstrates that there were those among the prophets of the Jews who did *not* embrace the Levite cult of animal sacrifice founded in Jerusalem.

Many attempt to say that the rebukes by the prophets were only against performing animal sacrifice, not against the practice of eating meat. However, the verse above from Jeremiah (7:21) disparages the priests who instructed followers to "eat flesh." (Deu. 12:7 below also refers to eating the sacrifices) These verses show that the understanding among ancient people was that they were one and the same thing and the practice of killing, burning (i.e., cooking) and eating burnt offerings was never meant by Moses to be continued when it was not a necessity.

> "...Bring all your ascent offerings, and sacrifices and tithes, and the heave offerings of your hand, and your vow offerings and voluntary offerings and the firstlings of your herds and flocks. *And you eat* there before YHVH Elohim..." Deu. 12:7

The Levites seized political and religious authority by aligning themselves with a foreign power against their own people, and revised the true history of Moses to satisfy their own motives, until it even went against the Ten Commandments. They murdered anyone who got in their way, repeatedly breaking the commandment "Thou shalt not kill." And yet somehow many people continue to respect the words they contributed to the Bible, not understanding Jerimiah's obscure warning about the scribes using their "lying pens" to rewrite Moses law. These misguided individuals still consider the Levite animal sacrifice cult's message as part of "God's" inspired word. Why would YHVH give a commandment like "Thou shalt not kill" then place the final editing of his words in the hands of murderers?

While everyone is obviously free to make their own decision as to whether to eat meat or not, everyone also has a right to know about all the information available on the historic, spiritual and health concerns this choice has in their lives. The information presented here shows that the debate over whether or not to eat meat did not just begin in recent times, rather the evidence in the Bible shows that it has been going on at least since the time of Moses.

TITHING

> "And concerning the tithe of the herd, or of the flock, even of whatsoever passes under the club, the tenth shall be holy unto YHWH." Lev. 27:32

Yeschu/Joshu/Jesus never asked for sacrifices or tithes, he taught his followers to hold all things in common. (Acts 2:44, 4:32, etc.) The concept of one tenth arose from the compensation originally given to the Levites for their work in slaughtering, cleaning and dressing the animal for sacrifice. Only those who brought animals to be sacrificed owed this payment; vegetarians who brought bread etc. brought their peace offerings to be shared among all the others out of love, not because the Levites had done any work to deserve a payment.

Later on, however, the Levite school also began to demand one tenth of whatever money or other wealth the people had. As the history of the period attests, the Levites were using the 'tithe' or one tenth 'rule' to finance real estate deals, businesses, building projects and cultural events. Wacholder, Eupolemus: *A Study of Judaeo-Greek Literature*, pp. 1-21

Since it was Ezra and the Levite scribes who insisted upon the reintroduction of animal sacrifice as a ritual practice, all the these false priests freely indulged their rapacious appetites (as Yeschu/Joshu/Jesus rebuked them for in Matt. 23:25), they thus even more so than many others, acquired the bloodlust for flesh foods.

Because of the effect indulging this bloodlust had on their brains and spirituality they became blind to the understanding of their originally assigned duty concerning hygienically performing animal sacrifice in times of hardship; for example, when after the Exodus the mixed multitude wandered forty years in the wilderness, unable to grow food and when such an act was ordained necessary by the elders of the tribe. Instead they turned it into a required regular practice, supposedly granting the people absolution from sin in exchange for the meat of animals and ordained themselves as priests over the ritual slaughter of animals for feasting.

THE TORAH REDACTED

> "While I (Moses) am yet alive and with you, you (the Levites) rebelled against YHWH, and indeed (you will again) after my death...I know that after my death you shall become corrupt, and withdraw from the way in which I instructed you." Deu. 31:29

Many scholars hold that the original Torah had probably been partly, if not completely lost, until after the Israelites were released from Babylon, at the time of Ezra (described as a scribe learned in the copy of the law found in an old temple). The Pentateuch or Torah was accepted as Law very early--according to tradition, since the time of Moses, usually dated around 1250 BC-1350[16] BC. ([16]see "The Exodus Decoded" documentary by Simcha Jacobovici,

<http://www.theexodusdecoded.net/index.html>)

Most documentary scholars say bits and pieces were accepted as Law from early times, but that the books did not take their final form until around 400 BC. Traditionalist scholars say the whole "Law" dates to Moses, (however, the chain of custody was, according to the Bible itself, broken so the copy Hilikiah found cannot be proven to exactly what Moses' wrote) but agree that Ezra did some "editing," thus the 400 BC date would also agree (roughly) with origin of the final form as we have it today. However, since the OT itself attests that the chain of custody was broken the authenticity cannot be proven, since Hilikiah 'found' the copy used it to support the claim of Levites to the priesthood (granted by King Josiah, who also enforced animal sacrifice upon the Israelites). Some have gone as far as hypothesizing a "Priestly Document" that has been incorporated into the OT, establishing the interests of the priests. *Who Wrote the Bible.* <http://www.straightdope.com/mailbag/mbible5.html>

> "P (priestly document) deals more with formal religion and worship, the priesthood and its regulations, genealogies, and sacrificial practices...the Priestly document is the last of the great pentateuchal documents. It comes out of the circle of priests who reassembled Israel, theologically speaking, after the tragedy of the Babylonian exile...usually dated to (587-539 BCE)...They sought to reinforce (so called) covenant practices in repentance for past neglect...(believing) Even when Israel alienated itself from God, there were sacrifices and rituals that could atone for faithlessness." *Priestly Document.* <http://www.hope.edu/bandstra/RTOT/PART1/PT1_TBC.HTM>

In the original Hebrew, the scroll of Ezra-Nehemiah was attached to the book of Chronicles. Because the last verses of Chronicles are identical to the opening of Ezra, he has been suggested as the author. Whoever it was, the "chronicler" viewed himself as an interpreter of history and included and excluded material according to how it fit with his ethical outlook. This emphasized the importance of the false Levite priesthood (as the evidence will show) and the scribes as interpreters, especially on the subject of the practice of animal sacrifice, from which the Levites and scribes fed themselves.

Scholars have suggested that the so-called prediction of Moses that the Israelites would come to "repentance in Exile" (Deu. 30:1) as a pre-condition of restoration, when according to the books of Ezra and Nehemiah it never did come about, was added later. More likely is the scenario that Ezra and the scribes made this prediction, hoping it would come about, attempting to put the words in the mouth of Moses.

Nehemiah refers to the fear of the restored nation, this contradicts the so-called prediction of Moses that the restored nation will subdue their enemies and have no fear of them upon restoration. With famine throughout the land the people are so desperate that they sell their lands and sell their children into slavery. This also contradicts the so-called prediction of Moses that upon the restoration God will prosper his people.

That these things never went on to happen makes it more likely that the time for them to occur had not yet happened at the writing, for the writer would not have knowingly made a liar of Moses, diminishing his authority and their supposed position as the heirs to the priesthood he established. And according to the biblical definition of a true prophet (Deu. 18:22) it also shows that the Levites who inserted these texts were not true prophets. Meyers, Eric M., and Robertson, John W., "World of the Ancestors," Kee, Howard Clark, et al, art. *The Cambridge Companion to the Bible,* Cambridge Univ. Press, 1997, 98, 99, p. 91.

<http://www.bibleorigins.net/PrimaryHistory562BCE.html>

Spinoza's biblical criticism in the *Tractatus Theologico-Politicus,* analyzed the biblical writings in an attempt to determine their authors (ibid., ch. 8-10) and concluded that Moses was responsible for some of the Pentateuch, but that together with Joshua-Kings they form a larger historical work whose editor/author was Ezra. They contain numerous repetitions and contradictions, e.g., of a chronological nature, that led to the conclusion the material was compiled from the works of different authors. De la Torre, Walter. M.A. *The Primary History An Exilic Composition.* <http://www.bibleorigins.net/PrimaryHistory562BCE.html>

Richard Friedman suggests that Ezra may have been the final redactor (editor) of the Torah, the first five books of the OT. Traditionalists usually say the entire written Torah had been lost, the people had strayed so far while exiled in Babylon. There is even an apocrypha account of Ezra's authorship in *2nd Esdras* or *4th Ezra*, in which Ezra purportedly describes himself telling the scribes what to write. <http://www.straightdope.com/mailbag/mbible2.html> & Bratcher, Dennis. *Hexateuch, Tetrateuch, and the Deuteronomic History.*

<http://www.crivoice.org/hexateuch.html> & *Ezra creates his "Law of Moses."*

<http://www.essene.com/History&Essenes/ezlaw.htm>

In this account Ezra states; "For thy law has been burned, and so no one knows the things which have been done or will be done by thee," (21) indicating that the true account by Moses was no longer available to the Israelites! So according to this account Ezra then feels inspired to rewrite or channel the version that has now come down to us.

"Prepare for yourself many writing tablets, and take with you these five (scribes) because they are trained to write rapidly...For my spirit retained its memory; and my mouth (Ezra's) was opened and no longer closed...and by turns they wrote what was dictated...So during the forty days ninety -four books were written." *2nd Esdras* or *4th Ezra,* 21,24,40,42-45

There is no doubt that the changes of YHVH to Adonai, and other changes, began around the time of Ezra, by the Sopherim, the scribes, since they left records of their changes. It is also established that Ezra was the first of these scribes who took upon themselves the job of interpreting various passages in the OT. Apparently the text was then passed on to the Massorites, by the Sopherim or scribes, whose work under Ezra and Nehemiah, was to transcribe and revise the text according to their own interpretations, after the return of the Israelites from their exile in Babylon.

"The Sopherim were the authorized revisers of the Sacred Text; and their work being completed, the Massorites were the authorized custodians of it." Bullinger, E. W. *The Companion Bible,* Appx. #30, p. 31.

It is accepted that the Massorites left behind records of their emendations, which are in the notes known as the Massorah, from whence is derived the name *Masoritic Text*. The word massorah is from the root *masar,* to deliver something into the hands of another, so as to commit it to his trust. When translators originally printed the Hebrew text, the small print of these changes was originally left out of the KJV, as it was found in the MSS from which the text was taken.

As mentioned in chapter one, the name Adonai is related to *adon*, the word for lord, meaning master, used throughout Egypt, the Mediterranean and the Middle East. The Syrian, Phoenician, and the Egyptian Adonis, also of Biblis was synonymous with the Adon or Adonis of Babylon, he later became the great Teutonic war-god, Odin or Wodan. Remember that it was also from the Teutonic 'heathens' that the Babylonian/Persian name "God" came into usage in the 7th century AD. Mead, G. R. S. *Did Jesus Live 100 Years BC,* pp. 104,135-138,177,256,334,335,408 &410. & <http://www.biblebelievers.com/babylon/sect41.htm>

The Egyptian Aton is equivalent to the Hebrew Adon. (remember the Egyptian T becomes D in Hebrew) In Hebrew the last two letters, "ai," added on to the end of the name Adon, is a Hebrew pronoun meaning 'my' or 'mine' and make it possessive. Thus Adonai means, Adon-Mine or My Lord. Many of the legends of Adonis also later derived from the original Aton/Adon. Gadalla, Moustafa. Egyptian-American Egyptologist, *Tut-Ankh-Amen: The Living Image of the Lord,* p. 33.

<http://books.google.com/books?id=NNj1rvFvkEkC&pg=PA43&lpg=PA43&dq=Tut-Ankh-Amen:+The+Living+Image+of+the+Lord,&source=web&ots=kMCNFsf4EA&sig=Cndsx8eO8vjd8V8zpGYmCoQ32Z4&hl=en>

One might wonder what caused the Levite scribes to choose a word that merely signifies 'master,' to represent the Supreme deity of the universe. Adonai Elohim could have been chosen because it signified to them the 'Master God'. However, it was understood by many learned men throughout the Middle East that there had earlier been another monotheistic 'God,' or 'Lord' of the Egyptians, known as Aton or Adon; Adon is a variation of Aton/Aten/Aden/Edon/Eden. However, as mentioned before Osman identified Levites as the select group of noble relatives of Akhenaten who made up the Egyptian priesthood of Aton and served in the temple of Aton in Egypt. There is a village in Egypt that still retains its name Mal-lawi or Mal-levi, meaning the city of the Levites. This information gives them a very clear motive, to supplant YHVH with the worship of Aton -Adon -Adonai the god they served in Egypt. *The Gospel According to Egypt.* Citing Ahmed Osman. <http://www.domainofman.com/ankhemmaat/moses.html>

> "The name Adon is also synonymous with Eden, and there was already at the time of Ezra a city by the name of Adon, in Tel-Assar, mentioned in Isa. 37:12, called Eden in the KJV. This city would have, therefore, been in existence before the Sopherim decided to substitute the name Adonai for YHWH. Now a Tel means a mound of an older city upon which the city was apparently built. Tel - mound and Assar – Asher/Asir/Osir (Osiris MHJ), a name derived, as was the names for Assyria, from legends that go back into the past even before the Egyptian Osiris." *Catholic Encyclopedia,* New Advent. <http://www.newadvent.org/cathen/06428c.htm>

There had been an attempt to establish a monotheistic religion before in Egypt (1367-1350 BCE) by Amenhotep (who changed his name to Akhen-aten). This, God, known as "the Only One" was held by some of the time to have a unique status among gods, he was not just a father god, at the head of a pantheon of lessor gods, he was the ONLY God. He had no image, just as the Adonai/Lord of the Levite priests likewise had no image. Mackenzie, Donald. quoting Prof. Petrie, *Egyptian Myth and Legend,* p. 333.

> "For behold! YHWH in fire he shall come as sweeping chariots of Him, to bring back the fury of Him and rebuke in blazes of fire....They that sanctify themselves, and cleaning for the gardens following 'ONLY ONE' (*Achad achth*[17]) in the midst, eating swine's flesh, and the abomination, and the mouse, shall be consumed together, avers YHWH." (Isa. 66:17) *Ten Gnostic Commandments.* <http://www.essenes.net/mathers.html>

[17]Consider also this passage from the Sepher Yetzirah: "*Achth Rvch Alhim Chiim*" *Achath* (feminine, not *Achad*, masculine) *Ruach Elohim Chiim*: One is She the Spirit of the Elohim of Life" 34. S. L. McGregor Mathers, *The Kabbalah Unveiled,* (remember also that *Chiim* is "the living" as in the "tree of the living ones") <http://www.morgane.org/unveiled.htm>

This verse has been changed from "following One" to read "behind one tree," but neither the word "tree" nor the phrase "behind one tree" occurs in the Hebrew text. "Hislop...and it is admitted by Lowth, and the best orientalists, that the rendering should be, "after the rites of Achad," i.e., "The Only One..." (*The Two Babylons*, Hislop, Rev. Alexander. footnote, p. 16)...Adam Clarke translates "behind one tree--," as "after the rites of *Achad* (One)" and goes on to explain that the Massorites tampered with Isaiah 66:17 by changing *Achad* to the feminine "Achath," given as moon. However *achth* is translated as the feminine of *achad* or one in the *Kaballah Unveiled. A Commentary and Critical Notes, Isaiah to Malachi*, Vol. IV, p. 246.

<http://www.essences.net/mathers.html>

& Franklin, Carl. *The Two Jehovah's of the Psalms.* <http://www.biblestudy.org/maturart/the-two-gods-of-psalms/introduction.html>

So the prophet Isaiah wrote that YHVH and His chariots of Elohim, would come *against* those who worshiped Aton/Adon-Adonai and ate swine and other abominations. (remember Isaiah condemned the eating of all animal sacrifices (Isa. 1:2-16) so no doubt he saw all animal sacrifice as an abomination) The later Levite Massorites wishing to use the words of this revered prophet had to change a few things if they wanted to include Isaiah's writings.

It would not have looked good, for Ezra and the Levites scribes, the Sopherim, and the Massorites to include something written by a famous prophet which appeared to castigate former members of their own group. So it was necessary to alter it so as to bring it into accord with their new worship of "the One God" Adon/Aton, Adonai.

These descendants of the Egyptian Levite servants of Aton/Adon had to make some adjustments to the text in their efforts to transform the worship of YHVH and *His* council of Elohim, the Elohim who had created the earth, into the worship of the limited Egyptian interpretation of the matter, the worship of the One God, Aton/Adon/Adonai. (My Lord God, a God in the form of a human.)

After their rise to power (granted to Ezra) they were in a position to extort sacrifices from the people, so they were no longer reduced to eating swine, mice and heaven knows what other abominations. Remember those were hard times with famine throughout the land and some of those who ate flesh had even sacrificed their own children to avert starvation. Hence their newfound position of superiority gave these later Levites a narcissistic belief in themselves, as being sanctified in eating the animals they perceived to be acceptable.

The Egyptian form of monotheism, the worship of Aton/Adon was (however unwittingly it may have been from association with the society of their time and what appeared to them to be accepted modes of thought) being adopted by the second order, the Levite Scribes turned priests. They lacked the knowledge that would have been passed on to them, had they received their training from the priesthood of first order, which Josiah and the Levite "priests" had destroyed.

These same Levite priests were the ones who rewrote the OT, and tried to eliminate all references that would give an understanding of YHVH's Elohim, replacing His name with, Adon-ai Eohim. Because they had murdered those who burned incense to YHVH's hosts of heaven, they were compelled to try to eliminate any appearance that the early Israelites had accepted a belief in the hosts of heaven, or a council of gods, YHVH Elohim.

The name of that monotheistic Egyptian Lord God was Aton/Adon/Aten/Aden. While the attempt to establish him as the "Only One God" in Egypt failed, since after Akhenaten's demise the Egyptians went back to polytheism; Aton's reputation, however, had not died completely and the Egyptian Adonis also went on to be derived from the use of the name Aton/Adon. Moustafa Gadalla, Egyptian-American Egyptologist, article; "The Living Image of the Lord" from *Tut-Ankh-Amen: The Living Image of The Lord,* p. 33.

It is clear that there must have been some reason for using the Adon/Adonai name which we now know as Lord, when according to Hebrew records it had always ranked below even the Elohim, sometimes even being used for mere mortal men, and surely nothing equal to the Supreme Creator of the universe, YHWH. *The Egyptian Pantheon;* Introduction to the Egyptian culture.

<http://www.icculus.org/~msphil/mythus/pantheolon/Egyptgod.txt>

The distinction Adon/Aton of the Egyptians had of being not just the head of a council of gods, but the only God, could not be allowed to stand unchallenged by the Levite scribes, the Sopherim, so they may have decided that the Levite YHWH could not be out done by any God claimed by the Egyptians. Not being privy to the teachings of the first priesthood, who communed with YHVH Elohim, they could not grasp that the universal mind of YHVH, that has always stood behind all of His Elohim who make themselves one with Him, throughout the universe, is already more magnificent than they could possibly imagine. He needs no titles shared by various Elohim or Egyptian gods, He stands alone as the unity of All in all. (1 Cor. 15:28)

Perhaps in their zeal to establish the God of the Israelites as the One and only god of their new definition of monotheism, including the attempt to eliminate even YHVH's council of Elohim, this God must have every quality that makes Him superior to all others, so they could not forgo also giving Him the title that had for millennia been synonymous with the Egyptian's One and only God. And so to make it appear that the God of the Israelites was "the Only One they also claimed for their "God" (from the Babylonian G-d/Gawd) the title Adon/Aton, modifying it only slightly to the Hebrew variation, Adon-ai, my Lord.

It might be wondered what difference does it make what name is used? Well aside from the loss of the most important historical record of the visitations to our planet by YHVH's Elohim, from elsewhere in the universe and our heritage from their interbreeding with us there was also the loss of the understanding of the importance of purity in diet. This is part of the knowledge that was carried and would have been taught by the priesthood of the first order, only now being rediscovered by science. In addition to these loses, YHVH does not want His glory given to any other name.

"I am YHWH; that is My Name: and My glory will I not give to another..." (Isa. 42:8).

Because of the years of tradition and indoctrination that followed the efforts of the Levite "priesthood" of the second order, it is still difficult for most people to believe that the "foods" that they have eaten all their lives are not good for them. We have lost our faith that if we maintain purity, YHVH's wrath will not be kindled against us in the form of chronic diseases. Humanity now sees life as fraught with the unfair infliction of disease, even on the innocent children, often asking why "God" allows such suffering. YHVH allows us the freedom of choice, and it is the impure choices of the ancestors of these children which has led to degeneration and suffering. It is these choices against the will of YHVH that cause disease, He does not inflict them, they are present by our own choices. Some of these diseases will be discussed in the chapter following.

DEUTERONOMY

There are many indications that Moses did not write all of the Pentateuch; saying "to this day," is the phrase of a later writer who is describing something that has endured. "Across the Jordan" (referring to someone who is on the other side from the writer), appearing to be in Israel, west of the Jordan, discusses what Moses did on the east side of Jordan; Moses was never in Israel. And

Moses statement that; "...he (Moses) was the humblest man on earth," would not in all likelihood have been written by Moses about himself, especially if he were really that humble. Friedman, Richard. *Who Wrote the Bible?,*1987, p.20.

And it is unlikely he would have referred to himself in the third person saying such things as "Moses said" Jer. 7:4 & 8:8 or "Moses came" or "YHWH spoke unto Moses" all found in Deu. 32. It especially would have been impossible for him to speak of his own death, as in Deu. 34:5; "So Moses the servant of YHWH died there in the land of Moab..." These writings seem clearly to have been written by someone other than Moses.

Richard Friedman makes the statement that; "The book that the priest Hilkiah found in the Temple in 622 BCE was Deuteronomy. This is not a new discovery. Early Church fathers, including Jerome, said that the book that was read to King Josiah was Deuteronomy....De Wette said, Deuteronomy was written not long before it was "found" and the "finding" was just a charade. The book was written to provide grounds for Josiah's religious reform...this brought all the influence and income of the religion to the Jerusalem Temple priesthood and it was a Jerusalem Temple priest who had found the book." Friedman, Richard. *Who Wrote the Bible?,* 1987, p.101-102.

> "The Deuteronomistic historian rates every one of the kings...Josiah and Josiah alone (rates) as unqualifiedly good...Cross thus argued that the original edition of the Deuteronomistic history was the work of someone who lived at the time of Josiah...And it was someone who was favorable to Josiah...Also it regularly refers to the well being of the Levites; it instructs the people to provide for the Levites...The Levites, Israel's priestly tribe seems a more likely group in which to look for the author of Deuteronomy than the royal courtiers...Halpern concluded that Deuteronomy's law code came from the Levitical priests of Shiloh." Friedman, Richard. *Who Wrote the Bible?,* 1987 pp.110,116,118,126.

In 1943, Martin Noth, showed that there was a strong unity between Deuteronomy and the next six books by the prophets following the five books of the Torah. It was not by one author, the finished product, nonetheless, was the work of one person. He constructed the work so that the laws of Deuteronomy would stand as the foundation of the history from Moses extending to the destruction of Judah by Babylon. Noth referred to the full seven book work as the *Deuteronomistic history...*The Deuteronomistic historian assembled his history out of the books available to him...Biblical scholars argue generally that, rather than one man, it was a "school" that produced the Deuteronomistic material. Friedman, Richard. *Who Wrote the Bible?* (1987) pp.103-104, 130, 145.

There are many references that show that the writings were done *before* the conquest of Judah by Babylon. For example why say that the poles, in the temple, for carrying the ark were; "there to this day" when the temple was burned down? Why would any person who had seen the fall of the kingdom in Judah write a work, after 587 BCE, claiming that YHWH had made a covenant claiming the kingdom would be eternal? Friedman, Richard. *Who Wrote the Bible?* (1987) p. 107.

I have to disagree with Richard Friedman's conclusion that Jeremiah was the Deuteronomistic historian, for the following reasons; Deuteronomy and the supporting insertions into the other four books of the Torah, emphasize the importance of animal sacrifice, whereas Jeremiah was against sacrifice. (Jer. 7:22-23) And it is not logical for him to participate in the rewriting of Deuteronomy and the other passages, to support the bringing of animals for sacrifice, then warn the people that the law had been altered by the "lying scribes." So it seems more reasonable to agree with the Biblical scholars and Halpern, and conclude that Deuteronomy was written or rewritten by individuals of one "school," specifically the school of Levite scribes who Jeremiah warns the people about. (Jer. 7:4 & 8:8)

In addition to the above reasoning there are other verses by Jeremiah that are in conflict with the establishment of the organized Levite animal sacrifice cult. They include; Jer. 5:31, 7:14 & 8:8, Jer. 5:30-31 & 7:14-15, Jer. 7:22-23, Jer. 7:8&21-23. Telling us; "Trust not in lying words...the lying pen of the scribes...The prophets prophesy falsely, and the priests bear rule by their means...For I spoke not unto your fathers...on matters of burnt offerings and sacrifices... from the prophets of Jerusalem is pollution going forth unto all the land...they are not speaking from the mouth of YHWH...I have not sent these prophets...I will bring an everlasting reproach upon you, and a perpetual shame which shall not be forgotten."

> "There is one more reason to be taken in to account to explain the success of the Aaronid priests in rebuilt Judah. That is the influence and power of one man: Ezra...It is likely that the book that Ezra brought from Babylon to Judah was the full Torah - the five books of Moses - as we know it...if Moses did not produce these books, who did? I think that it was Ezra...The person who assembled the four sources (J,E,D,P) into the Five Books of Moses is known as the redactor...The redactor was arranging texts that already existed." Friedman, Richard. *Who Wrote the Bible?*, 1987 pp. 158-159, 218.

In *The Christian Passover* by Fred R. Coulte, he says that Ezra and Nehemiah formed a group of Levites, "it was this group of Levites who compiled the Old Testament as we now know it. The Torah (the first five books) was translated, with special emphasis upon the commands in the book of Deuteronomy, which was updated, copied and sent throughout the Persian Empire." (539-512 BCE) <http://www.biblestudy.org>

The book of Deuteronomy, which has chapters that seem to have been inserted out of context, is much different from the other four books of the Pentateuch, both in terms of arrangement and content and in terms of how the material was presented. In Deuteronomy Moses appears to contradict his own instructions in his first four books too many times to include all of them, but what has been included in this book is enough to demonstrate a fairly clear case.

Martin Noth saw a much closer relationship between Deuteronomy and the rest of the historical books that followed. This left the four books of Genesis-Numbers, a Tetrateuch. Noth proposed that Deuteronomy was compiled during the exile in Babylon to deal with the crisis precipitated by the destruction of the temple and the loss of the land. There are some that see the book of Deuteronomy as standing alone, emphasizing the uniqueness of Deuteronomy. Bratcher, Dennis. *Hexateuch, Tetrateuch, and the Deuteronomic History.*

<http://www.crivoice.org/hexateuch.html>

Noth argued that instead of being composed from different sources, as some have hypothesized, blocks of material were developed around key experiences of the early Israelites. Noth saw the development as a process of reworking and expansion. He identified the Priestly source as the backbone of the Pentateuch to which the Yahwist and Elohist sources were added. *Priestly Document.* <http://www.hope.edu/bandstra/RTOT/PART1/PT1_TBC.HTM>

> "The final form of the Pentateuch may well lie with Ezra; but of course, on external, factual data, the origins of much of its constituent books lie much further back." Kitchen, K. A. *Last Things Last, A Few Conclusions, On the Reliability of the Old Testament,* Grand Rapids, Mich. William B. Eerdmans Pub. Co. 2003. ISBN 0-8028-4960-1, pp. 492-493.

The six books (Deuteronomy, Joshua, Judges, Samuel, and Kings I & II) are sometimes called the "Deuteronomistic History" because the editing and style of all six books are fairly uniform, and all are consistent with the book of Deuteronomy. Some scholars believe the Deuteronomistic historian was also the redactor of the Torah. Who was the Deuteronomistic historian and when did he flourish?

The insertions of material that would have been in the interests of the Levites centralized animal sacrifice cult, makes a fairly clear case that it was Ezra, perhaps with the help of the school of Levite scribes who compiled it. As the leader, their services were readily available to him, and this might have been necessary, for accomplishing what would have been a daunting task for any one man.

Most scholars place the work around 600 BC, with the books compiled and edited following the exile in 586 BC. (as recorded in Chr. and Ezra) Around 450 BC, Ezra and the governor Nehemiah re-established Judaism in Jerusalem. What ever Ezra may have done, tradition and at least some scholarship agree in assigning him an important editorial role. *Who Wrote the Bible.*

<http://www.straightdope.com/mailbag/mbible2.html>

Israel Finklestein also suggests that a substantial portion of the Pentateuch is a 7th century BCE construction, designed to promote the dynastic ambitions of King Josiah, portraying him as the legitimate successor the legendary David and thus the rightful ruler of Judah. (Silberman, Neil A., and Finkelstein, Israel, Simon and Schuster, NY, 2001)

Originally throughout the first four books of the Torah, instances where the priests and the Levites are mentioned in the same sentence as; "the Levites, the priests" it has generally been interpreted by the Levites themselves and later on others, to mean that the Levites were priests; since it does not say "the Levite Priests" it can just as well be interpreted as a way of listing all those who performed various functions, serving under Moses and Aaron, who were being instructed to follow some of YHVH's directions under Moses. Notice also that this phrase, "the priests, the Levites" first occurs in Deuteronomy, as stated before, it is not used in the first four books of the Torah.

> "When you are come to the land which YHWH gives you and you enjoy tenancy of her and dwell in her, and you say, I shall place over me a king as all of the nations around me...And it shall be, when he sits on the throne of his kingdom, that he shall make a copy of this book out of that which is before the priests the Levites." Deu. 17:9&18

Given all the other changes that were obviously made, it seems not too much more unlikely that the Levite scribe or scribes would add in a little here, to convince the king that he was predestined to give them the power they sought. They thus put the fear of God into him, that it was preordained that he should do so and support the Levites demand for centralized animal sacrifice and tithing. For it makes little sense for Moses to say this of the king, who would give power to the Levite scribes, then open the next chapter (18) by saying; "NOT he shall be for priests, the Levites" which is exactly what happens in Deu. 18:1, *if* it is read in the Hebrew line for line transliteration available at;

<http://www.scripture4all.org/OnlineInterlinear/Hebrew_Index.htm>

In the first chapter of Deuteronomy, it has Moses, after giving instructions that the Israelites should practice self rule, appointing judges and chiefs, he then goes on to say; "And I (Moses) commanded you at that time *ALL* the things you should do." (Deu. 1:18) So it makes little sense for him to then make mention of the time when the Israelites should place themselves in servitude to some king, without rebuking them for going against his instructions to practice self rule.

To suggest that Moses wrote Deu. 17:9&18, predicting Josiah's support and empowerment of the centralization of a Levite cult of animal sacrifice, would be to suggest that he predicted and condoned the re-establishment of kings, which would be at odds with his own orders. (Deu. 1:13-17) Such a statement would seem to suggest that he was reversing himself on his prior decisions, instructing the Israelites *to* elect ministers, judges, and chiefs, so at to rule themselves. (Num. 27:16-21, Jos. 1:1, Deu. 1:13-18)

The question also occurs to me to wonder if this were written by Moses, why would he, after going to all the trouble of freeing the Israelites, ever think free people would want to voluntarily give up self rule, to desire self imposed servitude under a king?

> "In those days there was no king over Israel: every man did that which was right in his own eyes." Judges 21:25

In Deu. 12:5 it appears to have Moses also reverse his decision to allow only those "*of the children of Israel which offered burnt offerings*" (Ex. 24:5) to do so, because it appears to have him then direct them differently, commanding everyone to offer sacrifices. "Thither you shall go and bring your burnt offerings and your sacrifices...You shall not do after all the things that we do here today, every man whatsoever is right in his own eyes." Deu. 12:5-8 If Moses knew they were to eventually do something more "right" why not implement it immediately? This is clearly the work of the animal sacrifice cult of the Levites, written in hindsight to lend authority to their movement.

The Levites even tried to make it appear that Moses reversed himself again by changing the laws concerning not eating unclean animals in (Deu. 14) to read that they *were* allowed to eat clean *and* unclean animals. (Deu. 12:15) Only in this case they choose to insert the contradictory passage *prior* to what is now known as the "Kosher laws."

Now it obviously makes no sense for Moses to tell them to eat unclean animals, then a couple of chapters later go to all the trouble of spelling out which animals were unclean and contradict that decision and forbid all those which were unclean to be eaten. That some animals were unclean was known as early as Noah. (Gen. 7:2) This addition of the earlier statement in Deuteronomy, in favor of eating unclean animals, clearly demonstrates that someone, serving their own self interest at some later point, added it to the original text.

> "And these are the kings that reigned in the land of Edom, before any kings reigned over the children of Israel" Gen. 36:31

Dennis McKinsey, concerning the above verse, Deu. 17:9&18, declared in his book, *Biblical Errancy*: "This passage could only have been written after the first king began to reign...(2000, p.521) The phrasing of the verse certainly seems to indicate that it was written after kings began to reign, saying "reigned" instead of "shall reign."

It is written in the past tense as though said by one looking back, rather than as one looking forward, which *would* have read somewhat more in this fashion; Now these are the kings of the land of Edom, and kings shall reign over the children of Israel again, when they will no longer be free to rule themselves.

> "He *is speaking* YHWH unto Moses...when you come into the land where I shall bring you, *THEN* it shall be that when you eat of the bread of the land, you shall offer up an heave offering unto YHWH. You shall offer up a cake of the first dough, for an heave offering, as you do the heave offering of the threshing floor, so shall you heave it. Of the first of your dough you shall give unto YHWH an heave offering, *in your generation."* Num. 15:18-21

The verses that follow this injunction commanded by YHVH in the above verse "He *is speaking* YHWH unto Moses" (spoken in the present tense) concerning the time when the Israelites reached the promised land, that they would *then* offer sacrifices of bread from the grain they would finally be able to grow, apparently suggests that Moses immediately again reverses himself, and contradicts YHVH's orders to then begin sacrificing bread, and goes on to order animal sacrifices in Num. 15:22. However, if one is paying close attention it will be seen that immediately following YHVH's commandment to sacrifice bread, a different writer obviously begins to speak, because this person speaks in past tense, as though in hindsight saying; "these instructions which *he spoke* YHWH to Moses." So given all the problems with Deuteronomy, it would seem prudent not to put too much faith in those purported instructions, given in Deuteronomy, which again show the handiwork of the Levites attempting to support animal sacrifice.

THE OLDEST SERIAL MURDER MYSTERY IN THE WORLD

> "<u>Woe to you scribes</u> and Pharisees, hypocrites! Because...you say, 'If we were in the days of our forefathers, we would not be sharers with them in the blood of the prophets. Wherefore you are bearing witness against yourselves that <u>you *are* the sons of those who murdered the prophets</u>." Matt. 23: 29-31

Yeschu/Joshu/Jesus knew of the murder of the true and original priesthood of Judah by the second priesthood of false Levite priests, because he had taught the story to Stephen who was also stoned to death just for mentioning it; "Which of the prophets have not your fathers persecuted? And they have slain them which showed before the coming of the just one; of whom you have been now the traitors and murderers...And when they heard these things ...they stoned Stephen" Acts 7:52

> "Woe unto you, scribes and Pharisees[18]!...for you build the sepulchers of the prophets , and your fathers killed them." Luke 11:44-54 ([18]The Pharisees are connected with the scribes 22 times in the NT. "One theory is that the Pharisees were descendants of the Diaspora (c. 722 B.C.–532 B.C.) scribes." *Jewish Religious Parties at the Time of Christ.* <http://www.sundayschoolcourses.com/pharsad/pharsad.htm>)

While these verses from the New Testament have been there for all to read, it is hardly ever mentioned that some of the prophets, who Yeschu/Joshu/Jesus clearly recognized as true prophets, were murdered by the Levite Priesthood just because they burned incense to YHVH's host of heaven and would not eat a Passover of sacrificial lambs. While other prophets were also murdered, these unleavened bread eating prophets of Judah are recorded in the Bible as having been murdered by the Levite scribes.

According to the Jewish tradition in the *Ascension of Isaiah*, the king Manasseh, who ruled before Josiah, murdered the prophet Isaiah in the 2nd year of his reign. The *Ascension of Isaiah* also mentions the murder of the Prophet Micah, Isaiah's contemporary. But Manasseh does not fit the profile of one of the murderers mentioned by Jesus, because he was not a Levite scribe, so he would not have been considered to be the forefather of those Levite scribes and the Pharisees, who descended from the Levite scribes.

The deaths of the prophets of Judah, the murders which Yeschu/Joshu/Jesus and Stephen were referring to, obviously had to be some prophets who were murdered by the forefathers of the Levites scribes (and the Pharisees who came from them) because Yeschu/Joshu/Jesus considered the Levite scribes and Pharisees, he was speaking to, to have been descended from the murderers.

This story of the unleavened bread eating priests of Judah, is one where the Levites scribes were the murderers, those murdered priests of Judah would have been considered prophets by Yeschu/Joshu/Jesus, as he was also from the tribe of Judah. (Heb. 7:14,16) In castigating the Levites and Pharisees as the sons of murderers, *Yeschu/Joshu/Jesus recognizes* the unleavened bread eating prophets of Judah to have been true and rightful prophets of YHVH of hosts, who are also mentioned in the NT; host of heaven;

> "Turns yet the Theos (translated as God) and beside (instead) gives them to be offering divine service to the <u>hosts of heaven</u> (*stratia ho ouranos*) according as it is written in the book of the prophets. <u>No slayed ones and sacrifices were offered to Me for forty years in the wilderness.</u>" (Acts 7:42)

This verse clearly states that Yeschu/Joshu/Jesus's followers understood that it *is* acceptable to offer divine service to the 'host of heaven' and that the animals that were sacrificed to feed the Levites and the mixed multitude, were NOT ordered as sacrifices offered to YHVH. This verse should demonstrate to all Christians that this was a later invention of the Levites in their interpretation of the laws of Leviticus (originally written by Moses to keep the Levites and mixed multitudes from spreading disease plagues throughout the rest of the people, from bacteria associated with meat). That the hosts of heaven are mentioned in the NT shows that they were recognized, taught about and divine service was offered to them, by Yeschu/Joshu/Jesus and his disciples.

> "O Jerusalem, Jerusalem, which killed the prophets, and stoned them that are sent to you." Luke 13:34

In the end, however, they got him too, those bloodthirsty Levite wannabe priests of Jerusalem, who hated Yeschu/Joshu/Jesus for exposing their rapacity and gluttony and their false claim to the priesthood. Fortunately, even though the mainstream redactors of the NT, while anxious to eliminate any references to Yeschu/Joshu/Jesus' teachings on diet (see the section on *broma* next chapter) were also not bright enough to obliterate every trace of these crimes by the Levites, so they too have also failed to notice the more subtle innuendos and missed the less overt references, indicating Yeschu/Joshu/Jesus' understanding in the area of fasting (Matt. 17:21 & Mark 9:29) and diet as an adjunct to spiritual healing.

What remains, however, has given us enough to piece together what would be called in a court of justice, a mostly circumstantial case along with their own confession, providing evidence that not only did the Levite false priests murder the prophets for being vegetarians, they also instigated the murder of the Nazarean vegetarian, Yeschu/Joshu/Jesus, when he began to expose the history of their crimes (committed so as to institute the animal sacrifice cult of the Levite scribes). Think of the verses presented here as a court case, and you are the jury, judge the evidence for yourself.

THIS KIND GOES NOT OUT BUT BY PRAYER AND FASTING

> "However, this kind goeth not out, but by prayer and *nesteia*-abstinence[19] or fasting." Matt. 17:21 [19]*Nesteia* is the Greek word meaning abstinence from food or fasting.
>
> <http://www.myetymology.com/greek/nesteia.html>

There has even been an effort in some manuscripts, to remove or alter the references to prayer and fasting as spoken by Yeschu/Joshu/Jesus (Matt. 17:21 & Mark 9:29); probably because it takes healing out of the realm of merely magical transformation and places the responsibility on ourselves. Unfortunately for them it is too late, that verse and all the others are known world wide, and there is no going back and rewriting history, as those editing the Bible have always liked to do (especially those who hate vegetarianism).

As discussed earlier in the section on Jesus/Yeschu of Nazareth, he was called a Nazarene. While any such references to the Nazarean views on diet have been excluded from the NT, historians have established that <u>the Nazarenes *were* vegetarian</u>. "The Nazarean - they were Jews by nationality...who kept all the Jewish observances, but they would not offer sacrifices or eat meat." Epiphanius *Panarion* 1:19

The Jewish Encyclopedia says of the word Nazarite, from Nazir or Nazar, to separate (Strong's 5144) which may actually be the meaning of the word Nazarean, "many abstained from wine and meat even without taking the vow" (B. B. 60b; Shab. 139a) *Nazarite.*

<http://www.jewishencyclopedia.com/view.jsp?artid=142&letter=N>

Yeschu/Joshu/Jesus himself tells us that the Levite lawgivers had corrupted the law ("For the priesthood being changed, <u>there is also the necessity of changing the law.</u>" Hebrews 7:11-14). But because it is the custom of many churches to take Bible verses and teach them one at a time, out of context, few people now understand the full implication of what he meant by the following statement;

> "Did not Moses give you the law (including "Thou shalt not kill") and yet none of you keep the law." John 7:20 "Thus by your own tradition, handed down among you (the Levite wanna-be priests) you make God's word null and void. And many other things that you do are just like that." Mark 7:13 (NEB)

That the changes making the Levites appear to be priests, had already taken place in the time of Yeschu/Joshu/Jesus is evidenced by the following verses; "For it is evident that the master came from out of Judah, of which tribe about priests Moses speaks nothing...Who not according to law of direction carnal (literally meaning flesh) has become, but according to ability of *life indissoluble[20].*" Heb. 7:14,16 [20]Health - see section on Life Not Subject to Destruction/Health.

> Paul spoke these words, to the Hebrews, and Paul had never met Yeschu/Joshu/Jesus. He was not aware, as Yeschu/Joshu/Jesus and his disciples were that Moses had in fact denied the priesthood to the Levites (Num. 16:8-10) and also said "<u>NOT</u> he shall be for priests, the Levites" (Deu. 18:1 see the Hebrew version of this verse at <<u>http://www.scripture4all.org/OnlineInterlinear/Hebrew_Index.htm</u>>). Yet while Moses rebuked them in Num. 16:8-10 "<u>and all your brothers the Levi with you *And You Seek The Priesthood Also*?</u>" the Levites themselves recorded that they murdered priests of Judah to acquire it, simply because they refused to attend an animal sacrifice and burned incense to the hosts of heaven.

Apparently Yeschu/Joshu/Jesus was well versed in the law, and being of a godlike intelligence, was also capable of distinguishing the same efforts at concealment by the Levites, that are revealed in this book. Even though they were for the most part craftily hidden by the Levite scribes in their efforts to mislead the people for their own gratification. Remember also that Moses and Elijah returned from the spirit world and visited Yeschu/Joshu/Jesus personally (Mark 9:4) so he had access to their story directly from them.

All this means that for about 2500 years there has been an ongoing conspiracy to cover up the murder of the true vegetarian prophets of Judah, by the Levites. First the vegetarian prophets of Judah were murdered, then Yeschu/Joshu/Jesus, who was a Nazarene vegetarian, from the tribe of Judah, was also murdered. When he began to reveal these murders as part of their plot to take over the priesthood, allowing the Levites to mislead the people into bringing them animals to kill and eat, he was also murdered at their instigation.

YESCHU/JOSHU/JESUS' PASSOVER OF BREAD AND WINE

> "If therefore perfection were through the Levite priesthood (for under it the people received the law) what further need was there that another priest (Yeschu/Joshu/Jesus)

207

should rise up of the order of Melchisedec (Gen. 14:18, Heb. 7:1) and NOT according to the order of Aaron? <u>For the priesthood being changed, there is also the necessity of changing the law</u>...For it is evident that out of Judah[21] the master (Yeschu/Joshu/Jesus) has risen." Hebrews 7:11-14 ([21]the very tribe of which, the Levite false priests of the second order slaughtered the original and rightful order of unleavened bread eating priests who burned incense to YHVH's elohim the host of heaven, the *zba eshmim*)

Remember also that it was Judah which included the tribe of Benjamin *tzoir*, the little people. Joshu/Yeschu/Jesus was closely related to the little people, and had their spiritual gifts and loving spirit of cooperation. Thus it could be easily predicted in olden times that a teacher descended from their bloodline would also have these spiritual gifts.

"And you Bethlehem Ephrathath *tzoir* (SHD 6819 little – see previous section on The Little People MHJ) to become mentors of Judah from you, for Me, he shall come forth to become one ruling Israel and going forth of him from aforetime from day of eon." Mic. 5:2

The reason the order of the Priesthood needed to be changed was because the Levites taught that animals <u>*must*</u> be sacrificed to obtain absolution from sins and/or receive healing whereas it is now well known to contribute to heart disease, cancer etc. Yeschu/Joshu/Jesus being god-like knew to the contrary, that some things had to be healed through prayer and fasting. (Matt. 17:21 & Mark 9:29) He knew that it is necessary to clean the inside as well as the outside, as he mentions in one of his parables (Matt. 23:25 following), and that kindness was necessary instead of sacrifices (Matt. 9:13&12:7).

"Nasareans meaning rebels, who forbid all flesh-eating, and do not eat living things at all...they hold that the scriptures of the Pentateuch were not written by Moses, and maintain that they have others...They claim that these books are fictions, and that none of these customs were instituted by the fathers." Epiphanius *Panarion* 1:18

That there was no need to ritually kill lambs, for Passover, was understood by Yeschu/Joshu/Jesus, as there was no meat, only bread and wine, at the last supper, which is mentioned as a Passover in three of the gospels of the NT. (Matt., Mark, & Luke) Some modern Jewish vegetarians celebrate a Seder at Passover, which is entirely vegetarian.

So it is little wonder that it was also the scribes who were among those Yeschu/Joshu/Jesus rebuked for hypocrisy. In Matt. 15:2, when the scribes and Pharisees rebuked his disciples for not washing their hands, he in turn rebukes them with a parable about cleaning the outside but not the inside.

"Woe to you, scribes and Pharisees, hypocrites[22]! ([22]the ancient Greek word for actors) For you clean the outside of the cup and the plate, but inside they are full of *rapacity* and self indulgence." (Matt. 23:25) Rapacity (from the Greek *harpage/harpyia* or like a harpy) is a word that implies a ravenous or voracious appetite, living on prey as does a raptor, a bird of prey. <<u>http://www.scripture4all.org/OnlineInterlinear/Greek_Index.htm</u>>

"Woe unto you, scribes and Pharisees, hypocrites! For you are like whitewashed tombs, which indeed appear beautiful outside, but inside are replete with bones of dead ones and every uncleanness." Matt. 23:27

It is established that he had angered many of the scribes, because along with the so-called Levite priests they were his staunchest accusers when he was brought before Herod and Pilate. "The chief priests and scribes stood by, vehemently accusing him." Luke 23:10 What had he done to incur their wrath? One, they accused him of claiming to be a god because he told them "I and my father are one." and after he told them, "Is it not written in the your law, I say you are gods?" (John 10:34) they had tried to take him so as to stone him but he escaped.

Besides the Levites efforts to change the name YHVH Elohim to Adonai Elohim, we may never know how many other references have been completely obliterated because of their hatred for the vegetarian priests they murdered, simply because they honored the host of heaven by burning incense and refused to attend and animal sacrifice. The hatred they felt when confronted, by Yeschu/Joshu/Jesus and Stephen, with these murders, is their own self loathing turned outward, just as many abusive persons still do when confronted with their crimes. But we must remember that they are in the throes of their insane rage, and as Yeschu/Joshu/Jesus and Stephen did, pray forgiveness for them, for it is true that 'they know not' what they are doing. They see only their desire to preserve their ego, by destroying any reminders of their own responsibility.

> "Once, Rabbi Yohanan ben Zakkai was walking with his disciple, Rabbi Y'hoshua (aka Yeschu/Joshu/Jesus) near Jerusalem after the destruction of the Temple. Rabbi Y'hoshua looked at the Temple ruins and said "Alas for us!! The place that atoned for the sins of the people Israel lies in ruins!" Then Rabbi Yohannan ben Zakkai spoke to him these words of comfort: 'Be not grieved, my son. There is another equally meritorious way of gaining ritual atonement, even though the Temple is destroyed. We can still gain ritual atonement through deeds of loving-kindness. For it is written; Loving kindness I desire, not sacrifice." (Hosea 6:6) Midrash Avot D'Rabbi Nathan 4:5

But also in addition to the above mentioned criticisms, Yeschu/Joshu/Jesus had no doubt angered them by driving out of the temple those who were selling sacrificial animals (sheep, oxen and doves for the mandatory sacrifices), that had been instituted by these false priests and Levite scribes (John 2:15-16) and he had at least twice, even according to the NT, criticized the practice of sacrifice, requiring it be replaced with kindness or compassion. (KJV, mercy)

> "For the law...can never with those sacrifices which they offered year by year continually make the comers perfect. For then would they not have ceased to be offered? For the worshipers once purged should have no more conscience of sins...For it is not possible that the blood of bulls and of goats should take away sin." Heb. 10:1-4

There is nothing about sacrificing or killing that logically seems to indicate that YHVH would forgive us if we killed an animal or his son as a sacrifice. This kind of twisted thinking arose out of the teachings of the Levite priests who promised absolution of sins, if people brought them animals to sacrifice and eat, and in earlier time of famine some even sacrificed children. This is not to say that Yeschu/Joshu/Jesus did not sacrifice his life, but his murder did not appease YHVH's wrath against the murderers (see Matt. 7:21), or give us the freedom to go do whatever we want, like destroying our health, and then simply be forgiven without first repenting, which means to 'turn away' and go the right direction.

This stance against animal sacrifice and in favor of inner hygiene, was one which the Jewish scribes no doubt found to be an insult to their continued rapacious appetites and greed, and his stance against sacrifice was also no doubt taken as a threat, to their freedom to continue gorging themselves on the sacrifices they demanded from the people in return for promises of absolution of sins, and the healing that the people so desperately sought and never received.

> "They that are whole need not a physician, but they that are sick. But go you and learn what that means, I will have kindness not sacrifice." Matt. 9:13 AND "For if you had known what this meant, "*I will have kindness and not sacrifice*" you would not have condemned the blameless." (for picking corn on the Sabbath to eat) Matt12:7 His meaning in these passages (that sacrificing and eating animals causes of sickness) has long been concealed because in Matt. 9:10 the KJV put it that Jesus "sat at meat" when in fact the Greek version says he was "lying (down) in the home."

<http://www.scripture4all.org/OnlineInterlinear/Greek_Index.htm>

The scribes and false priests surely did not want their way of living disrupted, and did not want any interference with their access to indulging their bloodthirsty "*rapacity*." (Matt. 23:25) Because of their desire for self indulgence" in the daily sacrifices, they had convinced the people that sacrifices were mandated by Moses to receive YHVH's blessings and healing rather than an occasional necessity to be performed attentively by trained servers, when needed for survival. Whereas in fact what YHVH states is necessary is just to hear His voice (what is now called conscience) rather than sacrifice. For clarification the following verse bears repeating.

> "I spoke not unto your fathers, nor commanded them in the day that I brought them out of Egypt, on matters of burnt offerings and sacrifices. But rather this thing I instructed them to say; Listen to my voice (speaking through our conscience MHJ) and I will become your Elohim, and you shall become my people." Jer. 7:8&21-23

The *dabar YHVH,* the word of YHVH, has been corrupted by the "lying scribes" and the false priests, teaching the Israelites to break the commandment, "Thou shalt not kill" some even going so far as to prescribe killing and sacrificing their own children (Jer. 7:8&21-23) after the manner of the Canaanites. Because of this many have lost faith in the version of the Bible that derives from the time of Ezra, as the inerrant word of YHVH and His Elohim. The many contradictions including, "to sacrifice or not to sacrifice" are one area that is scoffed at by Bible critics. *Bible Contradictions.* <http://www.evilbible.com/Biblical%20Contradictions.htm>

> "For if that first Covenant had been faultless, there would be no occasion for a second." Heb. 8:7

It should be obvious to any follower of Yeschu/Joshu/Jesus, that he was wiser than his disciples or apostles, so when there are various viewpoints on any given subject, Yeschu/Joshu/Jesus should clearly hold precedence. An example is the conflict between the words of Yeschu /Jesus/Joshu and his disciple John, in Matthew 7:21 and John 3:16, the later verse is popularly promoted in churches to provide a doctrine the masses would find easy to accept.

Whereas Yeschu/Joshu/Jesus says; "not everyone who comes to me saying, Lord, Lord, will enter the kingdom of heaven, but he who *DOES* the will of the Father." (Matt. 7:21) John, however, teaches the lesser light, "whosoever *believes* in him shall not perish, but have everlasting life." This is the most popular verse taught, by fundamentalists seeking to entice tithing members. It is one thing to enter the spirit world and have everlasting life, it is another to enter in amongst the most selfless spirits occupying the higher realms of the spirit world, the heavens of the heavens.

> "Who is able to build him a house, in that the heavens and heavens of the heavens are not able to contain Him?" II Chr. 2:6

PAUL THE APOSTLE WHO WAS NEVER A DISCIPLE

> "Let the reader contrast the true Christian standard with that of Paul and he will see a terrible betrayal of all that the Master taught...because the church has followed Paul in his error it has failed lamentably to redeem the world." *Christ or Paul* by Rev. V. A. Holmes-Gore.

> "The writings of Paul have been a danger and a hidden rock, the causes of the principle defects of Christian theology." *Saint Paul* by theologian Ernest Renan.

There are far more words of Paul in the NT than there are quoting Yeschu/Joshu/Jesus. Much has been said on the subject of Paul, who never even actually met Yeschu/Joshu/Jesus nor received instruction from him. His contributions to the NT, have occasionally skewed the original teachings. Especially on the subjects of advocating slavery (Eph. 6:7, Col. 4:1, 1 Tim. 6:1-2 Timothy was Paul's student); versus holding all things in common as Yeschu instructed; Yeschu had female disciples (Acts 9:36) who asked questions whereas Paul prohibits women's rights to even speak in church (Col. 3:18, I Cor. 11:3, 14:34-35, Eph. 5:22); and subverting the Essene-Nazarene teachings of purity in diet. Holmes-Gore, Rev. V. A. *In Christ or Paul?*

> "Paul declares that...the Elect may even eat meat sacrificed to idols...Whereas Jesus honored women and found in them His most devoted followers, Paul never tires of proclaiming their inferiority. He declares that, man is the head of the woman and she must always submit to his will...Whereas the Essenes proclaimed equality among the Brethren, Paul repeatedly declares that Christian slaves must be obedient to their Christian masters." Martin Larson, *The Story of Christian Origins.*

Yeschu/Joshu/Jesus was a great advocate of peace and pacifism. "Blessed are the peacemakers" (Matt. 5:9) and "Love your enemies." (Matt. 5:44) Yet there is one very famous verse which seems to contradict this stance (Matt. 10:34) seems to have Yeschu say; "I came not to send peace, but a sword." Yet the manuscript called the *Book of Kells aka Book of Columbia* (Dublin, Trinity College Library, MS A. I. 58) produced by Celtic monks around 800 AD translated this verse quite differently. This old MS gives the word *gaudium* which means joy instead of *gladium* meaning sword, rendering a quite different meaning. "I came not (only) to send peace, but joy."

> "I draw a great distinction between the Sermon on the Mount of Jesus and the Letters of Paul, Paul's letters are a graft on Christ's teachings." Gandhi, Mahatma, pacifist liberator of India from British Imperialism, in his essay, *Discussion on Fellowship.*

The Clementine Homilies and Recognitions by Apostle Peter explains; "But the reason why the demons delight in entering into men's bodies is that, being disembodied spirits and having perverted desires after meat and sex, but not being able to partake of these due to being spirits, and wanting organs fitted their enjoyment, they enter into the bodies of men in order to gain organs with which to satisfy their lusts, both meat and sex." Peter goes on...through the flesh diet, the demons are able to decrease the rate of vibration of your aura to the point they can pierce it and enter your body. then they attach themselves to your mind and "make suggestions" to you which you believe are from your own mind. Rev. Brother Nazariah. D.D. *Yashua or Paul.* <http://www.essene.org/Yahowshua_or_Paul.htm>

"Paul was the first corrupter of the doctrines of Jesus." Thomas Jefferson.

Paul himself tells us that following his "visions" of Jesus; "there was given me a thorn in the flesh, a messenger of Satan to buffet me." II Cor. 12:7 According to the Rev. Bro. Nazariah D.D. one of the Dead Sea Scrolls[23] *The Habukkuk Commentary* concerns Paul. He is referred to as "the Man of Lies." This would indicate that this scroll was written after the time of Paul and therefore also the time of Joshu/Yeschu/Jesus (remember that the Talmud also dates Joshu/Yeschu/Jesus to a century or so earlier than the year one). <http://www.essene.org/Yahowshua_or_Paul.htm> [23]..."the scrolls use 'house of Judah' to designate the Qumran community...there is no question that 'house of Judah' and 'those who observe the law' belong together, as both refer to the Essenes...Against the Man of Lies, 'who misdirected many with his deceptive words,' we find the Interpreter of Knowledge, whose words were not heeded. This is the Teacher of Righteousness..." Flusser, David. *Judaism of the Second Temple Period.* p. 256-257

"The Christianity that the nations of the world follow is the religion of Paul...because of his betrayal of the Master's teachings, the vision of true Christianity has been so dimmed that men have been able to defend war and a host of other evils, such as flesh eating and slavery, on the authority of the Bible." *Christ or Paul* Rev. V. A. Holmes-Gore.

"James[24] (Jesus brother) Peter, and the disciples were members of the *Essaei* (Essene MHJ) community, which Paul most assuredly was not...We see then, that Paul was the father of Pagan Christianity (Roman Catholicism) a *movement based on a concept completely foreign to Jesus, James, Peter and the Essaei* community..." Savoy, Gene. *The Essaei Document.* [24]"James the Lord's brother...drank no wine or other intoxicating liquor, nor did he eat flesh..." Hegesippus (Roberts-Donaldson translation)

<http://www.earlychristianwritings.com/text/hegesippus.html>

By the third century when the council of bishops under Constantine decided which manuscripts would be excluded, there were certainly objections made to the inclusion of any manuscripts that contained mention of Yeschu/Joshu/Jesus' diet. These were of the same type as those of whom Yeschu/Joshu/Jesus said, "You strain at a gnat but swallow a camel." (Matt. 23:24) They were adamant about pointing out anyone's failure in washing their hands or picking corn on the Sabbath, but constantly overlooked their own failure to keep one of the most important commandments, "Thou Shalt Not Kill." It does not say thou shalt not kill humans, it says Thou shalt not kill, period. Yet even Paul's writings in Rom. 14:21 teach that meat causes some people to develop infirmities. It is nowdays widely known that cholesterol, only found in animal foods, causes heart disease, the number one infirmity and cause of mortality in the United States.

<http://nutritionfacts.org/questions/how-can-i-avoid-the-top-10-leading-causes-of-death/>

"The ideal is not to be eating meat, nor drinking wine, nor anything which causes our brothers to stumble, become offended, or develop infirmities." Rom. 14:21 Note that the Greek words do in fact say "or is being infirm," NOT simply be made weak as the JKV has it. <http://scripture4all.org/OnlineInterlinear/NTpdf/rom14.pdf>

So while Paul's writing occasionally demonstrates some wisdom and insight as in (1 Cor. 15:28) it must be remembered that sometimes his wisdom and understanding of oneness with all life still falls short of that of Yeschu/Joshu/Jesus. And even Yeschu/Joshu/Jesus did not claim to have achieved perfect goodness as he reminds us "Why do you call me good? No one is good except God (Theos)." (Mark 10:18) Given all the changes made to the OT by the Levite scribes and the misunderstanding of the teachings of Yeschu /Jesus by Paul and others, we must therefore reexamine the suggestions given to us, that the Bible, OT and NT, is somehow the inerrant word of YHVH, perfect and unaltered, using discrimination and discernment when referring to it as a guide. Again we were not meant to worship the Bible we were meant to worship YHVH *Al Chimm* (YHVH All Life).

But the discriminating mind, having examined the mysteries of the earth, finds that evolution does not fit the evidence either. The best most can do is seek the grain of truth hidden in what remains to us and try to find written evidence that will help us find and rebuild YHVH's word, 'changing the law" back, by recognizing the falsehoods and misinterpretations that have been interjected into the Bible through the self interest, of the "lying scribes" and false priests, about whom the prophets wrote to warn us.

HISTORIC EVIDENCE

Because 5000 years ago in Greece, the Greeks also sacrificed goats and used its blood and/or flour (both symbols of life) sprinkled in the fields at springtime, as a sacrifice and to petition the Gods and the earth, to bless the future harvest, there is little question that some Israelites adopted this through association with the practices of their neighbors in the land of Canaan. When the Roman Legions conquered the Greeks, they took this celebration with them when they returned home and called this celebration "Lupercailis." (now celebrated as Valentines day) The Romans started the practice of masking and killed the fattened ox (*boeuf gras*) to commemorate the occasion. Participants who wished to become priests were allowed to let the warm blood flow over the worshipers to purify them and to wash away their sins. This misguided idea that blood can somehow purify also clearly shows up in the concepts promoted by the Levites. Cooper, David J. *A Kings History of Mardi Gras.* <http://www.mobile.org/vis_mardigras_king.php>

> "Most middle Paleolithic peoples must have eaten some vegetable foods, and in some habitats they probably consumed more plant foods than meat...First there are extensive cave or open-air occupations in which, given good preservation, both stone and bone remains may be very abundant. Next there are quite restricted scatters, sometimes in caves or rock-shelters, sometimes in the open, in which artifacts of all kinds and bone remains are very rare...little is known of the latter kind, partly because they are not considered rewarding to excavate...the smaller, ephemeral ones seem likely, as a rule, to

213

have been more specialized." *The Cambridge Encyclopedia of Archaeology*, p. 84.

"The neolithic man discovered in an Italian glacier in 1991 carried a bow and a quiver of arrows, leading archaeologists to label him a hunter. Chemical (hair) analysis indicated that the Iceman was a vegetarian..." (*Science News* Vol. 154, Nov. 7, 1998, p. 301) Later analysis of his colon contents showed that he had recently consumed animal foods, perhaps in a desperate attempt to survive the situation in which he found himself just before died. Baldia, Maximillian O. *The Iceman's Food Fight.*

<http://www.comp-archaeology.org/IcemanDiet.htm>

Australopithecus Africanus and *Sahelanthropus*, were all tool-less vegetarians, whereas *Homo erectus* was a crude toolmaker, with a more rounded skull, implying new brain areas. He appeared on the scene with a multitude of physical changes, which according to natural selection each one should have taken ages to take hold through natural selection and then become dominant. Instead these developments happened all at once with no transitional fossils. His use of tools and therefore flint weapons appeared when his newly rounded skull appeared, not before. If eating meat were the cause of the development of a larger brain, the signs of weapon use would have come first and gradually ushered in larger brains. Instead all the various new areas of the brain appeared all at once (with no fossil record of transitional types showing incremental changes).

So whether it is examined from the perspective of science or the understanding of the biblical history of the Garden of Eden, it is clear that before the appearance of tool-making and fire, our human ancestors were primarily vegetarians of a primate body style. It is from them that we have inherited our biology, one that allows eating the meat of small animals and then only intermittently, with a staple diet of non-animal foods. Anything more results in disease symptoms, discussed further in the chapter following.

Our basically primate biology is unable to easily adapt to things foreign to our biological type or anything that must be processed (cooking is processing), and those failures to adapt result in diseases, depending on what genetic weaknesses are present. After the advent of antibiotics, contagious diseases decreased, but chronic conditions are on the rise. Why are these diseases seen so frequently in humans but only rarely seen in animals that eat whatever their biology originally suited them to eat? It is because health is the natural state of each animal including those of us, who "does the will of the Father" (Matt. 7:21), practicing abstention from meat and its disease consequences. Our Creator, who established our biology, is the Great Holy Spirit He becomes the soul of all the living (Gen 1:24).

<http://scripture4all.org/OnlineInterlinear/OTpdf/gen1.pdf>

The habitual eating of flesh also resulted in the eventual loss of the natural foraging skills, acquired by the young observing their parents, as to what to eat while dwelling on the paradisaical young earth. This was all the various fruits, nuts, plants, and seeds, given to us for food in Gen. 1:29 at the time of the Garden of Eden, and will be again in YHVH's kingdom come (Isa. 11:6-9). When nothing is hurt or destroyed in all the earth Paradise will be again restored to the fruitful garden, through our active involvement in full consciousness of our role as tenants of the earth and caretakers of all creatures great and small.

Chapter Nine

THE ORIGINAL DIET IN THE GARDEN OF EDEN

"I have given you every herb (all edible plants were known as herbs) yielding seed upon the face of the earth,…and every tree with its fruit and seed (nuts), for you <u>He is becoming for food</u>[1]." Gen. 1:29 ([1]YHVH becomes every living thing and gives those suited to our biology to us for food) See <http://www.scripture4all.org>

BEFORE FIRE AND WEAPONS

The OT repeatedly addresses the recurring thread of what constitutes purity in diet. Because of the ongoing disputes between various Biblical prophets and the Levite animal sacrifice cult it is essential to address the question of the diet of the sons of the Elohim, as they and their wives from among the daughters of the Adam (Genesis 6:1-2) practiced around the time of the Garden of Eden.

Without an understanding of the ancient debate concerning the relationship between diet and the many plagues (which the Levitican laws were written by Moses in an attempt to control), the motives that the Levite animal sacrifice cult had for murdering the unleavened bread-eating priests cannot be clearly understood.

For it will be seen that it was by departure from that original diet that they brought a multitude of plagues, diseases, and untimely deaths upon themselves and for which they refused to accept responsibility. This chapter will present many verses that discuss these ongoing disputes between the Levite Sopherim (whose input was later incorporated into the OT long after Moses' time); and it will present Bible verses from many of the Old Testament prophets protesting the interpretation and alteration of Bible verses by these scribes.

Partaking in the heritage of the tree of knowledge allowed the Adam to exercise the freedom to use discernment (with their larger brains), and judge something to be good or bad. In so doing we become capable of participating in our own fate. But with freedom must also come responsibility for too much of any good thing becomes evil. Even water, so vital to life, can cause an overdose when taken in excess. And all self indulgence has the same potential for abuse or misuse.

Because humans had used this knowledge to learn eat some things which were used as food by other creatures so as to avoid starvation, they also learned that it was easier to make flint tools and hunt animals than to wait for a plant to produce fruit or grain. However excesses of biologically incompatible food sources, which might have served to prevent starvation in those early times, now brought about diseases.

Indulging the fear and aggression generated by the serpent brain breeds new problems, preventing starvation can bring about the problems of disease, self defense can cross the line to murder, the aggressive desire which some women find flattering can easily cross the line to rape, territorialism can develop into war, etc.

THE CURSE OF ALZHEIMER'S

"No curse comes without its cause." Prov. 26:2

Destruction of the neurons of the brain that lead to what is called Alzheimer's is now understood to result from *not* following the original diet that was given while "the Adam" lived in paradise on the pristine unspoiled earth. According to later verses from biblical texts the original diet was only modified after it was seen that the Adam was not continuing to be wise in following the original diet; these guidelines (called kosher) were meant to teach humanity that if they must eat animal foods to prevent starvation, to choose the "clean" over the "unclean." There is no such problem with vegetable food, as plants and fruits actually contain along with nutrients, anti-viral and anti-bacterial components, which actually help protect people from contagious diseases.

Vegetarians show statistically only half the incidence of Alzheimer's that occurs in omnivores (some say meat eaters are as much as three times more likely to develop senility). With the incidence of Alzheimer's on the rise perhaps it is time to reconsider our ancestors judgment call to begin introducing meat into humanity's diet after leaving paradise in of the Garden of Eden. (during which we ate the primarily vegetarian diet common to all higher primates) *Alzheimer's and Brain Health.* <http://www.goveg.com/alzheimers.asp>

Nelson, Jeff. *Alzheimer's: Losing your Mind for the Sake of a Burger.*

 <http://www.vegsource.com/articles/alzheimers_homocysteine.htm>

<http://www.google.com/search? hl=en&sa=X&oi=spell&resnum=0&ct=result&cd=1&q=vegetarians+%22senile+dementia %22+alzheimer%27s&spell=1?>

Magnesium is found most abundantly in dark green vegetation, fruit, and grains and is almost nonexistent in animal source foods. Remember phosphoric acid and sulfuric acid are highly corrosive to living tissue; and meat especially pig, has exponentially more of these acid forming minerals than any other food. The buffering effect of a diet abundant in alkaline forming minerals may help prevent damage to various cellular proteins (including DNA and RNA) and enzymes (which are comprised of protein). The presence of high levels of acid forming minerals may somehow prevent serum (blood) protein from carrying the alkaline forming mineral magnesium into the brain; where aluminum and other heavy metals build up in the brain and destroy neurons.

> "Evidence is presented indicating that dementias are associated with a relative insufficiency of Magnesium (Mg) in the brain. Such insufficiency may be attributable to low intake or retention of Mg; high intake of a neurotoxic metal, such as aluminum (Al), which inhibits activity of Mg-requiring enzymes; or impaired transport of Mg and/or enhanced transport of the neurotoxic metal into brain tissue. It is proposed that

Alzheimer's disease (AD) involves a defective transport process, characterized by both an abnormally high incorporation of Al and an abnormally low incorporation of Mg into brain neurons. The hypothesis is advanced that an altered serum protein contributes to the progression of AD by having a greater affinity for Al than for Mg, in contrast to the normal protein, which binds Mg better than Al. The altered protein crosses the blood-brain barrier more efficiently than the normal protein and competes with the normal protein in binding to brain neurons. Binding of the altered protein to the target neurons would both facilitate Al uptake and impede Mg uptake. Evidence suggests that albumin is the serum protein that is altered." Glick, J.L. *Dementias: the role of magnesium deficiency and an hypothesis concerning the pathogenesis of Alzheimer's disease.*

<http://www.ncbi.nlm.nih.gov/pubmed/2092675>

See also this info "Multiple studies implicate metals in the pathophysiology of neurodegenerative diseases...These data suggest that the conformation of α-synuclein can be modulated by metals, with iron promoting aggregation and magnesium inhibiting aggregation." Golts et al., *Magnesium Inhibits Spontaneous and Iron-induced Aggregation of alpha-Synuclein.*

<http://www.jbc.org/cgi/content/abstract/277/18/16116>

This brain deterioration may happens as a result of the folding of the neurons of the brain when the buffering alkaline presence of the magnesium found abundantly in green vegetation, especially in the presence of high iron and copper (both especially abundant in the blood, which in the OT was strictly forbidden), is suppressed by heavy metals. Evidence is piling up that iron and copper contribute to excess production of damaging reactive oxygen (free radicals) in the presence of a diet high in saturated fat (of which animal fat is a rich source) and contribute to Alzheimer's. Brewer, George J. *Iron and Copper Toxicity in Diseases of Aging...*

<http://www.ebmonline.org/cgi/content/abstract/232/2/323> & Rush Univ. Med. Ctr. *High Fat and Copper Rich Diets.* <http://www.sciencedaily.com/releases/2006/08/060816013125.htm>

"It shall be a perpetual statute for your generations throughout all your dwellings, that you eat neither fat nor blood." Lev. 3:17

It is no coincidence that animal fat, which amplifies the harmful effect of copper and iron on the brain; and blood containing iron and copper, were forbidden by YHVH's Elohim, since their understanding is and always was far in advance of humans[2]. Excess iron accumulation in the brain is a consistent observation in Alzheimer's disease. Conner, Milward, Moalem, Sampietro, Boyer, Vergani, Scott, & Chorney. *Is Hemochromatosis a Risk Factor for Alzheimer's Disease.* <http://www.ncbi.nlm.nih.gov/sites/entrez?cmd=Retrieve&db=PubMed&list_uids=12214033&dopt=Abstract>

Cutler, Paul. M.D. *Iron Overload - the Missed Diagnosis.*

<http://www.consumerhealth.org/articles/display.cfm?ID=19990303140150>

[2]Another occurrence of this foreknowledge occurred in the prohibition of incest, which by humans, was only recently proven by modern genetics to contribute to birth defects. Again with the practice of circumcision, foreknowledge is demonstrated, which has recently been shown to

reduce the risk of contracting HIV and AIDS and by association possibly other STD's as well. Russel, Sabin.. *Male Circumcision Shows Promise as Defense Against HIV Transmi magnesium protects against neural degeneration ssion.*

<http://www.sfgate.com/cgi-bin/article.cgi?file=/c/a/2006/12/14/AIDS.TMP&type=printable>

How could primitive humans, unfamiliar with methods of scientific proof, have known how to avoid these cause and effect scenarios or to avoid the effects of fat and the blood, without an advanced guide to teach them?

> "Vegetarian diets often contain more copper than do non-vegetarian diets, but observations of decreased plasma copper associated with vegetarian diets suggest that these diets have lower copper bioavailability than do non vegetarian diets" (Because they do not contain high levels of saturated fats, apparently increasing absorption of these elements MHJ). Hunt, Janet. and Richard A. Vanderpool. Apparent *Copper Absorption from a Vegetarian Diet.* <http://www.ajcn.org/cgi/content/abstract/74/6/803>

Extremely acid forming foods, with high levels of phosphorus, sulfur and chlorine, such as meat and dairy foods are known to have (milk has an 8:1 ratio of the acid forming phosphorus to the alkaline calcium, read the carton!!!) which, as any acid will do, depletes the bodies' reserves of alkaline minerals, including calcium and magnesium (for each extra mg. of phos. one mg. of cal. or mag. etc. is depleted from the body, brain and nerves) contributing to osteoporosis, tooth decay, and other degenerative diseases, as well as Alzheimer's.

Research from the two articles quoted below, as well as many other studies, show evidence concerning the importance of magnesium and therefore the vegetables which contain it. Quoted from the first article; "Significant lower magnesium scores were found in DAT Ss (Dementia of the Alzheimer's Type) than in controls; calcium:magnesium ratios were significantly different between the 2 groups…A possible causal relationship between low magnesium in hippocampal neurons and impairment of learning, as noted in aged rat experiments, suggests that magnesium protects against neural degeneration. (PsycINFO Database Record (c) 2006 APA, all rights reserved)

In the second study the author also discusses the importance of magnesium. "Reviews studies showing improvement of magnesium (Mg) levels and dementia with ethylene diamine tetraacetic acid and dietary supplements. The case of a 76-yr-old man with Alzheimer's disease treated with Mg oxide is discussed." The author also quotes the experiment with rats mentioned above.

> "Plasma magnesium decrease and altered calcium/magnesium ratio in severe dementia of the Alzheimer type." Lemke, Matthias R., Ingolstadt Medical Ctr, Dept of Psychiatry, Germany. Source: "Biological Psychiatry" Vol. 37, March 1995. pp. 341-343.

And: "Use of magnesium in the management of dementias." Glick, J. Leslie, Bionix Corp, Potomac, MD, US. Source: Medical Science Research, Vol. 18 (21), Nov 1990. pp. 831-833. <http://web.ebscohost.com/ehost/results?vid=5&hid=107&sid=1ae419ad-9b10-430b-b041-dd46ae75ffcc%40sessionmgr3>

Individuals who have entered a vegetative state and completely lost their understanding of language, i.e., "the word, logos or logic" no longer have a clear cut sense of self and know longer know who they are. When the Bible says "the dead know nothing" (Ps. 115:17; Ecc. 9:5-6) it may be the spirits of those people who, after progressing into a vegetative state have destroyed their brains and consequently their minds and memories by harmful diets, to which it is referring. To believe that when we enter the spirit world we automatically know everything would be absurd; it sets aside all the efforts of those who have worked to acquire their accumulated wisdom, knowledge working toward perfecting themselves. It would place those who have degenerated their understanding as instantly and automatically the equals of those who have worked to acquire wisdom by practicing self-improvement, purity and holiness, without any effort on the parts of those who have not.

It is from words that we form our internal description of our selves (which is always connected to what we want or don't want); animals do not develop the use of phonetic words unless taught, just as YHVH's Elohim taught us. As mentioned previously sociology has found that individuals who are raised without being taught to use words have a difficult time ever understanding all the words of their culture and socializing in general. This is also true of anyone who has lost the use of words. Because of deterioration of the brain, they are in a state of ignorance much like an animal, and often physically incapacitated as well, through health conditions brought on by related chemical processes, this is in turn because they cannot digest, assimilate or excrete the chemical by-products of a diet with which they are biologically incompatible.

The current evidence corroborating the health benefits of eating less red meat has been stated by numerous medical authorities including the American Heart Association. When they first announced their massively documented position concerning saturated fat and cholesterol (found only in animal products) they were threatened with multi-million dollar lawsuits by the dairy industry. In spite of this they bravely took their now famous stand against cholesterol and did not retract their position, now thoroughly understood by even the staunchest advocates favoring the consumption of animal foods. Robbins, John. *Diet for a New America.*

> "When you sit to dine with a ruler, understand what is before you. You place a knife in your throat, if you yearn for his meat (*lmtomuthiu*) for it is deceitful meat...Do not eat bread with one who has the evil eye nor desire his tasty meats." Prov. 23:1-6

> "You must not become like the ones carousing with wine and the ones being gluttons of flesh, for them that are carousing and being gluttons shall become destitute and tears shall clothe them in slumber[3]." Prov. 23:20

[3]Just as any one who has worked with Alzheimer's patients can attest to, they are sometimes barely conscious, and yet the hospitals and nursing homes continue to puree meat in blenders and force feed them something which robs them of their senses. Even those who have not reached this pathetic state often pass out after eating because of over-indulging and the difficulty digesting these foods, which takes all the blood away from the brain for work in the stomach.

> "If because of *broma* (actually the Greek word for food, not meat as given in KJV) your brother is grieved you are not walking with love. <u>Do not destroy any one with your (*broma*-food) for whom Christ died...It is not good to eat flesh, nor to drink wine, nor anything whereby your brother is made weak.</u>" Rom. 14:15&21 It is pretty clear these days, even to the most ignorant, that cholesterol makes many weak, since it cuts of the blood and oxygen supply to the brain and the limbs and that a high protein diet

contributes to incidence of cancer (see Cancer section following).

The Journal of the American Medical Association in Vol.176, # 9, 1961, p. 806, stated that; "A vegetarian diet can prevent 97% of coronary occlusions." And further after a massive governmental study, George Lundberg, editor of the Journal of the American Medical Association, went on to state that this 1984 study is the one "that secured the cholesterol theory in heart disease." Robbins, 1987, p. 245.

> "And YHWH spoke to Moses saying; Speak unto the children of Israel, saying, You shall eat no manner of fat, of ox, or of sheep, or of goat...For who so ever eats the fat of the beast, of which men offer an offering made by fire unto YHWH, the soul that eats it shall be cut off from his people[4]...Moreover you shall eat no manner of blood." Lev. 7:22&25-26 [4]The soul of Alzheimer's patients are definitely 'cut off' from the rest of us.

These guidelines were given by YHVH and His council of Elohim to Moses so that early man would be able to survive without completely destroying his intellect and health. Natural carnivores, like the feline and canine families, need no such restrictions; their biology allows them to eat blood and fat with impunity.

The very fact that meat must be specially prepared shows that it was not a natural food for humans. Anything that cannot be eaten raw and whole, is not something our human ancestors, who existed before fire, would have been naturally compatible with; as their descendants we would have inherited this incompatibility with flesh foods. Until the advent of the use of fire, it would have been necessary to eat meat raw, and before tools it would have been necessary to kill without the claws and fangs carnivores have. No other animal with primate biology kills and eats large bovine or porcine animals, as the larger feline and canine families can easily do, with their special teeth and claws. And even the small creatures primates do eat, are only killed rarely, and even then are not always indulged in by the females and non-dominant members of the troop.

Staunch defenders of remaining carnivorous, argue that because the Bible says the Elohim clothed the Adam with animal skins, in Gen. 3:21, this means the Elohim killed animals to do so. It seems the height of egotism and ignorance to assume that the act of skinning an animal, which could be learned by these primitive humans, was incapable of being demonstrated, on newly dead animals, by beings powerful enough to traverse the heavens in their "merkabah/chariots." To assume they killed animals to clothe the Adam, is to suggest they were not capable of flying over the massive herds in their "merkabah/chariots" and locating some dying animals to use as a demonstration, after the animal had died of its own accord. That the Elohim did not instruct the Adam to kill and eat animals is shown as Genesis goes on immediately thereafter to say;

> "You shall eat *from the ground*, being cursed for sake of you in grief, you shall eat from her (the earth) all the days of your lives. And thorns and weeds shall sprout for you and you will eat the herbage of the field. By the sweat of you nostrils, you shall eat *bread* until you return from the ground from which you came...And He is sending away him YHVH Elohim, from Garden of Eden to serve the ground from which you are made. For soil (minerals) you are and to soil you shall return" Gen. 3:17-1

A misunderstanding of the role of alkaline minerals, esp. magnesium, in the removal of acids like phosphorus (deposited along with calcium as calcium phosphate), is responsible for some of the misinformation proposed by defenders of an omnivorous diet. It is in fact the alkaline element magnesium (found in highest concentrations in greens and vegetable source foods), that facilitates the absorption and assimilation of calcium. It plays the role of keeping calcium where it belongs, which is bound to teeth and bones. (Without magnesium we would not have our strong tooth enamel and our teeth and bones would be like chalk.) <http://www.shirleys-wellness-cafe.com/magnesium.htm>

<http://www.mgwater.com/rod15.shtml>

If acid forming minerals were used to chelate out calcium deposits (some that combine with cholesterol; hardening of the arteries, kidney and gall stones, also joint deposits and heel spurs, inner ear deposits etc.) instead of magnesium, it would only result in more insoluble salts (as the teeth and bones also dissolve), which must be filtered from the blood by the kidneys (often resulting in kidney stones). These circulating salts in the bloodstream, resulting from magnesium imbalance, are responsible for arteriosclerosis, gall stones, joint deposits, and bone spurs. *Magnesium's Impact on Health and Vitality.* <http://adam.about.com/reports/000081_2.htm> Last, Walter. *Magnesium Chloride for Health and Rejuvenation.* <http://www.life-enthusiast.com/twilight/research_magnesiumchloride.htm>

Research has shown that magnesium is ideally to be consumed in a 2:1 ratio to calcium, the ratio that occurs naturally in dark green leafy vegetables. The caveat is that it is necessary to avoid greens high in oxalic acid. (an organic compound, not a mineral acid) The most common dark greens that meet this qualification are, dandelion, kale, mustard, collard, and turnip. Occasional consumption of those high in oxalic acid can, however, be used temporarily as a chelating agent to remove calcium deposits.

> "The one being yet unfirm in belief, you should not be getting into a discrimination of reasonings. Who indeed believes in eating all things? The one who is unfirm (ill) eats greens." Rom. 14:1-2

In the OT story about the time after the Adam could no longer live in the Paradisiacal Garden of Eden, they were compelled to begin farming to produce enough food to fuel their newly acquired larger brains, inherited from the sons of the Elohim. These large brains required abundant complex carbohydrates (bread) for the extra energy necessary and the protective alkaline minerals in vegetation, to function properly.

> "Vegetarians are more intelligent, says study"…"A study of thousands of men and women revealed that those who stick to a vegetarian diet have IQs that are around five points higher than those who regularly eat meat. Writing in the British Medical Journal, the researchers say it isn't clear why veggies are brainier - but admit the fruit and veg-rich vegetarian diet could somehow boost brain power. The researchers, from the University of Southampton, tracked the fortunes of more than 8,000 volunteers for 20 years." <http://www.thisislondon.co.uk/news/article-23378331-details/Vegetarians+are+more+intelligent,+says+study/article.do>

The argument that it was the act of eating animal protein that increased our brain size, and thus our intelligence, is now clearly disputed by the physical chemistry that has revealed the *harmful* effect of high levels of acids from meat, on brain health. It is now clearly understood that humans can acquire the eight essential amino acids, to make complete protein, from plant based foods that do not bring with it this consequence. So even if a high protein diet might contribute to the growth of the brain, it concurrently detracts from our very ability to continue using it, by creating early onset Alzheimer's. And intelligence has not been shown to be correlated with a larger brain; if larger brains meant greater intelligence then elephants would be smarter than humans.

It is perhaps this law of cause and effect concerning the effect on our souls, to which the ancients referred to in the following rebuke and warning given at the time when humans began to eat flesh after the flood."And fear of you and dismay of you shall be on all of animals of the earth...Every moving animal which lives, to you he is *becoming* for food, (just) as the green herbs I gave to you all. Flesh in which is the soul and blood you shall not eat. And yes, _your blood and souls, of you I shall require_ from hand of every of animal I shall require him." Gen. 9:2-5

Note that it was at this time that animals were becoming food for humans, as the green plants already were. It was also after man was told that if he must eat flesh, the directive to only eat clean animals was explained, and this was understood as far back as the time of Noah. (Gen. 7:2) After this the life span of humans lessened from the exceedingly long years attributed to humans from the time of the Adam. So while eating meat may have, at times, been a necessity for primitive man, after he no longer dwelt in the paradise of the new earth, abstaining from killing anything is the ultimate state to which we will return.

> "The wolf (now dogs) shall dwell with the lamb, and the leopard shall lie down with the kid, and the calf and the young lion and the fatling (domestic animal) together: and a little child shall lead them...They shall not _hurt or destroy_ in all my holy mountain: for the earth shall be full of the knowledge of YHWH, as the waters cover the sea." Isa. 11:6-9

Certainly at no time was man commanded to eat meat and even when clean animals were temporarily allowed, that act came with severe consequences. When the Israelites were in the wilderness, animals could only be slaughtered and eaten as part of the sacrificial service performed by trained servers. This was so that it would not be practiced, randomly without the proper hygienic precautions and removing the blood and fat, and then only when it was necessary for survival, and since without refrigeration it could not be kept, it was then distributed by the servers to those in need. (Lev. 17:3-5)

Aaron and his sons thereafter, were over the Levite servers in the tabernacle of the congregation who kept the laws concerning this practice of sacrifice among those of the Israelites who ate flesh. Lev. 1:7-8 And it was Aaron who clearly lacked an understanding of the power of YHVH and His Elohim to save His people, for Aaron then led the Israelites to fashion a golden calf, and pray to it.

This is an illogical act, that most anyone today would see as a somewhat stupid and futile recourse, but those whose judgment had been clouded by years of meat eating while in slavery, saw nothing illogical in believing that a golden statue of a calf could somehow save them.

This is an example of the power of graven images to influence the un-discerning. The power of images over the un-discerning is still prevalent today and has moved the whole world to worship the "movie stars" who are often no different from the person next door, but through promotion, lighting, makeup, fashion, wealth and other accouterments, they are made to appear so.

These "models" must appeal to the desire of males (to have a frail naive female, anxious to appear weak and so boost the male ego and his appearance of being an "alpha male") or conversely, the desire of females to find a powerful male who will provide for her and protect her from the necessity of facing her fears. All of these impulses arise from the fear generated by the reptile brain, not from the use of logic or the intelligence we acquired from the Elohim.

Prejudice against compassionate vegetarians is not something that ceased in the past, it continues to this day because of the hatred flesh addicts feel for themselves. This becomes magnified when they try to drown their negative emotions in the addictive pleasure they feel eating meat, so they often explode their self-hatred outward when discussing these issues. When they are placed in a position where they have to consider their cruelty, and their own self induced diseases, they project their own revulsion for themselves onto anyone who makes an effort to live a healthy lifestyle, rather than take responsibility for their own condition. This process of projection, as a defense mechanism, is well established in psychology.

Other forms of prejudice are no longer condoned, it is high time that society stops verbally attacking vegetarians, simply because they have found a healthier lifestyle, for the guilt and self-loathing felt by those indulging in the very cause of their self inflicted diseases. Diseases from which Yeschu/Joshu/Jesus tried to free them, when he taught forgiveness of sin, freeing each one from feeling bad because of their past sins and showing them the power this new start has to affect healing in conjunction with fasting (abstention) and prayer. (Matt. 17:21 & Mark 9:29)

This self-loathing (sometimes called boredom) is at the root of all addictions, whether it be for alcohol/drugs, food/gluttony, power/control, money/possessions, fame/attention/sex or any other form of escape from emotional pain. Instead of arguing philosophies, we all need to be open-minded enough to rationally debate ALL the evidence as to which lifestyle is healthier, and not just the rebuttal studies funded by vested interests[5] which surface every time another disease is attributed to diet and animal source "foods." Even then it is still a matter of choice, but society should not be expected to take care of individuals who destroy their own ability to remain functioning and coherent members of society, by consuming flesh "foods." [5]see Robbins, John. *Diet For a New America.*

B12 FROM MICROORGANISMS

Many will argue that the need for B12 would indicate a dependence on animal products for food. But this is due to a lack of understanding of the origin of B12; it *always* originates from microorganisms, even in the case of the B12 found in beef. It starts with micro-organisms, like lactobacillus acidophilus, found in the stomach of the cows, which is then absorbed by the cow, a completely vegetarian animal who manages to obtain an abundance of B12 without eating meat.

Proponents of eating meat often cite information showing that B12 deficiency has been correlated with Alzheimer's and also with smaller brain size in vegetarians. While it is true that modern vegetarians should probably supplement B12, because the source available to ancient man is contaminated. That source is the microorganisms on the surface of the vegetation eaten by the cow and other vegetarian animals. Since cooking and other forms of processing destroys these microorganisms modern vegetarians often need this supplementation but this does not mean that vegetarian animals have no source of B12 only that it is often no longer present in modern diets.

These microorganisms are present in breast milk and thereafter in the digestive tract of humans and when properly cultured in the presence of the mineral cobalt, without the presence of destructive artificial chemicals, chlorine etc., they can provide humans with B12, as well. Vegan humans and primates were tested for three years and found to have high to normal levels of B12 and in vitro the extracted organisms were shown to manufacture B12. *You Are What You Eat.* <http://community.channel4.com/eve/forums/a/tpc/f/258603069/m/5090081959>

These micro-organisms are found in rain water, in ground water, in the soil, on the surface of plants, and in various ferments. They are cultivated from ferments containing microorganisms to provide most of the B12 sold as supplements. Since we no longer drink ground water or rain water, nor is it fit to drink because of pollution, we are now dependent on cultivated forms, but this does not mean that humans were not originally capable of deriving B12 from vegan sources without resorting to flesh foods. *Vegan Fitness. B12 question.*

<http://www.veganfitness.net/forum/viewtopic.php?p=147393&sid=b5b80a64fe344cb6a77b...>

Adversaries of refraining from killing and eating animals have used the misinterpretation of *broma,* actually meaning food, but wrongly given as meat in the KJV of 1 Tim. 4:1-4&12 John 4:34 and elsewhere, to continue arguing the scribes stance in favor of killing animals for meat. Romans 14:15 & 21 make the distinction clear between the two words; using *broma* in verse 15 which is actually food in general and then deliberately changing to another word when specifying meat in verse 21, *kreas,* the Greek word used to specify meat as distinct from food in general. "The present Bible is translated from the Greek and all words in the Gospels, which have been translated as meat (fleshmeats) and appear to implicate the Master, do in fact mean no such thing. They are (used several times each): - *Broma,* which is simply food; *Brosimos,* that which may be eaten; *Brosis,* food or the act of eating; *Prosphagion,* any thing to eat; *Trophe,* nourishment, and *Phago,* to eat. All these Greek words have been rendered as meat, showing how a translator of no understanding of the attributes of a divine man can betray a vital aspect of truth." G.L.R. *Religious Considerations.*

<http://www.ivu.org/congress/wvc57/souvenir/religious.html>
<http://www.scripture4all.org/OnlineInterlinear/Greek_Index.htm>

> "In the latter times some shall depart from the faith, giving heed to spirits who have strayed and the teachings of demons. In hypocrisy of false sayings...Forbidding marriage and to be abstaining from *broma*-foods which God created...Every creature of God is good and *NOT* yet one 'cast from' (rejected) taken up with thanksgiving. It is holy through the word of God and in pleading these things you shall be to the brothers an ideal servant of Iesous anointed ..Become a model to those believing in this saying, in behavior, in love, in belief in purity. " 1 Tim. 4:1-4&12

This was incorrectly translated; "demons...forbidding marriage and *commanding to abstain from*

224

meats." In light of this correction it can be seen that the change in this verse was one of the very deceptions predicted by Timothy's warning about "giving heed to spirits who have strayed." When reinstated properly it clearly means not to abstain from the foods originally created, for humans in the beginning, that is, that health giving seeds and fruit were not to be abstained from, (as per Gen. 1:29 above). Another is in Luke 8:55 "And her spirit came again, and she arose instantly and he commanded to her to be given something to eat." This was changed to "he commanded to give her meat."

<http://www.scripture4all.org/OnlineInterlinear/Greek_Index.htm>

As mentioned in chapter one the residue of the acid ammonium, from a high protein diet causes a variety of symptoms in those individuals, born with a rhesus negative blood type, when their parents carried a recessive rhesus negative gene. When they are born with the biochemistry of the sons of the Elohim, without eating the same vegetarian diet the sons of the Elohim ate and that the Adam ate (as primitive primates do see previous section on CAIN AND ABEL) before they left the Garden of Eden, they suffer a variety of "dis-ease" consequences.

Until recently, no one knew the function of the Rhesus factor. In Nature Genetics, however, scientists from Belgium, France and Italy report that one of its components, RhAG, transports ammonium ions through the cell membrane. The Rhesus factor consists of several parts, RhD, RhCE and RhAG, and only RhD is missing in Rhesus-negative individuals. The researchers found that RhAG is similar in amino acid sequence to a family of ammonium ($NH4+$) transporters not found in vertebrates. RhAG was able to provide transportation to eliminate toxic methylammonium as well as excess ammonium out of the cells.

In humans, ammonium is mainly a waste product and becomes toxic at high blood concentrations. Because the Rh factor helps control levels of ammonia in the blood, persons with Rh neg. blood type often exhibit dis-ease symptoms when they attempt the consume the high protein diet consumed by modern man (ammonia is a by product of amino acids, which comprise proteins). That diet does not so rapidly create these dis-ease symptoms in Rh pos. persons. But over the course of time their bodies break down eventually when the correct ratio of alkaline to acid is not preserved. This coupled with the build up of cholesterol and antigen producing foreign proteins cause countless auto immune diseases and adds many chronic diseases to those contagious diseases often transmitted from animals to man. Karow, Julia. *A Role for the Rhesus Factor.*

<http://www.scientificamerican.com/article.cfm?chanID=sa003&articleID=000D1546-E506-1C67-B882809EC588ED9F>

Ammonia is a base. When ammonia (which has a chemical formula of NH_3) dissolves in water (chemical formula H_2O) it forms a solution of ammonium hydroxide (NH_4OH). Ammonium hydroxide is a chemical relative of other bases like sodium hydroxide (lye). However, the ammonium ion can act as a very weak Bronsted-Lowry acid in the sense that it can protonate a stronger base (alkaline) using any one of its hydrogen (H) atoms and convert back to ammonia. This means that the ammonium ion is a conjugate acid of the base ammonia. Wikipedia. *Ammonium.* <http://www.en.wikipedia.org/wiki/Ammonium>

The biblical story of Daniel is also one which many do not completely understand because the archaic word "pulse" is an ancient Hebrew term for vegetables, or rather seeds from vegetation, i.e. grains like oatmeal, with this understanding in place it is easier to see the significance of Daniel's challenge to the king's servants.

> "Daniel had determined that he would not defile his body with the king's meat, nor with his wine, therefore he requested of the chief eunuch that he be allowed to not pollute himself...And the chief of the eunuchs said; I fear the king, who has appointed your meat and drink...Then Daniel said...Put your servants to the test, but let us have pulse to eat, and water to drink...At the end of ten days their countenances appeared fairer and fatter than all who ate the king's meat.....And in all matters of wisdom and understanding, that the king inquired of them, he found them ten times better than all the magicians and astrologers that were in all the realm." Dan 1:8-20

> "Yes every pot in Jerusalem and in Judah shall be holy unto YHWH and all them that sacrifice shall come and take of them and seeth therein, and in that day there shall be no more Canaanite[6] (*Knoni*) in the house of YHWH of hosts." Zech. 14:21 ([6]SHD 6061 *anakim* in the OT, or Neanderthals, known as giants, another name for the Canaanites)

DISEASES WITH A CORRELATED AND STUDIED INCIDENCE, RELATED TO ANIMAL FOOD DIETS

¾Acidic conditions: Anxiety attacks[7], heartburn, ulcers, stress[7] and nerve damage, gout, muscle tension[7]. [7]Because alkaline minerals help in relaxation.

¾Auto immune disorders: Arteriosclerosis, Arthritic Rheumatism (increased incidence of swollen joints with milk allergies).

¾Congestion (primarily from milk products, just as drinking milk creates phlegm, this phlegm is white blood cells passing through mucus membranes in response to an allergen) : allergies, asthma, bronchitis, influenza, and pneumonia.

¾Cancer: colon, lung, pancreatic, prostrate, breast, uterine (see section on Cancer).

¾Constipation (from lack of fiber not present in animal foods): irritable bowel syndrome, diverticulitis, hemorrhoids, Candida, enzyme depletion.

¾Diabetes (high fat diets increase insulin resistance), pancreatic inflammation (from putrefying meat).

¾Food Poisoning from bacteria in meats, (low fiber also increases transition time and putrefaction leading to cancer etc.).

¾Gall stones (from cholesterol and calcium), kidney stones (from uric acid, found in high protein diets).

¾Heart disease, hypertension/high blood pressure (aggravated by cholesterol blocking arteries).

¾Leukemia (increased rate among those with a history of contact with animals like sheep, cow, and poultry) <http://semj.sums.ac.ir/vol9/jan2008/leukemia.htm>

¾Multiple sclerosis (damage to the phospho-lipid coating of the sclera, by free radicals and acid forming minerals, normally protected by healthy fats like vitamin E).

¾Obesity (accelerated by a high fat diet from animal fats).

¾Osteoporosis (the abundance of the acid minerals phosphorus,[8] sulfur, and chlorine actually leach calcium from bones). [8]Found in a 8:1 ratio to calcium in milk, leaving 7 extra mg of phos. for each mg of calcium, excess phos. leaches alkaline minerals like calcium from the body.

¾Psoriasis (itching and irritation is aggravated by the highly acid forming mineral content in animal foods, excreted through the skin) and a high protein diet accelerates plaque cellular growth rates.

¾Pesticide and hormone poisoning and DNA damage[9] leading to cancer ([9]from exposure to poisons).

¾Stroke (from lack of enzymes that keep blood from becoming too sticky).

¾Tooth decay (from the high acid mineral content in animal proteins which leach calcium and magnesium from tooth enamel).

¾Varicose veins (aggravated by pressure from constipation with low fiber diets, which prevents venous blood from returning easily to the heart).

¾Vision problems, blindness (low vegetable intake to provide vitamin carotenes; blindness associated with powdered milk consumption in poor countries caused so many cases of blindness that manufacturers of milk began supplementing milk with vitamins A & D).

For citations and references see *Diet for a New America,* by John Robbins; Prevention Magazine; *Food Reform our Desperate Need,* by Robin Hur; <http://www.goveg.com> The Meat-Disease Connection; <http://www.diseaseproof.com/archives/cancer-the-meatdisease-connection.html>

This video is especially informative on the subject of diet and disease. "Vegan diet benefits to the top 15 causes of death." <http://nutritionfacts.org/video/uprooting-the-leading-causes-of-death/>

LIFE NOT SUBJECT TO DESTRUCTION/HEALTH

"For if perfection had been according to the Levitical priesthood...what further need was there that another priest ...According to the likeness of Melchisedek, there is one standing up who is different. Who is not (teaching) according to the law of the precepts of the carnal (flesh) ones (the Levites) but according to the ability of <u>life indissoluble[9]</u> <u>(health)</u>...For the (carnal) law makes <u>high priests (of the Levites) who have infirmities</u>." Heb. 7:15-16 & 28, [9]this has been translated as life everlasting, but life everlasting is actually to be found elsewhere to be life "*eonian*" not life "*akatalutos,*" which means not subject to destruction. <http://www.scripture4all.org/OnlineInterlinear/Greek_Index.htm> *Akatalutos/Akatalutov.* <http://devel.searchgodsword.org/lex/grk/view.cgi?number=179>

It was an understanding of the relationship between diet and disease that moved Yeschu/Joshu/Jesus to make mention of the healing power of abstention. "These things cannot be healed except through prayer *and* fasting." (Matt. 17:21 & Mark 9:29) While most diseases are exacerbated by indulging in excesses, not everyone will develop the same "dis-ease" symptoms. This is because overindulgence will weaken each individual according to his genetically predisposed weaknesses, some may even escape with impunity right through to old age, but it is like playing Russian roulette, one can never completely predict which symptoms will arise.

Since fundamentalists like to claim that Jesus as God was all powerful (omni-potent) and interpret John 14:13-14, "And I WILL DO whatever you ask IN MY NAME, so that the Son may bring glory to the Father. You may ask ME for anything in my name, AND I WILL DO IT." This is taken to mean that he could do anything or heal anything. As mentioned before the verse about fasting and prayer has been taken out of some Bibles to avoid facing the understanding that Yeschu/Joshu/Jesus was subject to and could not overrule the Father's will (1 Cor. 15:28) and thus had to observe YHVH's laws just as other created beings. Interpreted in the light of Yeschu/Joshu/Jesus' inability to heal some diseases as in Mark 9:29, it clearly means that he was *willing* to do anything that he COULD do, i.e., anything that was in accord with the Father's will and His plan for us, but some things require fasting or abstention, or that is action on our part.

This is in direct conflict with the position of many in organized religion, by which they acquire followers looking for any easy way to be saved from the consequences of their own actions. Some representatives of various religious groups entice followers with the offer of an easy escape from responsibility for their own health and sins by depending on faith alone and salvation by faith without works. But the NT in James (brother to Yeschu/Joshu/Jesus) says "Faith without works is dead." James 2: 14-18

The traditional approach often interprets scripture to promote the position that all that is necessary is to believe, as the disciple John says in John 3:16, but even Yeschu/Joshu/Jesus himself says differently; "Not everyone who comes to me saying Lord, Lord will enter the kingdom of heaven, but he who DOES the will of the Father." Matthew 7:21 Do they really think YHVH, YHVH's Elohim, and/or YHVH's angels will continually keep coming back and healing them of their newly self inflicted illnesses in the kingdom come? A good example is those who must keep going back for bypass operations after they have clogged up their arteries again, do they think they will be able to eat cholesterol with impunity?

Persons afflicted with disease often rail against an unfair God thinking that it is He who causes people to suffer, asking how God could allow such suffering, including the suffering of innocent babies and children. But YHVH fairly warns, "…YHWH El, compassionate and gracious, slow to anger, and abounding in loving-kindness…yet He will by no means leave the guilty unpunished, visiting the iniquity of the fathers on the children and on the grandchildren to the third and fourth generations." (Exodus 34:6-7)

From this may be seen that the poor health we acquire by not following His laws, is also often inflicted on our innocent offspring in coming generations, (as in Toxoplasmosis) but this is our doing, not His. If we had chosen healthy lifestyles following the original diet in Gen. 1:29, this damage to our offspring and ourselves could have been prevented; this can be concluded also from information showing that diet alters our DNA.

National Jewish Health. *Mother's Diet Alters DNA...*

<http://www.nationaljewish.org/about/mediacenter/pressreleases/2008/asthma-epigenetics2.aspx>;

The Journal of Nutrition. *A Folate- and Methyl-Deficient Diet Alters the Expression of DNA...*

<http://jn.nutrition.org/cgi/content/full/136/6/1522>;

Baylor College of Medicine. *Mother's diet alters physical appearance in offspring...* <http://www.bcm.edu/news/item.cfm?newsID=696>;

NIEHS. *Diet and Genetic Damage.*<http://clinicaltrials.gov/ct2/show/NCT00340743>

Toxoplasmosis. <http://www.hpa.org.uk/infections/topics_az/zoonoses/toxoplasma/geninfo.htm> James and Yin. *Diet-Induced DNA Damage*

<http://www.carcin.oxfordjournals.org/cgi/content/abstract/10/7/1209>

<http://www.google.com/search?hl=en&q=diet+alters+DNA&btnG=Search>

It was the will of the Father, YHVH the Great Holy Spirit of the Infinite Creator, who decided the biological type of body we were to have, i.e., bodies are of the primate type (as apposed to bovine, canine, feline, equine, porcine, etc.). Primates rarely or never eat flesh and certainly *never* eat large cholesterol laden beasts. I.e., herbivores are healthy eating only plants; carnivores are healthy eating only meat; primates (like us) are perfectly healthy eating vegetation, fruits, and seeds as in Gen. 1:29. We cannot through belief change YHVH's creation of our body type, into a type that safely handles the diet of a natural born carnivore, like a lion, tiger or wolf, (of the feline and canine types) or for that matter to handle the diet of a horse or cow (equine and bovine herbivores who eat grass) since we are bound by the will of our Creator to follow our own biological limitations, that is, what we were created to be. So Yeschu/Joshu/Jesus could not overcome conditions that we continued to aggravate by refusing to change unhealthy diet habits, for that persons unhealthy diet would just change it right back again to a dis-ease condition.

Our body type is more like the other, mostly vegetation eating higher primates, than for example a herbivore designed to eat grass, or a large carnivore, designed to kill large animals. The level of stomach acid among carnivores is twenty times higher than ours, this kills the associated bacteria which causes food poisonings in humans. The level of anti bodies in the saliva of carnivores is also twenty times higher than ours, from which the myth of their clean mouth possibly arose.

They have a short, rapidly moving digestive tract that allows them to move decaying flesh quickly through, before it has time to become toxic. Fecal matter has been shown in animal studies to cause cancer when kept in prolonged contact with the skin. Rieger, Parlesak, Pool-Zobel, Rechkemmer, Bode. *A Diet High in Fat and Meat...*

<http://www.carcin.oxfordjournals.org/cgi/content/abstract/20/12/2311>

They have the teeth, jaws, claws and speed necessary to bring down large animals, something which no primate, not even a three hundred pound muscular gorilla can do. When the higher primates occasionally kill and eat meat, it is usually only small animals (lower in cholesterol) and then only rarely do they eat other creatures.

> "Doctor Group Estimates Real Price Of Meat. U.S. health care costs could be reduced by $29 billion to $61 billion a year if Americans cut meat out of their diet, according to researchers from the Physicians' Committee for Responsible Medicine. 'The health effects of an omnivorous diet may result from the presence of meat, the displacement of plant foods, or both.' wrote the researchers. In every study examined meat eaters were more likely to suffer from serious health problems." *Preventive Medicine Nov.* 1995

CANCER

It would be impossible in a book of this size to address every disease with a connection to dietary causes from animal foods but the big scare, cancer, certainly deserves some focus. Dr. Gio B. Gori, the Deputy Director of the National Cancer Institute's Division of Cancer Cause and Prevention, when asked what are the chief culprits involved in causing cancer, stated; "Until recently, many eyebrows would have been raised by the suggesting that an imbalance of normal dietary components could lead to cancer and cardiovascular disease...Today, the accumulation of evidence makes this notion not only possible but certain...(the) dietary factors responsible (are) principally meat and fat intake." (Robbins, 1987, p. 252, quoting Sussman, 1998)

The Journal of the National Cancer Institute reported; "There is not a single population in the world with a high meat intake which does not have a high rate of colon cancer." (54:7, 1975) That the cause was not hereditary was demonstrated by studies showing an increase in cancer incidence among Japanese who converted to a more American diet.

> "Red Meat Cancer Risk Found. Scientists at the MRC Dunn Human Nutrition Unit and the Open University compared red meat and vegetarian diets. Their study, published in Cancer research, found the red meat diet was associated with a higher level of DNA damage." BBC News. *Red Meat Linked to Cancer Risk.*
>
> <http://news.bbc.co.uk/2/hi/health/4088824.stm>

John Robbins took a stand that jeopardized his profits from the Baskin/Robbins empire to bring forward extensive information confirming that at every step of the way as medical science advanced its understanding, meat and dairy associations and national boards, funded "research studies" of their own countering the previous independent studies showing the harmful effects of animal source foods, that threatened to affect their profits; so if anyone can be said to not have a financial interest in diet research it would be him. This dis-information has now thoroughly confused the uneducated public, who after reading this propaganda, frequently revert to their original preferences, however harmful. Robbins, John. *Diet for a New America.*

"Carnitine, Choline, Cancer and Cholesterol: The TMAO Connection. A landmark new article in the New England Journal of Medicine shows that choline in eggs, poultry, dairy and fish produces the same toxic TMAO as carnitine in red meat, which may help explain plant-based protection from heart disease and prostate cancer... The TMAO story is such a fascinating twist. It helps explain, for example, Harvard's Meat and Mortality Studies. The role of the inflammatory "foam" cells (so-called because they're so packed with cholesterol they look foamy under a microscope) affected by TMAO is explained in my video series that starts with Arterial Acne and Blocking the First Step of Heart Disease."

<http://nutritionfacts.org/video/carnitine-choline-cancer-and-cholesterol-the-tmao-connection/?utm_source=rss&utm_medium=rss&utm_campaign=carnitine-choline-cancer-and-cholesterol-the-tmao-connection&utm_source=NutritionFacts.org&utm_campaign=bfb9e35001-RSS_VIDEO_DAILY&utm_medium=email>

Since the connection between diet and disease could fill many books, for the purposes of the present discussion, rather than go into further details in that area it seems wiser to simply point the reader in the direction of some of the pre-existing reports to be found in published books (in most health food stores) mentioned above especially the writings of John Robbins. He stood only to gain from following in the footsteps of his family's Baskin/Robbins empire and defending the benefits of animal foods, yet, commendably, in the interest of truth he choose to inform the world of the harmful effects of animal foods.

Besides the arguments against eating a plant based diet mentioned previously, it has been pointed out that many plants contain toxins harmful to humans. While this is true, it should be noted that these occur in the parts of the plant which the plant wants to protect from being consumed, not in the parts of plants which (because of their symbiotic relationship with animals) the plants have actually made enticing to any creature who will carry and cultivate the seeds (through attractive fragrances, flavors, nutrients, and colors).

These are the fruits and nuts in the high growing trees, these are among the very foods mentioned in the Bible as our first foods. Fruits and nuts do not contain the kinds of toxins seen in the body of the plant. Some seeds, like peanuts which grow in the ground may contain toxins, and develop mold toxins; and cashews may be problematic for some as they contain allergens being members of the same family as poison ivy and sumac.

Grains and legumes were included in the first allowed foods in Gen. 1:29, as well as the fruit of trees and the seeds in them (nuts); humans were given the herbs (plants) and the seed (grains and beans) of plants for food. While grains and legumes contain some toxins (like pyrrolizidine alkaloids and legume toxins like hemagluttins and anti-trypsin, they are not deadly) they do not contain the high levels of fat and the iron and copper that meat contains. They are thus prevented from destroying our intelligence, making it possible for the elders to be the teachers they were meant to be.

So fruit and nuts are ideal foods for human primates, because they contain no harmful toxins and actually include helpful substances that fight many diseases, including anti-virals (like in concord grapes and elderberries) and natural antibiotics (like in grapefruit and cranberry).

The reason no fresh raw fruits and vegetables are ever considered as "comfort foods" is because the desire for comfort foods arises from the fear and insecurity generated by the reptile brain, when there is no fear there is no need for comfort. The desire to be secure and comforted brings memories of times of plenty and "feasts" and the tendency to lethargy and "slumber[10]" induced by heavy foods These memories trigger digestive enzymes and insulin etc. that accompanies voracious appetites. In order to overcome the impulses of the reptile brain, it is first necessary to come to terms with psychological insecurities. [10]Prov. 23:20

PLACEBOS, FAITH AND PRAYER

"According to your faith be it unto you." Matt. 9:29

For healing any disease that has arisen from addiction, faith is necessary, and the importance of faith was emphasized by Yeschu/Joshu/Jesus. This is why he said that it was according to ones faith; he did not just grant healing without repeatedly making it clear that the person's own faith was a factor (Matt. 8:13; Matthew 9:21-22). The importance of faith has been demonstrated repeatedly by science. It was because of the power of faith or belief that the "double blind placebo controlled study" became necessary. Just the belief that one will get well influences the outcome of trials of experimental drugs. Even the belief or faith of the practitioner can influence the outcome of a trial; so the doctors as well must be kept from knowing who is to receive the medicine and who the placebo, hence the term "double blind."

Prayer has been tested and found to accelerate healing in studies. In various experiments it was found that prayed for rye-grass grew taller, yeast resisted cyanide toxicity, bacteria grew faster, and seeds germinated better. In his 1994 book, "Healing Words" Larry Dossey, M.D. says, "I adore these experiments because they don't involve humans, you can run them with fanatical precision and you can run them hundreds of times." These experiments show that it is not all in the minds of the subjects, or psycho somatic, since these living things cannot be accused of having religious beliefs. The experiments showed that a simple, "Thy will be done." approach was quantitatively more powerful than when specific results were held in mind. *The Proof that Prayer Works.* <http://1stholistic.com/Prayer/hol_prayer_proof.htm>

<http://archinte.ama-assn.org/cgi/content/abstract/159/19/2273>

The segments of the OT that address the understanding that YHVH desires mercy (rather than for us to sacrifice animals and fulfill an appetite for flesh), are among the hidden mysteries that Yeschu/Joshu/Jesus referred to. Also included are the power of faith, and an understanding that we are descended from the "gods" and have inherited their power to be intelligent and use discernment when considering what is "good and evil."

If we are to advance we must not continue allowing ourselves to be ruled by the serpent brain. Again teaching humanity of this lost knowledge will help us restore our oneness/*echad,* our power, through supplication of YHVH and His council of Elohim, and through removal of unnecessary so-called "foods" we can restore our mental and physical health.

232

These "foods" are not really human food at all but simply a temporary recourse to which humanity had access in primitive times, these must be put aside when YHVH's kingdom of the Heavens comes on earth, for then we shall no longer hurt the animals as killing them for food does;

> "The lion shall lie down with the lamb... and <u>they shall not hurt or destroy</u> in all my holy mountain: for the earth shall be full of the knowledge of YHWH, as the waters cover the sea." Isa. 11:6-9

JUDGE NOT

> "Judge not lest you be judged." Matt. 7:1

The understanding of the effects of diet upon health should not be used to cast others into despair, hate the sin not the sinner. To explain the power of YHVH's original plan, is meant to free others; to hatefully criticize can only reinforce the heritage of sin, which is self judgment, depression and addictive escapes. Rather we should reinforce and remind each other "know ye not that ye are gods?" to bring out the highest that each should remember to reach for, remembering that no one is perfect, only YHVH the Great Holy Spirit is All Perfect.

> "Why do you call me good? No one is good except God (Theos)." Mark 10:18 This is Yeschu/Joshu/Jesus speaking.

But we also must not demand others to avoid speaking of the understanding of the disease consequences of food choices because we are in denial about our addiction to certain habits. Responsibility for our "sins" (a word which literally means mistakes) may not be the easy way out some are looking for, to bring about the kingdom come to earth, but how can anyone think they will acquire the power to become like the "gods" if they do not accept responsibility for maintaining the their own health and therefore also the condition of their brains? Do they think YHVH's Elohim will endlessly repair the damage their addictions continue to do?

Acceptance of our oneness and equality in YHVH, going beyond the opinions of our world, having faith that YHVH and His Elohim will help us in our times of distress, if we only begin to call on them, this is the answer to freedom from that heritage of sin, "the knowledge of good and evil," felt as self-loathing, depression, fear, suffering and addictive escapes including 'food' abuse. YHVH Elohim will turn the winds and change the minds of those in our paths, making our way smooth, whenever our will is submissive to YHVH and our goal is the betterment of our world, through the establishment of His kingdom.

THE HIDDEN MYSTERIES

> "The knowledge of the mysteries of the kingdom of heaven has been given to you, but to them it is not given." Matt. 13:11 also Mark 4:1

233

The changes made by the scribes in order to re-institute the regular practice of consuming flesh, demanding it of the people, in exchange for the so-called blessings of these false priests, and the lost understanding of the meaning of YHVH's holy name and our relationship to His council of Elohim, and that they visit us in their rides/merkabah/'chariots' are among "the hidden mysteries" to which Yeschu referred in his attempts to initiate his disciples.

> "Unto you it is given to know the mysteries of the kingdom of God: but to others in parables; that seeing they might not see, and hearing they might not understand. Now the parable is this: The seed is the word of God...For nothing is secret that will not be made manifest: Neither hidden that shall not be known and become apparent." Luke 8:10-11

Being godlike he understood that the adrenaline that floods the animal's body at its death, stimulates fear, paranoia and aggression generated by the reptile brain, when humans absorb the hormone adrenaline from the animals flesh. He therefore understood how dangerous the temper of meat-eaters can be, so he told his disciples that he could teach them the hidden mysteries but that he must teach the masses in parables so, "though hearing, they may not understand" Luke 8:10, and turn on him, killing him, before he had finished giving his message to the world. And it is for attempting to spread these clarifications of the obfuscations of the scribes and the false priests among the Jews, that he was murdered.

> "The Talmud declared categorically that Jesus had lived a century earlier. Quoting from the Talmud; 'When King Jannai...(who reigned over the Jews 104-78 BC)...directed the destruction of the Rabbis...Jechu went to Alexandria...And the Teacher has said; Jeschu had practiced sorcery...'. This famous passage taken by itself, would...fully confirm the hypothesis of a 100 years BC date for Jesus...(rather) than the date assigned to him by evangelists, and that instead of his being crucified in Jerusalem he was stoned at Lud." Mead, G. R. S. *Did Jesus Live 100 Years BC*, pp. 104,135-138.

The "black arts" that Jeschu was accused of studying, in those days were so named and understood to refer to the study of chemistry in Alexandria, because Egypt was known as "the black"; not because there was something sinister about them, that connotation came later. Half of Alexandria's extensive library, including their early knowledge of chemistry, was burned by Julius Caesar in 47 BC and a subsidiary library was later burned by Christians in 391 AD. (*Encyclopedia Britanica* Vol. 1 1984, p. 479) The word chemistry derives from a name for Egypt, in those times, Al-Khemet or Khamet/Hamet (from the descendants of Ham) *khemia* which meant "the black" was so named because of the black soil (and perhaps also because of the black people who lived there MHJ). This was combined with the Greek *kymatos,* meaning to pour, as a double entendre. It was ``from this word that the word alchemy was coined and from whence we derive the word chemistry. *Alchemy.*

<http://www.etymonline.com/index.php?search=alchemy&searchmode=none>

> "For nothing is hidden which shall not become apparent, neither is any thing hid that should not be known and become apparent." Luke 8:17

The Greeks, Chinese, and Indians usually referred to what westerners call alchemy as "The Art" or by terms denoting change or transmutation. Most historians, however, agree that the Egyptians were the first chemists. Their symbol the eye of Ra, became the Rx, meaning to take, and it is

234

still used to denote prescriptions. *Eye of Horus.*

<http://www.themystica.com/mystica/articles/e/eye_of_horus.html>

> *Earliest Reference Describes Christ as 'Magician'.* "A bowl, dating to between the late 2nd century B.C. and the early 1st century A.D., is engraved with what may be the world's first known reference to Christ. The engraving reads, 'DIA CHRSTOU O GOISTAIS[11],' which has been interpreted to mean either, 'by Christ the magician' or, 'the magician by Christ.'" (<http://dsc.discovery.com/news/2008/10/01/jesus-bowl.html>) Remember that the word magic derives from the magi of Zarathustra, see previous section on The Star That the Zarathustrian Magi Followed . [11]From the Greek <u>goēs</u>

St Austin (c. 380) asserted that it was generally known in church circles that Rabbi Jesus had been initiated in Egypt, and that "he wrote books concerning magic." According to an account of Celsus (from 117-138 AD, during Hadrians reign) preserved in a refutation of Origen, written sometime in the third century, one of the accusations leveled at Yeschu/Joshu/Jesus, called Rabbi by the Jewish scribes, was that he had gone to Alexandria in Egypt and learned magic, sorcery etc. According to Origen this was a common accusation among Jews. (Mead, G. R. S. *Did Jesus Live 100 Years BC,* p. 128) The Gospel of Nicodemus, the Jews brought the same accusation before Pontius Pilate, "Did we not tell you that he was a magician?" Adams, Robert. *What Was the Church Trying to Hide?*

<http://www.conspiracyplanet.com/review.cfm?rtype=22&reviewid=27&page=2>

> "Plato distinguished between two kinds of magic: popular magic, which is denigrated as sorcery, and authentic or "Persian magic" (from the magi) which is considered to be a form of religion, "the worship of the gods."...In ancient texts it was "*Ostanes the Magi*" who taught Democritus the art of alchemy...A comparable document from Hellenistic Egypt has convinced some investigators that Egyptian alchemy was rooted in Babylonian practices of a far greater age." Settegast, Mary. *When Zarathustra Spoke,* 2005, pp. 120 & 132 citing; Forbes, R. J., *The Origin of Alchemy in Studies in Ancient Technology I;* Eisler, R., *L'origine Babylonienne de l'Alchimie;* & Rey, A., *La Science Orientale Avant les Grecs.*

As mentioned previously the word magic derived from the "Magi" those wise men who had knowledge of the prediction of the appearance of a "star" (attrib. to Zarathustra) at the birth of a cosmic savior. The Magi and Chaldeans were renowned for their teachings of magic and alchemy, including the use of minerals and herbs, in those times these forms of "magic" were considered synonymous with science (by the Levites it was held to be heresy, they advocated faith in their religion of 'Adonai Elohim' and their priesthood practice of animal sacrifice, as the only acceptable remedies for illness.

Contrary to popular knowledge Alchemy was not all about changing lead into gold, another goal was the quest for immortality or as the NT calls it life indissoluble. (7:15-16) At least some of the Magi had inherited the understanding of Zarathustra's teaching of the importance of not eating meat, to the preservation of the brain and the life force within the body. *Wisemen of the East.* <http://www.thedyinggod.com/chaldeanmagi/index.html>

Without an understanding of chemistry, it is not possible to fully realize the effects of the intake of phosphoric acid and sulfur acid, in animal foods; and the prayer and the benefits of eating greens and fasting (little else remains of the teaching on life immutable of Yeschu/Joshu/Jesus in the NT). The taste of meat is salty (from the blood), which initially satisfies the craving for alkaline minerals to balance the high levels of acid residues from previous meat meals. Unfortunately this is only temporary since sodium cannot satisfy the deep cravings for magnesium, calcium and potassium which then accumulate ever greater deficiencies. Natural carnivores know to chew on bone and cartilage to address their need for these alkaline minerals but humans not being true carnivores do not do this.

The fact that the NT mentions that unfirm persons need to eat greens (Rom. 14:1-2) shows that Yeschu/Joshu/Jesus and his disciples were aware of the healing power of this incredibly alkaline food. His teachings on the necessity of prayer and fasting (Matt. 17:21 & Mark 9:29) also support his acceptance of the necessity of physical healing remedies in conjunction with prayer and spirituality.

It does no good to heal someone without teaching them anything about what they did to make themselves sick. So any good healer must also be a teacher, his patients must be taught to keep the "cup clean on the inside" and go and sin no more, if he does not want to keep redoing his work. So even if the charges of learning magic or alchemy in Egypt were true, a knowledge of chemistry and healing principles would simply be a complementary skill to augment the ability to heal spiritually, the exact combination of fasting and prayer that Yeschu/Joshu/Jesus advocated. (Matt. 17:21 & Mark 9:29)

THE SECRET OF THE KINGDOM OF HEAVEN

> "To you it has been given to know the secret of the kingdom of heaven" Matt. 13:11; Luke 8:10

The secret of the kingdom of heaven included the true rendering of all the miss-translations by the Levites, which Yeschu began to reveal before he was murdered, including his mention of our becoming "gods" when he quotes Ps. 82:6 (which uses the term Elohim-gods), in John 10:30-35. These mistranslations concealed who YHVH's Elohim were and the hidden knowledge of the murder of the first order of the true prophets of the host of heaven. Through those prophets the truth of our status as "gods" would have constituted our (now lost) connection to YHVH's Elohim and their periodic visitations to us.

The final reason why Yeschu/Joshu/Jesus was murdered, was in fact because when he said; "I and my father are one." He was trying to teach them of oneness "That all one they may be; as you, Father in me, and I in you, that they in us may be (All One)." (John 17:21), but they twisted his words and accused him of making himself god. Even after they sought to stone him he tried to teach them that even they are gods. (John 10:30-35) Besides understanding the true interpretation of Moses Record of Testimony carried in the ark, the unleavened bread-eating priests also knew the importance remaining vegetarian had to healthful chemistry. The efforts to cover-up this murder has held the world in darkness for the two and half millennium, and concealed the health advantages that can heal the world of most of their self-inflicted diseases.

This return to health will also help prevent DNA damage that will affect innocent children as we can also prevent many birth defects that contribute to inherited diseases. With the elimination of Alzheimer's far more earthlings will continue to retain their intelligence into old age and will thus be able to solve a great many other health problems. And last but not least the power of faith and prayer will again be able to help cure those diseases which are aggravated by psycho[12]-somatic influences. [12]Remember that psyche is Greek for soul.

Through surrender of self will to the Universal mind of All Truth, YHVH, the Great Holy Spirit of our Living Universe, and through oneness with His Elohim, we will regain the power to move the earth forward into a new age of peace, health, and through oneness we will achieve knowledge and power beyond any science can now even grasp. When earthlings see that all their opinions are conditioned, that their myriad likes and dislikes are as counterproductive as their reptile brain, creating only conflict, and a pointless waste of energy, then they can go beyond their own opinions and focus on facts and evidence concerning religion, rather than just perpetuating beliefs based purely on tradition.

Instead of focusing on the mere pursuit of pleasure, the unity of mind and the power that can then arise from uniting the consciousness of earthlings with the Light of YHVH and His Elohim, will result in a new condition capable of bringing about a system of health, unity and peace. That will be the kingdom come on earth as it is practiced throughout the heavens, by YHVH's Elohim, our lost brothers and sisters. That unity of mind and advanced state of knowledge will include the return of our ability to communicate with the spirit dimension. We must seek out and actively reintroduce the genetics of the Elohim who, like the early prophets could see and hear psychically, seeing and hearing in spirit. Only then will we come to understand and acquire the power to materialize and dematerialize ourselves and our starships, giving us the means to traverse the otherwise imponderable distances of interstellar space, as they have done forever.

Later still we will participate in the formation of new planetary systems from interstellar dust, becoming like the Elohim before us, helping YHVH prepare planets for The Great Holy Spirit to create new life-forms and even other Elohim-like humanoids. This understanding of our destiny, on the path to oneness with YHVH and his Elohim is perhaps the greatest of the hidden mysteries which has been concealed by those whose self interest has opened them up to the carnal influences of earth-bound spirits, with their limited earthbound viewpoints.

This collection of evidence supports only the version being presented here, obviously there are a great many other records and "gospels" etc. written by those who were not in a position, as Yeschu/Joshu/Jesus was, to know the secrets of the Kingdom of Heaven. Those are not addressed here, as they support the traditional interpretation which has been used, *ad nauseum,* to attract followers by teaching them to rely on faith alone and not teaching them to control the indulgence of their self-interests and appetites as Yeschu/Joshu/Jesus did when he taught "prayer *and* fasting." This has led to a multitude of diseases in their followers and a loss of faith in a God that brings suffering to the innocent; rather than realizing they have done it to themselves and their children by not following the will YHVH.

Chapter Ten

THE GREAT FLOOD

"These genealogical annals of Noah, *Noah man* (*nch aish*) righteous flawless he became in generations of him, with Elohim he walks, Noah." Gen. 6:9

WORLDWIDE SURVIVORS OF THE FLOOD

This chapter will discuss evidence concerning the flood story in the Bible and other flood stories found around the world. The Dead Sea Scrolls, 4Q370, tells much the same story of the great flood as the OT, but rather than the story of Noah and his ark, it simply tells how YHVH saw that the people of earth were evil, and so He flooded the earth.

> "And YHVH covered the land with fruits and gave them plenty of food and made every living thing content with the fruit. "May everyone who does as I ask be filled with food and be satisfied (1) ...But now they have done things that I believe are evil (2)...And the entire earth shook, and the waters overflowed from the gorges; all the entrance gates of the heavens opened up and the abysses overflowed from the strong waters;...And they were destroyed by the flood...everyone (3) died in the waters...Not even the strongest escaped...And YHVH made a (contract) and put a rainbow (in the clouds) to remember the contract he made with the people..." *Dead Sea Scrolls* 4Q370
>
> <http://www.history.upenn.edu/~humm/Resources/StudTxts/4Q370.html>

Does any of this mean that the story of the flood in biblical texts is not complete? The account found in the Dead Sea scrolls proves that there *was* more than one version of the account of the flood. Parts of the biblical flood story seem to indicate that it was not compiled directly from one single account by the survivors. The number of days of the Flood story does not add up right for one thing; and while Noah takes two of each animal; at another point, he takes two of some, seven of others.

That there are so many different statements as to how long it took before land appeared seems to indicate that there were originally many stories that someone attempted to combine. Gen. 8:3 says; "the waters were abated at the end of a hundred and fifty days" 8:4 says; "the ark rested, in the seventh month" whereas 8:5 says; "in the tenth month the mountain tops appeared" and 8:6 says; "at the end of forty days, and Noah...sent out a dove...it returned to him to the ark...he waited seven more days...the dove came to him...an olive leaf in its mouth...seven more...and it did not return...in the second month...the earth dried." (56-58)

The biblical Noah story begins by telling us that it is a genealogical annal of "Noah man" *nch aish,* and the righteous and flawless generations of *nch aish* (man-'iysh SHD 376 i.e., Noah man, humans of that era) who walked with the Elohim (note the plural predicator). Gen. 6:9 Rather perhaps it should be seen as one account of the great flood, compiled from the various accounts present with the Noah-man, *nch aish,* of Shem/India, Ham/Africa and Jaffeth/China. These stories they shared with each other, and being in general agreement in their understanding of the great flood, the variations later got compiled into one story of the three great peoples, the Shem/Semites, the Ham/Khemet (the ancient name for Egypt) and the Jaffeth/Asians descended from the *nch aish.*

More than 500 deluge legends are known around the world and, in a survey of 86 of these (20 Asiatic, 3 European, 7 African, 46 American and 10 from Australia and the Pacific) the specialist researcher Dr. Richard Andree concluded that 62 were entirely independent of the Mesopotamian (Encyclopedia of Religion, on Mesopotamian Religions, *The Atrahasis Epic,* from which the later Epic of Gilgamesh derived, p. 456) and Hebrew accounts. Each story was only told from the point of view of the survivors, believing they alone survived unaware that there were others far removed from themselves. <http://www.deusdiapente.net/science/flood.php>

THE FLOOD STORY OF THE AMERICAS

> "Memories of a terrible flood...are preserved in the *Popul Vuh* (from ancient Central America)...the Great God decided to create humanity...These creatures fell out of favor because they did not remember their Creator *And so a flood was brought by the Heart of Heaven...the face of the earth darkened and a black rain began to fall by day and by night*...Like the Aztecs and the Mechoacanesecs, the Maya of the Yucatan and Guatemala believed that a Noah figure and his wife...had survived the flood to populate the land anew." Hancock, Graham. *Fingerprints of the Gods,* p. 191-193.

The story of the Bering Straight crossing conveniently supports white history, making all Native Americans immigrants as well, thereby justifying the take over by Europeans. But the *Popul Vuh,* one of the few precious records not deliberately destroyed by the invaders represents red history, and that history has it that the red race has been here since the flood. Massive book burnings were carried out by zealous missionaries, of these irreplaceable records, because they were considered satanic or some such nonsense. However written in Native South American hieroglyphics, this story was already in existence before Columbus landed, so it is not possible that it was plagiarized from the Bible.

> "Paintings retracing the deluge...fixed by symbolic and mnemonic paintings before any contact with Europeans...have been discovered among the Aztecs (who speak Guatemalan), Miztecs, Zapotecs, Tiascaltecs, and Mechoacaneses. Corliss, William. *Unknown Earth,* p. 817, quoting F. Lenormant in *Contemporary Review.*

DNA has actually provided support for a combination of both stories. While there are sufficient markers to indicate an assortment of migrations from various places, there are also DNA markers that are unique to Native Americans that diverged as early as 30,000 years ago. Some Bering Straight theorists have tried to hypothesize a period of 15,000 years where the ancestors of Native Americans lived isolated from the Asians before populating the Americas. But if they succeeded in doing so they would have been the only people on the Asian continent to achieve such a state of genetic purity, a most unlikely and illogical assumption. (The Japanese achieved something close to this but they were island bound, and were not exclusively ancestral to Native Americans.) It is far more reasonable to suppose that the original red race also crossed the ocean in boats. Science Daily. *New Ideas About Human Migration from Asia to Americas.*

<http://www.sciencedaily.com/releases/2007/10/071025160653.htm>

"When did humans first come to the Americas." It's agreed that the majority of the first Americans were from Asian. How and when they got here is constantly changing. Up until a few years ago, 10,500 years ago was the standard. Now dates of 16,000 years ago are common and some go as far as 38,000 or 50,000 years back...Several of the theories share similar facts...The Pacific Route suggests that people sailed the South Pacific to colonize first South America, then migrated north into what is today North America." <http://answers.yahoo.com/question/index?qid=20080711071705AAZfhur>

> "Native American artifacts tell story of primitive cultures. University of South Carolina archeologist Albert Goodyear has discovered artifacts that, he says, indicate that there may have been humans in the area as long as 37,000 years prior to the Clovis people that were said to have arrived in America 13,000 years ago. While controversial, his discoveries are opening scientific minds to the possibility of pre-Clovis occupation of America." (Ross, 2012) <http://www.independentmail.com/news/2012/jan/29/native-american-artifacts-tell-story-primitive-cul/>

> "Humans in North America earlier than thought. The recent discovery of ancient tools in a Texas creek bed shows human settlers arrived in North America about 2,500 years earlier than originally believed, say archeologists. "We have found evidence of an early human occupation … 2,500 years older than Clovis," Michael Waters from Texas A&M University said in a release..."People [who lived at the site] could have experimented with stone and invented the weapons and tools that we now recognize as Clovis … In short, it is now time to abandon once and for all the 'Clovis First' model and develop a new model for the peopling of the Americas." (CBS New, 2011)

<http://www.cbc.ca/news/technology/story/2011/03/24/tech-clovis-texas-archeology.html>

> "New Signs In Brazil That Humans Landed In Americas Long Before We Thought. A scientific article by French and Brazilian researchers brings major new findings to the discussion on the date humans arrived to the American continent. It analyzed three archeological sites in Piauí, in northeastern Brazil, and shows evidence that the region was inhabited by humans 22,000 years ago. The researchers' discoveries, published in the "Journal of Archaeological Science", are yet other empirical evidence against the so-called "Clovis first" paradigm, the oldest theory of the occupation of the American continent. (Paulo, 2013)

<http://www.worldcrunch.com/tech-science/new-signs-in-brazil-that-humans-landed-in-americas-long-before-we-thought/brazil-excavations-archeology-piau-ice-age/c4s11488/#.UXfrGcqgCf0>

Who were the First Americans? The emerging answer suggests that they were NOT Asians who crossed a land bridge into Alaska eleven thousand five hundred years ago, as the textbooks say, but different ethnic groups, from places very different from what scientists thought even a few years ago. Characteristics include medium skin pigmentation, straight black hair, spare body hair, and a very low frequency of male pattern balding. In addition to the presence of blood type O, rather than the Asian B, in half the American Indians tested several other characteristics of their blood types set them apart from the Mongoloid peoples, with who they were sometimes classed in the past. Most Mongols have blood type B, this blood type only accounts for half of the picture among Native Americans.

Blood type B shows up in the Zuni, in "The Zuni Enigma" (2000) Nancy Yaw Davis. Because of other corresponding cultural influences, artistic designs etc., suggests it resulted from Japanese contact. This appears to be supported by Betty Megger's Jomon in Ecuador proposals (1995) (Jomon pottery from Japan, dates to 10-16,500 BCE, this implies the invention of the wheel at least 10,000 years BCE). As was mentioned before there are no genetic markers of the type found among the Jews, in the blood of American Indians, making a problem for the Mormon theory that Native Americans are a lost tribe of Israel. Blood type A, rare among Indians who are mostly type O, shows up in the North Peigan the South Peigan, the Blood, and the Siksika tribes (Blackfoot), Lenni Lenape (Delaware) and Algonquin. Guisepi, R.A. ed. *Where Did the Indians Come From?*

<http://www.history-world.org/american_indians_or_native_ameri.htm>

The Blackfoot, Delaware and Algonquin (possibly the largest inclusive group of Indians with the most widespread language group in Native Americans of North America MHJ) are possibly at least partially descended from the nomadic Lapps in whom blood type A commonly shows up. This blood type shows up in Scandinavians, it may also have been left by Vikings who arrived 2000 years before Columbus. (*Vikings Came Before Columbus* <http://webexhibits.org/vinland/archeological.html> see the story of Leif Erickson and subsequent archaeological evidence found in Newfoundland, Canada) However, the forensic evidence of blood typing has shown that 6,000 to 10,000 years ago a strain of DNA was introduced into the Indians of the Amazon basin, that clearly also shows a relationship to Pacific Islanders. Recently one woman[1] in a rowboat, rowed from Peru to French Polynesia, if one woman can do it surely ancient teams of skilled rowers could do likewise. ([1]Maud Fontenoy 2003) Keyser, John D. *The Story of the Algonquin Indians.*

<http://www.hope-of-israel.org/algonqun.htm> & *Vikings Came Before Columbus.*

<http://webexhibits.org/vinland/archeological.html>

> "What's more, stone tools, hearths and remains of dwellings unearthed from Peru to South Carolina suggest that Stone Age America was a pretty crowded place for a land that was supposed to be empty until those Asians followed herds of big game from Siberia into Alaska. Because if the evidence from stones and bones (from 15,050-12,500yrs ago) 3,500-100yrs before the original Americans supposedly flocked across the Bering strait, scientists are reconsidering the Bering Strait theory. Any new theory must account for charcoal, stone tools and woven material, 14,000 and possibly 17,000 years old. Apparently America was a veritable Rainbow Coalition of ethnic types, some lived in caves-but they were pretty smart, smart enough to have navigated the oceans, the Asians of the West may have been seafarers." *Newsweek Magazine,* 4/26/1999, p. 50-57.

"There are Japanese traditions according to which the Pacific islands of Oceania were formed after the waters of a great deluge had receded." Graham Hancock, *Fingerprints of the Gods,* quoting Sykes, E. *Dictionary of Non-classical Mythology,* p. 194.

"As Siberia and the Soviet Far East were devoid of human occupation, it must be *assumed* (italics mine) that the colonization of Japan took place via Korea, to which southern Japan was connected throughout the Pleistocene, for virtually all of the faunal changes of mainland north-east Asia are found also in southern Japan. Occasional edge-ground tools occur in early contexts and one edge-ground axe from Sanrizuka site, east of Tokyo, is dated about 30,000 years ago, earlier even than the edge-ground axes of northern Australia.

"After 20,000 years ago there is evidence for larger populations in southern Japan, and for an increasing tempo of cultural change with the development of micro blades by about 15,000 years ago and pottery by 12,000 years ago. The best evidence for this final Paleolithic occupation comes from Fukui cave in northern Kyushu, where in Horizon 3, dated to 12,500 years ago, pottery appears associated with the assemblage of microblades." *The Cambridge Encyclopedia of Archaeology,* p.155.

The Jomon people survive as the Ainu of Hokkaido and northern Honshu. Jomon pottery containers are the oldest known, dated slightly later than 12,750. In the rest of Europe, Asia and Africa the oldest are Turkish, about 10,500 years old. Joseph B. Lambert, *Traces of the Past.*

"Japanese archaeologists report in the New Scientist (March 2000) that they have uncovered the remains of what is believed to be the world's oldest artificial structure… the site has been dated to half a million years ago[2]…" Communication Studies, Univ. of Los Angeles. Paleoanthropology. [2]see later section on Radiometric Dating inaccuracies. <http://www.aeroman.de/html/paleoanthropology.html>

THE COUNTRIES OF SHEM, HAM AND JAFFETH

"At one point our species may have been down to as few as 2,000 individuals...'The assumption has always been that the original population [in sub-Saharan Africa] was very small but probably a single population,' said Spencer Wells, head of the Genographic project which oversaw the study. 'Turns out, that is not the case.'" Avasthi, Amitabh. for National Geographic News. *After Near Extinction, Humans Split Into Isolated Bands.*

The names Shem, Ham and Jaffeth are considered by many ancient historians and by the people of many ancient cultures all the way from China to Africa to be the names of their countries and their peoples. Many of them claim decent from one or the other of these races and the respective names figure prominently in the history and myths of those cultures.

INDIA/VINDJA

> "One of the most ancient legends of India...relates that several hundred thousand years ago there existed in the Pacific Ocean an immense continent which was destroyed by geological upheaval." Louis Jacolliot, *Histoire des Vierges: Les peuples et les continents desparus.*

Vimanas, flying machines described in ancient Sanskrit literature and the huge roaring may be descriptions of the same vehicles called in the Bible; "the chariots of the Elohim." The god Vishnu, "the Preserver," who is celebrated in India to have miraculously preserved a righteous family when the world was flooded, it not only has the story of Noah and the flood legend, but the hero is called by the same name. Vishnu is just the Sanskrit form of the Chaldee "Ish-nuh," or that is "the man Noah," in the OT he is called *"nch-aish,* Noah man." Gen. 6:9

SHEM/SHUM/SEMITES/SHUMERIA

As for this son of Noah, Shem is a word for land in the Middle East and India; It is also the root of the name of the Semitic peoples and a Hebrew word used to mean a "name" so possibly the "name" of a people or that is, a country. *Eerdmans Bible Dictionary,* p. 923.

> "The Sumerians were, as we all are, a mixture of races and probably of peoples." (Roux, George. *Ancient Iraq,* p. 89) the "Land of the Guardians." (Shum or Shem means land, & Ur or Ir - guardians. Sitchin, Zechariah. *Divine Encounters,* p. 7) "It was, in fact, the biblical Land of Shin'ar...the Egyptian *Ta Neter* - Land of the Watchers, the land from which the gods had come to Egypt." Sitchin, Zechariah. *Stairway to Heaven.*

> "One reason for guessing that there may have been Semites in South Iraq when the Sumerians first arrived is that some of the earliest Sumerian inscriptions contain words undoubtedly taken over from Semitic speech." *Everyday Life in Babylonia & Assyria,* p. 30.

In one Assyrian-Babylonian Creation story uncovered at Nineveh, the first man was fashioned out of blood, flesh and clay. In the ancient Akkadian language, *Adami* meant red clay...a goddess pinched off clay, spit in it, and created Eaboni; other tablets refer to him as *Adami.* Drohan, Francis Burke. *Jesus Who? The Greatest Mystery Never Told,* p. 10.

The earliest Sumerian history is related in the *Sumerian King List,* it begins like this; "After the kingship descended from heaven, the kingship was in *Eridug.* (followed by the names of various kings, the places of their kingdoms and the lengths of their rule) after which is says; "then the flood swept over." In the Sumerian *Atrahasis Epic, Enlil*[3] and the council of gods decide, because of the "noise of mankind" becoming too loud, that a flood will be caused to wipe out mankind. The hero of this story is Atrahasis. (known in similar Sumerian accounts as Ziusudra or Utnapishtim) quoted from Peter Goodgame, *The Spirit World and Civilization.*

<http://www.redmoonrising.com/Giza/SpiritCiv5.htm>

[3]*En*-Lord, *lil*-sky, *lil* is also perhaps related to the Assyrian word *ilu* which corresponds to the Hebrew *El or Al* meaning God, which would make it also "Lord God,") *Brown Driver Briggs Hebrew Dictionary* # 410, and perhaps to the Assyrian word for bright, *ellu,* # 1984

HAM/KHEM/KHEMIT/EGYPT

Another son of the Biblical Noah was Ham, it is well known by Biblical scholars, who will be familiar with the name Ham. Ham, Kem, or Khemet was a name for ancient Egypt." *Eerdman's Bible Dictionary*, p. 437.

While some have said the Egyptians have no record of the flood, the following account of the sinking of the original birthplace of humanity may not only be the origins of the story of Atlantis, mentioned by Plato as having its origins in Egypt, but another account of the flood, if the sinking of this birthplace of humanity, *translated as an island,* was actually a continent large enough to affect the rest of the world when it sank.

The first mention of Atlantis occurs in Plato's book, Timaeus, when a character named Kritias tells of an account of Atlantis that has been in his family for generations. According to the character, the story was originally told to his ancestor, Solon, by a priest during Solon's visit to Egypt. It is well known that the Greeks acquired many of their stories from the nearby Egyptian legends, following is one such legend taken from the temple walls at Edfu.

> "The first record...of the Sanctified God who came into being at the First Occasion, sets out a picture of a primeval island (*iw*). This island has a principal name Island of Trampling (or Crushing) (*iw titi*)...the name of a region in which the creation took place, is known to us only from the first Edfu cosmogonical record...The sacred place *Djeba* in *Wetjeset-Neter* having been created, the Sanctified Ruler...appeared. He came from the underworld...as a protector, and is said to resemble the *Nefer-her.* (The sanctified {*nefer* also means beautiful} falcon- hr or *Hor*-Light, much more on this meaning of *Hor* as light in the section on The Shemsu Hor Followers of Light) ...Then the Lord of the Wing (*ndm ndb*) arrived in the island...the Place-of-Uniting-of-Company. The meaning of the name...might refer to a group of divine beings who had died...(the word *smd* describes the arrival of gods in which a new settlement was to be founded) *Wetjeset-Neter*...is interpreted as...restoring the Ancestors." Reymond, E. A. E. *Mythical Origin of the Egyptian Temple,* p. 12-22.

> "The domain of the *Wetjeset-Neter* is now attacked by the enemy-snake (elsewhere known as a symbol of corpor and the serpent brain drive for corporeal things) and *Heter-Her* (Hor/Horus/Or-Light) is hard pressed...When the enemy, the snake, appeared at the landing stage of that domain, a *bw-titi*, Place-for-crushing, was planned and protective guards of the god were formed...Another fight took place at the same time in the sky, in which the Falcon (Hor) was believed to fight against the snake named *sbty[4]*." Reymond, E. A. E. *Mythical Origin of the Egyptian Temple,* p. 23,34,35.

*Note from the section on ' The "Turning Point" Judgment Day, that in Old Persian Satan was Sheitan. Beside the similarity to the correlation between the 'snake' and Satan-the adversary (having the same general meaning as enemy) this story of a snake involved in the creation of the earth is also somewhat cognitive of the Babylonian story of *tia maat,* another snake story involving the creation of the earth.

"The Edfu cosmogonical records begin with a picture of the primaeval island where the gods were believed to have lived first...We know from the Edfu texts that the Earth-Maker created the grounds for the domains of the gods (*niwt*) ...by virtue of *the word* of the Earth-Maker...He is said to be the snake who created the Primaeval Ones...who created the Earth (corporeal matter)...This quotation seems to reveal a tradition according to which the first creative power, represented eventually as a snake, was believed to be the Earth-God...the Sole Unique One without peer, who was first to fashion the Earth upon his (potters) wheel (keep in mind that a pot is round and spinning thus dispelling the myth that the ancients did not know the world to be round, MHJ) who created men, gave birth to the Gods, Lord of the Universe, Ruler of the Primaeval Ones, the First Primaeval One who came into being before the Primaeval Ones." Reymond, E. A. E. *Mythical Origin of the Egyptian Temple,* p. 59-61.

"This text seems to imply a belief in the existence of a group of nameless (*shmw,* Shem? MHJ) deities who existed before the origin of the world, and who were believed to act as a single creating power...these powers are described as the Primaeval Ones...the lords of the light...The Ghosts, the Ancestors...These nameless Creators of the Earth seem to have been regarded as its original inhabitants...they are also described as the Great *Ennead* (Remember from the section on Shem/Shum/Semites/Shumeria that in Assyrian these 'Lords' of Creation are referred to as 'En' just as they are in Egyptian.) ...the Sanctified Ones who...created their own bodily form for themselves, who fashioned themselves as their (own) work...divine beings described as...the word Company...(it) may have been the name of some divine beings who eventually formed the company of the nameless god described as *Pn*...The name *Pn* as a divine name is known to us...as a subsidiary name of *Ptah*." Reymond, E. A. E. *Mythical Origin of the Egyptian Temple,* p. 63,74,77,78,94,95.

"The general tone of the beginning of the first record seems to convey the view that an ancient world, after having been constituted, was destroyed, and as a dead world it came to be the basis of a new period of creation...life developed within the island; this then became the scene of various mythical events, such as, for instance, the *titi.* Theoretically *titi* can be interpreted as trampling or aggression. It may be surmised that there was a fight in the island...the result that the divine inhabitants died. This interpretation accords with other parts of the first Edfu record which alludes to the death of the Company...A further important fact that emerges...the allusion to the underworld...makes it clear that the underworld was believed to have existed before the world was created...the Underworld of the Soul (the spirit world, MHJ)." Reymond, E. A. E. *Mythical Origin of the Egyptian Temple,* p. 106,107,114.

"The Pn-God...is to be linked with the gnn, the Weak One...the first act of creation...in the Island of Trampling was solely an act of recreation of a divine world which once existed...Then appeared on the scene a large company of divine beings...the whole

245

company (*tt*) was then divided into four groups; each group was placed along one side of the *bw-titi*...Thereafter the snake was overthrown and the victorious gods are said to have settled (*sndm*) beside him...The divine powers who were believed to have acted in this phase of creation were the deities who took part in the former process; they were the Progeny of the Earth-God." Reymond, E. A. E. *Mythical Origin of the Egyptian Temple*, p. 125,195,214.

"It looks as though the Egyptians believed that there was one land only in which all the orders of creation were effected...in which the Lord of All was the Earth-God and his immediate successor the Winged One." Reymond, E. A. E. *Mythical Origin of the Egyptian Temple*, p. 215,262,263,274.

Notice that the Egyptian story does not name the ocean where this primeval land existed, this may become important, in light of recent discoveries beneath the Pacific Ocean off the coast of Okinawa. These discoveries will be explored further in a later section. Since the Greeks, and therefore Plato as well, were only familiar with the Atlantic ocean it is reasonable to hypothesize that they assumed the flood and sunken continent stories from that part of the world to have taken place in the Atlantic or surrounding areas. Then from that misunderstanding arose the fictional account of Atlantis written by Plato, and later taken up by others.

JAPHETH/JAVA/JAPAN/ASIA

Now as for Jaffeth/Japheth, the name Japheth etc. is to be found on many ancient maps in the area of China, Java and Japan. "The Moguls trace their pedigree, with each particular ancestor specified, from Japhet (or Jaffeth)...Gengis Khan marched into China in 1211 AD...all Asia knows that the Khan of Cara-corum is the lineal descendant of Japhet." Higgins, Godfrey. Vol. 2 *Anacalypsis*, p. 353&359.

These three separate peoples, the Shem/Shemites, the Ham/Khemetic people of Egypt, and the Japhethians/Asians traded and carried the understanding of their survival after the flood, with them. This understanding they also traded amongst themselves and it resulted in a proliferation of stories about the flood from the time of Noah man, from whom they all understood themselves to be descended.

This intermingling resulted in a new race, the Ghans (Khans MHJ), the remnant of this name is found in the name Afghanistan. "The inhabitants of China are known to the world as Chinese. They speak of themselves as the "people of Han, or T'ang." Bing, Li ung. *Outlines of Chinese History*, p. 1.

F. Hirth...suggested the identification of the Han with the Huns who were believed to be Turks...Hirth's idea was that the various names...reveal a common root...the old pronunciations (of Han/Ghan) Kwan, Gun, Kun etc. presented reproductions of the word Xun, the real name of the Huns. Hirth, F. *Chinese Statelets and the Northern Barbarians in the Period 1400300 BC*, p. 911.

Ja-phung is Chinese for Jappeth, possibly the origin of Java, and the name Japan, which is not the name the people of Japan knew their country by, is an ancient name by which the ancient Middle Eastern countries referred to Asia." Java has produced the earliest evidence of Homo sapiens in South East Asia: remains of c.40,000 BC." *Times Atlas of World History*, p. 132.

"They came all Noah (*al Nch*) to all the ark (*al ethbe*) male and female as which He instructs Elohim (ath-with) Noah." Gen. 7:9&15

THE SUNKEN CONTINENT IN THE PACIFIC

"It has been said that "A hypothesis that is appealing for its unity or simplicity acts as a filter, accepting reinforcement with ease but tending to reject evidence that does not seem to "fit" (Grad, 1971, p. 636)…Geological, geophysical, and dredging data provide strong evidence for the presence of Precambrian and younger continental crust under the deep abyssal plains of the northwest Pacific (Choi, Vasil'yev, and Tuezov, 1990; Choi Vasil'yev, and Bhat, 1992)…There is also evidence of paleolands in the southwest Pacific around Australia (Choi, 1997)…" Pratt, David. *Plate Tectonics: A Paradigm Under Threat*. 2000. <http://ourworld.compuserve.com/homepages/dp5/tecto.htm>

It is my proposed intention to provide scientific evidence substantiating another hypothesis, and difficult as that may be to prove, one that includes evidence of spiritual intervention on this planet. And not only spiritual intervention but evidence of extraterrestrial spiritual intervention. This would mean that YHVH's Elohim can and do travel throughout the universe. It seems improbable that YHVH would create a universe and not allow his angels or the powerful Elohim to travel or dwell, as those who existed before the creation of earth must have, anywhere beyond this planet. It is hoped that the evidence in this book may, for those individuals of both a scientific and spiritual bent, provide a "new" filter through which the evidence may be viewed. Perhaps others will go forward and fill in new evidence that supports such a hypothesis, and inspire even those scientifically minded persons without "spiritual" gifts to inquire into possible scientific methods by which to search for ways to investigate and demonstrate the influence of a universal "spiritual" dimension.

Obviously those who start by closing their mind to such possibilities will never pursue such avenues, but for the rest of mankind, investigation of such avenues may inspire faith in just such a presence, and help lift humanity out of the materialistic pursuits which threaten to ruin us. In the face of the lack of spiritual faith many place their faith in the material realm only, and the consequential competition for material security could eventually drive us to the brink of self-extinction. If the hypothesis of a sunken continent can be connected to the prevalence of stories of a world wide flood in ancient times, such material evidence may provide a beginning place for many to seek and find solid evidence of interference in human history, from the spirit world. The reason this is suggested will become more clear after reading the section on Modern Evidence of the Presence of the Elohim.

The feminine name Noah, according to Brown, Diver, Briggs, means to shake to and fro. But what is the significance of this to a worldwide flood? Let us explore some modern discoveries of a lost continent beneath the pacific, and the shaking to and fro, which accompanied its sinking.

247

Survivors sailed to the surrounding lands where their individual stories then survived (the Middle East, Japan, India, Asia, and So. America)

Besides underwater ruins near Okinawa which display quarry marks, cleared paths, and other signs of human intervention in natural processes, an enormous number of anomalous conditions exist beneath the Pacific Ocean. Along with the presence of a large percentage of earth's islands, these anomalies are all signs that a continent existed in that area at one time, just as numerous legends in surrounding areas have attested to. If the anomalies given in the this section, are indications that a one-time continent in that area sank, it would also offer an explanation for a worldwide flood. It would thus explain the Egyptian legends of the sunken birthplace of mankind (that Plato may have adopted in his original story of Atlantis, from which all the others derive). Consider the following evidence and judge for yourself.

> "<u>The Pacific contains the only tectonic plate without a continent on it</u> and it is surrounded by the famous "Ring of Fire"; geological activity...in the form of earthquakes and volcanic eruptions... (it is) concentrated in distinct zones which are usually not located at the boundaries of continents and oceans." Andel, Tjeerd. *New Views On An Old Planet*, p. 122&132.

Distribution of deep-sea sediments in the area of the Pacific Ocean from the equator northward (from Alaska to Indonesia including Japan across to Tahiti and back up, including Hawaii, to Alaska), unlike the rest of the worlds oceans, does *not* contain calcareous mud. This calcareous mud is from the shells of crustaceans settled to the bottom over long ages. Gross, M. Grant. *Oceanography*, p. 32&37.

Lack of calcareous mud is only one of many mysterious anomalies of the Pacific. "About 80 percent of all the islands in the world lie within a triangle whose apexes are Tokyo, Jakarta and Pitcairn." (p. 21) "Lost Paradise" by Ian Cameron. (to see a topographical map of these islands and the pacific ocean floor see page 1177 of the "Readers Digest Illustrated Encyclopedic Dictionary" or "National Geographic" magazine 10/69) "Harry Hess ...reported the discovery of 160 (hundreds more have since been mapped)...drowned islands of the Pacific basin...from 3000 to 4000 meters...rarely closer than 1000 meters to the waters surface. He named the flat topped ones "guyots"…in 1956 it was found that sediments retrieved from the tops of some mid-Pacific guyots contained fossils of *shallow-water species* (italics mine) dating from the relatively recent Cretaceous Period,...What, Hess wondered, could possibly have submerged these mountains to such great depths in so short a time? <u>It was also discovered that some of the sea mounts are tilted on the edges of oceanic trenches...though having been formed upright.</u>" Menard, H. W. *Continents in Motion, the New Earth Debate*, p. 61,62.

"The flat-topped guyots, high level terraces, and submarine canyons may have been cut by oceans miles lower and/or thousands of feet higher than those that roll against today's shores." Page 285 "Unknown Earth" by William Corliss. When the flat-topped mesas, of Monument Valley, Arizona for example, are observed above water it is fairly obvious that their flat tops are all of similar height and most likely represent a former surface of the land before aeons eroded it away, first to become islands and until eventually the receding the water level left them standing completely exposed. Similar processes must have originally formed those under the Pacific.

> "Recent geophysical and geological investigations of the floor of the deep Pacific

indicate that this area has been the scene of large-scale geologic activity during relatively late stages of earth history...Mesozoic or Early Tertiary...the apparently slight thickness of deep-sea sediment suggests that relatively rapid deposition did not begin until the Mesozoic." Page 717 "Unknown Earth" by William Corliss quoting Roger Revelle in "Geological Society of America, Bulletin 1951.

"In a great swath of death around the edge of the Arctic Circle the remains of uncountable numbers of large animals have been found - including many carcasses with the flesh still intact,...Hundreds of thousands of individuals must have been frozen immediately after death and remained frozen, otherwise the meat and ivory would have spoiled...stone artifacts have been frozen in situ at great depths, and in association with Ice Age fauna, which confirms that men were contemporary ...The animals were simply torn apart and scattered over the landscape like things of straw and string, even though some of them weighed several tons....mixed with piles of bones are trees, also twisted and torn and piled in tangled groups; and the whole is covered with a fine sifting muck, then frozen solid. "Obviously we have here victims of an immense catastrophe which swept continents and left the debris in the far northern latitudes piled in jumbled masses that now form decent-sized islands. L. Taylor Hansen, *The Ancient Atlantic*.

If glaciers caused this, why are there no similar signs in the southern hemispheres, and how could glaciers move animals from a temperate to an Arctic zone? The direction would be the reverse. "The last glaciation...{is} called the Mankato by geologists and placed by Antevs at about 25,000 BC." Brion, Marcel. *The World of Archaeology; India, China, America.* p. 130.) ...of the 34 animal species...no less than 28 were adapted *only to temperate conditions*...Grasses, bluebells, buttercups, tender sedges, and wild beans have been found, yet identifiable and un-deteriorated, in their mouths and stomachs. ...such flora does not grow anywhere in Siberia." Pages 213-216 "Fingerprints of the Gods" by Graham Hancock.

"Some anomalous aspects of the (theory of glacial) drift are: Drift deposits and apparent glacial striations well south of the charted ice sheets. Striations indicating northward motion of the supposed ice sheets. Boulder trains and associated erosion that seem to demand cataclysmic flooding." Page 32 "Unknown Earth" by William Corliss. "One of the coldest regions of the earth is Siberia...Here if anywhere, we should find the Drift; here if anywhere, was the ice-field, "the sea of ice"...and yet there is no Drift in Siberia!" Corliss, William. *Unknown Earth*, p. 104, quoting Ignatius Donnelly, *Ragnarok: The Age of Fire and Gravel.*

"The south sea islands are covered by Triassic plants. These living fossils, not found elsewhere, demand some type of explanation." Furthermore, ...by the end of the Jurassic, Japan and the Philippines had been isolated from the mainland and consequently have Jurassic flora." Page 136&237 "Red Earth, White Lies" by Vine Deloria Jr.

This makes it most likely that those South Sea islands have been above sea level from the Triassic onward and were not formed in their entirety by volcanic activity, as is sometimes suggested. "The rim of the Pacific basin is marked by a succession of trenches that cut into its floor like deep gashes....By the 1950s the trenches (and the strangely weak gravity above them) had emerged as one of the most remarkable features of the earth's surface...some of them extending farther below sea level than Everest rises above it by a margin of a kilometer or more....materials recovered "resemble...deposits laid down in shallow water." What implacable forces could have caused such large-scale distortions of the sea floor? Why are they so narrow so long and so deep?...What is the significance of the fact that they lie along the Pacific ring of fire?...The most prominent ones are all about the same depth - ten kilometers (six miles) below sea level-suggesting they were all products of a similar, uniform process. If the floor of the Pacific was old compared to that of the Atlantic...why is the average thickness of Atlantic sediment twice that of Pacific sediments? If trenches mark where sea floor, moving away from a central ridge, descends beneath the continents, where are the trenches on either side of the Atlantic? If the trenches on the rim of the northwest Pacific are swallowing sea floor manufactured along a mid-ocean ridge, ...*where is that ridge*?" Sullivan, Walter. *Continents in Motion,* pp. 58-60 & 109

> "Materials which are usually supposed to be deposited only in shallow water have actually been found on the floor of some of the deep trenches....The Question remains: Where are the trenches of yesteryear? Are we living in an exceptional geologic era; are the apparently young trenches...unusual formations that have had no counterparts during most of geologic time? ...The continents and ocean basins are distinctly different aspects of the earth's crust. Some areas of the earth's crust are neither strictly continental (sialic; i.e., mostly granite) nor strictly oceanic (simatic; i.e., basaltic) - they seem to combine a little of both! These areas are the island archipelagoes ...Japan...the Philippines...the East Indies and New Guinea...and the West Indies. The principal islands in such chains have a dominantly continental character." *Continents Adrift Readings from Scientific American,* pp. 15-17.

> "The volcanic rocks of Easter Island, rising from the East Pacific Rise, were suspiciously continental also. The quakes in the Gulf of Alaska were also in a "continental area." H.W. Menard, *The Ocean of Truth.*

In 1987, pyramids and structures with enormous square, hewn, stone blocks, were discovered off the coast of Yonaguni, Japan, under the Pacific Ocean." (see article in "Ancient America" magazine vol. 3 #17). Except for some knowledge of the above water islands all the information in the preceding notes concerning the Pacific ocean floor was unknown in 1882, the date of the publication of the book *Oahspe. Oahspe* includes a map of this sunken continent called "Pan" and said to have sunken 24,000[6] years ago. It includes the area of Japan, but it is *not* included in the areas of the maps of Mu; closer to the equator, or Lemuria; the land bridge between Africa and India.

> [5]"Lemuria commenced its life as a scientific hypothesis to explain the existence of lemurs...in Madagascar...Africa and tropical Asia. William Blandford suggested...a land bridge connecting southern Africa and Asia. ("The Fauna of British India" published 1888) This idea was taken up by the German biologist Ernst Haeckel, who suggested that this land bridge was the method by which the lemurs populated the various continents...The name Lemuria, is simply derived from the connection with the Lemurs...The most famous exponent of the lost continent of Lemuria was the founder of the Theosophist movement, Madame Blavatsky, who used it in her weird cosmos...Mu is derived from James Churchward ("The Lost Continent of Mu" published 1926)." Page

176 "Gods of Air and Darkness" by Richard Mooney.

[6]"There are no archaeological (fossil) finds that can be placed in the period between 20,000 and 25,000 BC., although we have finds from before and after those dates...It seems feasible that an event that modified the concentration of carbon 14 in the atmosphere took place in those days." Pauwels and Bergier, *The Eternal Man,* p. 65.

Numerous photographs now exist showing the underwater ruins off the coast of Okinawa spreading over more than 300 sq. miles of ocean floor. They show massive stone monuments, one in the form of a human head with either a headdress or a flowing mane of locks of hair, round cisterns drilled into solid rock, steps and arched passage ways also carved into solid rock, and a huge stone platform with a pathway cleared of rubble around the base, rocks carved with strange hieroglyphics and animal shapes, and perfectly square blocks cut with 90% angles. Cites showing dramatic photos of these ruins include;

<http://www.mysteriousworld.com/Journal/2003/Autumn/Fragments/>

<http://www.conspiration.cc/sujets/archeologie/japon_construction_sousmarine.htm>

<http://www.cyberspaceorbit.com/phikent/japan/japan2.html>

<http://www.altarcheologie.nl/index.html> <http://www.crystalinks.com/lemuriajapan.jpg>

<http://www.freewebs.com/histrynow/okinawaunderwaterruins.htm>

<http://www.damninteresting.com/?p=725>

Unlike the other oceans of the world, trenches (deeper than Everest is high) border the Pacific. These trenches have yet to be explained. *Oahspe* offers the explanation that the continent in the Pacific was deliberately sunken by YHVH's gods because this birthplace of humanity had decayed into such a state of corruption. This included cannibalism, and so many other evils that the Creator ordained it to be destroyed, just as numerous flood stories from around the world have recorded. According to *Oahspe* this was done by a circle of starships/merkabah/'chariots' of the Elohim-gods who broke through the earth around the sides of Pacific plate in that area. Whatever happened it would obviously have taken more force than humanity can presently imagine, to have carved these trenches around the Pacific plate.

"Ocean-basin studies show that island-arc trench fills, where "subduction" supposedly takes place, are undeformed. The volumes of undeformed sedimentary rocks in layer 1 indicate (1) that sea-floor spreading has not taken place since Mesozoic or earlier time; or (2) that subduction must take place seaward from the island-arc trenches; or (3) that there is no such process as "subduction." Page 461 "Unknown Earth" by William Corliss quoting A. A. Meyerhoff in "American Association of Petroleum Geologists, Bulletin 1972."

There also exists the presence of a layer of ash which must have been deposited in a brief moment in geological history. This layer and the presence of strange molten glass tektites seems to attest to some volcanic and explosive catastrophe that occurred in relatively recent geological time.

"The great extent of a sub-bottom echo at depths of 0 to 40 meters below bottom in the tropical Eastern Pacific has been demonstrated...The first sub-bottom echo is well correlated by cores throughout the area with a white ash layer. Since the layer is fairly near the surface and is not discolored and contains nothing but the glassy ash material, it must have been laid down fairly quickly...The great extent of the ash and its shallow cover would imply a great amount of recent activity for a short time. Corliss, William. *Unknown Earth,* p. 283, quoting J. Worzel in *National Academy of Sciences, Proceedings* 1959.

"Tektites are a silica-rich obsidian glass different from terrestrial obsidian. The greatest number has been found in Australia, Indochina, the Philippines, and Moldavia. They are usually jet-black and take the form of button shapes, spheres, and dumbbells. Some consider that they are extraterrestrial in origin and have gained their shapes by aerodynamic ablation through high-speed flight and kinetic heating on their passage through earth's atmosphere ...modern nuclear weapons have failed to produce tektites." Mooney, Richard. *Gods of Air and Darkness,* p. 110.

Gondwana is the portion of Pangaea (the ancient land mass that results when all the continents are fitted back together, theorized to have separated due to continental drift), that contained the continents; Africa, Antarctica, Australia, So. America and India. "Some geologists speculate ...of a lost continent they call Pacifica. They suggest that Pacifica broke off from Gondwana about 220 million years ago and drifted into the Pacific basin. National Geographic, *Exploring our Living Planet,* p. 321.

"Lynn Rose and a number of others have noted that the continental mass of the world would not end up in one place for no reason, and that it would have to be pulled into one place by some titanic force of attraction. Rose notes that the antique solar-system alignment which did this also pulled the earth into a spun cam, or egg shape. He notes that the Tethys sea is therefore an anomaly; if the land mass is pulled into one place by an attractive force, you expect it to be pulled into a circle or pie shape, and Pangaea was more like a pie with one wedge (Tethys[7]) cut out and eaten." [7]This triangular area corresponds well with the continent *Oahspe* calls "Pan" (on the Pacific Plate) which is also given as a triangular shape. *The Anomaly of Pangaea.*

<http://www.bearfabrique.org/Catastrophism/rose.html>

"Yonaguni's most experienced diver Kihachiro Aratake...(whose) lifetime project (is) to explore...the coast of Yonaguni...made a discovery which some scholars believe could be of immense and disturbing historical significance...What Aratake found was an apparently man-made structure, carved out of solid rock in complex shapes and patterns, that lay with its base on the ocean bed at a depth of 27 metres. More than 200 metres long, it rose gracefully before his eyes in a series of pyramid-like steps to a summit platform just 5 metres beneath the surface...Professor Masaaki Kimura, a leading Japanese geologist from Okinawa University...has studied the monument intensively, making hundreds of dives to it over many years of research...he adamantly insists that it is a man-made object...Blocks carved off during the formation of the monument are not found lying in the places where they should have fallen if only gravity and natural forces were operating; instead they seem to have been artificially cleared away to one side and in some cases are absent from the site entirely...two metre-deep circular holes, a stepped, cleanly angled geometrical depression, and a perfectly straight narrow trench...Between its north and south walls the 4-metre-wide floor at the foot of the trench was littered with the debris of large apparently quarried blocks that seemed to have fallen from above...A series of steps rises at regular intervals... a distinct "wall" encloses the western edge of the monument...it consists of limestone blocks not indigenous to the Yonaguni area. What looks like a ceremonial pathway winds around the western and southern faces of the monument...That such stark differences of topography can be observed side by side is therefore strong evidence in favor of artificiality...If only natural erosional forces had been at work, one would expect them to have acted uniformly on the same member of rock in the same locality of the monument." Pages 201-220 "Heavens Mirror" by Graham Hancock.

"At the eastern end of the platform we found a straight channel, approximately three-quarters of a metre wide and half a metre deep, running for 8 metres through a raised plinth...We noted that the bearing of the trench was very insistently east-west...In our view it may well be significant that the structure incorporates characteristics that would unhesitatingly be recognized as astronomical if it stood above sea-level. It is oriented due south, towards the meridian, and features a massive east-west trench targeted to sunrise and sunset on the spring and autumn equinoxes. It stands at a latitude...that there have been times...when the Yonaguni "monument," located at 24 degrees 27 minutes north latitude, would have stood exactly astride the Tropic of Cancer...9000 & 9900 yrs ago." Hancock, Graham. *Heavens Mirror,* pp. 201-220.

Also it could correspond with dates going back at the 21,600 year cycles it takes for the earth to wobble the relative position of the Tropic of Cancer; 30,600 & 31,500 and 52,200 & 53,100 years ago. *Oahspe* gives the date of the sinking of Pan at 24,000 years ago. This would mean the structure could have been built anywhere from 6-7000 years before it sank all the way back to 28,000 years before it sank. This is somewhat after the time of the first colonies on the continent Pan described in *Oahspe*, which it places as beginning 72,000 years ago.

"We have found that the destruction of an entire mid-ocean ridge, known as the Izanagi Ridge, initiated a chain reaction of geological events," said Joanne Whittaker, a doctoral student at the University of Sydney's School of Geosciences who led the research. Using geophysical data gathered by scientists from Australia and Russia, the team confirmed that the ridge plunged underneath a plate of Earth's crust that stretches between the Korean Peninsula and Japan...The cause of (this) major change in the motion of the Pacific plate has long puzzled scientists," Whittaker said." Ryall, Julian. *Ancient Cataclysm Rearranged Pacific Map, Study Says.*

<http://news.nationalgeographic.com/news/2007/10/071024-tectonics.html>

Chapter Eleven

MODERN EVIDENCE OF THE PRESENCE OF THE ELOHIM

"And He is answering, YHWH...where were you when I laid the foundations of the earth...and the morning stars jubilated together and all the sons of the Elohim shouted for joy?" Job 38:1-7 Were some the Elohim at one time beings who could have occupied or visited the morning stars, Venus and/or Mars?

ARE THE ELOHIM STILL WATCHING?

A great deal of evidence has been accumulated suggesting the human race descended from some extraterrestrial source, some of the best are works by; Eric Van Daniken; Graham Hancock; Zechariah Sitchen; and of special note although it is more obscure is; "Mankind-Child of the Stars" by Flindt & Binder. These authors have been quoted and referenced in the writing of this book. This chapter will also briefly consider another extremely obscure book.

What if there was a very obscure communication that not only gave an account that correlates with all the historical and etymological evidence presented in this book including all the evidence of the Elohim-gods, *and* the Hebrew data when accurately translated (according to established Hebrew dictionaries written by accredited scholars)? What if there were a book, published before the Nag Hammadi library and the Dead Sea scrolls were discovered, and before Dalman printed the Talmud texts concerning Yeschu in 1891, that has since been confirmed by them in many area? And what if it also gave preemptive information on since discovered scientific discoveries (like the sunken continent in the Pacific) unheard of at the time it was published in 1882; and actually predicted its discovery?

What if, unlike the vague metaphorical prophecies of Nostradamus or others, it predicted numerous examples of precise and specific historical and scientific information that is has only since been discovered and confirmed, by the recent archaeological discoveries of ancient documents? What if it predicted the formation of the Olympics; the underwater discoveries of sunken remnants in the Pacific ocean; plasma physics (http://www.holoscience.com); and the numerous sightings of starship/UFOs that were to take place in the next two hundred years following its publication. This being in 1882, at a time when UFOs were not yet so called and were thus simply referred to as starships?

Such a book exists, it follows the same story line as the evidence presented in this book, and more. It not only gives information on our earthly history (that follows the evidence given in this book), which version of history, as given here, has been possible to confirm in part by studying the remains of our own past. However, the book in question also gives a history of the spirit dimension around us, and some of YHVH's council of holy Elohim, speaking of these gods and goddesses by name. These areas of knowledge of events in the spirit world are of course, impossible to confirm, but the fact that the amazing book under discussion gives so many areas of foreknowledge in earthly concerns certainly makes it deserving of examination.

That book is the Kosmon (from the Egyptian spelling *kosmos* i.e., cosmos) bible *Oahspe,* which was written as a spiritually channeled guide and message from the YHVH's Elohim, who are Gods and Goddesses dwelling in the spirit dimension. The name means O-Sky (etherea/interstellar space), Ah-Earth (corpor/matter) and Spe-Spirit or, "Thought which may be likened to the soul." (p547/537v30 the 2nd # refers to Eng. version) "These three entities, which constitute the universe, being emblematical of Jehovih." (p841/818v25) It has given voluminous information, later correlated by science and disinterested parties; these were persons not even familiar with *Oahspe.* It provides numerous clues, as to where to look for evidence and information concerning inaccuracies in the Bible, thus helping in the discovery of the changes made to the Hebrew Bible discussed in this book.

Some of these principle Elohim (gods and goddesses) through their actual materialization and through the appearance of their starships, and through the knowledge of oracles, mediums and prophets who possessed spiritual abilities, apparently became known by name to earthlings in the past. This was when mankind's bloodline, from the sons of the Elohim was more pure, and so still possessed many spiritually gifted people, and thus their names crept into history. Others, gods and goddesses and the events of the spirit world are not possible to confirm by material knowledge. Yet the fact that this book is correct in so many areas that are possible to confirm warrants its consideration by those seeking such spiritual knowledge.

Oahspe recounts the story of the writing of the current version of the Bible, as having been masterminded by Ezra, founder and first of the school of Levites historically known as the Sopherim; the evidence presented here now demonstrates that this was indeed the case. Evidence supporting *Oahspe*'s account has surfaced in a multitude of areas, and as time has progressed, myriad bits and pieces have also eventually proven to be true or at least as reasonable as other theories and dogmas. Even then *Oahspe* does not claim to be infallible, as according to itself it was channeled from spirits on the other side; these beings make no claim to be omniscient, as only YHVH *Al Da'at* is All Knowing (the universal mind of the Great Holy Spirit) .

Oahspe's account, published in 1882, of the appearance of a starship at the birth of Yeschu/Joshu/Jesus, was confirmed in 1947 by the discovery of the Dead sea scrolls. The Dead Sea Scroll account (by the Essenes) of this visitation, mentioned previously, is so significant and beautiful that it bears repeating again in this context in comparison with *Oahspe*'s account;

> "The Cherubim praise the vision of the Throne-chariot above the celestial sphere, and they extol the radiance of the fiery firmament beneath the throne of His glory. And the Holy Angels come and go between the whirling wheels, like a fiery vision of most holy spirits; and around them stream rivulets of molten fire, like incandescent bronze, a radiance of many brilliant colors, of exquisite hues gloriously mingled, the Spirits of the living God move in constant accord with the glory of the Wonderful Chariot (*mrkb* vehicle)." (Allegro, 99)

This is very close to the account given in *Oahspe* p662/or 643 verse 5; "Jehovih raised up from the Asenean (Essenean, or Es'ean) one Joshu, (i.e., Yeschu/Jesus) an iesu, in Nazareth. p726/707v11 And he was the child of Joseph and his wife Mara, devout worshipers of Jehovih, who stood aloof from all other people except the Es'eans. v13 The time of the birth of the child

255

was three days after the decent of a heavenly ship from the throne of God. And many Es'eans looked up and saw the star,...And they said, one to another: Jehovih remembers us. (17) When the birth was completed the angels of heaven re-entered their star-ship and hastened back to paradise."

Oahspe also gives a record that explains the creation of the NT that follows the extraneous historical evidence that many have since used to cast doubt on the NT account and/or on the existence of Yeschu/Joshu/Jesus. This includes a time line for his birth that corresponds to the Talmud's prior mention of his existence in the second century BCE, as he was already alive at that time. There is no way this historical account of his birth could have been plagiarized since it appeared *before* the date accepted by Constantine's Catholic council. This new date for his birth also appears to correlate with information on the Dead Sea Scrolls Essene "teacher of righteousness" who taught the version of the beatitudes mentioned previously.

> "(Quoting from the Talmud); "When King Jannai...(who reigned over the Jews 104-78 BC)...directed the destruction of the Rabbis...Jeschu went to Alexandri." This famous passage taken by itself, would...fully confirm the hypothesis of the 100 years BC date of Jesus...The Talmud declared categorically that Jesus had lived a century earlier than the date assigned to him by evangelists, and that instead of his being crucified in Jerusalem he was stoned at Lud." Pages 104,135-138,177,256,334,335,408 &410 "Did Jesus Live 100 Years BC" by G. R. S. Mead.

Many Christians have objected to *Oahspe*'s account of Yeschu/Joshu/Jesus' life (where his name is given as the English form of *Yeschu*-Joshu) because *Oahspe* explains that the word Christ also meant knowledge. The presently recognized etymology defines the word Christ as "the anointed." However, information was given in the section on the *Krst*, on the previous usage of the title *Krst* to refer to Horus and others. The usage of the Egyptian/Coptic term *rexit*, translated as "Christ" in the Bruce Codex Schmidt translation of *The Book of Ieou*, p. 270-271, may explain this usage. The presence of the Coptic word *rexit* as meaning Christ, in this early Christian writing, seems to make it possible that to the Egyptian Christians at least, their Coptic word *rexit* meaning "Christ" or *krst* may have also had some association with the Egyptian word for knowledge, *rkh*.[1] *Rexit* meaning Christ in these Gnostic texts, could then be a related form of the Egyptian word *rkh* meaning "know." The word *Rexit* is from Coptic, which is a later form of the Egyptian hieroglyphic language, one that would have been in use among the "Christians" of Alexandria, the Gnostics, and people throughout Egypt, at the time of Yeschu/Joshu/Jesus. [1]Wallis Budge, *Egyptian Language,* p. 165&194.

<http://www.thekeep.org/~kunoichi/kunoichi/themestream/glyphs_2b.html>

There is also a difference in interpretation as to how salvation is achieved that may offend some Christians reading Oahspe; even though the NT says "Wherefore, my beloved, as ye have always obeyed, not as in my presence only, but now much more in my absence, <u>work out your own salvation with fear and trembling</u>." (Philippians 2:12) *Oahspe* agrees with the concept presented earlier that Yeschu/Joshu/Jesus knew from his own name that YHVH saves, or that is, YHVH offers salvation to all His children who practice oneness in Him, as proclaimed in Isa. 43:10. "<u>I (even) I YHWH and besides Me there is no savior</u>." Also see Psalms 9:14 "Show me favor O YHWH...that I may be joyful in your salvation." However in contrast to John's teachings, in

John 3:16 (so intensely promoted by fundamentalist teachings), Joshu/Yeschu/Jesus himself says that "not everyone who comes to me saying, Lord, Lord, will enter the kingdom of heaven, but he who *DOES* the will of the Father." (Matt. 7:21) Since to Christian's Joshu/Yeschu/Jesus understanding should be taken as superior to John's, the teachings of Joshu/Yeschu/Jesus in the NT clearly express the understanding that belief alone is not enough.

> "The word mummy is perhaps derived from the Egyptian mum, to "initiate into the mysteries." This origin would suggest that the elaborate procedure of mummification was inaugurated to typify the whole broad meaning of the incarnation, as a submerging of high spirit in the dense state of mortal matter...Attention must now be given to the Egyptian word which was used to designate the mummy. It was usually marked upon the coffin lid. It may offer a connection of great potential fruitfulness for knowledge. It consisted of the consonants K R S with a suffix T, giving K R S T. The voweling is indeterminate, as it always was in ancient writing. Scholars have introduced an A before the R and another after it, making the word K A R A S T as generally written. There is probably no authoritative warrant for this spelling, but there has ever been a stout resistance to all suggestions that the alternative vowels, E, I, O or U be used in the form. Yet scholarship would be hard put to substantiate any objection to the spellings Karist, Karest, Kerast, Kerist or Krist. Indeed, as the root is very likely a cognate form with the Greek kreas, flesh, there would be more warrant for writing it Krast, Krest or Krist than the usual Karast. If we know how easily a "Kr" consonant metamorphoses into the Greek Chr, we can not dismiss the suggested closeness of the word to the Greek Chrestos or Christos as an absurd improbability. This may indeed be the Kamite origin of our name Christ, whatever be the outcry against such a conclusion." Kuhn, Alvin Boyd. *The Lost Light.* <http://www.theosophical.ca/LostLight2.htm>

Oahspe has the following to say about the substitution (by the Levites who served Aton) of Adonai[2]-Lord in place of YHVH's sacred name ([2]deriving originally from the Egyptian word Aton). "Moses being old, said: Above all things preserve the sacred pass-word, E-O-Ih (as it is pronounced, however, now transliterated as YHWH) inviolate; neither suffer it to come to the unlearned lest they be confounded by the subtlety of the God of the Egyptians. Was it not because the unlearned desired a form or figure to worship that the "Lord" (Osiris) ruined Egypt?" (From *Oahspe*'s book on Etymology, *Saphah*, Tablet of Biene, verse 22) This use of Adonai to mean the Creator and its associated etymology with the Egyptian "Lord" (Aton/Adon) is now clear from modern studies in Egyptology; as discussed previously referring to the work of Moustafa Gadalla in *Tut-Ankh-Amen,* the Hebrew word Adon/Adonai/Lord can be seen to be a cognate of Aton/Adon, meaning Lord in Egyptian. This has the meaning of a God in shape and form of a human, far less than YHVH who becomes the soul of all the living (Gen. 1:24 <http://scripture4all.org/Online Interlinear/OTpdf/gen1.pdf>) and who is the only One who may be All in all (1 Cor. 15:28). These verses are reflected in the teachings of Yeschu/Joshu/Jesus to those who embraced his teachings of oneness with YHVH as the only salvation (Isa. 43:10) And he knew from his own name (Yah saves[3]) and had first chosen and then shown others as the way to salvation (John 17:21). [3]<http://biblefocus.net/theology/Yeshua/index.html>

The historic evidence presented in this book, concurs with *Oahspe*'s account, however, *Oahspe* also contains much from prehistoric times, prior to the appearance of phonetic writing, that therefore can not all be confirmed or denied from written history (however, some evidence has been found through paleontology and geology). Oahspe discusses the time of the existence of dinosaurs and other reptiles as all collectively grouped, and named as types of "serpents," in ancient times; some were described as "four-legged," just as discussed in the Bible. These were mentioned previously in the section on Serpent Brain (as mentioned in the Bible), after which the only serpents left had to "crawl on their bellies." It also includes much from the Bronze age and on that cannot be verified, thanks to the destruction of libraries, in Egypt, the Middle East, China, and South America by religious fanatics of the past who sought to obliterate any records of spiritual information outside their own religion.

Oahspe includes records of the history of many other ancient religions and cultures including the history of the now gone "little people" called in *Oahspe* the *Ihin*. (SHD 5869, 6030, 6031 & 6041 *Ayin* in Hebrew means humble, knowledge, looked down upon, lowly, etc. Their presence in Hebrew history may account for the extremely frequent biblical references to "the humble" as being especially in need of YHVH's protection; some of these references, therefore, may actually refer to a people known by that name.) They were known for their devotion to and inspiration from the spirit world by YHVH Elohim, the Creator's council of holy gods and goddesses, and like them dwelt in oneness. These gods and goddesses, the Elohim are still here offering inspiration to help bring mankind in various parts of the world to understand the Creator's Will and Universal Mind of all Truth. This is the Great Holy Spirit, YHVH, in whom All Truth (*Al Emeth*) and All Knowledge (*Al Da'at*) is known, so that every mind which reveres the truth, albeit perhaps unconsciously, already shares a part in the understanding and knowledge of the infinite universal mind of YHVH the Great Holy Spirit.

It is through reexamining and reclaiming the history of these little people, our ancestors (and the original continent in the Pacific on which they first lived), that we can once again reestablish the history of our descent from the Elohim and through them our connection to the rest of the cosmos. *Oahspe* explains that the original beings, the sons of the Elohim who procreated with humans, the daughters of the Adam, while able to exist with actual bodies in the physical realm, (some) had not fully experienced a mortal existence. Understanding little about the responsibilities of procreation, they engendered modern humans, now distinctly different from the previous race of hominids. These earlier hominids lacked a knowledge base (such as later acquired by humanity through an understanding of "the word" of YHVH, *DABAR IEVE*, i.e., the truth*). The Elohim communicated or taught the understanding of "the word" (spoken and written language/symbols) to their offspring; without this communication, like people raised without human contact, our ability to communicate would have remained much closer to the same levels as other higher primates who have not been trained to understand spoken commands, signs and symbols. That humans and other primates do not spontaneously develop a social sense of self, when raised without human contact, provides evidence that we received this instruction elsewhere.

Visitation from little pale "grays" and the out of body experiences remembered by some abductees (like Betty Andreasson), and their descriptions of these little people as having comparatively large heads and undeveloped sex organs corresponds with some abduction experiences. This larger brain size is what some scientists suggest would result if infants were grown outside of a womb. The brain and skull would continue to grow, as possibly the brain size is presently limited by the restriction of the uterus. In more advanced beings, *in vitro* development may be an alternative to abortion.

To be scientifically accurate it is necessary for any theory that can be logically assumed to be correct, to fit all the evidence, not just exclude anomalous evidence from textbooks or from limited definitions of religion because one theory or system of dogma has a standing tradition and/or supporters. It must account for information that does not fit, even if the presence of the evidence excluded disputes some longstanding interpretations and destroys some reputations in the process.

In addition to other information, corresponding to the evidence, time line and religious history presented in this book, *Oahspe* demonstrated foreknowledge of information about the continent sunken at the time of the flood; including the underwater archaeological discoveries off the coast of Okinawa. These exhibit many signs of human presence like, stairways, artifacts, quarry marks and a cleared path around the base of the site. *Oahspe*'s foreknowledge not only predated the predictions of the Lemurian and Lost continent of Mu concepts (published after the publication of *Oahspe*'s account of this lost continent), it also included the areas of the recent discoveries off the coast of Okinawa, not included in the maps of Lemuria or Mu (by James Churchward).

Information on genetics has shown that Native Americans were not just derived from one stock that crossed the Bering Straight. It is now seen that South Sea Islanders contain genetic traces related to American Indians, showing that ocean travel by boat obviously occurred at some time. This confirms *Oahspe*'s account that the original people on this continent were capable of crossing the ocean in boats. The lack of Middle Eastern genes in Native Americans also disproves the Mormon account, of Indians being a lost tribe of the Israelites, which *Oahspe* stated beforehand to be untrue.

Additionally the account of the pre-Columbian Native American record in the Popul Vuh mentioned earlier, adds confirmation to *Oahspe*'s story that the original stock of Native American ancestors had knowledge of a flood that destroyed mankind after they had incurred the disapproval of the Creator. The original inhabitants were only later added to by other people, perhaps crossing the Bering Straight, or sailing across at later times.

This amazing bible (*Oahspe*) contains an account of human history, from interbreeding with the Elohim, now confirmed by many the discoveries in paleontology mentioned in the section on Evolution and the Forensic evidence of two types of humans, one of which has no rh neg. DNA as found other large primates. The palentological evidence concerns the sudden concurrent appearance of the multiple changes; changes like our sharp chin, weak brow, with no thick brow ridges, high vaulted forehead, thin skull, diminished teeth, less ponderous jaw, smaller eye orbits, streamlined pelvis, and redesigned vocal tract. These features heralded the first of the Homo species, without any transitional fossils from the Australopithecus line posited by the theory of evolution.

There are presently no Oahspe readers who completely practice Oahspe's position on living in communal oneness, so there are no leaders duly authorized by such a communal group. However, there are some among the Oahspe readers who object to this research on the concurrent singular and plural use of the word Elohim, as indicating the existence of a council of Elohim serving YHVH/Jehovih. This is based on the presence of one case where Elohim is translated to mean the Creator (The words Jehovih and Eloih are used instead of Elohim throughout the main body of Oahspe). According to my research this instance using Elohim to mean the Creator would have occurred *after* the time I suggest the confusion arose between the singular and plural pronunciations. This instance is present in the linguistic book of Saphah in Oahspe. Most of the other cases where the word Elohim occurs in this linguistic book of Saphah, in Oahspe, are in the rites of Emethachavah. But the presence of the words Christ, Christians, Buddha, Mohammed, the Koran, etc. date these rites to the time of Yeschu/Joshu/Jesus not the Emethachavah rites used as far back as Abraham. John B. Newbrough mentions Higgin's research on the word elohim (SHD 430) in his "Commentary on Oahspe" from the 1882 Oahspe. Newbrough quotes (and the glossary directs the student to study) Higgin's research on elohim including Higgin's statement; "it is by no means singular."

Oahspe also takes a stand on nutrition, supporting the health benefits of a vegetarian diet that has now been repeatedly proven in many areas of medical research. It is universally understood that eating foods containing animal fat contributes to the formation of plaques, comprised of cholesterol and calcium, leading to arteriosclerosis, high blood pressure and heart disease. Additionally the linking of red meat to so many other diseases including cancer, demonstrates that depending on the person's genetic weaknesses it is almost universally impossible to avoid some kind of disease consequences when consuming meat on a regular basis. Whether considering the Garden of Eden or evolution theory, there must have been time before mankind used fire or weapons. A time when mankind's earliest ancestors did not kill, cook or eat large animals; therefore indicating that the ancestors from whom we inherited our genetic makeup would not have had the necessary biochemistry to perfectly adapt them to eating meat. This lack of adaptation is now called disease.

> "Beginning with Upper Cretaceous Chalk...found [extending] from...the Soviet Union...Egypt...Texas and Australia. Under present theories about how sediments are deposited, it is not possible to explain the wide spread occurrence of this facies. Coal Measures... extend in essentially the same form all the way from Texas to...the U.S.S.R....red sandstone...limestone, gravel conglomerates, and other formations are shown to extend over exceedingly wide geographical areas. The problem posed by these strata is that they suggest a blanketing of the planet from extraterrestrial sources. Sedimentary rocks are something more than we have been taught. Ager notes that "even in such classic areas as the Mississippi delta, where sediment is thought to be accumulating rapidly, there is plenty of evidence to suggest that, after building up for a while, much of it is carried away again."...we cannot begin to explain the origin of what we have called sedimentary strata because there are no processes of deposition that we can observe that would create anything resembling what we see in rock formations today. Since it is almost impossible to create a fossil by gradual burial by sediment, we should examine the idea that our planet has been blanked by much extraterrestrial matter in previous times, burying almost all of the life that then existed." Deloria, Vine Jr. *Red Earth, White Lies*. p. 182,183,237.

In the area of geology, *Oahspe* also included foreknowledge of recently discovered information, like these veins of material, too large to have been formed by sedimentary processes; thus demonstrating the presence of the fall of belts of material from the protostellar disk. This material originated from the slow collapse of the proto-stellar cloud. This is a concept discussed in *Oahspe*, while long after its publication many so-called scientists continued to embrace theories such as those that the material forming the earth was thrown off by the sun, and the moon was thrown off from the earth.

"The public's most widely known piece of geological knowledge - how petroleum and natural-gas deposits formed on Earth - is false, a noted scientist says...some geologists...acknowledge that petroleum's origins may be dramatically different than what people believe....Thomas Gold, a scientist at Cornell University. ...presented evidence that oil and gas deposits on Earth are primordial. That means they came with the planet....Gold...and associates drilled...into a kind of rock that was not sedimentary, not associated with the sediments believed to produce oil deposits. At a depth of about 4 miles, they encountered a hydrocarbon oil...this single site contained "more petroleum than all of Saudi Arabia."...Petroleum originating from plant matter decayed by bacteria,...would resemble a microbial product. Instead, petroleum is chemically similar to a pure hydrocarbon that has been contaminated with microbial material...Michael Carr,...a scientist with the U.S. Geological Survey in Reston, Va. "Dr Gold has some very, very good evidence"...Carr said geologists plan to reconsider the conventional theory about petroleum formation at a major meeting later in the year." from an article entitled "Fossil-fuel Theory Debuncted" accredited to the "Toledo Blade" page A26 2/23/97 "The Arizona Republic."

This is just one more area where *Oahspe* shows preemptive knowledge, for the discovery of these oil beds, deeper than the layers of the earth that supported organic life, were only recently discovered. Their presence at this level would make it impossible for organic material to have caused them. This material is said by *Oahspe* to have originated from the collapse of a belt of cellulose, called semu or "gelatine" (*Oahspe*'s Cosmogony ch. 4:18), cellulose is the most abundant material in interstellar space, accumulated from interstellar dust present long before life ever formed on earth.

"Cellulose is not only the most abundant organic molecule on Earth. Interstellar dust consists in the main of cellulose, or of some related polysaccharide." Hoyle, Fred & N. C. Wickramasinghe. *Lifecloud*. p. 44&94.

Oahspe predicted the presence of polarized needle shaped interstellar particles, which when un-polarized, prevent the travel of light. "The polarization of the counter-glow is surprising, Pure {i.e., 180 degree} back-scattering from randomly oriented irregular, amorphous or spherical particles should give zero polarization. The existence of a marked polarization effect in our observations implies scattering by elongated preferentially oriented particles. Needle like particles are possible,...One is tempted to think of a magnetic field as the arranging agency." *Dark Nebula, Globules and Proto-stars* p. 801 & 802.

"Until 1949 no one expected the light of distant stars would become polarized... To produce interstellar polarization in the light of distant stars requires not only a preponderance of somewhat elongated particles in interstellar space, but further, some powerful mechanism to align these particles over great distances." Bartand, Pricilla Bok. *The Milky Way*, p. 200.

Oahspe also mentions the difficulty of seeing stars outside of earth's atmosphere; which lack of visible stars can now often be seen in photos of earth from space. "Well that may have been one small step for Neil, but it's a heck of a big leap for me...Just for the record, I don't see any stars out here." Astronaut Nary Captain Bruce McCandless II during the first un-tethered space walk. Feb. 7 1984. Science Digest Magazine 1/1985

Confirmation of *Oahspe*'s description of the solar system as shaped like a somewhat flattened cone shape has only recently been discovered to be true, this was done by astrophysicists completely unfamiliar with *Oahspe*'s prediction in that area. "The findings, detailed in the May 11 issue of the journal Science,...Data recently received from the Voyager 1 and 2 spacecraft reveal the heliosphere's shape is deformed in another way: the northern hemisphere bulges outward while the southern hemisphere is pressed inward.
<http://www.space.com/scienceastronomy/070515_st_mag_field.html>

There is such a prodigious amount of information now confirming *Oahspe* that it would be impossible to mention all of it in this book. However, in the ebooks by myself, *Oahspe Confirmation and Cosmo online* evidence in other areas that conflicts with orthodox religion, history and science, and evidence confirming *Oahspe's* account can be viewed online in the file section of the Oahspe Confirmation group at;
 <http://groups.yahoo.com/group/Oahspe_Confirmation/>

The file names are *Ospcnfrm* and the companion volume of scientific information confirming *Oahspe*'s *Cosmology* is called; *Cosmo online*. Citations for all the information mentioned above concerning *Oahspe* can be found in these books. Additional new evidence confirming *Oahspe* may also be found at the second url above and at the *Oahspe Confirmation* group by doing a search for recent updates in the groups search function by typing in the words; *Oahspe* confirmation.

My book has been an effort to provide an easy reference to historical facts and scientific evidence not usually considered by fundamentalists, evolutionists, scientists and historians. While the evidence previously given in this book mostly corresponds to a biblical time line and to scientific interpretations not in conflict with the majority of the forensic evidence revealed by paleontology, some does not. The principle remaining conflict between the scientific theory and the interpretation of the biblical data (record) given here (and also with *Oahspe*) is one of dating, so let us examine radiometric evidence logically and scientifically, eliminating anything that is based on assumption or guesswork.

PROBLEMS WITH RADIOMETRIC DATING

Science News 9/16/95, p. 191, reports that the space probe, Galileo has encountered a third unforeseen dust storm as it neared Jupiter. The probability of large amounts of very old matter periodically falling during the early stages of the earth when the proto-stellar cloud was still very dense is usually not taken into consideration by scientists when calculating the age of the earth using radiometric processes. To assume that the proto-stellar cloud condensed from new material, all at the same time into planetary bodies is not reasonable by even currently understood laws of physics. One factor used to calculate the age of the earth is the amount of time it would have taken to form the many layers of rock through the process of sedimentation. This means of calculation fails to take into account the possibility of huge amounts of material falling to earth when the proto-stellar cloud was denser.

> "Radiometric dating involves at least 8 untestable assumptions; (1) Beginnings conditions known. (2) Ratio of daughter (element) to natural. (3) Constant decay rate. (4-7) No leaching or addition of parent or daughter (element). (8) All assumptions valid for billions of years. If we assume that (1) a rock contained no Pb206 when it was formed; (2) all Pb206 now in the rock was produced by radioactive decay of U238; (3) the rate of decay has been constant; (4) there has been no differential leaching by water of either element; and (5) no U238 has been transported into the rock from another source, then we might expect our estimate of age to be fairly accurate...It is obvious that radiometric technique may not be the absolute dating methods that they are claimed to be." (anti-creationist) Stansfield, W. D. Prof. Biological Science, Cal. Polyt. State U, *The Science of Evolution,* p. 84.

According to *Oahspe* at the time *Homo sapiens sapiens* first came to exist, the earth was already 9,470,500 years old (p41/42 note #2). This figure lies somewhere between the extreme views held by science and the biblical fundamentalists based on the idea that it took only seven actual days to create every living species. This interpretation of Genesis can logically be seen to have been impossible since according to their interpretation of the creation story there were "days" and green plants appeared on the third "day" before there was a sun. The traditional biblical explanation posits the sun to supposedly have been made on the fourth "day." There could be no 24 hour period divided into light and dark without a sun to shine in the daytime. So based on the information in the section on Genesis Revisited it seems more likely that the atmosphere cleared in the forth *ium* (incorrectly translated as a 'day').

Science has based its theories of the age of the earth on radiometric dating processes, where the assumption is made that the earth, and consequently the material they use for dating, was not contaminated with older material. *Oahspe* explains to us that material, previously formed, in an already ancient universe, was re-gathered up by the vortex of the proto-stellar cloud that formed the solar system and the planets.

> "According to the U.S. Geological Survey, each year tens of thousands of tons of interstellar dust falls to Earth, carried mostly in IDPs (interplanetary dust particles). Science & Technology. *Dust that's Worth Keeping.*

> <https://www.llnl.gov/str/September05/Ishii.html>

Meteorites dating to 4.5 million years ago have fallen in recent times. (Chapman & Morrison, *Cosmic Catastrophes,* p. 205) If material from an admittedly ancient universe was collected by the proto-stellar cloud which formed the earth and the solar system, the possibility of accurate dates becomes impossible, because of contamination by older material. The tendency for older dates becomes more likely the farther back one goes, based on the presence of the higher ratios of decayed elements used in radiometric dating that would be present due to the immense stretches of time interstellar particles would have had in which to decay. The different elemental compositions of interstellar clouds in the past to those in which we presently find the earth, have also not been considered when calculating the age or history of the earth. The possibility of contamination makes current theories at best highly suspect and logically unacceptable.

William Corhillis has recorded the dates of many "dark days" (pp. 30-34) *Handbook of Unusual Atmospheric Phenomena,* and says (p. 31); "Almost all...dark days during which the sun *and* stars are blotted out can be explained in terms of: (1) forest fires; (2) volcanic eruptions; (3) dust storms; and (4) intense storms, perhaps augmented by natural or artificial air pollution. When the stars appear during a dark day, one must search for extraterrestrial sources, such as cosmic material veiling the sun."

> "Petrifying springs...The dripping waters are used for the purpose of petrifying...A sponge is petrified in a few months, a book or cap in a year or two, cat or bird a little longer...One cat shown in the museum had the head broken off at the neck, showing the whole was limestone throughout, with not a trace of the organic structure." (Corliss, William. *Unknown Earth,* quoting I. Charles King in *Scientific American*, p. 760) The significance of this information is, in some areas processes of fossilization may not have taken the millions of years hypothesized, a factor scientists have used when calculating dates for the history of the earth.

Recently scientists have proposed difficulty in dating objects having contact with electricity because it could also distort the accuracy of radiometric dates. "There have been some studies that suggest that an electrical field of high concentration can alter decay rates. These findings probably have a greater impact on longer-lived isotopes like uranium or potassium-argon, but they are an issue that has to be considered in calculations. The older the sample is, the less likely it is that our estimate of age is going to be accurate." Clayton, John N. *Carbon 14--Friend or Foe?* <http://www.doesgodexist.org/NovDec05/Carbon14-FriendofFoe.html>

There have been numerous discoveries of artifacts; gold chains, nails, human teeth, a spark plug etc., in solid rock and coal dated millions of years before Homo-sapiens sapiens existed. (Readers Digest, *Mysteries of the Unexplained,* p. 46-47; and Cremo & Thompson, *Forbidden Archeology,* p. 798-828) If these artifacts were buried in interstellar dust that had formed millions of years before it fell to earth, it would account for these unusual finds.

> "The upper age limit for conventional radiocarbon dating...varies from laboratory to laboratory but is typically in the region of 40,000 years." (Bowman, Sheridan. *Radiocarbon Dating,* p. 37) "A rock that had an early form of an organism was clearly older than rocks containing later form. Furthermore, all rocks that had the early form, no matter how far apart those rocks were geographically, would have to be the same age...fossil successions made it possible to say that the Cambrian rocks are older than the Ordovician rocks. In this way our geologic time table came into being...Without the theory of evolution and the interdisciplinary science of paleontology, it could not exist." Putman and Bassett, *Geology,* p. 544

> "This poses something of a problem; If we date the rocks by their fossils, how can we then turn around and talk about patterns of evolutionary change through time in the fossil record?" Eldridge, Niles. "Time Frames" p. 52.

"Tree ring work supported by radiocarbon analyses shows that the <u>concentration of radiocarbon in the atmosphere, and hence in living things, has in fact varied considerably - 6000 years ago it was much higher than it is today</u>....In 1956 it was realized that changes in the strength of the earth's magnetic field in the past would have changed the intensity of cosmic radiation reaching the earth, as this magnetic field has the effect of partially deflecting the cosmic rays. Since it is this radiation which produces radiocarbon in the atmosphere, the atmospheric concentration of radiocarbon would have been altered." Renfrew, Colin. *Before Civilization*, p. 70&76.

"<u>Radiohalos occur</u> when radioactive matter infiltrates a mineral deposit during the early stages of its formation...<u>the radioactive particle continues to emit radiation and produces rings of discoloration</u>...The problem from a geologist's point of view is that the radiohalos are too small. Given the energy of the radiating particle and the length of time it has been enclosed in its mineral matrix, the radiohalos should be larger than they are. <u>From the physicist's point of view, the implication is that the mineral matrices are nowhere near as old as the geologist tells him they are. ...it seems that radical revisions of scientific chronology may soon be in order</u>." Readers Digest, *Mysteries of the Unexplained,* p. 55.

EPILOGUE

The purpose of this book has been to demonstrate that the historical evidence from the Bible and all the ancient cultures included recognition of the gods; the false gods *and* YHVH's holy Elohim. And to show that variations of these most ancient versions of humanity's history of the gods, often have continuity from prehistoric times on; once differences of language, and the alterations of time are taken into account. This is also true of the original writings of Moses, as from the evidence presented, he obviously understood that the "holy gods" were one in YHVH.

The evidence presented here demonstrates that the misinformed Levites later altered the original account in their quest to justify murder and then discredit YHVH's true Judean prophets; those who inquired of YHVH's host of heaven the Elohim, seeking guidance as YHVH had ordained (Ps. 14:2). There is never enough evidence to convince the hardened skeptic, but there is evidence. Hopefully it will help those who are seeking to inquire further into the mysteries of our spiritual history.

I have written this book not to pretend to be better than anyone else[t]; I am still far from being a goddess in YHVH's kingdom. Rather I have written this book because if the information it contains was available when I was younger I think I would have lived differently, for I was always looking for proof or at least evidence. [t]As the master Yeschu/Joshu/Jesus said when someone called him good master, "There is no one who is good except Theos (KGV God)." (Mark 10:18)

Yet I knew enough about the KJV to know that it was fraught with contradictions, illogic, murder, and mayhem in the name of religion. Had it stood as Moses originally intended or included all the teachings of Yeschu/Joshu/Jesus, and been embraced by others following the teachings of loving kindness (to animals also not sacrificing them), oneness and purity I might have grown up in a world that had faith and thus learned to have faith also.

Instead I grew up, with little but abuse, among those who could not love the truth because it would have revealed their own motives. For the sake of all YHVH's children who have no one to love them, the profits from this book will go toward the purchase of property to be held in trust for any of YHVH's little ones who have no one to care for them. It will be open to anyone that wishes to surrender worldly desires and serve YHVH by caring for them. The purpose will be to further all efforts to promote YHVH's kingdom on earth as it is in the heavens. Anyone who also wishes to thus serve the All in Oneness may participate in such efforts by donating to those working for this goal or through participation and may contact me. @; lordessoflight@yahoo.com (Martha, from the Hebrew var. of Maharaj-Lord/Lordess, Helene, Greek for light/torch and Jones from Yohanns, favored by YHVH). I believe that the reason my name was given to me was that the angels knew being born to abusive parents, I would need something to inspire me to rise above the disabling trauma in my life.

My hope is that for those who look for reason and consistency, along with purity and ethical teachings, the evidence and information presented here may help others find a reason to remain faithful to seeking the All Truth (*El or Al Emet/Emeth*). For only those who seek shall find, and not lose faith as I did in my childhood. My hope is that it may help free some from the misery of disappointment and resulting loss of faith in YHVH the All Life (*Al Chi*). May this help others find their way back to freedom from the serpent brain and from worldly values. Returning to YHVH's light (*Aur*), i.e. wholistic intelligence, restores oneness with the Great Holy Spirit of the All One *YHVH Echad,* through the knowledge that though the world is unkind and unfair, YHVH is All Holy (*Al Hakadosh*).

> "Now also when I am old and grey-headed, O Elohim, forsake me not; until I have showed your strength unto this generation, and your power to everyone that is to come" Ps. 71:18

The power of YHVH's Council of Elohim is still present and to whom we may appeal in times of distress and adversity. They will aid in forwarding all those who surrender to oneness in service to YHVH. A return to power to help change the world will be restored to humanity, if we again understand that when we are granted an opportunity to affect change, we must remember YHVH's Council of Elohim and practice calling on Him and them. If we do so they will help smooth the way for His purpose and further His will.

The essence of Yeschu/Joshu/Jesus' teaching in the *Book of Ieou* bears repeating again at this point. "To send the earth to heaven is that he has ceased to have the understanding of a man of earth, but has become a man of heaven, his understanding has ceased to be earthly...by means of the hidden mysteries which show the way to the chosen race." This means that one is free, no longer bound by worldly opinions. Whatever earthlings see as good or desirable is no longer seen subjectively, freeing one from the circular limitation of desire and its accompaniment, suffering. That which is seen as evil or ugly is also no longer feared, for through acceptance of any temporal state, it too is understood to be subjective and is therefore no longer resisted through violence. Herein lies the reconciliation of good and evil, and the return of peace and oneness.

The act of partaking of the fruit of the "tree of the knowledge of good and evil" aka "tree of the living ones" (Gen. 3:22), was partaking of the genetic heritage of the Elohim and the sons of the

Elohim by humans. This began the process of cause and effect, that has put us all at odds with each other. In the reconciliation of good and evil lies the understanding that our values are subjective, and not lasting. In this understanding is freedom from suffering, since then there is no longer an agenda and therefore it is possible to go beyond the fear generated by the reptile brain and live from moment to moment in faith (not, however, meaning a hedonistic living *for* the moment). The power of faith must be called forth if one is to let go of this fear and trust in YHVH *Al Echad Al Emet,* the All One, All Truth. This is the inner journey that must be taken to obtain freedom from the world and from misleading teachers motivated by self-interest.

Yet as long as members of every religion point to each other as the godless evil-doers, we will all be antagonists and war will continue on earth. Yeschu/Joshu/Jesus said "Love your enemies." (Matt. 5:44) and if one looks deeply every great religion has the message of peace somewhere in its teachings, it is the failure to practice this brotherly and sisterly love that creates conflict. Satan the collective consciousness of warriors and adversaries lives off the power of adversity. Freedom from war, evil, conflict and adversity begins with non-attachment to the things of the world. This must include the attachment to imposing the so-called rights to ownership of the earth, gaspingly coveting all the open land at the expense of the indigenous peoples, whose rights and freedoms are taken away so that political interests can dominate mother earth.

Just as peace can only result from non-attachment to controlling the earth, freedom from disease must also begin with non-attachment, to pleasure and indulging the desire for it, from this freedom arises a state of energy, balance, harmony, and thankfulness. In individuals thus freed from strife and disease are the seeds of oneness, the chosen race of peaceful healthful earthlings who will bring about the new age in the foundation of YHVH's kingdom on earth as it is practiced throughout all the heavens of the universe.

We must let go of fear driven ambitions and desires driven by the serpent brain and find a purpose for our lives that is motivated by love, especially for the innocent orphaned and abused children. And we must become an example for those who have been misled by all worldly opinions, which does nothing to create health and sanity. Not for tithes, recognition or personal gain, but to be able to know that we have helped to make our world sane and free from the Satan's rule through the serpent brain. To become godlike is not to acquire followers, wealth, property, power, or fame to glorify ego. It is to master the serpent brain drives and instead cultivate the individual talents each one possesses, through which we can contribute to *Al Echad* the All One.

> "YHWH will become king over all the earth, in that day, YHWH, He shall become One (Achad/Echad) and His name One." Zech. 14:9

In order for any theory to represent the truth it must account for all the evidence, not just exclude unaccountable evidence to support some favored dogma, and teach some partial theory merely because someone's reputation depends on it. To exclude anomalous evidence and out of place artifacts, is to try to make a theory fit when it does not. This is just as blind and ignorant as superstitious religious beliefs. We must eventually come to see the truth of visitation from other sentient beings, and account for their interest in us.

The purpose of this book is not to prove beyond a doubt, which is impossible, as some other reason than the truth, can always be found by the doubter. But this book provides evidence and substantiation, for those whose faith falters because science has taught us to have faith in accounts so radically different from the orthodox interpretations of the Judeo/Christian religion that the Great Holy Spirit has been forgotten. Perhaps it may also awaken the interest of those who have never found documentation to support their faith in that One they have believed in, but had no faith in the account religion traditionally has given. The purpose is also to glorify the Great Holy Spirit and the legions of light, the Holy Elohim who have been laboring to preserve the truth, and bring all this evidence to light.

Our spiritual history has been rewritten so many times, in the interest of earthly religions seeking followers, authority, power, and influence, that it is almost unrecognizable when compared to the evidence. But the evidence is still there in the Hebrew stories, and other religions. Because the ancients could only stand in awe of those powerful gods, the Elohim, who could appear and disappear, occasionally intervening in human affairs, to rescue the faithful who practiced oneness, the council of Elohim were acknowledged to be one with YHVH and so were called YHVH Elohim.

> "That all one they may be; as you, Father in me, and I in you, that they in us may be (All One)." John 17:21

Because the ancients recognized the oneness of YHVH Elohim, they were written of by earthlings as One unified being. We too can embrace and recognize oneness with this unified being, the Great Holy Spirit, of whom each is a small part. Thanks to all those who embraced oneness and carried the history of the Elohim forward for all humanity, our history can be rediscovered. This history is the lost data of the visitation of chariots (vehicles or rides) carrying YHVH's Elohim, our older brothers and sisters, who are still watching over us. For those who give up the desire for worldly things and inquire of the Elohim, as per Ps. 14:2, their assistance and protection will help bring a new age in which YHVH's kingdom will come on earth, as it is done in oneness throughout the heavens. Aho (Lakota, thank you) Aumen

Ho hecetu yelo (Lakota, "I have spoken") *Aho Mytake Oyasin* (Lakota; "thank you all my relations") Martha Helene Jones (from the Maine Kickapoo, "wanderers" and the Rh neg. sea-people who settled Ireland etc.) Thunderbirds, which spewed fire as they traveled across the sky of ancient North America, may represent attempts by native culture to depict the starships of the Elohim. Rock carvings of UFO shaped objects abound in North America and one was the inspiration for my decision to begin collecting evidence. In a pair of twin rock petroglyphs, of stick figure people with bows and arrows, following antlered deer, above which is what appears to a domed flying saucer, and in one of the pair, a small stick figure man appears to be represented in the craft. There is a modest reward offered for anyone who can track down the book on North American Archaeology or Artifacts, containing photographs of these Native petroglyphs, from which I was first inspired by this Native American record. Contact me at the above email.